STABILITY AND CONTINUITY IN MENTAL DEVELOPMENT

Behavioral and Biological Perspectives

STABILITY AND CONTINUITY IN MENTAL DEVELOPMENT

Behavioral and Biological Perspectives

EDITED BY

MARC H. BORNSTEIN
National Institute of Child Health and Human Development
and
New York University

NORMAN A. KRASNEGOR
National Institute of Child Health and Human Development

LEA
1989
LAWRENCE ERLBAUM ASSOCIATES, PUBLISHERS
Hillsdale, New Jersey Hove and London

Lawrence Erlbaum Associates, Inc., Publishers
365 Broadway
Hillsdale, New Jersey 07642

Library of Congress Cataloging-in-Publication Data

Stability and continuity in mental development : behavioral and biological perspectives / edited by Marc H. Bornstein, Norman A. Krasnegor.
p. cm.
Includes bibliographies and index.
ISBN 0-8058-0203-7
1. Child development. 2. Child psychology. I. Bornstein, Marc H. II. Kasnegor, Norman A.
[DNLM: 1. Child Behavior. 2. Child Development. 3. Infant, Newborn. 4. Infant, Premature. 5. Mental Processes—infancy & childhood. WS 105.5.D2 S775]
RJ131.S668 1989
155.4—dc19
DNLM/DLC
for Library of Congress 89-1581
CIP

Printed in the United States of America
10 9 8 7 6 5 4 3 2 1

For

Anita

and

for

Daniel Gideon and Joshua David

Contents

Contributors

Dr. Margaret L. Adams Eliot-Pearson Department of Child Study, Tufts University, Medford, MA 02155

Dr. Lauren B. Adamson Department of Psychology, Georgia State University, Atlanta, GA 30303

Dr. Heidelise Als Neurobehavioral Infant & Child Studies, Enders Pediatric Research Laboratories, The Children's Hospital, Enders Main Room M29, 300 Longwood Avenue, Boston, MA 02115

Dr. Mark I. Appelbaum Department of Psychology, University of North Carolina, Chapel Hill, NC 27514

Dr. Nathlie Badian Neurobehavioral Infant & Child Studies, Enders Pediatric Research Laboratories, The Children's Hospital, Enders Main Room M29, 300 Longwood Avenue, Boston, MA 02115

Dr. Roger Bakeman Department of Psychology, Georgia State University, Atlanta, GA 30303

Dr. Leila Beckwith Department of Pediatrics, School of Medicine, UCLA, Los Angeles, CA 90024

Dr. Richard Q. Bell Department of Psychology, University of Virginia, Charlottesville, VA 22901

Dr. Marc H. Bornstein Section on Child and Family Research, National Institute of Child Health and Human Development, Building 31, Room B2B15, 9000 Rockville Pike, Bethesda, MD 20892

Dr. Robert H. Bradley Center for Research on Teaching, and Learning, University of Arkansas, 2801 South University Avenue, Little Rock, AK 72204

Dr. Sarah H. Broman Developmental Neurology Branch, National Institute of Neurological and Communicative Disorders and Strokes, Federal Building Room 8C06, National Institutes of Health, Bethesda, MD 20892

Dr. Josephine V. Brown Department of Psychology, Georgia State University, Atlanta, GA 30303

Dr. Margaret R. Burchinal Frank Porter Graham Child Development Center, Highway 54 Bypass West 071A, Chapel Hill, NC 27514

Dr. Sarale E. Cohen Department of Pediatrics, School of Medicine, UCLA, Los Angeles, CA 90024

Dr. Bruce A. B. Cooper Harold E. Jones Child Study Center, Institute of Human Development, University of California, 2425 Atherton Street, Berkeley, CA 94704

Dr. Frank H. Duffy Neurobehavioral Infant & Child Studies, Enders Pediatric Research Laboratories, The Children's Hospital, Enders Main Room M29, 300 Longwood Avenue, Boston, MA 02115

Dr. Melvin Eldridge Department of Psychology, Georgia State University, Atlanta, GA 30303

Dr. David H. Feldman Eliot-Pearson Department of Child Study, Tufts University, Medford, MA 02155

Dr. Jane V. Hunt Child Study Center, 2425 Atherton Street, Berkeley, CA 94704

Dr. Norman A. Krasnegor Human Learning and Behavior Branch, Center for Research for Mothers and Children, National Institute of Child Health and Human Development, Executive Plaza North—Room 633C, 6130 Executive Boulevard, Rockville, MD 20852

Dr. Marvin W. Lee Frank Porter Graham Child Development Center, Highway 54 Bypass West 071A, Chapel Hill, NC 27514

Dr. Gloria B. McAnulty Neurobehavioral Infant & Child Studies, Enders Pediatric Research Laboratories, The Children's Hospital, Enders Main Room M29, 300 Longwood Avenue, Boston, MA 02115

Dr. Arthur H. Parmelee Department of Pediatrics, Center for Health Sciences, University of California, Los Angeles, CA 90024

Dr. Robert Plomin 211 South Henderson, Human Development Building, The Pennsylvania State University, University Park, PA 16802

Dr. Craig T. Ramey Frank Porter Graham Child Development Center, Highway 54 Bypass West 071A, Chapel Hill, NC 27514

Dr. Susan A. Rose Department of Pediatrics K-215, Albert Einstein College of Medicine, 1300 Morris Park Avenue, Bronx, NY 10461

Dr. Linda S. Siegel The Ontario Institute for Studies in Education, Office of the Assistant Director—Academic, 252 Bloor Street West, Toronto, Ontario M5S 1V6, CANADA

Dr. Marian Sigman University of California, Department of Psychiatry and Biobehavioral Sciences, School of Medicine, Neuropsychiatric Institute, The Center for the Health Sciences, 760 Westwood Plaza, Los Angeles, CA 90024

Dr. Robert A. Terry Department of Psychology, University of North Carolina, Chapel Hill, NC 27514

Dr. Ina C. Užgiris Department of Psychology, Clark University, 950 Main Street, Worcester, MA 01610

Dr. Mary F. Waldrop 5802 Johnson Avenue, Bethesda, MD 20817

Introduction

Norman A. Krasnegor
National Institute of Child Health and Human Development
National Institutes of Health

An enduring interest of theoreticians is whether behavior developmental processes are *stable* and/or *continuous* during ontogeny. If they are stable, an individual should maintain his or her relative position with respect to others on psychological or behavioral dimensions through time. If, for example, intelligence is a stable dimension, one should find that individual babies measured for intelligence, however defined in infancy, retain their ranks relative to each other across the life span. Similarly, if psychological and behavioral dimensions are continuous they should be found to persist without essential change throughout life. Operationally, this implies that a dimension such as intelligence tracks through infancy, childhood, adolescence, and into adulthood.

A basic understanding of stability and continuity is of central importance to help elucidate fundamental scientific and clinical questions concerning the care and behavioral development of neonates and young infants. Studies of stability and continuity are of great theoretical relevance in posing questions for gaining deeper insights into what principles govern normal behavioral developmental processes. These concepts are also of great relevance for those scientists who study development of "at risk" populations of children. Of particular importance, in this regard, to the National Institute of Child Health and Child Development are those babies who are born small for gestational age or at low birth weight. The field of neonatal medicine has pioneered research during the past two decades that has resulted in the capacity to routinely deliver and sustain babies weighing less than 2500 grams. Indeed, current neonatal intensive care centers have begun to master both clinical and physiological problems associated with maintaining viability and development of babies weighing less than 1000 grams.

Along with this success in the biological realm, behavioral scientists have begun to investigate the consequences of premature birth on social, emotional, cognitive, and behavioral development. Using longitudinal designs and a diverse array of methodologies and instruments, they have attempted to both characterize the early development of these children and predict behavioral outcomes related to premature status at birth. The capacity for early identification of those babies, born at risk, who will develop normally from those who will not is an issue of great scientific and clinical interest. Success in this domain of behavioral science will provide parents, neonatologists, pediatricians, and child development specialists with a better estimate of the population of children who can benefit most from early intervention.

The ideas and data contained in this book are at the cutting edge of research on stability and continuity in behavioral development. The work presented provides exemplars of both the range and depth of studies conducted and of the innovative methodological approaches required to address the complexities inherent in this field of inquiry. A major feature of the volume is its focus on prospective longitudinal studies designed to demonstrate the capacity to predict behavioral outcome data in childhood from knowledge of predictor variables in infancy. The book is divided into two parts: (1) Empirical Studies of Stability and Continuity, and (2) Commentary.

EMPIRICAL STUDIES OF STABILITY AND CONTINUITY

The first part of the book is composed of twelve chapters organized around five themes: Neurobehavioral Functioning; Physical Status; Traditional Infant Tests; Information Processing Capacities; and Experience. These domains are central for testing ideas concerning stability and continuity of mental development.

Neurobehavioral Functioning

The first chapter in this section is by Heidelise Als, Frank H. Duffy, Gloria B. McAnulty, and Nathlie Badian, whose research concentrates in the field of behavioral development of premature infants. It summarizes their studies on methodological approaches to classification and periodic testing of children from the point of their premature birth to five years of age. The work is both theoretically rich and indicative of a highly original set of innovative approaches that combine biological and behavioral techniques to measure status and to predict outcome. The second chapter is by Marian Sigman, Leila Beckwith, Sarale E. Cohen, and Arthur H. Parmelee. Their focus is on stability characteristics inherent in the biosocial development of the preterm infant. They describe research on the infant's capacity to self-regulate with regard to internal stimuli and to interact with the external environment with a particular emphasis on caregiver-infant interactions. As in the previous chapter, Sigman and co-workers provide the reader with a summary of the outcome data on subjects in their eighth year of life. Their findings demonstrate associations between characteristics measured in infancy for later development and thereby provide strong support for the concept of stability.

Physical Status

This section of the book contains two chapters, respectively, by Sarah H. Broman and by Richard Q. Bell and Mary F. Waldrop. Broman's work summarizes data from the Collaborative Perinatal Project, a prospective multidisciplinary study of the developmental consequences of complications in pregnancy and the perinatal period of development. Her work highlights findings concerning relations between physical status of the newborn (birthweight, head circumference, brain abnormality, neonatal seizures, Down's syndrome, motor disability, and congenital heart disease) and cognitive tests at preschool and in school (four and seven years of age).

Bell and Waldrop detail their research on the relations between minor physical anomalies at birth and later IQ and school achievement. Their findings indicate that such anomalies serve as markers for disorders in embryonic development and predict school performance problems. There are no clear-cut relations between the predictor variables and achievement. Their review of the literature also shows that anomalies correlate with distractibility in both boys and girls. Boys with high anomaly scores have high activity levels; girls so identified have low levels of activity. They conclude that, although their data argue for discontinuity in development, a more thorough understanding of developmental processes and more finely tuned intervals of measurement might lead to a reinterpretation of the data in favor of the continuity hypothesis.

Traditional Infant Tests

The theme of this section is the predictive validity of traditional infant testing and its value in assessing theoretical and clinical issues related to stability and continuity. In her chapter Linda S. Siegel argues that traditional tests of intelligence conducted during infancy and early childhood are predictive of later measures of intelligence. She asserts that discrepancies in the literature concerning the failure of infant tests to predict lie not with the tests but with an analytic strategy that employs correlation coefficients. She argues that one should use a measurement strategy focusing on the prediction of range rather than exact score. Siegel also indicates that, for the purposes of assessing stability, more specific tests should be employed in contrast to global scores. Her reconceptualization of prediction should serve to stimulate research agendas associated with studies of stability and continuity.

Jane V. Hunt and Bruce A. B. Cooper's chapter describes their research on a prospective study of very low birthweight babies designed to determine what the behavioral risk is to such children. Their subjects were followed from birth to age 8 years and tested periodically during that time span. Parental education level was found not to influence the probability of normal outcome but did influence the severity of the problem. Their results also indicate no evidence for developmental continuity across ages two to eight years, which is defined as developmentally appropriate changes in behavioral characteristics that, nevertheless, distinguished outcome groups. They assert that these data also support the conclusion that there is little evidence for continuity in developmental rates across ages as defined by steady changes in trajectory that differentiate groups under study over the time frame used.

The chapter by Ina Č. Užgiris, presents the reader with an overview of critical theoretical issues and their implications for measurement of stability and continuity. Her thoughtful analysis brings a number of points into focus that must be considered before fully realized definitions of stability and continuity can be achieved. This chapter is a must for both researchers in this field of behavioral science and all students of development.

Information Processing Capacities

In this fourth section, two chapters are organized around the issue of the predictive validity of the information-processing capacities of human babies. The first work is that of Marc H. Bornstein. Bornstein provides an overview of information processing in the context of his research on habituation. He parametrically analyzes this measure and reports systematic research using it to demonstrate its value for predicting stability of intellectual functioning. This chapter defines habituation from both theoretical and empirical perspectives and provides the reader with evidence for the reliability of the measure as well as its validity. Bornstein interweaves results from his own and others' research to demonstrate the power of habituation studies of babies to predict intelligence test scores in school-age children.

Susan A. Rose's chapter details her work on measuring infant intelligence. She provides the reader with a review of evidence for the existence of rudimentary forms of information processing in human infants. She, as does Bornstein, argues that assessment of intelligence early in life can lead to a relatively accurate prediction of outcome during middle childhood. Rose presents data on the stability and psychometric properties of her measures (including concurrent and predictive validity). The chapter is data rich and, together with the work of Bornstein previously described, makes a strong case for the availability of a new and scientifically rigorous test for assessing stable cognitive attributes of human infants.

Experience

The last section of Part I focuses on the theme of experience. It is comprised of contributions by Robert H. Bradley, Craig T. Ramey and his associates, and Roger Bakeman and his colleagues.

Bradley's chapter details his research on relations between the home environment and child development during infancy. He describes his major measurement instrument (the HOME) that is designed to assess the quality and quantity of cognitive, social, and emotional support available to a child in the home environment. The instrument was employed in the context of the Little Rock Study initiated in 1970. The author indicates that stability in the environment is frequently found to be correlated with stable patterns of development. Furthermore, he points out that extreme environmental conditions can predict stable patterns of development, particularly when they mirror initial developmental status. Bradley concludes his chapter by outlining a research agenda that provides guidance for future directions in studies designed to investigate relations between environment and stability in development.

The next chapter by Craig T. Ramey, Marvin W. Lee, and Margaret R. Burchinal describes their research on the consequences of modifying social ecologies for the intellectual development of socially defined high-risk children. The data reveal that, in general, educational intervention changes the average level of cognitive performance but not the cross-time predictability of intellectual development. The results further demonstrate individual predictability or stability in the relative ranking of individuals along with between-group plasticity when the same dimension is examined across time in separate analyses. Ramey et al. therefore conclude that the data support the idea of plasticity of development predicated on interactions between the individual and the environment. This research makes a strong case for the efficacy of early educational intervention in preventing the decline of intellectual development of high-risk children.

Roger Bakeman, Lauren B. Adamson, Josephine V. Brown, and Melvin Eldridge focus on individual differences in social and cognitive competencies based on mother-infant interaction (as measured by the HOME) early in life. Early social interactions were rated and used to predict cognitive and social functioning later in life. Although no significant predictions ensued, the authors are not willing to conclude that no important relations exist. Rather, they urge that investigations be undertaken to determine specific aspects of interaction (e.g., contingent responsiveness or reciprocal interaction) that may improve prediction. They speculate that the failure to find the expected outcomes will stimulate research to pinpoint what specific aspects of social interaction can have an impact on later cognitive and social development.

COMMENTARY

The second part of this volume is composed of three chapters. Each provides a different context for the reader to assess the foregoing empirical studies. These frameworks are, respectively, quantitative methodologies, developmental behavior genetics, and theories of intelligence.

The chapter by Mark I. Appelbaum, Margaret R. Burchinal, and Robert A. Terry reflects a crucial aspect of stability and continuity, namely quantitative assessment of the phenomena. They discuss the three measurement approaches most frequently used to model and analyze these data. These are, respectively, regression and correlation, growth curve modelling, and scaling procedures. They highlight the fundamental strengths and limitations of each approach. In addition, the authors provide an overview of the issues inherent in estimating parameters and the precision of measurement possible. This chapter guides those researchers who have an interest in a priori and post hoc quantification issues that could well determine experimental designs for longitudinal research to evaluate stability. The work provides an essential point of reference for the reader to help interpret the conclusions reached by the authors in Part I of the book.

The chapter on developmental behavior genetics by Robert Plomin focuses on the idea of individual differences. Plomin employs the terms *stability* and *instability* to refer to changes in individual differences. He emphasizes that measures of variance and covariance are the essential statistics, rather than the mean, for gaining a deeper understanding of individual differences. He asserts that data on heritability support the conclusion that as development proceeds, variance accounted for by heretibility increases. This finding is counter-intuitive because a majority of developmentalists might well argue that, as children encounter more diverse environments, this aspect of variance should account for more phenotypic variance. The author also provides a cogent discussion on the relevance of covariance measures for characterizing developmental change. This chapter is of great theoretical interest and gives the reader a unique filter for viewing the concepts of stability and continuity.

The final chapter by David H. Feldman and Margaret L. Adams provides an overview of crucial theoretical issues inherent in the concepts of intelligence and stability. They review the work and ideas of Jean Piaget and their implications for the continuity-discontinuity conceptualization of intelligence. This treatise also focuses on the work of three other theorists who have written extensively on the topic of intelligence during this decade: Sternberg, Gardner, and Feldman. The authors review Sternberg's theory and its central theme of metacomponents, which emphasizes "executive processes" such as planning, devising strategies, and allocating resources for problem solving. They provide an incisive summary of Gardner's theory of multiple intelligences. Gardner is quite critical of a psychometric approach to defining intelligence and is skeptical of a "central mental organization that controls the functioning of the child's mind." Rather,

Gardner posits seven distinct intelligences that are described for the reader. The authors also describe Feldman's theory of nonuniversal development. The theory, although not specifically about intelligence, has direct implications for defining stability. Feldman's central thesis posits that individuals have the potential for expressing their capacity in "uniquely satisfying ways." Feldman and Adams help the reader to gain new perspectives on what intelligence is and how possibly to redefine stability and continuity.

In summary, *Stability and Continuity in Mental Development* is unique because it gives the scientific community broad coverage on the topics of stability and continuity in mental development. The data sets described are representative of the longitudinal designs necessary to test theories of stability based on prediction models. In addition, the critical commentaries included serve to enlighten the reader concerning theoretical frameworks for interpreting the data presented and the conclusions drawn about stability based on prediction models.

PART I
EMPIRICAL STUDIES OF STABILITY AND CONTINUITY

Section 1:
Neurobehavioral Functioning

1 Continuity of Neurobehavioral Functioning in Preterm and Full-Term Newborns

Heidelise Als
Frank H. Duffy
Gloria B. McAnulty
Nathlie Badian
Harvard Medical School
and
The Children's Hospital, Boston

INTRODUCTION

Recent advances in the care of premature infants have led to rapid improvement in survival rates. The ensuing demand for early support of these infants necessitates early assessment strategies on which to base appropriate support and with which to assess individual progress. This demand reflects the clinician's conviction that assessment and support at this early stage of life can result in greater functional competence in a child beginning in infancy, and continuing into childhood and possibly adult life.

The work presented here focuses on assessment of the newborn's competence, adaptations, and early developmental process in a framework of behavioral organization, in concurrence with Parmelee and others (Arend, Gove, and Sroufe, 1979; Harmon, 1979; Jennings, Harmon, Morgan, Gaiter, and Yarrow, 1979; Morgan, Harmon, Gaiter, and Jennings, 1977; Sigman and Parmelee, 1979; Sroufe, 1979), that in comprehensive constructs of competence may lie an understanding of individual organisms' continuity of development. How can one assess the newborn infant's competence, and how can one foster it? How can one therewith document continuity of development?

These questions have been a challenge to the researcher. Both the clinician and the parent typically state that a child who is referred, for instance, with behavior problems or learning disabilities in the early school years has "always been that way." Clearly they do not mean that the specific behaviors exhibited by the child are those the child exhibited as an infant. They are referring to an underlying organizational pattern of functioning that has characterized the child since birth, which takes different manifestations as the child matures. We have formulated a functional model that attempts to specify the subsystems of functioning, which, in their respective interplay, in the manner in which they move from stable to disorganized functioning, and in the flexibility with which they maintain organized functioning in the face of varied exogenous and endogenous events, may exemplify a person's long-term individuality of behavioral functioning. Based on this model, we have attempted to develop systematic assessments, the APIB and the Kangaroo-box Paradigm, to quantify the degree of differentiation and modulation of these behaviorally defined subsystems of functioning. We hypothesize that the behavioral differences documented via these assessments are brain-based, i.e., part of the child's biological make-up. They are, of course, a response to environmental influence, but exhibit a recognizable pattern along a defineable trajectory.

In the first part of this chapter, we sketch theoretical considerations about development and assessment, the objective being a quantifiable understanding of individual behavior. The two research instruments designed to assess competence and behavioral organization in both the preterm and fullterm child are described. In the second part of the chapter, we present the results from two studies utilizing these instruments.

THEORETICAL CONSIDERATIONS AND INSTRUMENT DEVELOPMENT FOR THE ASSESSMENT OF CONTINUITY

Theoretical Basis for a Process-Oriented, Synactive Theory of Development

Various disciplines analyze human development from a number of perspectives and at different levels of organism functioning. We have drawn upon four principles of development from which we have formulated a new principle.

Principle of species adaptedness. The first principle, drawn from ethology, concerns the individual organism as a member of a species in evolution. From the construct of adaptedness, as described for humans by Blurton Jones and others (1972, 1974, 1976; Hinde, 1970; Hinde and Spencer-Booth, 1967), we see that each organism at any stage of development is evolved to not only a species-specific, but also a species-parsimonious level of adaptedness to its particular niche. The process of selection takes place at the level of behavior, and, over generations, many essentials of a species' repertoire become hardwired, as experimental animal studies have shown (Duffy, Mower, and Burchfiel, 1978; Freedman, 1964, 1974, 1979; Lettvin, Maturana, McCulloch, and Pitts, 1959; Spinelli and Jensen, 1979; Winter and Funkenstein, 1973).

The principle of adaptedness can sharpen one's observations in terms of the organism's behaviors at each stage in the species' adaptation. In this view, the human newborn emerges as a biologically social partner in a feedback system with the caregiver, eliciting and seeking the physiological, motoric, state, and attentional interaction from the environment that is needed to progress on the course of self-actualization (Als, 1975, 1977; Grossman, 1978).

Principle of continuous organism-environment interaction. From neuroembryology comes a second principle of development: continuous organism-environment interaction. The key characteristic of the central nervous system, as Palay (1979) pointed out, is differentiation and development by interaction with environment. This begins at the unicellular stage and continues thereafter (Bunge, Johnson, and Ross, 1978; Landis, 1980; Patterson, 1979; Patterson, Potter, and Furshpan, 1978). The importance of organism-environment interaction has long been recognized by motor system physiologists. We have discussed it in the context of motor system differentiation in the preterm infant (Als, in press). The human developmental process relies on continuous actualization and refinement of internalized feedback loops by experience and their impact on the organism's optimal development.

Principle of orthogenesis and syncresis. From organismic psychology comes a third principle: orthogenesis and syncresis (Werner, 1957), which is derived in turn from principles of cellular embryology. This principle has been applied specifically to the embryology of behavior by, among others, Bruner (1968, 1974), Coghill (1962), Gesell (1946; Gesell and Armatruda, 1945), Hooker (1936, 1942), and McGraw (1945). Wherever development occurs, it proceeds from a state of relative globality to a state of increasing differentiation, articulation, and hierarchic integration. Qualities of functioning that are fused and apparently unifocal (Herzog, 1979) at one developmental level become discrete, multifocal, and differentiated at another. Application of these principles to the study of the human newborn has led Sander (1964; Sander, Stechler, Burns, and Julia, 1970) to identify the interplay of various subsystems of functioning within the organism. He sees the main task of the newborn as synchronization of these systems. One would infer that poorly timed inputs penetrate and disrupt this subsystem synchronization, whereas appropriately timed inputs enhance functional integration and support growth.

Principle of dual antagonist integration. From motor system neurophysiology comes a principle of development that furthers understanding of the early growth process. According to Denny-Brown (1962, 1966), the organism always strives for smoothness of integration. Underlying this endeavor is a tension between two basically antagonistic physiological types of response: the exploratory or approaching, reaching out and the avoiding or withdrawing, defending. At times the two are released together. If a threshold of organization-appropriate stimulation is passed, the approaching and exploratory behavior may abruptly switch into defending and avoiding behavior. If an input is compelling to the organism and matches internal readiness, the organism will approach the input, react and interact with it, and become sensitized to it. If the input overloads the circuitry of the organism it will defend itself and actively withdraw. The responses are mutually modulating. Schneirla and Rosenblatt (Rosenblatt, 1976; Schneirla, 1959, 1965; Schneirla and Rosenblatt, 1961, 1963) discussed this principle in the differentiation of adaptive behaviors of altricial mammals.

Principle of synaction. A synthesis of the four principles of development outlined results in the principle we call SYNACTION (Als, 1982, 1986), which proposes that development proceeds through the continuous balancing of approach and avoidance, yielding a spiral potentiation of continuous intraorganism subsystem interaction and differentiation and organism-environment interaction aimed at bringing about the realization of hierarchically ordered species-unique developmental agenda.

Behavioral Organization of the Newborn Infant

Assessment of individual newborn infants' functioning in this model requires identification of their current standing on the filigree matrix of subsystem development in interplay with the environment. This conceptualization of development focuses on the way individual infants handle the experience of the world around them rather than on skills. The infant's functioning is seen in a model of continuous intraorganism subsystem interaction, and the infant, in turn, is seen in continuous interaction with the environment. We have termed this view of development synactive, because at each stage in development and at each moment the various subsystems of functioning are existing side by side. They are often truly interactive and at times costly to each other when development is proceeding disorganizedly. They are mutually supportive (synactive) when development proceeds smoothly. These systems include:

(1) the autonomic system,
(2) the motor system,
(3) the state organizational system,
(4) the attention and interaction system within the state system, and
(5) a self-regulatory, balancing system.

The functioning of all these systems is reliably observable in the behavior of the organism. The autonomic system is behaviorally observable in the pattern of respiration, color changes, tremulousness, and visceral signals such as bowel movements, gagging, and hiccoughing. The motor system is observable in the posture, tone, and movements of the infant. The state organizational system is observable in the range of states of consciousness of the infant, from sleeping to aroused, in the distinctness versus diffuseness of states, and in exhibited patterns of state transition. The attention and interaction system is exemplified in the infant's ability to regulate the robustness and differentiation of an alert, attentive state and to utilize this state to take in cognitive and social-emotional information from the environment and, in turn, elicit and modify inputs from the surrounding world. The regulatory system is behaviorally exemplified in the observable strategies the infant utilizes in maintaining a balanced, relatively stable and relaxed state of subsystem integration or in returning to such a state if internal subsystem desynchronization, imbalance, or stress has occurred. A further parameter of functioning is identifiable in the kind and amount of facilitation from the caregiver or environment that is necessary to aid infants' return to balance in situations when their own regulatory capacities are exceeded.

The synactive approach to assessment of organism functioning is appropriate throughout the human life span. At each state of development, newly salient agenda are being negotiated on the backdrop of previously accomplished subsystem differentiation and modulation. Figure 1.1 is a schematic conceptualization of the synactive perspective of development, applied to the fetal and neonatal stages.

Assessment of Behavioral Organization

In the synactive conceptual framework, an assessment tool requires a systematic situation or sequence of manipulations that bring out:

(1) The infant's current level of balance and smoothly integrated functioning. In what situation and with what facilitative inputs does this infant function smoothly?

(2) The threshold of disorganization indicated in the behaviors of defense and avoidance. The degree and kind of stress and the intensity of frustration or defense serve as indicators.

(3) The degree of differentiation within the level of integrated functioning. For instance, given that the infant is well-integrated if flexed and maintained quietly and held upright on the mother's shoulder, how much leeway is there to this maintenance?

(4) The degree of modulation and regulation in the actualization of the current level of differentiation. For instance, one infant will handle the shift from shoulder to crib without any disruption of either the physiological, motor, or state organization, whereas another infant will show changes in color, respiration, movement, and state.

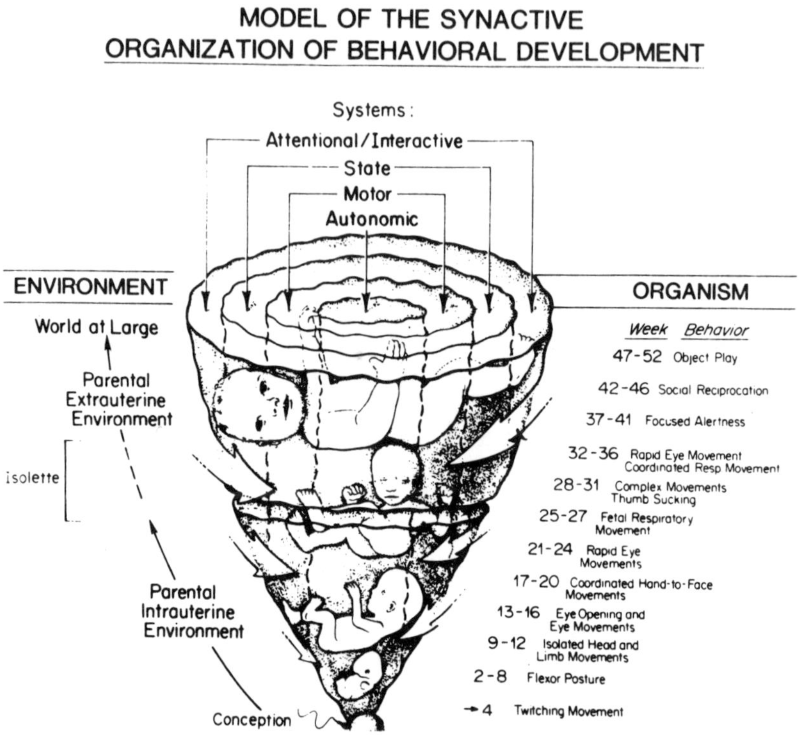

FIGURE 1.1. Model of the synactive formulation of behavioral development (From "Toward a Synactive Theory of Development" by H. Als, 1982, *Infant Mental Health Journal, 3*. Reprinted by permission).

(5) The strategies and the effectiveness of self-regulation an infant is capable of and the degree of elicitation or facilitation required of the caregiver.

(6) The degree and kind of environmental structuring, support, and facilitation necessary, not only to reestablish smooth functioning, but also to facilitate optimal functioning and the realization of the next step.

We postulate, and have shown some evidence (Als, Lawhon, Brown, Gibes, Duffy, McAnulty, and Blickman, 1986), that bringing about optimal functioning is critical for the organism's realization of new pathways. It is also important for the social interactors with the organism (parents, caregivers), who, in turn, require positive social elicitation and feedback from the infant. Freeing up the small strands of the next functional level sets the path of development in a positive direction and avoids the unwitting reinforcement of the disturbing, negative, and distorted behaviors, which are ready concomitants of the discrepant organism-environment interaction in a premature infant and lead to a cycle of increasing and reverberating distortion (Herzog, 1979).

The elements of synaction, integrative level, threshold, and cost have guided the construction of (a) a systematic behavioral assessment procedure for the preterm and full-term infant, referred to as Assessment of Preterm Infants' Behavior (APIB) (Als, Lester, Tronick, and Brazelton, 1982) and (b) an experimental play paradigm with versions appropriate for the 9-month, 18-month, 3-year, and 5/6 year-old levels, referred to as the Kangaroo-box Paradigm (Als, 1984; Als and Brazelton, 1981; Als, Lawhon, Brown, Gibes, Duffy, McAnulty, and Blickman, 1986). These assessment strategies are designed to evaluate continuity of functional differences in these developmental parameters over time.

Description of Instruments

The assessment of preterm infants' behavior (APIB). In the APIB, the maneuvers of the Brazelton Neonatal Behavioral Assessment Scale (Brazelton, 1973) are seen as a graded sequence of increasingly demanding environmental inputs or packages, moving from distal stimulation presented during sleep to increasing tactile stimulation gradually paired with vestibular stimulation. Other behaviors are also assessed by the APIB. The social interactive attentional package is administered at the point in the examination when the infant's behavioral organization indicates readiness for this sequence. During each package, one monitors the infant's reactions and behaviors along the five systems of functioning: autonomic system, motor-organizational system, state-organizational system, attention/interactive system, and self-regulation system. One also monitors the extent to which examiner facilitation is necessary to bring the infant to optimal performance and/or to help return to an integrated, balanced state. The system parameters are scaled from 9 (disorganized performance) to 1 (well-modulated performance). The APIB is described in greater detail elsewhere (Als, Duffy, and McAnulty, 1988a, 1988b; Als, Lester, Tronick, and Brazelton, 1982).

The Kangaroo-box Paradigm. The assessment of behavioral organization of the older child is based on a paradigm again designed to assess the degree of subsystem differentiation and modulation in the synactive formulation (Als, 1982; Als and Brazelton, 1981). Again, the systems considered are autonomic organization and more differentiatedly gross and fine motor organization, cognitive organization, vocalization pattern, affective organization, self-regulation, object play, social interaction, required facilitation, and pleasure/pride among others. The paradigm involves a toy task using a transparent plexiglass box accessible through porthole latch doors and containing a wind-up hopping kangaroo. Parent and child are asked to play with the toy in whatever way they most enjoy. They are videotaped with a two-camera split-screen system through one-way mirrors for six minutes. Then the parent is asked to sit against the wall of the room looking at the child, but not interacting in any way. The behavior of the child is observed in this "still-face" situation for six minutes. Then a

3-minute reunion in play is observed. Three specific versions of this apparatus are used, differing in the degree of complexity appropriate to increasing ages.

TESTING THE CONTINUITY HYPOTHESIS

If it is true that differentiation and modulation of functioning are parameters that have continuity across an individual's development, then assessment of behavioral organization in specially constructed paradigms, which are purported to identify an individual infant's organizational patterns, should be able to uncover developmental connections between the infant's performance on sequential assessments. We report two studies: first, a study to demonstrate the stability and consistency of behavioral functioning in the newborn period as measured with the APIB; and, second, a study of the consistency of APIB-measured newborn functioning to neuropsychological, neurobehavioral, and neuroelectrophysiological functioning at 5 years post-term.

Study 1: Stability and Consistency of Newborn Functioning

As previously described, we have developed an assessment instrument of preterm and fullterm infants' behavior, the APIB, in order to quantify not only the skill repertoire of the preterm and fullterm infant, but foremost, the infant's reactivity and threshold of disorganization and stress to environmental input. The instrument focuses on areas of autonomic, motoric, state organization, attentional functioning, self-regulatory capacity, and the degree of environmental facilitation necessary to help the infant maintain or regain synchronization of internal subsystem stabilization.

We consider differentiation and modulation along these parameters to be the newborn analogues of later integrative capacity. The task is to differentiate the baby who can muster alertness, but only with extreme stress to the autonomic and motor system, from the baby who has leeway and modulation to do so without difficulty.

Sample. We have studied 98 newborns who were selected because they were, as far as was known, free of neurological compromise, major medical problems in infant and mother, and severe social hardships in the family. All infants had a high likelihood of normal development. The infants spanned the gestational age continuum in approximately equal numbers as follows: 33 infants were 32 weeks gestational age at birth or less and are referred to as PPTs, or very preterm infants. These infants were selected to be free of intraventricular hemorrhage, perinatal asphyxia, seizures, bronchopulmonary dysplasia, necrotizing enterocolitis, and unresolved retinopathy of prematurity, the major medical conditions associated with early prematurity. Another 31 infants were between 33 and 37 weeks gestational age at birth and are referred to as PTs (middle preterm). They met all the criteria that the PPTs met and were healthy preterms. Finally, 34 infants were between 38 and 41 weeks gestational age at birth and are referred to as FTs (fullterm). They were selected to have Apgar ratings of seven or better at 1 minute and eight or better at 5 minutes, and were healthy, fullterm newborns. All twins were excluded, as were any infants with any kind of congenital or chromosomal abnormalities or intrauterine infections.

Behavioral differences by gestational age group. All infants were healthy and at home with their parents by 41 weeks and were examined with the APIB at 42 weeks postconception. All APIB examiners were trained to reliability by the first author and were unfamiliar with the gestational age group status of the infant.

The APIB yields 30 mutually exclusive summary scores, six of which are "systems scores" that identify the differential subsystem stability of the infant. The others quantify other parameters of functioning. Results of behavioral differences on the APIB by gestational age and gender show that the gestational age group differences were most pronounced. All six APIB systems scores show PPTs as the least well-organized and most reactive, with PTs in the middle, and the FTs the best organized. Of the remaining 24 APIB parameters, 13 yield similar results, evidencing the early-born preterms as less well-modulated in performance than the middle preterms and the fullterms. The parameters involved are largely motor system, state organizational, and attentional/interactive parameters. There were very few sex and gestational age-by-sex interaction effects.

To explore the behavioral differences among FT, PT, and PPT group members further, individual group comparisons were undertaken as follows: All 34 fullterms were compared to all 64 preterm infants (PT and PPT combined, referred to as PPPT) via the 30 variables of the APIB. Univariate student's t-tests were performed on all variables to assess their differentiating ability. Of the 30 variables, 21 achieved significance at the $p < 0.05$ two-tailed level. There appears to be a significant difference between all fullterm and preterm infants, as assessed by the APIB. The results indicate the continued reactivity and threshold to disorganization of the preterms as a group in responding to their environment. The fullterms at 42 weeks were autonomically and motorically stable, had good state control and better ability to maintain themselves in balance, stayed well-organized, and required much less help from the examiner. Overall, the preterms as a group at 42 weeks still had moderate difficulty with autonomic, motor, and state organization and considerable difficulty coming to a steady focussed alert state. They displayed much more autonomic lability, motoric stress signals, and inability to come to a robust crying state. Differences between fullterm infants and subgroups of the preterms were also analyzed. These results are reported in greater detail in Als et al. (Als, Duffy, and McAnulty, 1988a).

Prospective classification test. It is important to know how consistent these group differences are across populations. We examined data on 40 infants previously studied with the APIB, 20 of whom were fullterms (group FTMN) and 20 preterms (PTMN). The FTMN group matched our current FT group well. Likewise, the PTMN group best fit our PPT group, but had a slightly wider gestational age window (i.e., under 34 rather than 32-week preterm). The plan, therefore, was to initiate a prospective classification test to see if discrimination rules based on groups FT and PPT could accurately classify members of groups FTMN and PTMN. A training-set, test-set procedure was employed. Diagnostic rules were generated by the TICAS program CLASIF, a multigroup classification algorithm, which uses Geisser's equal dispersions, small samples procedure, as described by Cooley and Lohnes (1971). This program develops rules and thereby assigns subjects to one of several categories based on probabilistic measures derived from considerations of variance and covariance matrices. The data from the six-system sheet APIB summary features were analyzed. The training set consisted of FT and PPT and the test set FTMN and PTMN. Surprisingly, 100% of the FTMN (20/20) and 90% of the PTMN (18/20) were correctly classified, for an overall success of 95% (38/40). To be sure that the choice of PPT did not overly bias our results, we repeated the analysis using PPPT (all preterms) along with FT as the training set. Once again, prospective test set classification was successful, with FTMN classified 100% correctly (20/20) and PTMN classified 85% correctly (17/20), for an overall success of 92.5% (37/40). It can be concluded that APIB-derived classification rules generated on one population to discriminate fullterms from preterms can accurately discriminate on another population. The results speak to consistent behavioral differences between full and preterm infants, as well as the sensitivity of the APIB to these differences (Als, Duffy, and McAnulty, 1988a).

Behaviorally defined clusters of infants independent of gestational age group. Although the gestational age group differences at 2 weeks after due date are striking, it is well-known that there are early-born PPTs who will do well and fullterms who will not do so well. We therefore asked whether the APIB data allow us to subgroup our 98 infants into behaviorally defined, functionally distinct subgroups, cutting across the gestational age continuum. If this was possible, we would have functionally defined groups of infants whom we can track across time.

To see whether such natural groupings existed in our current data set, we employed cluster analysis (Anderberg, 1973). The major problem with cluster analysis is not in finding putative clusters, but in determining whether any given cluster configuration has meaning. TICAS program PINDEX was used in our studies. It employs a unique test of cluster configuration significance developed by Bartels, Bahr, Calhoun, and Wied (1970). Basically, it generates clusters and then determines whether the clusters identified are significantly separable from each other or are part of a homogeneous group of subjects. Once their separateness is established, it identifies which number of clusters is the most parsimonious representation of the data structure. The ultimate proof of cluster representation lies in the demonstration of similar clusters on two independent data sets. Accordingly, we randomly split our 98 subject group into halves of 49 each. We took care only that the numbers of FT, PT, and PPT subjects were similar in each half. Each set was separately submitted to program PINDEX. The six APIB summary sheet variables were used. For each group, using a statistical significance level of $p < 0.03$ as the cutoff, a configuration of three clusters was shown to be more significant than any other number. We then assessed whether these three-cluster groupings represented stable entities. Our approach was to develop classification rules on the three clusters of the first 49 subjects (training-set) and see if these rules would categorize the second 49 subjects (test-set) into the three clusters previously established. TICAS program CLASIF was used, again employing the six summary sheet variables. The results were remarkable. Forty-four of the 49 test set group members were correctly assigned over the three independently derived clusters, for an overall 89.8% classification success. Thus, there is a demonstrated consistency of cluster configurations when our population is split in half. These results are discussed in detail elsewhere (Als, Duffy, and McAnulty, 1988b).

What is the meaning or clinical significance of such clusters? To investigate this, we submitted the entire population to the PINDEX program and, as anticipated, three clusters emerged as more significant than other cluster configurations. Because the behavioral variables are scaled from 1 (well-organized) to 9 (poorly organized), we rank-ordered the clusters on the basis of the mean of the six variable means per cluster. We refer to rank-ordered clusters as *nimbuloids* (little cloudlike configurations), with number I indicating the most well-organized nimbuloid and higher numbered nimbuloids denoting increasing disorganization. Nimbuloid I infants show well organized (between 2 and 3) autonomic scores and state organizational and self-regulatory capacity scores, with relatively little need for examiner facilitation. Attentional capacity is in the focused, well-organized range, yet showing the largest standard deviation. This correlates well with our model of development, which perceives alertness as the most recently emerging subsystem in the newborn period, reflected in the relatively greater variability in comparison to the other subsystems. Nimbuloid I membership reflecting well-modulated behavior is shared by 19 FTs, 6 PTs, and 3 PPTs. It is pleasing to see that although the majority of infants in this top nimbuloid includes fullterms, there are also 9 preterms, 6 middle borns, and 3 very early borns who are also well-organized.

Nimbuloid II is characterized by relatively steady autonomic and motor functioning and by substantially less organized state modulation, self-regulatory ability, and higher facilitation necessary to maintain integration. Of interest is the disproportionately poorer attentional capacity of the Nimbuloid II infants. Relatively equal shares of subgroups, 12 FTs, 12 PTs, and 10 PPTs, occur in the nimbuloid.

Nimbuloid III scores reflect greatest disorganization autonomically, motorically, and state-wise, with the most poorly organized self-regulatory capacity and requiring increased examiner facilitation. Again the attentional system is proportionately the least well-organized. Nimbuloid III membership is shared by 3 FTs, 13 PTs, and 20 PPTs. The picture that emerges shows that the three nimbuloids cut across the gestational age grouping of FT, PT, and PPT and cluster the babies by quality of behavioral organization, grouping those preterms who are behaviorally well-organized with those fullterms who are poorly organized. This then gives us the desired subject grouping by behavioral functioning beyond that by gestational age grouping (Als, Duffy, and McAnulty, 1988b).

Given the behavioral data structure, it was of interest to know whether medical background variables in infant or mother and demographic background variables in the family are associated with nimbuloid status. A one-way ANOVA was developed for pertinent medical variables across all three APIB nimbuloids. The most dramatic differences were in the variables gestational age at birth, birthweight, height, and head circumference. These show significant differences between all three pairs of nimbuloids ($p < 0.001$). Weight, height, and head circumference at 42 weeks and Ponderal Index at birth, among others, discriminate primarily between Nimbuloids I and III, and discriminate between I and II, but not between II and III. Number of medications and postnatal complications differ in all three groups. It, thus, appears that infants in Nimbuloid III, as a rule, are earlier born, smaller, and continue to stay sicker than infants in Nimbuloids II and I. There were no sex distribution differences in the three nimbuloids. Inspection of maternal variables shows that the two variables that differentiate the nimbuloids are the obstetric complication scale score (Littman and Parmelee, 1974) and number of abortions. Obstetric complications show significant differences between mothers of Nimbuloid I and of Nimbuloid II infants, yet also significant differences between the other two pairs, Nimbuloid I and II and Nimbuloid II and III infants. Number of abortions significantly differentiates mothers of infants in Nimbuloid I compared to Nimbuloids II and III, but not II compared to III. No other differences (e.g., social class, maternal age, parity, etc) were found to differentiate nimbuloid status. It appears that mother's obstetric history and previous abortion history relates to infant behavioral functioning. These associations are discussed more fully elsewhere (Als, Duffy, and McAnulty, 1988b).

In summarizing Study I, it can be concluded that there is an intrinsic structure to the data set (three clusters) and that this can be defined reliably by behavioral measures. It can furthermore be concluded that the APIB identifies behavioral differences in a normal population of 42 weeks postconceptional age newborns, some of which are determined by the infant's gestational age at birth and others of which appear to reflect behavioral functional differences as assessed by the APIB. We are very enthusiastic about this beginning definition of the neuropsychological functioning of the newborn.

Study 2: Long-term Follow-up from APIB Assessment in the Newborn Period to Neuropsychological and Neuroelectrophysiological Assessment at Age Five Years

The key question, in the context of continuity, is whether our synactive model of differentiation and modulation of behavioral functioning has any meaning for later functioning. Having established that the APIB can identify behaviorally defined, stable subgroups of newborns the next step is to reassess the meaning of these behavioral configurations at a later age. Of the 40 infants used for the test of prospective classification (20 fullterms and 20 prematures born below 34 weeks gestation), we have recently completed an extensive re-evaluation of 28 of these infants, 14 fullterms and 14 preterms at age 5 years post EDC. The neuropsychological assessment battery is detailed in Table 1.1. It was designed specifically to assess bihemispheric, right and left hemispheric, and frontal capacities. It also includes an extensive timed motor examination based on the work of Denckla (1979). Furthermore, to assess our primary concern, subsystem integration, the children were studied in the previously described Kangaroo-box Paradigm, a play observation focussed on the integration of autonomic, motor, spatial, attentional, cognitive, social and affective skills. A full neurophysiological assessment (BEAM) was also performed on each child, based on a range of brain activation states including resting, listening, watching, and visual and auditory evoked response (VER) paradigms.

Newborn functioning. We first cluster-analyzed the 28 children's APIB systems sheet data. The children had been examined with the APIB at 40 weeks and 44 weeks postconceptional age. Three clusters were identified at each age point. Cluster membership concordance was highly significant. Thus, mean scores of the two assessments were utilized for final cluster analysis. Figure 1.2 shows the three APIB nimbuloids.

Nimbuloid I, reflecting the most well-organized performance, contains only fullterms. Nimbuloid III, reflecting the least well-organized performance, contains only preterms. Nimbuloid II, a middle position, has five fullterms and four preterms.

TABLE 1.1

5-Year-Old Neuropsychological (Nψ) Battery & Timed Motor Examination (TME)

Left Hemisphere		*Right Hemisphere*		*Frontal*		*Bihemispheric*		*TME (D)*	
[SEQP	HANDMVT., WORD &	[SIMP	GESTALT CL, SPAT. MEM.,	VFLU	VERBAL FLUENCY (M)	PA	PAIRED ASSOC (V)	TTR	TOE TAPPING R
	NUMBER RECALL (K)]		MATRIX ANAL., ΔS (K)]	RANC	RAPID AUTOM. NAMING—	LQ	LATERALITY Q	TTL	TOE TAPPING L
BADT	COLOR, SHAPE, NO. NAM.	SPAT	PICT. COMP, GEO. DES,		COLORS (D)			HTR	HEEL TOE TAP. R
	ABC-RECIT., NAM. WRIT.		BLOCK DESIGN (W)	RANN	RAPID AUTOM. NAMING—			HTL	HEEL TOE TAP. L
INFO	INFORMATION (W)	MAZE	MAZES (W)		NAMES (D)			HPR	HAND PATTING R
VOCAB	VOCABULARY (W)	VMIS	VMI SCALED SCORE	RANO	RAPID AUTOM. NAMING—			HPL	HAND PATTING L
SIML	SIMILARITIES (W)	MVTQ	MOT. FREE VISUAL PERCEP.		OBJECTS (D)			PSR	PRON.-SUPIN. R
COMP	COMPREHENSION (W)	RDISC	RECOGN.-DISCRIM. (F)	BEDF	BEAD NAMING—FORWD.			PSL	PRON.-SUPIN. L
ACH	FACES & PLAC, ARITH.,	DAPT	DRAW A PERSON (M)	BEDB	BEAD NAMING—BACKW.			FRR	FING. REP. TAP. R
	RIDDL., READ. DECOD. (K)	FACE	FACE RECOGNITION (B)	DS	DIGIT SPAN (K)			FRL	FING. REP. TAP. L
BNT	BOSTON NAMING TEST	FINGR	FINGER LOCAL (B)	FFD	ARITHMET. SENTENC.			FSR	FING. SEQ. TAP. R
AAS	AUDITO. ASSOC. ITPA	FLY	MAP WALKING		ANIMAL HOUSE (W)			FSL	FING. SEQ. TAP. L
PPVT	PEABODY PICT. VOCAB	RECT	RECTANGLES (S)	CNRS	CONNERS R SCALE				
TOKN	TOKEN TEST	PAPR	PAPERFOLDING (S)						
GCS	GRAMMATIC CLOS. ITPA								

Note. D = Denckla; K = KABC; W = WPPSI; B = Benton; F = Florida Batt.; M = McCarthy; S = Stanford-Bin.; V = Vellutino.

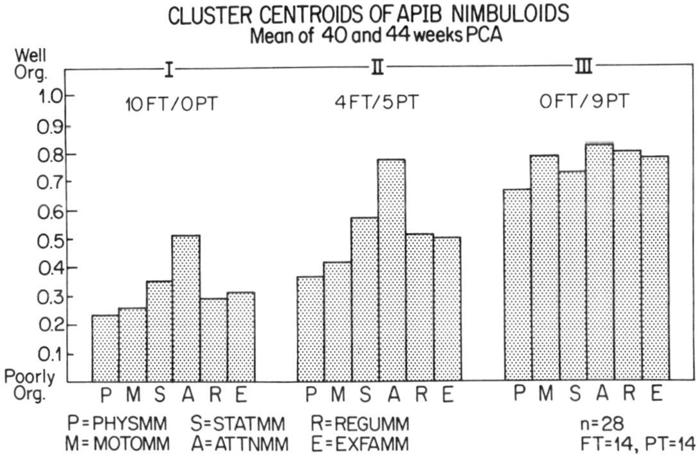

FIGURE 1.2. Cluster centroids of APIB Nimbuloids, mean of 40 and 44 weeks PCA (postconceptional age). Three nimbuloids emerged from the six APIB System scores for the 28 preterms. Scores range from 0.1, representing well-organized behavioral indices, to 1.0, representing poor organizational status. The six APIB System scores are: (1) PHYSMM—mean of autonomic reactivity scores, (2) MOTOMM—mean of motoric reactivity scores, (3) STATMM—mean of state organization reactivity scores, (4) ATTNMM—mean of attentional reactivity scores, (5) REGUMM—mean of self-regulation reactivity scores, and (6) EXFAMM—mean of examiner facilitation scores.

Five-Year-Old Functioning. An ANOVA testing for gestational age, sex, and gestational age by sex interaction effects was performed on the variables of the neuropsychological battery (Table 1.1). Gestational age differences were minimal and expected by chance. Sex differences favored the girls in the Paired Associate Task, Digit Span, and Draw-A-Person tests, whereas the boys performed better on six of the fourteen Timed Motor Exam variables.

Of interest is the large number of parameters (11 out of 47 summary variables) that show gestational age by sex interaction effects, as Figure 1.3 demonstrates. With the exception of Verbal Fluency (VFLU), which is considered an attentional, frontal measure, these results tend to show pronounced male–female differences in the fullterms, favoring the females, and minimal or no male–female differences in the preterms. This may be explained by Geschwind's hypothesis (1965) that the male brain may be left-hemispherically disadvantaged due to the prolonged chorionic gonadotropin exposure eliciting testosterone production in utero, a condition that the preterm male escapes.

To assess continuity over time, we first analyzed the neuropsychological data for underlying structure via cluster analysis (PINDEX). To accomplish this, the neuropsychological battery data were first condensed into summary variables, and four variables were chosen on an a priori basis. Freedom from Distractability

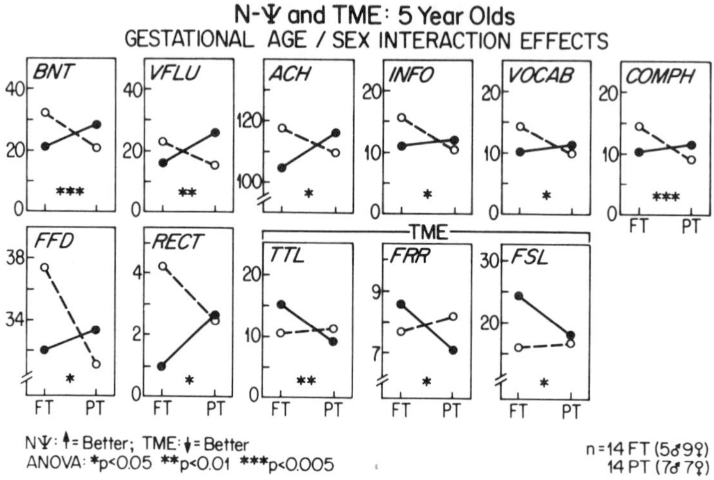

FIGURE 1.3. N-Ψ and TME: 5-year-olds, gestational age/sex interaction effects. Ninety-four neuropsychological (NΨ) and timed motor examination (TME) variables were analyzed, of which eleven showed significant gestational age by sex interaction effects. The eleven parameters shown in the figure are defined in Table 1.1. See also text.

(FFD) (WPPSI) was taken as an attentional, frontal measure, Badian Test Total Score (BADT) as a risk measure—probably largely left-hemispheric, Spatial Factor (SPAT) (WPPSI) as a right hemisphere measure, and Sequential Processing (SEQP) (K-ABC) as a left-hemisphere measure. We were guided in this variable selection by our clinical experience with children in the three- to seven-year-old age group. To our satisfaction, this first choice resulted in three parsimonious clusters. Figure 1.4 shows the three five-year-old clusters with the variables that formed them, each scaled from 0 to 1, with 1 being the best score. The five-year-old cluster ranking is obvious, and the nimbuloids are shown as I, II, and III. We performed an ANOVA on all 94 neuropsychological variables across the three five-year-old clusters. Forty-eight variables reached the $p < 0.05$ level, and, of these, 27 reached the $p < 0.01$ level. The five-year-old nimbuloids were differentiated on the basis of a number of attentional measures as well as achievement measures, the Badian Risk Battery, and some right hemisphere spatial ability measures. Our results on the neuropsychological batteries led us to ask whether our between-group differences could further be validated via neurophysiological assessment. For this analysis, we used the BEAM (Brain Electrical Activity Mapping) technique, a computer-based tool that interprets electroencephalographic and evoked potential data and displays results using rainbow scaled topographic images of differential electrical activity in the brain (Duffy, 1981, 1982; Duffy and Als, 1983; Duffy, Burchfiel, and Lombroso, 1979; Duffy, Denckla, Bartels, and Sandini, 1980; Duffy, Denckla, Bartels, Sandini, and

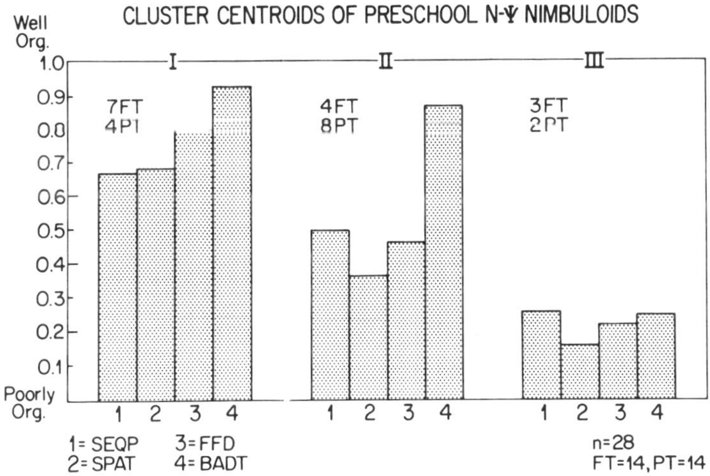

FIGURE 1.4. Cluster centroids of preschool N-Ψ Nimbuloids. Three nimbuloids emerged from the four neuropsychological (N-Ψ) battery summary variables selected. Scores range from 0.1 to 1.0, 1.0 being the best organized. See text for variable definitions.

Kiessling, 1980; Duffy, Jensen, Erba, Burchfiel, and Lombroso, 1984). An adjunct statistical methodology, significance probability mapping (SPM) (Duffy, Bartels, and Burchfiel, 1981), provides images capable of comparing group neurophysiological data. Using the F-test SPM, the electrophysiological tests of the five-year-olds (BEAM) were analyzed for the various brain activation states. These neurophysiological results were statistically significant in differentiating the three neuropsychologically defined nimbuloids, as seen in Figure 1.5. It appears that widely distributed large regions of cortex are involved in the group differences. The correlation of BEAM findings with behavioral functioning and the prediction of neuroelectrophysiological functioning are the subject of reports currently in preparation.

Having established three neuropsychologically defined subgroups that show strongly associated electrophysiological correlation, we asked whether there might be cluster concordance between the original newborn APIB nimbuloids and these five-year-old nimbuloids. Our analysis of cluster membership concordance indicated significance at a low level, with a Kendall's Tau of .21 ($p < .059$).

We also studied the 28 five-year-old children in the Kangaroo-box (K-box) Paradigm. The five-year-old paradigm consists of a large, three-tiered plexiglass box in an otherwise empty playroom. On the top and bottom tiers sit wind-up kangaroos. There are tools, a key, and a footstool available. The Kangaroo-box Paradigm follows the procedures described earlier. Video tapes of each episode are scored on five-point, behaviorally specified parameters. The parameters include autonomic, gross and fine motor, attentional, spatial, affective, and social

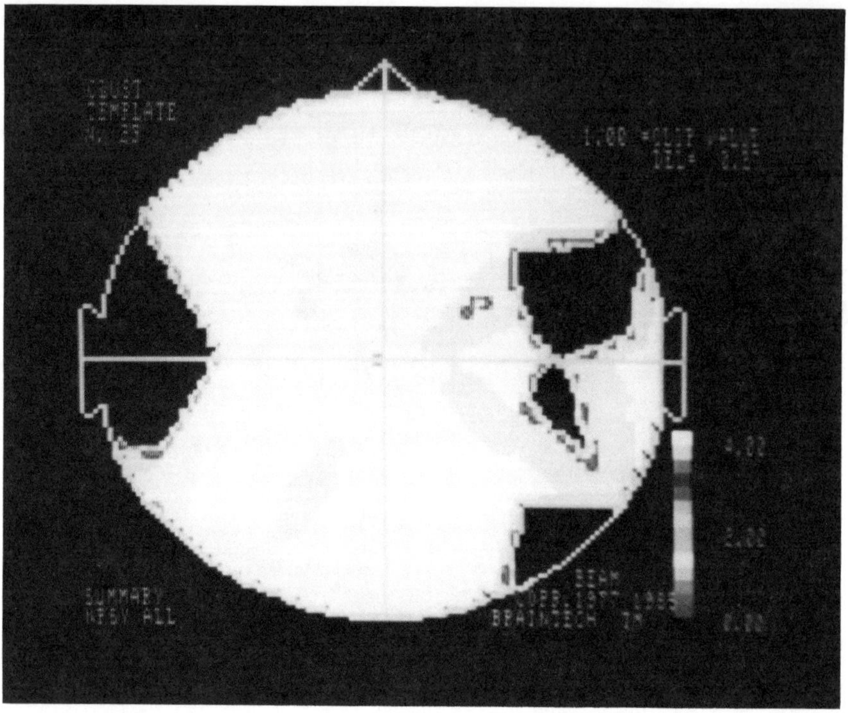

FIGURE 1.5. Summary BEAM SPM differentiating the three neuropsychological Nimbuloids.

interactive dimensions, again assessing modulation of performance beyond specific skill. The lack of a structured sequence in the paradigm and the need to combine motor with social planning in the spatially complex situation may make this paradigm a test of right hemisphere and frontal lobe functioning. Figure 1.6 shows a five-year-old with (a) pronounced over-reaching; (b) poor appreciation of himself in space, with generalized whole body movement, in relation to the toy; and (c) poor gross motor modulation, evidenced in awkward stance. The K-box data of the 27 children (one child missing due to mother's illness), unlike the neuropsychological data, showed pronounced preterm/fullterm differences at five years of age, consistently favoring the fullterms. Five of the 18 play episode variables and almost twice as many stillface episode variables (9 out of 17) showed significant gestational age group differences, primarily involving the motor domain, verbal capacity, and spatial and attentional functioning. It appears that the stillface episode considerably lowers the threshold of the preterm children's behavioral modulation. They are more dependent on their parent's structuring of the situation. There are few sex differences, favoring the females; these are, not unexpectedly, in the vocal, social, and affective display domains.

FIGURE 1.6a. 5-year-old Kangaroo-box Paradigm, overreaching with marked finger splay.

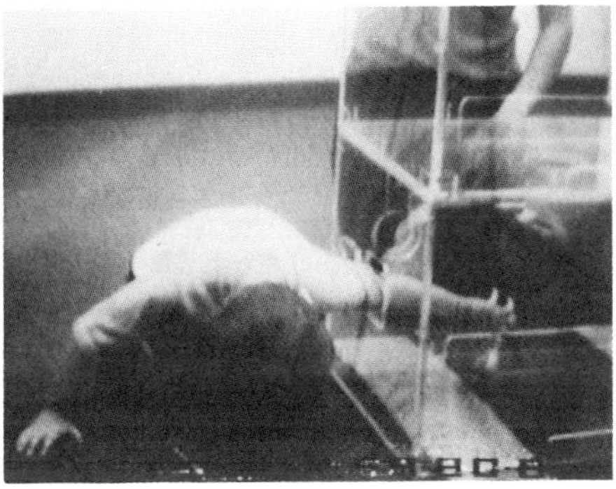

FIGURE 1.6b. 5-year-old Kangaroo-box Paradigm, whole body flexor generalization in reaching.

FIGURE 1.6c. 5-year-old Kangaroo-box Paradigm, awkward stance.

There are also few gestational age by sex interaction effects, with a trend to less differentiation in the preterms than in the fullterms and with preterm girls showing less adept performance than fullterm girls, whereas preterm–fullterm boy differences appear negligible.

When Kangaroo-box features were subjected to PINDEX clustering, two clusters emerged. These were ranked and therewith designated as nimbuloids. As Figure 1.7 shows, the grouping parameters are gross and fine motor modulation, motoric overflow and modulation of tempo of motoric action. Nimbuloid I children are relatively well-modulated, whereas Nimbuloid II children are very poorly modulated on these parameters.

In Nimbuloid I are 12 out of 14 fullterms and only 1 preterm, whereas in Nimbuloid II there are 2 fullterms and 12 of the 13 preterms. The BEAM data collected on the 28 five-year-old children showed consistent, highly significant correlations to the two Kangaroo-box nimbuloids. Referring to Figure 1.8, right hemispheric and frontal lobe involvement is more pronounced than left hemispheric involvement. Cluster membership concordance from the APIB in the newborn period to the K-box at age five years is very high, with a Tau of .69 ($p < 0.0003$).

To summarize Study 2, it appears not only that statistically separate and clinically meaningful behaviorally defined groups can be developed at differing

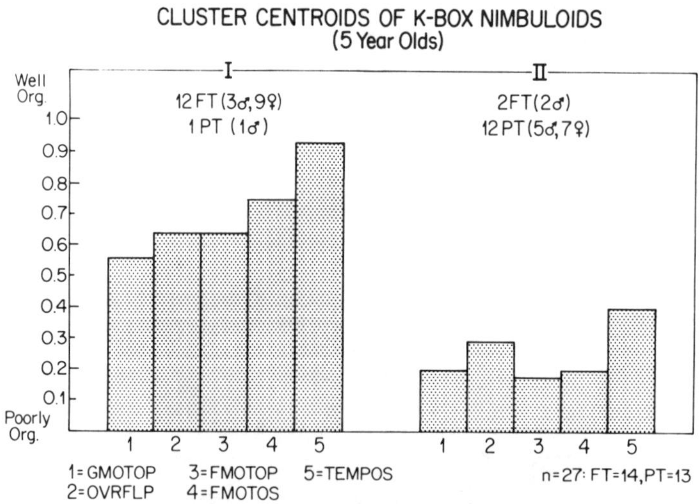

FIGURE 1.7. Cluster centroids of K-box Nimbuloids (5-Year-Olds). Two nimbuloids were formed on the basis of five K-box variables. The variables are: (1) GMOTOP—Gross motor modulation, play episode, (2) OVRFLP—Motoric overflow, play episode, (3) FMOTOP—Fine motor organization, play episode, (4) FMOTOS—Fine motor organization, stillface episode, and (5) TEMPOS—Tempo of motoric action, stillface episode.

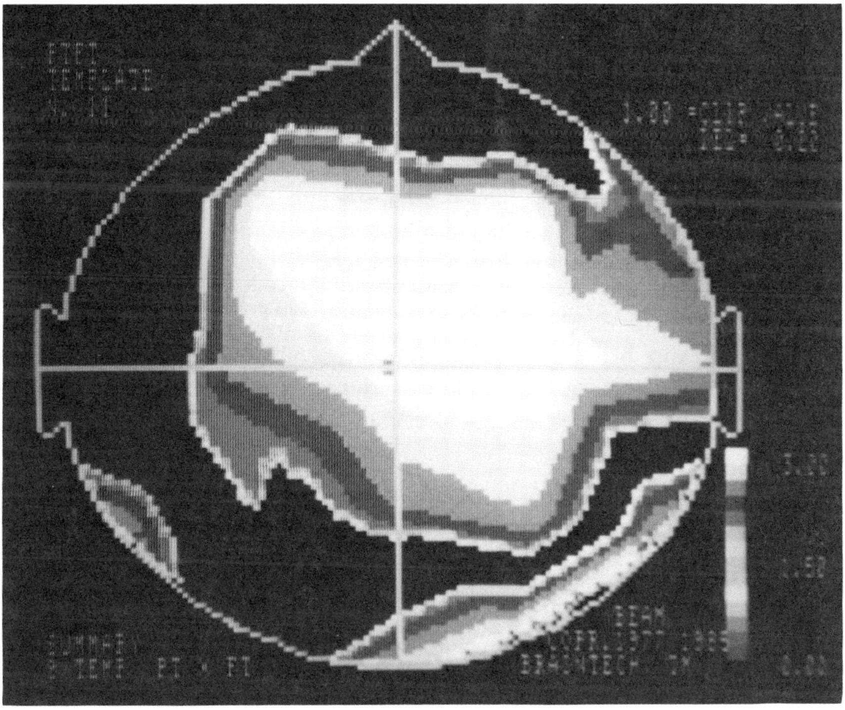

FIGURE 1.8. Summary BEAM SPM differentiating the two Kangaroo-box Nimbuloids.

age points, but that group membership tends to remain consistent over time. The spatial and attentional findings that keep emerging in our analyses warrant further examination, and we look forward to the analysis of our larger data sets. The very encouraging finding of the continuity relation of behavioral hyperreactivity and low threshold to disorganization in the newborn period (as measured by the APIB) to the later functional differences in motor, attentional, and spatial competence of these children (as measured by the K-box Paradigm) helps us to further understand the neurophysiological makeup of the young child in our synactive formulation of functioning.

CONCLUSIONS

The studies reported in this chapter show the following: Newborn behaviors of neurologically normal preterm and fullterm babies not only show differences by gestational age group, but also allow one to group infants reliably into low threshold, highly reactive, sensitive babies; moderately well-modulated babies; and well-modulated babies. Further, behavioral organizational group membership in the newborn period predicts to neuropsychological functioning at age 5 years, with the low threshold reactive newborns showing much greater difficulties in spatial organization, attentional capacity and sequential processing. Moreover, newborn behavioral group membership accurately predicts to differentiation and modulation of functioning in an unstructure challenging play situation involving high demands on motor and spatial planning, as well as on social interactive capacity, with low threshold newborns showing much greater difficulty in those domains. Electrophysiological correlates to five-year-old behavioral functioning are highly significant.

We are looking forward to further assessment of our study children during their school age years, in order to identify relations between early behavioral configurations in our synactive model of functioning and specific diagnoses at school age, such as attentional deficit disorder, specific learning disabilities, emotional disturbances (e.g., autism) and more global behavior problems. We are convinced on the basis of our clinical work that our research findings will bear out documentable connections from newborn functioning to later functioning. This work brings us, therewith, closer to early diagnosis of developmental difficulties and to the possible opportunity for amelioration. Thus, the behavioral organization of the infant as studied in the framework of our synactive formulation may provide a promising avenue for capturing some aspects of development germane to each individual from birth that show continuity over time.

ACKNOWLEDGMENTS

This work was supported in part by NICHD Grant RO1HD18654 to H. Als, Grant RO1HD18761 to F. H. Duffy, and the Mental Retardation Grant P30HD18655 to C. F. Barlow. We would like to express thanks to our assistants D. Moir, S. Phillips, S. Gillis, A. Rossow, M. Kennefick, and S. Papo; our EEG technologists A. Mirabella, S. Katz, E. Burke, and S. Manganaro; as well as our research secretaries C. Murray and C. B. Taymor for their patient and dedicated efforts; D. McAnulty for his superb editorial review; our Department Chiefs S. Walzer (psychiatry) and C. F. Barlow (neurology) for their unflagging support; M. F. Epstein, Director, Joint Program in Neonatology, and the medical and nursing staff for their continued facilitation of our research efforts; as well as C. T. Lombroso, emeritus Chief of the Seizure Unit, for sharing his expertise in pediatric EEG. Foremost, we thank all our study families for their generosity in participating in our research and giving us the privilege to observe their children so closely over such an extended period of time.

REFERENCES

Als, H. (1975). *The human newborn and his mother: An ethological study of their interaction.* (Doctoral dissertation, University of Pennsylvania, 1975). *Dissertation Abstracts International, 36,* 5.

Als, H. (1977). The newborn communicates. *Journal of Communication, 27,* 66–73.

Als, H. (1982). Towards a synactive theory of development: Promise for the assessment of infant individuality. *Infant Mental Health Journal, 3,* 229–243.

Als, H. (1983). Infant individuality: Assessing patterns of very early development. In F. Call, E. Galenson, and R. L. Tyson (Eds.), *Frontiers in infant psychiatry* (pp. 363–378). New York: Basic Books.

Als, H. (1984). *Manuals and scoring system for the assessment of children's behavior: Kangaroo-box paradigm.* Unpublished manuscripts, Children's Hospital, Boston.

Als, H. (1986). Synactive model of neonatal behavioral organization: Framework for the assessment and support of the neurobehavioral development of the premature infant and his parents in the environment of the neonatal intensive care unit. In J. K. Sweeney (Ed.), The high-risk neonate: Developmental therapy perspectives. *Physical and Occupational Therapy in Pediatrics, 6,* 3–35.

Als, H. (in press). Self-regulation and motor development in preterm infants. In J. Lockman & N. Hazen (Eds.), *Action in social context.* New York: Plenum.

Als, H., and Brazelton, T. B. (1981). A new model of assessing the behavioral organization in preterm and fullterm infants: Two case studies. *Journal of the American Academy of Child Psychiatry, 20,* 239–269.

Als, H., Duffy, F. H., and McAnulty, G. B. (1988a), Behavioral differences between preterm and fullterm newborns as measured with the APIB: I. *Infant behavior and development, 11,* 305–318.

Als, H., Duffy, F. H., and McAnulty, G. B. (1988b), Assessing functional competence in preterm and fullterm newborns with the APIB: II. *Infant behavior and development, 11,* 319–331.

Als, H., Lawhon, G., Brown, E., Gibes, R., Duffy, F. H., McAnulty, G., and Blickman, J. G. (1986). Individualized behavioral and environmental care for the very low birth weight preterm infant at high risk for bronchopulmonary dysplasia: Neonatal intensive care unit and developmental outcome. *Pediatrics,* 78, 1123–1132.

Als, H., Lester, B. M., Tronick, E. C., and Brazelton, T. B. (1982). Manual for the assessment of preterm infants' behavior (APIB). In H. E. Fitzgerald, B. M. Lester, and M. W. Yogman (Eds.), *Theory and research in behavioral pediatrics (Vol. 1,* pp. 65–132). New York: Plenum.

Anderberg, M. R. (1973). *Cluster analysis for applications.* New York: Academic Press.

Arend, H., Gove, F. L., and Sroufe, L. A. (1979). Continuity of individual adaptation from infancy to kindergarten: A predictive study of ego-resiliency and curiosity in preschoolers. *Child Development, 50,* 950–959.

Bartels, P. H., Bahr, G. F., Calhoun, D. W., and Wied, G. L. (1970). Cell recognition by neighborhood grouping techniques in TICAS. *Acta Cytologica, 14,* 131–324.

Blurton Jones, N. (1972). Characteristics of ethological studies of human behavior. In N. Blurton Jones (Ed.), *Ethological studies of child behavior* (pp. 3–37). Cambridge: Cambridge University Press.

Blurton Jones, N. (1974). Ethology and early socialization. In M. P. M. Richards (Ed.), *The integration of a child into a social world* (pp. 263–295). Cambridge: Cambridge University.

Blurton Jones, N. (1976). *Growing points in human ethology: Another link between ethology and the social sciences.* In P. P. G. Bateson and R. A. Hinde (Eds.), Growing points in ethology (pp. 427–451). Cambridge: Cambridge University Press.

Brazelton, T. B. (1973). *Neonatal Behavioral Assessment Scale.* Clinics in Developmental Medicine, No. 50. Philadelphia: Lippincott.

Bruner, J. S. (1968). *Processes of cognitive growth in infancy*. Worcester, MA: Clark University Press.

Bruner, J. S. (1974). Nature and uses of immaturity. In K. Connolly and J. Bruner (Eds.), *Growth of competence* (pp. 11–49). New York: Academic Press.

Bunge, R., Johnson, M., and Ross, C. D. (1978). Nature and nurture in development of the autonomic neuron. *Science, 199,* 1409–1416.

Coghill, G. E. (1962). *Anatomy and the problem of behavior*. New York: Macmillan.

Cooley, W. W., and Lohnes, P. R. (1971). *Multivariate Data Analysis*. New York: Wiley.

Denckla, M. B. (1979). Development of coordination in normal children. *Developmental Medicine and Child Neurology, 16,* 729–741.

Denny-Brown, D. (1962). *The basal ganglia and their relation to disorders of movement*. Oxford: Oxford University Press.

Denny-Brown, D. (1966). *The cerebral control of movement*. Springfield, IL: Charles C. Thomas.

Duffy, F. H. (1981). Brain electrical activity mapping (BEAM): Computerized access to complex brain function. *International Journal of Neuroscience, 13,* 55–65.

Duffy, F. H. (1982). Topographic display of evoked potentials: Clinical applications of brain electrical activity mapping (BEAM). *Annals of the New York Academy of Science, 388,* 183–196.

Duffy, F. H., and Als, H. (1983). Neurophysiological assessment of the neonate: An approach combining brain electrical activity mapping (BEAM) with behavioral assessment (APIB). In T. B. Brazelton (Ed.), *New Approaches to Developmental Screening of Infants* (pp. 175–196). New York: Elsevier.

Duffy, F. H., Bartels, P. H., and Burchfiel, J. L. (1981). Significance probability mapping: An aid in the topographic analysis of brain electrical activity. *Electroencephalography and Clinical Neurophysiology, 51,* 455–462.

Duffy, F. H., Burchfiel, J. L., and Lombroso, C. T. (1979). Brain electrical activity mapping (BEAM): A method for extending the clinical utility of EEG and evoked potential data. *Annals of Neurology, 5,* 309–321.

Duffy, F. H., Denckla, M. B., Bartels, P., and Sandini, G. (1980). Dyslexia: Regional differences in brain electrical activity by topographic mapping. *Annals of Neurology, 7,* 412–420.

Duffy, F. H., Denckla, M. B., Bartels, P., Sandini, G., and Kiessling, L. S. (1980). Dyslexia: Automated diagnosis by computerized classification of brain electrical activity. *Annals of Neurology, 7,* 421–428.

Duffy, F. H., Jensen, F., Erba, G., Burchfiel, J. L., and Lombroso, C. T. (1984). Extraction of clinical information from electroencephalographic background activity—the combined use of brain electrical activity mapping and intravenous sodium thiopental. *Annals of Neurology, 15,* 22–30.

Duffy, F. H., Mower, G. D., and Burchfiel, J. L. (1978). Experimental amblyopia production by random monocular shifts of visual imputs. *Society for Neuroscience Abstracts, 4,* 625.

Freedman, D. G. (1964). Smiling in blind infants and the issue of innate versus acquired. *Journal of Psychology and Psychiatry, 5,* 171–184.

Freedman, D. G. (1974). *Human infancy: An evolutionary perspective*. New York: Wiley.

Freedman, D. G. (1979). *Human sociobiology: A holistic approach*. New York: Macmillan.

Geschwind, N. (1965). Disconnection syndromes in animals and man. *Brain, 88,* 237–294.

Gesell, A. (1946). *The ontogenesis of infant behavior*. New York: Wiley.

Gesell, A., and Armatruda, C. (1945). *The embryology of behavior*. Westport, CT: Greenwood Press.

Grossman, K. (1978). Die Wirkung des Augenoffnens von Neugeborenen auf das Verhalten ihrer Mutter. *Geburtshilfe und Frauenheilkunde, 38,* 629–635.

Harmon, R. J. (1979). *Play, mastery, and attachment in term and preterm infants*. Paper presented at the meeting of the American Academy of Child Psychiatry, Atlanta, GA.

Herzog, J. M. (1979). *Attachment, attunement and abuse, an occurrence in certain premature infant-parent dyads and triads*. Paper presented at the meeting of the American Academy of Child Psychiatry, Atlanta, GA.

Hinde, R. A. (1970). *Animal behavior*. London, New York: McGraw-Hill.

Hinde, R. A., and Spencer-Booth, Y. (1967). The behavior of the socially living rhesus monkeys in their first two and a half years. *Animal Behavior, 15,* 169–196.

Hooker, D. (1936). Early fetal activity in mammals. *Yale Journal of Biological Medicine, 8,* 579–602.

Hooker, D. (1942). Fetal reflexes and instinctual processes. *Psychosomatic Medicine, 4,* 199–205.

Jennings, K. D., Harmon, R. J., Morgan, G. A., Gaiter, J. L., and Yarrow, L. J. (1979). Exploratory play as an index of mastery motivation: Relationships to persistence, cognitive functioning and environmental measures. *Developmental Psychology, 15,* 386–394.

Landis, S. C. (1980). Developmental changes in the neurotransmitter properties of dissociated sympathetic neurons: A cytochemical study of the effects of medium. *Developmental Biology, 77,* 349–361.

Lettvin, J. Y., Maturana, H., McCulloch, W., and Pitts, W. (1959). What the frog's eye tells the frog's brain. *Proceedings of the Institute of Radio Engineers, 47,* 1940–1951.

Littman, B., and Parmelee, A. H. (1974). *Manual for Obstetrical Complications*. Unpublished manuscript, UCLA.

McGraw, M. B. (1945). *The neuromuscular maturation of the human infant*. New York: Haffner Press.

Morgan, G. A., Harmon, R. J., Gaiter, J. L., and Jennings, K. D. (1977). A method of assessing mastery in one-year-old infants. *J.S.A.S. Catalog of Selected Documents in Psychology, 7,* 68.

Palay, S. L. (1979). *Introduction to the nervous system: Basic neuroanatomy*. Lecture delivered at the Harvard Medical School, Boston.

Patterson, P. H. (1979). Epigenetic influences in neuronal development. In S. O. Schmitt and F. G. Worden (Eds.), *Neurosciences Fourth Study Program* (pp. 929–936). Cambridge, MA: MIT Press.

Patterson, P. H., Potter, D. D., and Furshpan, E. J. (1978). The chemical differentiation of the nerve cells. *Scientific American, 239,* 50–59.

Rosenblatt, J. S. (1976). Stages in the early behavioral development of altricial young of selected species of non-primate mammals. In P. P. G. Bateson and R. A. Hinde (Eds.), *Growing points in ethology* (pp. 345–385). Cambridge: Cambridge University Press.

Sander, L. W. (1964). Adaptive relationships in early mother-child interaction. *Journal of the American Academy of Child Psychiatry, 3,* 231–264.

Sander, L. W., Stechler, G., Burns, P., and Julia, H. (1970). Early mother-infant interaction and 24-hour patterns of activity and sleep. *Journal of the American Academy of Child Psychiatry, 9,* 103–123.

Schneirla, T. C. (1959). An evolutionary and developmental theory of biphasic processes underlying approach and withdrawal. In M. R. Jones (Ed.), *Nebraska Symposium on Motivation*. (pp. 1–42). Lincoln: University of Nebraska Press.

Schneirla, T. C. (1965). Aspects of stimulation and organization in approach and withdrawal processes underlying vertebrate development. *Advances in the Study of Behavior, 1,* 1–74.

Schneirla, T. C., and Rosenblatt, J. S. (1961). Behavioral organization and genesis of the social bond in insects and mammals. *American Journal of Orthopsychiatry,* 31, 223–253.

Schneirla, T. C., and Rosenblatt, J. S. (1963). "Critical periods" in the development of behavior. *Science, 139,* 1110–1115.

Sigman, M., and Parmelee, A. H. (1979). *Longitudinal evaluation of the preterm infant*. New York: Spectrum.

Spinelli, D. N., and Jensen, F. E. (1979). Plasticity: The mirror of experience, *Science, 203,* 75–78.

Sroufe, L. A. (1979). The coherence of individual development. *American Psychologist, 34,* 834–841.

Werner, H. (1957). The concept of development from a comparative organismic point of view. In D. B. Harris (Ed.), *The concept of development* (pp. 125–148). Minneapolis: University of Minnesota Press.

Winter, P., and Funkenstein, H. H. (1973). The effect of species-specific vocalization on the discharge of auditory cortical cells in the awake squirrel monkey (Saimiri Sciureus). *Experimental Brain Research, 18,* 489–504.

2 Stability in the Biosocial Development of the Child Born Preterm

Marian Sigman
Departments of Psychiatry and Psychology, UCLA

Leila Beckwith
Sarale E. Cohen
Arthur H. Parmelee
Department of Pediatrics, UCLA

INTRODUCTION

A major task of the infant in the early months of life is to regulate responses to stimulation from endogenous and exogenous sources (Sander, Stechler, Burns, and Julia, 1970). With only limited neurological control mechanisms, the infant must integrate varied experiences including those stemming from internal states of arousal and more environmentally mediated visual, auditory, gustatory, olfactory, and tactile sensations. Furthermore, with development, the infant increasingly seeks out sensory experiences with what seems like an innate motive to interact with and assimilate the environment (Haith, 1980; Piaget, 1952).

Infants appear to begin postnatal life with varying capacities to regulate both their own endogenous states as well as their responses to exogenous stimuli (Als, 1983, chapter 1 in this volume; Anders, Keener, and Kraemer, 1985; Korner, Zeanah, Linden, Berkowitz, and Agras, 1985; Thoman, 1982). These individual differences stem from genetic, prenatal, and perinatal influences. Whatever the basis for these individual characteristics, they are likely both to affect the quality of the adaptation of the infant to the environment and to have consequences for infant development.

The central question of this chapter is the extent to which these individual characteristics remain stable over development. Based on the data presented, we argue that there is considerable stability in the child's capacity to regulate responses to internal stimuli and to engage with and process exogeneous stimuli.

Although the behaviors involved in learning seem quite discontinuous from infancy to childhood, there may be an underlying similarity in the psychological mechanisms required. The evidence presented bears principally on the issue of stability of individual characteristics but, in some cases, heterotypic continuity (Kagan, 1980) in processes may be inferred.

Early infant characteristics are unlikely to be the only determinants of development because all human infants mature in a social context. The relationship between the infant and the primary caregiver, shaped by characteristics of both caregiver and infant, should have an important influence on the nature of the child's development.

The purpose of this chapter is to review what we have learned about issues of infant stability and environmental influence over the last 15 years as we have followed a cohort of preterm infants from birth to early adolescence. We examine the cognitive development of these children at 8 years of age, because our current assessment in early adolescence is still in progress. The focus is on two assessments of newborn capacities for self-regulation and responsiveness to stimulation and on observations of caregiver-infant interactions over the first two years of life.

The subjects were a group of preterm infants born at the University of California Hospital or transferred to the nursery shortly after birth between July 1972 and the end of 1974. Prematurity was defined by a gestational age at birth of 37 weeks or less based on maternal report of last menses and a birth weight of 2500 grams or less. Infants with obvious congenital anomalies or syndromes were not enrolled in the study. This chapter focuses on the infants from families in which English was the predominant language used in the home. Although this subsample was culturally more homogeneous than the entire sample, the group is quite varied in terms of socioeconomic status. The mean Hollingshead index is 42.8 with a standard deviation of 13. The sample size varies at different ages because children could not be tested or located, but, in general, about 60 to 65 children were tested at each age.

The first question to be addressed is the extent to which the infant's neurological integration manifested in sleep, the infant's responses to visual stimuli when awake, and ongoing relationships between infants and caregivers over the first two years of life each separately influence development. The first section of this chapter reviews and integrates previously published findings. The second question is the nature of the associations between newborn characteristics measured in the laboratory and the relationship that the caregiver and infant form over the first two years of life. Finally, we describe the interactive effects of the infant's characteristics, measured in sleep and in response to visual stimulation when awake, and the ongoing relationship between infant and caregiver in influencing cognitive functioning assessed during the mid-school years.

THE RELATION OF INDIVIDUAL FACTORS TO LATER DEVELOPMENT

Design of the Study

Families were recruited into the study before the infant was discharged from the hospital. The family was contacted by a public health nurse after discharge and a home visit was conducted. All infants were provided with free medical care through the Well-Baby Clinic at UCLA during the first two years of enrollment in the study. Age was computed from expected date of birth to correct variations in gestational age. Standardized developmental tests—the Gesell and Bayley—were administered on five occasions during infancy, the Stanford-Binet was administered at five years of age, and the WISC-R was administered at eight years. For the purposes of this chapter, the eight-year WISC-R IQ is used as the principal outcome measure.

The sleep state and attention measures were conducted on the same day, at 40 weeks conceptional age. All infants had been discharaged from the hospital at this time and had been home for about 1 month. The family brought the infant to the laboratory and testing began after a short physical and neurological examination. The visual attention assessment was conducted first; the infant was fed, electrodes were attached, and then the baby was put to sleep by the caregiver in a small crib.

Sleep State Integration

For the study of sleep states, a single sleep polygraph recording was made for each subject at term, 40 weeks conceptional age, during a day nap in a sound-attenuated laboratory room (Beckwith and Parmelee, 1986). The recordings were bipolar from the frontal temporal, frontal central, temporal occipital, and central occipital positions over both hemispheres following the 10-20 system (Anders, Emde, and Parmelee, 1971). Respiration and heart rate were monitored electronically, eye movements and body movements were noted by direct observation.

The recording time was 90 minutes with the final 60 minutes used for analysis and the first 30 minutes considered to be adaptation to the strange situation. Records were visually analyzed by 20-second epochs with state and EEG codes determined independently, without knowledge of the subject's medical history or subsequent development. Data were coded for each 20-second epoch on the basis of observable behavior and physiological functioning: awake (eyes open); quiet sleep (eyes closed, no eye movements, no body movements except for occasional body jerks, and regular respiration); active sleep (eyes closed, eye movements, body movements irregular respirations); and, indeterminate sleep (eyes closed but not fitting either of the other two sleep states). Each 20-second epoch was coded in terms of the state that prevailed for most of the period.

The EEG was coded without knowledge of sleep states using a three-digit numbering system, and the last digit in the code identified the general nature of the pattern, and the first two digits indicated the specific form of the pattern expected at 40 weeks conceptional age (Anders et al., 1971). At this age, the EEG patterns of preterm and fullterm infants are very similar with only a scattering of immature EEG patterns in the preterm infants that are not found in the fullterm infants (Parmelee and Sigman, 1983). In our previous studies and in studies by others (Parmelee et al., 1968), four patterns have been readily identified in the sleep of the infants at term. These patterns are as follows: (1) 402-LVF, low voltage fast activity; (2) 403-M, mixed low voltage, fast and slow waves; (3) 405-HVS, high voltage, slow waves; (4) 407-TA, alternating burst of high voltage, slow waves with attenuated periods, known as tracé alternant.

We initially focused on quiet sleep as a marker of neurophysiological variation in the newborn period (Beckwith & Parmelee, 1986). This is a state that requires a high level of cybernetic control to suppress body and eye movements and maintain regular respiration concordant with each other for sustained periods of time along with specific EEG patterns. In the first months of life, quiet sleep rapidly increases in amount and in the strength of concordance of the determining parameters (Parmelee and Garbanati, 1987; Parmelee and Stern, 1972). Furthermore, this developmental process seems to be more a function of brain maturation than environmental circumstance in the early period (Anders, Keener, and Kraemer, 1985). In the analyses of quiet sleep it is particularly important to include the specific EEG pattern, 407-TA (tracé alternant), as a criterion of normal development, because lethargic infants secondary to illness or neurological problems can have long periods of no movement and regular respiration and appear to be in quiet sleep. Such infants, however, generally lack the expected EEG pattern, tracé alternant. Therefore, the total amount of quiet sleep independent of the specific EEG pattern is not an adequate marker of normal brain development, whereas that with the tracé alternant EEG pattern is a sufficient indicator.

More recently, we have been considering the relation of the amount of active sleep in the newborn period to later outcome. Active sleep rapidly decreases in amount in the first months of life as the amount of quiet sleep and waking increase. Neurophysiologically and behaviorally, active sleep appears to be a disorganized state because it is characterized by irregular respirations and heart rate, frequent body movements often of a twitching nature, and rapid eye movements. This state, however, does have an underlying distinctive neurophysiological organization and, even though it decreases in amount with maturation, it also develops increasing concordance and organization of the determining parameters (Parmelee and Garbanati, 1987; Parmelee and Stern, 1972). In the infants in our study, the expected EEG patterns 402-LVF and 403-M were so consistently present in active sleep that we have used the total amount of active sleep independent of EEG for our analyses. Active sleep is considered to be influenced by environmental circumstances (Anders et al., 1985) and related to the neurophysiological mechanism involved in wakefulness, particularly, to the alert awake state (Denneberg and Thoman, 1981) and, specifically to the alert orienting awake state in animals (Morrison, 1983).

On the average, the infants were asleep 93% of the observed time. About half the sleep time (mean = 56%), was coded as indeterminate sleep and half as more organized states of quiet and active sleep. Active sleep (26% of the sleep time) exceeded quiet sleep (18%) as expected at this age. The EEG pattern of 407-TA was predominant in quiet sleep, but the range of individual variability was wide. For example, infants had from 0% to 100% of quiet sleep with 407-TA as the associated EEG pattern. This EEG pattern was manifested in quiet and indeterminate sleep and almost never in active sleep.

The proportion of sleep time that the infant spent in quiet sleep without the specific EEG criterion was unrelated to IQ at eight years, but the percentage of quiet sleep with the 407-TA EEG pattern was significantly correlated with eight-year IQ (Beckwith and Parmelee, 1986). This was the only EEG pattern in all the different states to show an association with intelligence. Thus, the findings supported the expectation that the degree of state control in sleep, as manifested in the amount of this highly organized quiet sleep pattern, was positively associated with later intelligence in childhood.

The proportion of sleep time that the infant spent in active sleep was also associated with WISC-R Full Scale IQ at eight years (Beckwith and Parmelee, 1986). In addition, those children who suffered learning disabilities at eight years showed significantly less active sleep at term than children without learning disabilities (Cohen, Parmelee, Sigman, and Beckwith, in press).

Responsiveness to Visual Stimuli

The infant's responsiveness to a single 2 × 2 checkerboard was observed (Sigman, Kopp, Parmelee, and Jeffrey, 1973). In order to minimize the variations due to state differences, a standardized procedure preceded the observation. All infants were tested with a ten-minute neurological assessment that tended to leave them in the awake, alert state. In order to calm the babies somewhat, they were fed a small amount of milk. With the eyes still open, the infant was placed in an infant seat facing a white screen and the three-minute observation commenced. After the first one-minute trial, the checkerboard was illuminated with a series of flashing lights during the second one-minute trial. On the third trial, the checkerboard was again unilluminated. The infant's eyes were observed through a peephole at the side of the stimulus, and fixations were recorded and decoded in half-second intervals.

These studies indicated that preterm infants showed longer fixation durations at expected date of birth than full-term neonates (Sigman, Kopp, Parmelee, and Littman, 1977). We followed a small sample of full-term infants from birth to two weeks of age and found no change in the total fixation time, although other studies have found a decline in fixation time to unchanging stimuli as full-term infants mature (Brennan, Ames, and Moore, 1966; Fantz, 1965; Lewis, Goldberg, and Campbell, 1969; Wetherford and Cohen, 1973).

Preterm infants appear to process visual stimuli somewhat more slowly than full-term infants when these children are compared at four to twelve months of age (Caron and Caron, 1981; Rose, 1980; Rose, Gottfried, and Bridger, 1979; Sigman, 1976; Sigman and Parmelee, 1974). The longer fixation durations shown by preterm infants at term may therefore reflect a similar slowness in the rate of visual processing. Alternatively, preterm infants may be less able to modulate states of arousal so that they are not able to inhibit looking at the unchanging visual stimulus. Whatever the basis for the long fixation durations, preterm infants who look for long periods of time are expected to develop cognitively less well over time.

Support for this hypothesis has been presented in a number of publications (Cohen and Parmelee, 1983; Sigman, 1983; Sigman, Cohen, Beckwith, and Parmelee, 1986). A significant negative association was found between fixation duration and WISC-R IQ at eight years. The particular measures showing correlations are the length of the first fixation to each new stimulus, the total fixation time in the first trial, and the total fixation time over all trials. Infants who showed longer fixations were less cognitively competent later in life.

Infant-Caregiver Interaction

Assessments of the rearing environment were derived from naturalistic home observations made when the infants were one, eight, and twenty-four months (Beckwith and Cohen, 1984; Beckwith, Cohen, Kopp, Parmelee, and Marcy, 1976). At the one-month visit, the infants were observed on an average for 73 minutes of awake time; at eight months, 90 minutes of awake time, and at 24 months, 50 minutes of play time. The observer used a precoded check list, and every 15 seconds recorded presence of a set of infant behaviors, caregiver behaviors, and events defined as contingent or reciprocal interactions between caregiver and child, as well as behaviors of other persons towards the infant.

Certain interactive events were selected a priori for study as indicators of responsive caregiving. At one month, these were maternal positive attentiveness to the infant, face-to-face talk, mutual visual regard, maternal contingency to distress, and infant held upright; at 8 months, contingency to distress was omitted and contingency to nondistress vocalization and floor freedom were added, at twenty-four months, positive attentiveness, reciprocal interaction, and time spent in intellectual tasks (dramatic play, books, puzzles, and blocks) were used. The codes of each of these indices were converted at each age to standardized scores that assessed the degree to which the infant-caregiver interaction was facilitative.

Correlations were computed between these summary scores and IQ at age eight years. Generally, the individual summary scores obtained at one month had little association with later cognitive development. However, the frequency of total talking to the one-month-old infant was significantly related to eight-year IQ. The eight-month caregiver-infant interaction summary score was predictive of later competence in childhood for the female infants but not the male infants. The 24-month summary score was associated with childhood intelligence scores for both males and females (Beckwith and Cohen, 1984).

The competence of the infants who experienced consistently responsive caregiving over the first two years of life (in that their standardized scores were above the median at one, eight, and twenty-four months) was contrasted with that of infants whose interactional experiences were either consistently unresponsive or inconsistent. Consistently good relationships between caregiver and infant over the entire two-year period were clearly advantageous for the child's development. Almost one-third of the sample engaged in consistently responsive caregiver-infant interaction and most of these dyads were middle or upper socioeconomic status. However, the pattern of interaction altered the children's developmental test performance regardless of socioeconomic status. If the infant and caregiver were consistently and positively engaged, the child tended to perform significantly above the average, even within the poorer families (Beckwith and Cohen, 1984).

ASSOCIATIONS AMONG NEONATAL MEASURES

An association between the two neonatal measures might be expected, because both measures are thought to reflect the infant's capacity for self-regulation. In order to assess the extent of shared variance, correlations were computed among the percentage of sleep time that the infants at term date showed the tracé alternant pattern during quiet sleep, the proportion of active sleep, the proportion of quiet sleep, total attention time to the visual stimulus in the first minute, and total attention time in all three trials. There were no significant associations between the sleep and attention measures. Two possible explanations suggest themselves. First, the kind of state regulation required to maintain sleep states may be different from the kind of state regulation needed to focus and turn away from a visual stimulus. Thus, the measures may reflect different kinds of state regulation. Second, the sleep measures may assess state regulation whereas the attention measure may assess an early form of alertness to stimulation or information processing. The infant, then, may start life with capacities for sleep state

TABLE 2.1
Correlations Between Neonatal Measures with Factor Scores on the 8-Year WISC-R

	WISC-R Factors		
	Verbal Comprehension	*Perceptual Organization*	*Freedom from Distractability*
Quiet Sleep—%	—	—	—
Active Sleep—%	—	—	.30*
%407 in Quiet Sleep	—	.32*	—
Fixation Time—Trial 1	−.30*	−.28*	—
Fixation Time—Total	−.33*	—	−.29*

*$p < .05$, $df = 57$ to 59

functions and responses to external stimuli that are somewhat independent of each other.

One way to specify the processes captured by each of these infant measures is to compare prediction to different aspects of development. Intelligence tests can be considered to reflect a variety of intellectual processes. Performance on the WISC-R is often viewed in terms of the child's abilities on three factors: verbal comprehension, perceptual organization, and freedom from distractibility (Kaufman, 1975). In order to determine whether the attention and sleep measures tapped different processes, correlations were computed between the five newborn measures and the three WISC-R factors (see Table 2.1). The percentage of time that the child was in active sleep was significantly correlated with the freedom from distractibility factor and neither of the other two factors. The amount of time that the infant showed the EEG pattern, 407-TA, in quiet sleep was correlated with perceptual organization and neither of the other factors. The attention measures were associated with all three factors with, perhaps, somewhat stronger associations with verbal comprehension. Thus, there were differential relations between the state regulation and attention measures with IQ outcome in the school years.

ASSOCIATIONS BETWEEN THE NEONATAL MEASURES AND CAREGIVER-INFANT INTERACTION

The characteristics of the infant are likely to be associated with the nature of the relationship between infant and caregiver. Infants who have better modulated states may be easier to care for so that their social interactions may be more harmonious. Infants who are in more harmonious interactions may be better able to maintain organized sleep states because of the assistance provided to them by their caregiving environments. In order to confirm or disconfirm these hypotheses, correlations were calculated between the proportion of time in active sleep, the proportion of time in quiet sleep, and the duration of 407-TA in quiet sleep with a number of variables reflecting the caregiving environment. The three caregiving variables were the 1-month summary score, the percentage of time that the caregiver talked to the infant at one month, and the number of visits over the first 2 years in which the caregiver-infant interaction was observed to be good. In addition, a measure of socioeconomic status, the Hollingshead Index, and maternal IQ were also included.

There were no significant associations between the environmental measures and those sleep measures, the percentage of active sleep and of quiet sleep with 407-TA, associated with later outcome. On the other hand, the proportion of time that the infant spent in quiet sleep, irrespective of the EEG pattern, was correlated significantly with all three later interaction measures. Those preterm infants who spent more of the laboratory time in quiet sleep had caregivers who talked to them less, $r(74) = -.27, p < .05$, and showed less responsive caregiving, $r(74) = -.33, p < .05$, in the home at one month of age. Moreover, infants with more quiet sleep also continued to be involved in less satisfactory interactions over the two-year period, $r(63) = -.26, p < .05$. Thus, sleep organization and interaction were associated. However, the sleep measure related to home interaction was not predictive of later development, whereas the predictive sleep measures were unassociated with the caregiver-infant interaction patterns.

In order to assess the associations between early attention and the caregiving relationship, correlations were computed between total fixation time in the first trial and across all three trials with the 1-month home summary score, the percentage of time that the mother talked to the child, and the number of visits in which the caregiver-infant relationship was observed to be responsive. In addition, the Hollingshead Index and maternal IQ were also used. There were no associations between the attention measures and the interaction measures, but maternal IQ was associated with total fixation time, $r\ (43) = -.39, p < .05$. Infants who looked for less time had mothers with higher IQs than infants who fixated the stimulus for longer periods of time.

The home measures were not associated with attention measures for the sample as a whole, but associations between the caregiving environment and the infant's attention have been documented when individual factor scores were used separately for males and females (Sigman and Beckwith, 1980). Both male and female infants who showed brief fixations were involved in more optimal relations with their caregivers at one month of age, but the exact variables differed according to the infant's sex. To summarize these findings, female infants who showed brief fixations were held more by their caregivers, were talked to more, and were involved in somewhat more mutual gaze than female infants who showed long durations of fixation on the black and white checkerboard. Males who showed brief fixations received more responsive holding and were stressed less motorically. The direction of effects is impossible to ascertain with these data, because the laboratory measure was always administered at 40 weeks conceptional age and all the infants had been living at home for at least 1 month by that time.

CONTRIBUTION OF LABORATORY AND HOME INTERACTION MEASURES TO PREDICTION OF LATER OUTCOMES

We have previously shown that a consistently positive relationship between the caregiver and infant can buffer the child's development against problems in neurological integration (Beckwith and Parmelee, 1986). For the purpose of this chapter, we wished to examine the relative contribution of early neurobehavioral functioning and home interaction to later development across the entire range of relations rather than comparing an optimal group to all others. A set of multiple regressions was calculated with WISC-R Full Scale IQ measured when the children were eight-years-old. The total frequency that the caregiver talked to the one-month-old, percent of 407-TA in quiet sleep, proportion of time in active sleep, total duration of attention, and Hollingshead Index were entered into a multiple regressions with WISC-R Full Scale IQ as the dependent variable. Three variables predicted the eight-year IQ (Adjusted $R^2 = .26$), active sleep time, total fixation time, and total talking by the caregiver. Socioeconomic status did not contribute significantly to the regression. The amount of 407-TA in quiet sleep did not enter the regression once active sleep had entered. When the

TABLE 2.2
Regression between the Term and 1-Month Measures and WISC-R IQ at 8 Years

Variable	R^2	*df*	*F*	R^2 *Added*	*df*	*F*
% Active Sleep	.13	1,57	8.57*	.13	1,57	8.57*
Total Fixation Time	.21	2,56	7.16*	.07	1,56	5.13*
Total Talks—1 Month	.26	3,55	6.46*	.06	1,55	4.24*
With % Active Sleep Omitted from Independent Variables						
Total Talks—1 Month	.11	1,57	7.17*	.11	1,57	7.17*
Total Fixation Time	.19	2,56	6.47*	.08	1,56	5.23*
% 407 in Quiet Sleep	.26	3,55	6.32*	.07	1,55	5.05*

Note. The order in which variables entered was stepwise. Hollingshead Index did not enter into the equations.

*$p < .05$

multiple regression was calculated without active sleep as an independent variable, 407-TA in quiet sleep, total fixation time, and total caregiver talking all enter. Thus, measures from all three domains contribute independently to the variance in intelligence at eight-years of age.

CONCLUSION

Our program of research reveals that infants' sleep state organization, visual behaviors, and social relationships with caregivers exert independent effects on childhood intelligence. These results attest to the influence of infant characteristics on later development and, therefore, support the evidence for stability.

Sleep organization appeared to link to cognitive development in two different ways. The capacity for the infant to maintain a highly regulated form of quiet sleep seemed to reflect the level of neurological integration of the infant at term, to be relatively independent of environmental influences, and to have had a continuing impact on the individual's perceptual cognitive capacities. In addition, the proportion of sleep time in active sleep in this brief laboratory session was somewhat linked with characteristics of the family and was predictive of the child's capacities for sustained attention. In line with this, we have reported that the infant's tendency to engage in active sleep at term is related to the presence of learning disorders at age eight years (Cohen et al., in press). Thus, the infant's engagement in active sleep has a rather specific link to future attentional capacities. In this light, it is interesting that the duration of active sleep in the young rabbit is correlated with exploratory behavior one year later (Waite, DeSantis, Thoman, and Dennenberg, 1977).

Attention to visual stimuli appears to follow yet another path in its interconnections with the environment and its influence on development. The infant's tendency to fixate a stimulus for long periods of time was related to maternal intelligence, somewhat tied to the caregiving relationship, and was predictive of childhood intelligence. The association between neonatal attention patterns and later cognitive skills appears to be rather general. The lack of association between the sleep state and attention measures indicates that somewhat different processes are tapped by these assessments. Infant attention has been hypothesized to reflect three different processes, modulation of arousal, information processing, and early precursors of motivation (Bornstein and Sigman, 1986). We are currently testing the same subjects at age twelve years with a variety of measures of attention engagement, control, and selectivity. One of the aims of this study is to discriminate between the processes assessed by the early sleep state and attention measures. Some preliminary evidence from this follow-up suggests that infant attention patterns, as we have measured them, predict the efficiency of information intake.

Although the concurrent caregiving environment is associated to some degree with the characteristics of the infant, both infant and caregiver behaviors are independently associated with outcome. The ongoing relationship between the caregiver and infant can overcome neonatal characteristics, but this relationship is shaped by the abilities and limitations of both partners. It is clear clinically that intervention efforts must be focused on this relationship rather than individually on the caregiving environment or the infant. The difficulties incurred in bringing about change arise from limitations of both caregiver and infant, and the possibilities for change must emerge in their relationship. The evidence presented in this research points to both stability and a great deal of plasticity in the biosocial interaction that shapes development.

REFERENCES

Als, H. (1983). Infant individuality: assessing patterns of very early development. In J. Call, E. Galenson, & R. L. Tyson (Eds.), *Frontiers in infant psychiatry*. New York: Basic Books.

Als, H., Duffy, F. H., McAnulty, G. B., and Badian, N. (in press). Continuity of neurobehavioral functioning in preterm & fullterm newborns. In M. H. Bornstein and N. Krasnegor (Eds.), *Stability and continuity in mental development*. Hillsdale, NJ: Lawrence Erlbaum Associates.

Anders, T., Emde, R., and Parmelee, A. (Eds.). (1971). *A manual of standarized terminology, techniques and criteria for scoring of sleep and wakefulness in newborn infants*. UCLA, Brain Information Service, NINDS Neurological Information Network.

Anders, T. F., Keener, M. K., and Kraemer, H. (1985). Sleep-wake state organization, neonatal assessment and development in premature infants during the first year of life. II. *Sleep, 8,* 193–206.

Beckwith, L., and Cohen, S. E. (1984). Home environment and cognitive competence in preterm children in the first five years. In A. W. Gottfried (Ed.), *Home environment and early mental development*. New York: Academic Press.

Beckwith, L., and Cohen, S. E. (1978). Preterm birth: Hazardous obstetrical and postnatal events as related to caregiver-infant behavior. *Infant Behavior and Development, 1,* 403–411.

Beckwith, L., Cohen, S. E., Kopp, C. B., Parmelee, A. H., and Marcy, T. G. (1976). Caregiver-infant interaction and early cognitive development in preterm infants. *Child Development, 47,* 579–587.

Beckwith, L., and Parmelee, A. H. (1986). EEG Patterns of preterm infants, home environment, and later IQ. *Child Development, 57,* 777–789.

Bornstein, M., and Sigman, M. D. (1986). Continuity in mental development from infancy. *Child Development, 57,* 251–274.

Brennan, W. N., Ames, E. W., and Moore, R. W. (1966). Age differences in infant's attention to patterns of different complexities. *Science, 151,* 354–356.

Caron, R., and Caron, A. (1981). Processing of relational information as an index of infant risk. In S. L. Friedman and M. Sigman (Eds.), *Preterm birth and psychological development*. New York: Academic Press.

Cohen, S. E., and Parmelee, A. H. (1983). Prediction of five year Stanford-Binet Scores in preterm infants. *Child Development, 54,* 1242–1253.

Cohen, S. E., Parmelee, A. H., Sigman, M., and Beckwith, L. (1988). Antecedents of school problems in children born preterm, Journal of Pediatric Psychology.

Denenberg, V. H., and Thoman, E. B. (1981). Evidence for a functional role for active (REM) sleep in infancy. *Sleep, 41,* 185–1981.

Fantz, R. (1965). Visual experience in infants: Decreased attention to familiar patterns relative to novel ones. *Science, 146,* 668–670.

Haith, M. (1980). *Rules that babies look by.* Hillsdale, NJ: Lawrence Erlbaum Associates.

Kagan, J. (1980). Perspectives on continuity. In O. G. Brim and J. Kagan (Eds.), *Constancy and change in human development.* Cambridge, Ma: Harvard University Press.

Kaufman, A. S. (1975). Factor analysis of the WISC-R at 11 age levels between 6½ and 16½ years. *Journal of Consulting & Clinical Psychology, 43,* 135–147.

Korner, A., Zeneah, C., Linden, J., Berkowitz, R., and Agras, S. (1985). The relation between neonatal and later activity and temperament. *Child Development, 56,* 38–42.

Lewis, M., Goldberg, S., and Campbell, S. (1969). A developmental study of information processing within the first three years of life: Response decrement to a redundant signal. *Monographs of the Society for Research in Child Development, 34.*

Morrison, A. R. (1983). Paradoxical sleep and alert wakefulness: Variations on a theme. In M. Chase and E. Weitzman (Eds.), *Sleep disorders: Basic and clinical research.* New York: Spectrum.

Parmelee, A. H., Jr., and Garbanati, J. A. (1987). Clinical neurobehavioral aspects of state organization in newborn infants. In H. Yabuuchi, K. Watanabe, and S. Okada (Eds.), *Neonatal brain and behavior.* Nagoya, Japan: University of Nagoya Press.

Parmelee, A. H., Jr., Shulte, F. J., Akiyama, Y., Wenner, W. H., Schultz, M., and Stern E. (1968). Maturation of EEG activity during sleep in premature infants. *EEG and Clinical Neurophysiology, 24,* 319–329.

Parmelee, A. H., and Sigman, M. (1983). Perinatal brain development and behavior. In M. M. Haith and J. J. Campos (Eds.), *Handbook of child psychology; Vol. II. Infancy and developmental psychology.* New York: Wiley.

Parmelee, A. H., Jr., and Stern, E. (1972). Development of states in infants. In C. Clemente, D. Purpura, and F. Meyers (Eds.), *Sleep and the maturing nervous system.* New York: Academic Press.

Piaget, J. (1952). *The origins of intelligence in children.* New York: Norton.

Rose, S. A. (1980). Enhancing visual recognition memory in preterm infants. *Developmental Psychology, 16,* 85–92.

Rose, S. A., Gottfried, A. W., and Bridger, W. H. (1979). Effects of haptic cues on visual recognition memory in full-term and preterm infants. *Infant Behavior and Development, 2,* 55–67.

Sander, L. W., Stechler, G., Burns, P., and Julia, H. (1970). Early mother-infant interaction and 24-hour patterns of activity and sleep. *Journal of the American Academy of Child Psychiatry, 9,* 103–123.

Sigman, M. (1976). Early development of preterm and full-term infants: Exploratory behavior in eight-month olds. *Child Development, 47,* 606–612.

Sigman, M. (1983). Individual differences in infant attention: Relations to birth and intelligence at five years. In T. Field and A. Sostek (Eds.), *Infants born at risk: Physiological, perceptual and cognitive processes.* New York: Grune and Straton.

Sigman, M., and Beckwith, L. (1980). Infant visual attentiveness in relation to caregiver-infant interaction and developmental outcome. *Infant Behavior and Development, 3,* 141–154.

Sigman, M., Cohen, S. E., Beckwith, L., and Parmelee, A. H. (1986). Infant attention in relation to intellectual abilities in childhood. *Developmental Psychology, 22,* 788–792.

Sigman, M., Kopp, C. B., Littman, B., and Parmelee, A. H. (1977). Infant visual attention in relation to birth condition. *Developmental Psychology, 13,* 431–437.

Sigman, M., Kopp, C. B., Parmelee, A. H., and Jeffrey, W. E. (1973). Visual attention and neurological organization in neonates. *Child Development, 44,* 461–466.

Sigman, M., and Parmelee, A. H. (1974). Visual preferences of four-month-old premature and full-term infants. *Child Development, 45,* 959–965.

Thoman, E. (1982). A biological perspective and a behavioral model for assessment of premature infants. In L. Bond and J. Joffee, (Eds.), *Primary prevention of psychopathology, Vol. 6: Facilitating infant and early childhood development.* Hanover, NH: Universities Press of New England.

Waite, S. P., DeStantis, D. S., Thoman, E. B., and Denenberg, V. H. (1977). The predictive validity of early sleep development on later behavioral characteristics of the rabbit. *Biology of Behavior, 2,* 249–261.

Wetherford, M., and Cohen, L. (1973). Developmental changes in infant visual preferences for novelty and familiarity. *Child Development, 74,* 418–424.

PART I

Section 2: Physical Status

3 Infant Physical Status and La Cognitive Development

Sarah H. Broman
National Institute of Neurological and Communicative Disorders and Stroke

INTRODUCTION

This chapter examines stability and continuity in relations between physical status in the first year of life and cognitive abilities assessed longitudinally through age seven years. Results are drawn from the Collaborative Perinatal Project, a prospective multidisciplinary study of the developmental consequences of complications in pregnancy and the perinatal period (Broman, 1984). The healthy infant, one who is getting off to a good start, is highly valued both within the family and in the broader community. The physical state and responsiveness of the newborn and the newborn's subsequent growth and adaptation to environmental demands in the first years of life are issues of great importance to parents and students of human development. On both theoretical and empirical grounds, some degree of stability is expected from infant physical status to childhood cognitive development although the interactive processes are not yet fully understood (Sameroff and Chandler, 1975). Theoretically, it is generally accepted that all behaviors have a biological base (Scarr-Salapatek, 1975) and that cognitive functioning reflects the integrity of the central nervous system with environmental influences acting as modulating factors. Empirically, there is the consistent finding, replicated in the Collaborative Perinatal Project, that measures of physical and intellectual development are positively related (Garn, 1966; Tanner, 1970).

Early biomedical complications can affect mental as well as physical domains of functioning. They may be broadly classified as risk factors for nonoptimal cognitive development, such as low birthweight, or as established antecedents of cognitive deficit, such as Down's syndrome or major malformations of the central nervous system. During development, relations between the physical and mental domains may remain stable or they may change reflecting a pattern of recovery from biological insult or, less frequently, a worsening of cognitive impairment. Longitudinal data from the Collaborative Perinatal Project offer an opportunity to examine relatively long-term effects of infant physical status on childhood cognitive ability.

The major goal of the Collaborative Perinatal Project, funded and directed by the National Institute of Neurological and Communicative Disorders and Stroke, was the significant one of identifying causes of abnormal outcomes of pregnancy. The outcomes most central to the investigation were named in the original title, which was the Collaborative Study of Cerebral Palsy, Mental Retardation, and Other Neurological and Sensory Disorders of Infancy and Childhood. Other goals of this longitudinal study beginning in pregnancy were to determine etiologies of perinatal death, prematurity, congenital malformations, and more generally, to identify the important biological and environmental influences on physical and cognitive growth.

A series of retrospective studies published in the 1950s provided the background and rationale for the Collaborative Perinatal Project that began its 16-year period of data collection in 1959. Lilienfeld and Pasamanick and their colleagues (Lilienfeld and Pasamanick, 1955, 1956; Pasamanick and Lilienfeld, 1955; Pasamanick, Rodgers, and Lilienfeld, 1956) reported an excess of complications in pregnancy, labor and delivery, and the newborn period in birth histories of children with cerebral palsy, epilepsy, mental retardation, and behavior disorders. Little had made a similar connection for cerebral palsy approximately 100 years earlier (Little, 1862). Pasamanick and Lilienfeld developed the concept of a "continuum of reproductive casualty" that attributed a gradient of abnormal outcomes, from fetal and neonatal death to mild neurological deficit, to the brain injury resulting from complications in the pregnancy and perinatal periods. The Collaborative Perinatal Project was designed to investigate these relations prospectively thus avoiding the known biases of retrospective study. This goal committed the research program to its most unique characteristic, which is a longitudinal study population of more than 50,000 pregnancies.

In this chapter, following a description of methodologies, relations between 13 selected indices of neonatal and infant physical status and IQ scores at ages four and seven years are examined individually in samples of white and Black children followed to age seven years. Retention of each variable in multivariate analyses of cognitive outcome at the two ages is indicated. To place these results in perspective, an overview is presented of analyses of a wide range of precursors and correlates of mental development indicating their contribution to individual differences in childhood cognitive performance.

METHODS

The methods and procedures of the Collaborative Perinatal Project have been described in detail elsewhere (Broman, 1984). The essential elements of the research design were recruitment of a study population large enough to include adequate samples of rare, catastrophic outcomes and the collection of detailed systematically recorded data on the events of pregnancy and the perinatal period. Further sampling requirements were representation of a wide range of pregnancy conditions and the feasibility of completing longitudinal studies of the children.

Between 1959 and 1974, the offspring from 53,043 pregnancies were followed from gestation through age eight by multidisciplinary research teams in 12 medical centers. Over the six-year period of enrollment that terminated in 1965, over 7,000 of the women registered for more than one pregnancy. In both social and medical characteristics, the registrants were representative of patients receiving prenatal care in the collaborating medical centers, all of which were in urban areas and all but one of which served clinic patients. Guided by a sampling frame, some centers enrolled all eligible women registering for prenatal care (the most common exclusion was walk-ins on the day of delivery) and others selected random samples (Broman, 1984). Sample sizes by study center or institution and ethnic group are shown in Table 3.1.

In the original study population, 45% of women were white and 47% were Black as self-reported at time of enrollment. Mean socioeconomic index scores

TABLE 3.1
Sample Size by Institution and Ethnic Group
in the Collaborative Perinatal Project Population

	Ethnic Group				
	White	*Black*	*Puerto Rican*	*Other*	*Total*
Boston Lying-In Hospital	10,803	1,198	25	167	12,193
Providence Lying-In Hospital	2,096	672	5	49	2,822
Children's Hospital, Buffalo	2,383	59	12	15	2,469
Columbia-Presbyterian Medical Center	633	876	602	27	2,138
New York Medical College	269	1,558	2,630	17	4,474
Pennsylvania Hospital	882	8,580	316	14	9,792
Johns Hopkins Hospital	798	2,744	1	6	3,549
Medical College of Virginia	831	2,367	0	6	3,204
University of Tennessee College of Medicine	22	3,501	0	0	3,523
Charity Hospital, New Orleans	0	2,582	0	0	2,582
University of Minnesota Hospital	2,986	19	2	140	3,147
University of Oregon Medical School	2,216	861	1	72	3,150
Total	23,919	25,017	3,594	513	53,043

on a 95-point scale based on head of household's education and occupation and family income were 57 (± 19) for whites and 38 (± 18) for Blacks. The median age of women in the white and Black samples was twenty-four years and twenty-three years, respectively. Eighty-eight percent of whites and 64% of Blacks reported that they were married at the time of registration for prenatal care.

Sample loss occurred over the 16 years of data collection. The problem of maintaining adequate follow-up is a typical one in longitudinal studies, and the large-scale Collaborative Project was no exception. Follow-up rates for survivors in the population of 53,043 pregnancies were 88% at one year, 75% at four years, and 79% at seven years. At ages three and eight years, speech, language, and hearing examinations were administered in selected study centers only with follow-up rates of 48% and 47%, respectively (Broman, 1984). The number and characteristics of children lost to the study have been presented elsewhere (Broman, Nichols, and Kennedy, 1975; Hardy, Drage, and Jackson, 1979; Niswander and Gordon, 1972). The cohort for the present investigation of infant physical status as an influence on cognitive development is composed of the 17,432 white children and the 19,419 Black children who were examined at age seven years with a battery of psychological tests. Characteristics of the cohort are described in detail in the parent study of mental retardation in young school-age children (Broman, Nichols, Shaughnessy, and Kennedy, 1987).

The major points of data collection in the Collaborative Perinatal Project were during visits to the prenatal clinic, at delivery, in the newborn nursery, and at the follow-up ages of four, eight, and twelve months, four years, and seven years. In this chapter, the measures of interest are indices of biomedical status of the infant and the tests of mental development given in childhood. The predictor variables include abnormal conditions with low frequencies as well as continuously distributed biomedical characteristics.

Neonatal Measures

The neonate was observed initially in the delivery room and examined by a pediatrician at 24-hour intervals in the newborn nursery. A neurological examination was performed at two days of age. Other information from the nursery period included nurses' observations and the results of laboratory tests. A diagnostic summary of the nursery period was completed by a study physician. The following indices of neonatal status are examined in this chapter for their association with cognitive test scores at later ages:

(1) *Birthweight.* Recorded in the first hour of life. Mean values were 3284 (± 532)g in the white sample and 3055 (± 534)g in the Black sample.

(2) *Head circumference.* Recorded in the first day of life. Mean values were 34.0 (± 1.5)cm and 33.4 (± 1.7)cm in the white and Black samples, respectively.

(3) *1 minute Apgar score.* Recorded 1 minute after delivery by an independent observer. The score is the sum of five subscores, each ranging from 0 to 2, that evaluate heart rate, respiratory effort, muscle tone, reflex irritability, and color of the neonate. Mean values were 7.6 (± 1.9) in the white sample and 7.9 (± 1.9) in the Black sample.

(4) *Brain abnormality.* A clinical judgement made by a pediatrician after review of newborn nursery records for signs of seizures or spasms, abnormal muscle tone, hyperactivity or lethargy, and abnormal reflexes. The proportion of newborns affected was 0.4% in each sample.

(5) *Neonatal seizures.* Any seizure occuring within the first 28 days of life. The relative frequency was 0.3% in each sample.

The following diagnoses made in the newborn nursery were confirmed at one year of age and again at age seven years.

(1) *Down's syndrome.* Clinical diagnosis made by two examiners independently. Chromosome studies were optional. The proportion of infants with Down's syndrome was 0.1% in the white and also the Black sample.

(2) *Other genetic or post-infection syndromes.*[1] Includes 23 rare disorders of which the most frequent were post rubella syndrome ($N = 13$) and von Recklinghausen's syndrome or neurofibromatosis ($N = 7$). The relative frequency of this group of conditions was 0.2% among whites and 0.1% among Blacks.

(3) *Major malformations of the central nervous system.*[1] Of the eight malformations in this category, the most frequent was hydrocephaly ($N = 14$). The proportion of affected infants was 0.2% in the white sample and 0.1% in the Black sample.

Infant Measures

After the neonatal stage, follow-up examinations were conducted at specified intervals. At each visit, the mother or caretaker was interviewed about the child's interval history, with medical records obtained when indicated, and the child's physical measurements were recorded. During the first year, infants were given a pediatric examination at age four months, an evaluation of psychomotor abilities at age eight months, and a pediatric neurological examination at age twelve months. A diagnostic summary of the first year of life following nursery discharge was prepared by a study physician. The following biomedical characteristics of the infant were analyzed for their association with IQ scores at ages four and seven years.

[1]Syndromes and major CNS malformations are described in more detail in Broman et al. (1987).

(1) *Head circumference.* Recorded during the twelve-month medical examination. Mean values were 45.8 (± 1.5)cm in the white sample and 45.6 (± 1.5)cm in the Black sample.
(2) *Nonfebrile seizures.* Any nonfebrile seizure occuring between the ages of one and twelve months. The proportion of infants affected was 0.3% among whites and 0.2% among Blacks.
(3) *Delayed motor development.* Failure to walk with support or abnormal gait or posture as observed during the twelve-month pediatric-neurological examination. Infants judged to be delayed were 1.6% of the white sample and 1.5% of the Black sample.
(4) *Cerebral palsy.* A chronic motor disability of mild, moderate, or marked degree diagnosed at age one year in 0.4% of the white sample and 0.6% of the Black sample.
(5) *Congenital heart disease.* Both cyanotic and acyanotic types documented by laboratory tests at age one year. Among whites, 0.4% of infants were affected and among Blacks 0.5%.

Tests of Mental Development

Following the first developmental assessment at age eight months with the research version of the Bayley Scales of Mental and Motor Development (Bayley, 1965), cognitive abilities of children in the Collaborative Perinatal Project were evaluated in the preschool and early school-age periods. At age four years, the abbreviated version of the Stanford-Binet Intelligence Scale, Form L-M was administered (Terman and Merrill, 1960), and at age seven years, the Wechsler Intelligence Scale for Children (Wechsler, 1949). The abbreviated version of the Stanford-Binet consists of four of the six items at each age level. Mean IQ scores in the white and Black samples were 104.5 (± 16.5) and 91.4 (± 14.0), respectively. The Wechsler Intelligence Scale for Children was shortened to four of five verbal subtests and three of five performance subtests. Mean IQ scores at age seven were 102.4 (± 14.7) in the white sample and 89.5 (± 13.1) in the Black sample. Slightly less than 1% of children in the study population were unable to take the WISC at age seven years (N = 334). The substitute tests most often given were the Stanford-Binet and the Leiter International Performance Scale (Broman et al., 1987).

The stability of IQ scores from age four to age seven years was moderately high. In the Black sample, $r = .59$ ($N = 16616$) and in the white sample, $r = .63$ ($N = 14458$).

Several methods were adopted to increase the reliability of the data collected in the Collaborative Perinatal Project. These included conducting and recording examinations blind (that is, without prior consultation of the subjects' records), editing completed protocols twice (once at the study site and again at the Perinatal Research Branch), and the retesting of small random samples of children after a three-month interval by examiners from a different institution. These latter "quality control trials" were complex in both design and logistics but produced needed reliability coefficients for the four- and seven-year psychological examinations, and served as workshops to maintain comparable techniques of test administration and scoring among examiners at the different study centers. Adequate reliability was demonstrated for the psychological test batteries as exemplified by test-retest correlations of .83 for the Stanford-Binet IQ score at age four years ($N = 140$) and .85 for the WISC full-scale IQ score at age seven years ($N = 416$).

Analytic Techniques

Associations between the quantitative characteristics of the infant and mental test scores at subsequent ages are expressed in Pearson correlation coefficients. For the low frequency qualitative characteristics, often rare abnormalities, mean IQ score of the affected groups at ages four and seven years are presented. As Rutter (1984) pointed out, the correlation coefficient is an inappropriate measure of association or continuity when the independent variable involves a small proportion of the population.

Methods used in the multivariate analyses cited are described in detail in the original studies of cognitive outcome at age four years (Broman et al., 1975) and age seven years (Broman et al., 1987; Broman and Nichols, 1988). Basic procedures relevant to this chapter are summarized. In the four-year study, independent variables were selected in a correlation screen. The criterion for retention was a Pearson correlation with IQ score significant at $p < .001$ in the white sample ($N = 12210$) or the Black sample ($N = 14550$). In the technique used to regress predictors against IQ (BMD02R), a sequence of multiple lincar regression equations was computed in a stepwise manner (Dixon, 1973). At each step one variable was added to the regression equation. The variable added was the one with the highest partial correlation or partial F with IQ, holding constant variables already added. It was also the variable that made the greatest reduction in the error sum of squares. Variables were automatically removed when their F values became too low. The significance level selected for inclusion and deletion of variables was .01. The regressions were computed separately for boys and girls in each sample.

In comparisons of children with low and normal IQs at age four years (with low IQ defined as two standard deviations below the ethnic-sex group mean), the predictor variables were entered in a forward stepwise linear discriminant analysis (BMD07M). One variable was either added to or removed from the equations until optimum discriminant functions were achieved. The variable added was the one that would make the greatest reduction in the ratio of the within to the total generalized variances. Equivalently, it was also the one that, when partialed on the previously entered variables, had the highest multiple correlation with the groups. It was also the variable that, if added, would have the largest *F* value. The value of the *F* statistic for inclusion or deletion was 6.63, $p < .01$.

In the study of severe and mild mental retardation at age seven years, independent variables were screened by comparing the mean value in a retarded group with that in comparison groups in the white and Black samples (*N*s of 17432 and 19419, respectively). The comparison groups were four higher IQ levels for the severely retarded and three higher levels for the mildly retarded. The *t* and chi-square tests were used for quantitative and qualitative variables, respectively. Group differences were considered significant at $p < .05$. Variables passing the univariate screen in each of the seven comparisons were entered in SPSS stepwise two-group discriminant function analyses (Hull and Nie, 1981) and retained at $p < .05$.

In analyses of factors related to IQ score at age seven years, independent variables were selected in the white and Black samples in a correlation screen. The criterion for retention was a Pearson correlation of .06 or greater with IQ score. Stepwise multiple regressions for boys and girls in each sample were computed using the SPSS New Regression Program (Hull and Nie, 1981). The significance level for inclusion and deletion of variables was .01.

SINGLE INDICES OF INFANT PHYSICAL STATUS AND COGNITIVE DEVELOPMENT

Correlations of birthweight with IQ scores at ages four and seven years are shown in Figure 3.1. Values were low ranging from .07 to .12 in the two samples. As a consequence, birthweight played only a modest role in multivariate analyses of factors related to cognitive outcome. At age four, birthweight was retained as a predictor of IQ for Black girls (Broman et al., 1975) and at age seven years for children of both sexes in the Black sample (Broman and Nichols, 1988). In the study of mental retardation at age seven years, birthweight was a minor discriminator in the white sample between severely retarded children and those with IQs in the average range (Broman et al., 1987).

Because low birthweight is a widely used index of prematurity, a condition placing the neonate at some degree of risk for later motor and/or mental handicap (Parmelee and Haber, 1973), its contribution to a low level of cognitive functioning was further evaluated. The population attributable risk or PAR (Rothman, 1986) was calculated for birthweight less than 2000 grams and IQ score less than 70 at ages four and seven years in the white and Black samples.[2] At both ages, the PAR was 5% in each sample indicating that low birthweight, and its associ-

[2]Sample sizes used in calculating the population attributable risk were 14,445 and 16,595 for whites and Blacks, respectively, at age four years and 17,414 and 19,305 at age seven years.

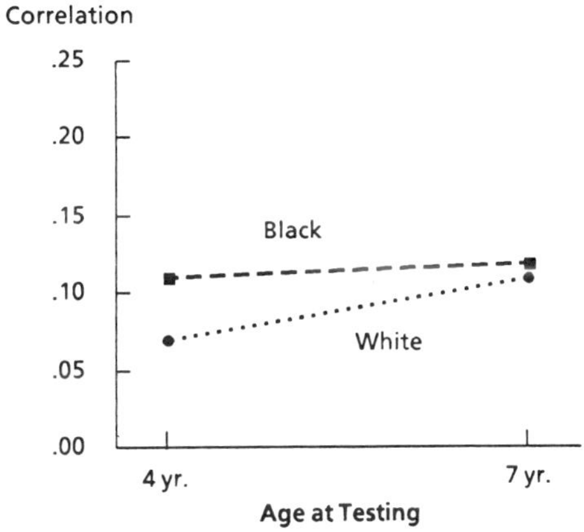

FIGURE 3.1. Correlation of birthweight with IQ scores in childhood.

ated complications, was a small but not negligible causal factor in cognitive deficit in this study population.

Head circumference at birth had correlations with later IQ scores comparable to those of birthweight ranging from .08 to .14 (Figure 3.2). Head circumference at 1 year of age, also shown in Figure 3.2, became increasingly correlated with childhood IQ scores, especially among whites (from .12 at age four to .21 at age seven), a trend suggested in the neonatal period. In contrast to birthweight, head circumference at birth was frequently retained in multivariate analyses indicating a greater independent contribution to cognitive outcome at both ages. It was a predictor of IQ score and low IQ level at age four for boys and girls in the white sample and a predictor of IQ score at age seven for boys and girls in both samples. In analyses of cognitive deficit at age seven, head circumference at birth was a discriminator for the severely retarded and for the mildly

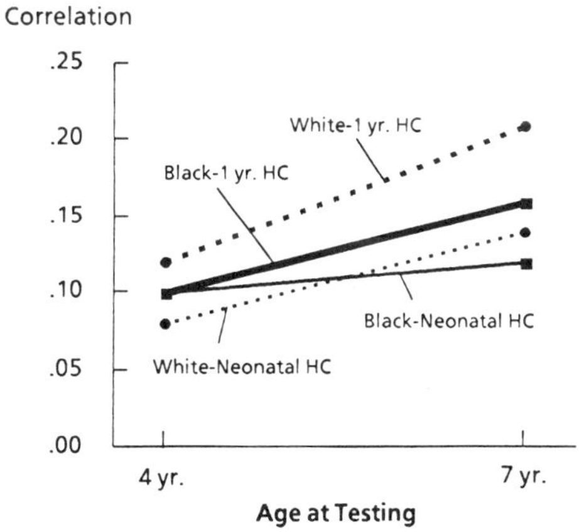

FIGURE 3.2. Correlation of head circumference at birth and age one year with IQ scores in childhood.

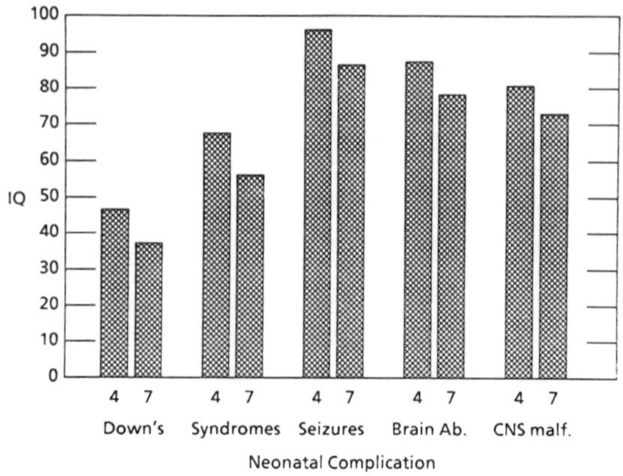

FIGURE 3.3. Mean IQ scores at ages four and seven years by neonatal complication: White sample.

retarded in comparisons with nonretarded groups. Head circumference of the older infant at age one year was consistently related to IQ score and to low IQ levels at both ages in each sample.

Apgar score at one minute after delivery was uncorrelated with IQ scores in the Black sample and had very low correlations of .03 and .04 with scores at ages four and seven years in the white sample. This index of neonatal physical status was a minor predictor of IQ at age four years for boys and girls in the white sample and a minor discriminator between low and normal IQ groups at this age for girls in both samples. At age seven years, 1-minute Apgar score made a small

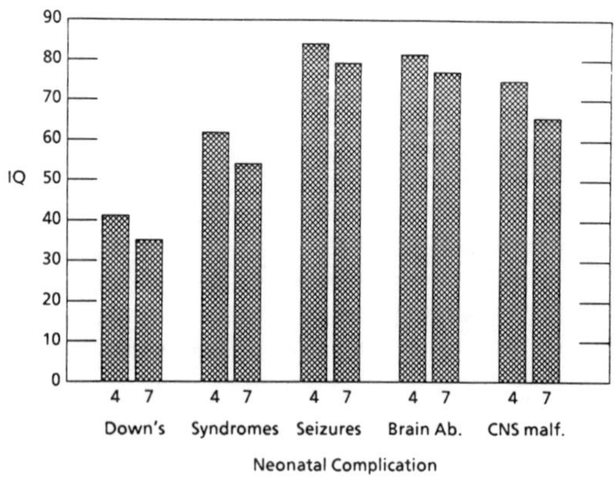

FIGURE 3.4. Mean IQ scores at ages four and seven years by neonatal complication: Black sample.

contribution to discrimination between the severely retarded and the average and above average IQ groups in the white sample.

Continuity in mental development of children with serious neurological complications as neonates is shown in Figures 3.3 and 3.4. Each condition, including the clinical impression of brain abnormality, was associated with a decline in IQ score from age four to age seven years. Decreases in mean scores of eight to eleven points among affected white children and five to nine points among affected Black children exceeded the two-point decrease in the total samples described earlier. The largest decrements occurred among children in the white sample with diagnoses of Down's syndrome, other genetic and postinfection syndromes, and neonatal seizures. The first two conditions, or the syndromes, were associated with the most depressed levels of cognitive functioning at both ages. In multivariate analyses of IQ at age four years, the category of neonatal seizures was not available for inclusion. Some of the other neonatal complications were extremely rare in the four-year samples that had been restricted to "first study registrants" (Broman et al., 1975). Those most often retained in analyses of IQ score and low IQ level were Down's syndrome and neonatal brain abnormality. In the larger samples at age seven years, each neonatal complication was retained consistently as a predictor of IQ score and as a major discriminator for the severely retarded. Down's syndrome among whites, other syndromes, and major CNS malformations were also discriminators for the mildly retarded at age seven years.

Trends present in the neonatal data were accentuated in relations between indices of physical status at age one year and mental test scores at ages four and seven years as shown earlier for head circumference. Mean IQ scores of children with neurological and other biomedical complications identified at one year of age are shown in Figures 3.5 and 3.6. Declines in mean score from age four to

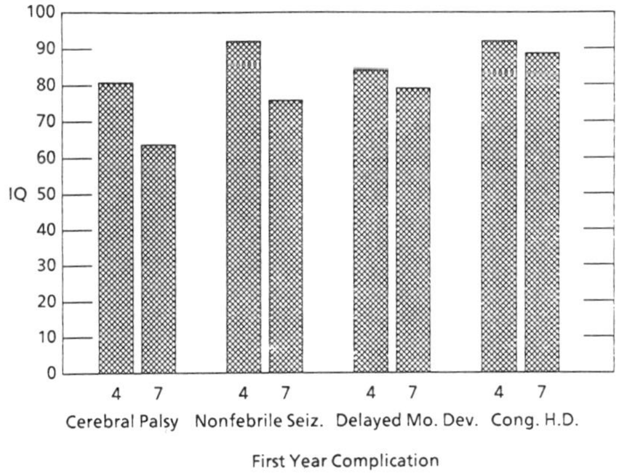

FIGURE 3.5. Mean IQ scores at ages four and seven years by first year complication: White sample.

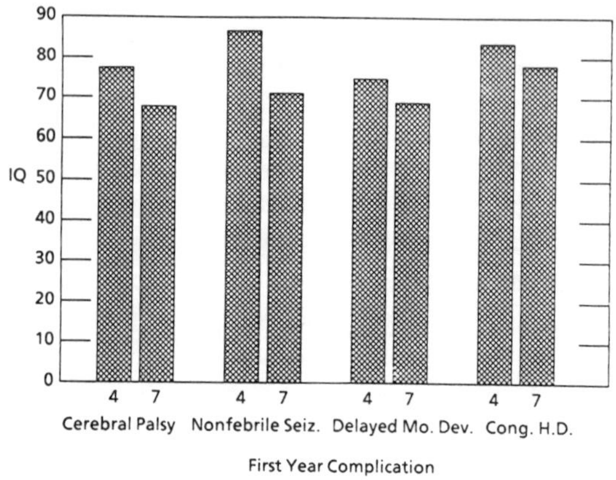

FIGURE 3.6. Mean IQ scores at ages four and seven years by first year complication: Black sample.

age seven years were only four to six points for children with congenital heart disease or delayed motor development at age one year, but for those with cerebral palsy or nonfebrile seizures in the first year declines were sixteen or seventeen points in three of the four subgroups. Level of functioning was lowest (mean IQs of 64 and 68) for the seven-year-old children given a diagnosis of cerebral palsy at age one (Nelson and Ellenberg, 1982). In multivariate analyses, all four of the infancy complications were consistently related to IQ and to severe mental retardation at age seven years. These conditions were also related to mild retardation among whites; only delayed motor development, an important discriminator, was retained in the Black sample. At age four years, delayed motor development and, among whites, cerebral palsy were the more consistent predictors.

INFANT PHYSICAL STATUS AND COGNITIVE TEST SCORES: AN OVERVIEW

To provide a context for evaluating the significance of the relations reported between selected indices of infant physical status and cognitive development, more comprehensive findings from the Collaborative Perinatal Project are briefly reviewed.

Low birthweight has long been considered a potent risk factor related to survival and to mental and motor development. The control of birthweight and of preterm delivery has been described as central to improving fetal and perinatal health, a major goal of pediatric research (Court, 1980). Unexpected findings emerged from an early study of birthweight, infant psychomotor development, and IQ scores in the preschool period (Broman, 1981). Although mean raw scores at 8 months of age on the research version of the Bayley Mental and Motor Scales increased linearly with birthweight as predicted, with the lightest group (≤ 2000 grams) scoring about two standard deviations below the heaviest group (≥ 3501 grams), birthweight explained only 5% to 6% of the variance in test scores in this population of 31,000 infants. Other variables in the multiple regression analyses were gestational age and sex of child, and ethnicity and education of the mother. Together, these variables explained only an additional 2% to 3% of the variance in Bayley mental and motor scores. These results show that, although low birthweight is a risk factor for delayed psychomotor development, the effect of birthweight on developmental outcome is small. Most of the variance in infant test scores was unexplained in these analyses.

The relation between birthweight and Stanford-Binet IQ scores at age four years was examined within four demographic subgroups because of the moderately high correlations between ethnicity and educational level of the mother and the child's IQ (r_s of .41 and .33, respectively).[3] The samples of 11,475 white children and 12,300 Black children were dichotomized at maternal education less than twelve years. Mean IQs increased with birthweight but differences were smaller than at eight months of age. In both subgroups of the white sample and among Black children whose mothers had at least a high school education, the lightest birthweight group scored about one-third of a standard deviation below the heaviest group (five to six points). The largest difference of nine IQ points was found among Black children whose mothers had not completed high school. In a regression analysis with six covariates, birthweight explained less than 1% of the variance in IQ scores at age four years. Ethnicity and maternal education were the best predictors, accounting for 16% and 6% of the variance, respectively. These results show that birthweight has less of an effect on measures of cognitive development at age four years, when verbal skills are assessed, than at age eight months. The most important predictors of preschool IQ were cultural and social characteristics of the family.

Perinatal anoxia, or reduction in oxygen level below the physiological requirements of the organism during labor and delivery, has been recognized as a possible cause of mental and physical handicaps in childhood for over a century. Studies of the association between perinatal anoxia and intellectual functioning were reviewed by Gottfried (1973), who found that inconsistencies in findings were related to important variations in research design. Some of the methodological issues raised were addressed in an investigation of ten clinical signs of perinatal anoxia as risk factors for cognitive deficit among children in the Collaborative Perinatal Project (Broman, 1979). Bayley Mental Scale scores at eight months were consistently lower within demographic subgroups for infants with a

[3]Birthweight and number of years of education completed by the mother were only weakly related with correlations of .06 in the white sample and .03 in the Black sample.

clinical judgement of respiratory difficulty in the newborn nursery, and for those who had suffered multiple apneic episodes. In multiple regression analyses, the ten signs of perinatal anoxia together explained only 2% to 3% of the variance in Bayley Scale scores in the white and Black samples.

At age seven years, IQ scores on the Weschler Intelligence Scale for Children (WISC) were lower among children with respiratory difficulty as newborns and among those with low Apgar scores of three or less at one minute after birth, although these differences were not consistently significant within demographic subgroups. The 10 clinical signs of perinatal anoxia explained less than 1% of the variance in seven-year IQ scores in the white and Black samples. In summary, prediction of cognitive outcome from signs of perinatal anoxia alone or in combination with other predictors resulted in an estimate of the magnitude of the relation which was very small in infancy and even smaller in childhood. Results from other methods of analysing these data, including lower mean scores for anoxic groups and a higher frequency of the clinical signs among the retarded, indicate that anoxia accounts for so little of the variance in cognitive test scores not because it is unrelated to outcome, but because relatively few newborns are affected.

A large-scale study of prenatal and postnatal factors related to IQ at age four years among 26,760 white and Black children examined 169 potential demographic, obstetric, and developmental predictors (Broman et al. 1975). The variables most highly correlated with IQ in the white sample, with coefficients ranging from .38 to .20 were maternal education, socioeconomic index, maternal nonverbal intelligence test score (SRA), Bayley Motor and Mental Scale scores, number of prenatal clinic visits, and length of gestation at registration for prenatal care (the only negative relationship). In the Black sample, variables with the highest correlations with IQ (.25 to .21) were the Bayley Motor and Mental Scale scores, the socioeconomic index, and maternal education. The mean IQ score was 13 points higher among whites than Blacks as indicated earlier. Within ethnic group, IQ scores increased with socioeconomic status and were slightly higher for girls than boys.

Many of the 80 maternal and child characteristics that passed the initial correlation screen ($p < .001$ in one or both samples) remained significantly related to IQ within demographic subgroups including neonatal complications, size at birth, eight-month Bayley Scale scores, and delayed motor development and neurological abnormalities at age one year. In stepwise multiple regression analyses conducted separately for boys and girls in each sample, all predictor variables accounted for a maximum of 28% of the variance in IQ among whites, and 17% among Blacks. Prenatal variables alone accounted for 20% of the IQ variance among whites, and a maximum of 11% among Blacks, with maternal education and the socioeconomic index contributing the largest proportion of explained variance not only in the analysis of the prenatal epoch but also when neonatal and childhood variables were added. The neonatal variables accounted for an additional 1% to 2% of the variance, and those from infancy and childhood added 4% to 6%.

The factors most highly related to low IQ scores at age four years (two standard deviations below the ethnic-sex mean) in stepwise discriminant analyses were a diagnosis of delayed motor development at one year, Bayley Mental and Motor Scale scores at eight months, maternal education, and relatively rare conditions associated with neurological impairment in the first year.

In analysing influences on cognitive development of children in the Collaborative Perinatal Project at age seven, major emphasis was placed on the groups that were severely or mildly retarded as defined by the traditional IQ cutoffs of scores less than 50 and those between 50 and 69 (Broman et al., 1987). Retarded and higher IQ groups were compared in stepwise discriminant function analyses in the white and Black samples. As expected, in the period from gestation through infancy, the factors most highly related to severe retardation were the rare but devastating conditions exemplified by Down's syndrome, malformations of the central nervous system, and cerebral palsy. Neonatal and infant seizures and delayed psychomotor development in the first year were other major predictors of severe retardation. Characteristics of the severely retarded as neonates included congenital malformations other than those of the CNS, apnea, clinical signs of brain abnormality, and smaller size than children in the comparison groups.

There were very marked differences between the largest risk factors for severe and for mild retardation. Prominent among the discriminators for the mildly retarded were socioeconomic descriptors and maternal intelligence test score, the only discriminator retained throughout the first year in all comparisons in both samples. Major CNS disorders were, as expected, much less important as discriminators for the mildly retarded and, when they occurred, were mostly confined to the white sample. Neonatal characteristics of the mildly retarded included non-CNS malformations, small size, respiratory difficulty, low Apgar score, and multiple birth.

The Bayley psychomotor scores at eight months were highly related to intellectual level at age seven years as was the diagnosis of delayed motor development at 1 year. These variables discriminated between the retarded and normal groups and between the severely and mildly retarded.

Findings from a prospective study of factors accounting for individual differences in IQ score at age seven years show a high degree of stability from the preschool to the early school-age period (Broman and Nichols, 1988). Results from the correlation screen and stepwise regression analyses at the two ages were very similar. Predictors from the prenatal period through the first year of life accounted for 34% of the variance in IQ at age seven years among whites and 22% among Blacks. Prenatal variables alone accounted for 23% of the IQ variance among whites and 12% among Blacks with socioeconomic status, maternal intelligence test score, and maternal education contributing the largest proportion of explained variance not only in the prenatal analysis but also in the summary regressions through age one year. In both samples, neonatal variables accounted for an additional 5% to 6%, whereas those from the infancy period added 5%.

In a study of early academic delay, another dimension of cognitive development, children who were low achievers at age seven were found to differ little in infant physical characteristics from normally achieving, IQ-matched comparison children (Broman, Bien, and Shaughnessy, 1985). An exception was lower weight at age one year among low achievers in the Black sample.

CONCLUDING COMMENT

In examining stability and continuity in relations between infant physical status and cognitive development in the preschool and early school-age periods, some intriguing but not major changes were found and mental development itself had a moderately high degree of stability. This set of relations contrasts with those obtained when the periods of infancy and childhood are compared as, for example, at ages eight months and four years. Measures of mental development in these two periods have an unstable relation (correlations less than .25; Broman et al., 1975) and a relatively large change occurs as the influence of physical status of the infant declines over this transitional period. In a study of risk and resilience in mental development, Wilson (1985) described the waning influence of prematurity and the increasing importance of home environment as represented by socioeconomic status and maternal education.

Although mental development was generally stable from age four years to age seven, some unexpected changes appeared in the predictive power of the infancy antecedents examined. Early physical growth as represented by head circumference at age one year became more predictive of IQ score over the interval from age four to age seven years. Similarly, serious neurological complications identified in the neonate and older infant had increasingly detrimental effects on childhood cognitive development. These findings underscore the importance of the preschool period as a time for interventions that foster the development of cognitive skills whether a child is at risk from poor nutrition or from fetal insult.

The relation between infant physical status and childhood cognitive development is for some indices a modest one. This is illustrated in results from a stepwise regression of 14 prenatal and neonatal variables on IQ score at age four years in the sample of white boys (Broman et al., 1975). Head circumference at birth was estimated to have a small incremental effect of slightly less than one IQ point (b = .90) per centimeter. In the same analysis, however, the estimated effect of the clinical diagnosis of brain abnormality in the newborn was a decrement of 14 IQ points. Estimated effect sizes are, of course, to some extent dependent on the factors included in the analysis.

The mechanisms through which biological processes influence psychological ones are not well-understood, as noted earlier. For children with overt or suspected neurological disorders, the ultimate goal is to identify the different underlying pathophysiologies. New research is needed on measures of central nervous system and autonomic nervous system functioning as contributors to individual differences in learning and performing cognitive tasks. Concurrent as well as predictive relations should be studied because, as Wilson noted (1985), an initial deficit is often offset by recovery, although at different rates, during the processes of development.

REFERENCES

Bayley, N. (1965). Comparisons of mental and motor test scores for ages 1–15 months by sex, birth order, race, geographical location, and education of parents. *Child Development, 36,* 379–411.

Broman, S. H. (1979). Perinatal anoxia and cognitive development in early childhood. In T. Field (Ed.), *Infants born at risk.* Jamaica, NY: Spectrum.

Broman, S. H. (1981). Risk factors for deficits in early cognitive development. In G. Berg and H. Maillie (Eds.), *Measurement of risks.* New York: Plenum.

Broman, S. H. (1984). The Collaborative Perinatal Project: An overview. In S. A. Mednick, M. Harway, and K. M. Finello (Eds.), *Handbook of longitudinal research (Vol. I).* New York: Praeger.

Broman, S. H., Bien, E., and Shaughnessy, P. (1985). *Low achieving children: The first seven years.* Hillsdale, NJ: Lawrence Erlbaum Associates.

Broman, S., and Nichols, P. L. (1988). *A prospective study of developmental influences on IQ at age 7.* Unpublished manuscript.

Broman, S. H., Nichols, P. L., and Kennedy, W. A. (1975). *Preschool IQ: Prenatal and early developmental correlates.* Hillsdale, NJ: Lawrence Erlbaum Associates.

Broman, S., Nichols, P. L., Shaughnessy, P., and Kennedy, W. (1987). *Retardation in young children: A developmental study of cognitive deficit.* Hillsdale, NJ: Lawrence Erlbaum Associates.

Court, S. D. M. (1980). Context and priorities for pediatric research in the eighties. *Pediatric Research, 14,* 1290–1994.

Dixon, W. J. (Ed.) (1973). *BMD biomedical computer programs.* Berkeley: University of California Press.

Garn, S. M. (1966). Body size and its implications. In L. W. Hoffman and M. L. Hoffman, (Eds.), *Review of child development research* (Vol. 2). New York: Russell Sage.

Gottfried, A. W. (1973). Intellectual consequences of perinatal anoxia. *Psychological Bulletin, 80,* 231–242.

Hardy, J. B., Drage, J. S., and Jackson, E. C. (1979). *The first year of life.* Baltimore, MD: Johns Hopkins University Press.

Hull, C. H., and Nie, N. H. (1981). *SPSS update 7-9: New procedures and facilities for releases 7-9.* New York: McGraw-Hill.

Lilienfeld, A. M., and Pasamanick, B. (1955). The association of maternal and fetal factors with the development of cerebral palsy and epilepsy. *American Journal of Obstetrics and Gynecology, 70,* 93–101.

Lilienfeld, A. M., and Pasamanick, B. (1956). The association of maternal and fetal factors with the development of mental deficiency. II. Relationship to maternal age, birth order, previous reproductive loss, and degree of mental deficiency. *American Journal of Mental Deficiency, 60,* 557–569.

Little, W. J. (1862). On the influence of abnormal parturition, difficult labor, premature births, and asphyxia neonatorum on the mental and physical condition of the child, especially in relation to deformities. *Transactions of the Obstetric Society of London, 3,* 293–344.

Nelson, K. B., and Ellenberg, J. H. (1982). Children who "outgrew" cerebral palsy. *Pediatrics, 69,* 529–536.

Niswander, K. R., and Gordon, M. (Eds.) (1972). *The women and their pregnancies.* Philadelphia: Saunders.

Parmelee, A. H., and Haber, A. (1973). Who is the "risk infant"? *Clinical Obstetrics and Gynecology, 16,* 376–387.

Pasamanick, B., and Lilienfeld, A. M. (1955). Associations of maternal and fetal factors with development of mental deficiency. I. Abnormalities in the prenatal and paranatal periods. *Journal of the American Medical Association, 159,* 155–160.

Pasamanick, B., Rogers, M. E., and Lilienfeld, A. M. (1956). Pregnancy experience and the development of behavior disorder in children. *American Journal of Psychiatry, 112,* 613–618.

Rothman, J. K. (1986). *Modern epidemiology.* Boston: Little, Brown.

Rutter, M. (1984). Continuities and discontinuities in socioemotional development: Empirical and conceptual perspectives. In R. N. Emde and R. J. Harmon (Eds.), *Continuities and discontinuities in development.* New York: Plenum.

Sameroff, A. J. and Chandler, M. J. (1975). Reproductive risk and the continuum of caretaking casualty. In F. D. Horowitz (Ed.), *Review of child development research* (Vol. 4). Chicago: University of Chicago Press.

Scarr-Salapatek, S. (1975). Genetics and the development of intelligence. In F. D. Horowitz (Ed.), *Review of child development research* (Vol. 4). Chicago: University of Chicago Press.

Tanner, J. M. (1970). Physical growth. In P. H. Mussen (Ed.), *Carmichael's manual of child psychology* (Vol. 1). New York: Wiley.

Terman, L. M., and Merrill, M. A. (1960). *Stanford-Binet Intelligence Scale.* Boston: Houghton Mifflin.

Wechsler, D. (1949). *Wechsler Intelligence Scale for Children: Manual.* New York: The Psychological Corporation.

Wilson, R. S. (1985). Risk and resilience in early mental development. *Developmental Psychology, 21,* 795–805.

4 Achievement and Cognitive Correlates of Minor Physical Anomalies in Early Development

Richard Q. Bell
Department of Psychology,
University of Virginia

Mary F. Waldrop
Bethesda, Maryland

INTRODUCTION

An instructive exercise in the study of continuity and discontinuity is provided in the succession of events starting in early pregnancy by which minor physical anomalies lead to later hyperactivity. The anomalies most often assessed in research are 18 unusual morphological features of the head, hands, and feet, which are part of a larger set originally described by J. Langdon Down (1866). They are not medically or cosmetically serious. In fact, except in the case of Down's syndrome, in which all or most of the 18 anomalies are present, they do not result in any lowered attractiveness (Rapoport and Quinn, 1975; Rosenberg and Weller, 1973; Schexnider, Bell, Shebilske, and Quinn, 1981; Von Hilsheimer and Kurko, 1979). Even though they do not produce detectable differences to the untrained eye, they serve as important markers of disorders with far-reaching consequences. This is because the anomalies develop from the same embryological layer as the central nervous system, and at the same time as sexual differentiation of the fetus occurs, so that whatever affects physical development is also likely to affect sex differences and neural structures important in control of behavior. If identification of the anomalies makes it possible to form a risk group, developmental pathways may be identified, and from this knowledge the optimal timing and mode of intervention can be devised (Bell, 1986). With the exception of severe psychopathology, most outcomes that are reviewed in this chapter are clearly within the range of behavioral or medical treatment. Thus, the anomalies point to problems that need help and can probably be helped, and not to the predestination implied by the studies of physiognomy, phrenology, and body types that characterized earlier research on biological contributors. Not only may research on anomalies lead to risk groups and prevention, there are some indications, to be discussed later, that they may help us understand the basic process of normal sex-role development (Halverson, 1981).

In this chapter we review studies of cognition and information processing in individuals with high anomaly counts. Other than studies of historical interest, the review is limited to the period from 1968 to date and to studies that yield findings pertinent to these areas in which a sufficient number of studies have been carried out to provide some cumulative and generalizable conclusions (Bell and Hertz, 1976). As in most areas of social and behavior research, individual studies may be exciting and stimulating, but research progress largely depends on trends that can be observed across many studies.

The review presents basic data on the nature of the samples and results, as well as an evaluation of the extent to which two important requirements have been met—achievement of behavior aggregation, as described by Epstein (1980), and the extent to which the measurement of the independent variable, the anomalies, and the dependent variable, the behavior, have been insulated from each other. The importance of avoiding the latter contamination is self-evident, but it is less widely recognized that a substantial number of studies in the social and behavior sciences simply fail to measure a sufficient amount of behavior over a long enough time period to yield meaningful results.

MEASUREMENT OF THE ANOMALIES

Before proceeding with the review of findings, the measurement of minor physical anomalies is described, as well as some problems of methods to which the potential user needs to be sensitized. Waldrop and Halverson (1971) provide a manual for assessing the anomalies, pictures of some anomalies for which verbal description is inadequate, norms for physical characteristics, and a weighting system to reflect degree of presence of each anomaly and its discriminating power. The examination takes ten minutes, and can be carried out (with minor adjustments for anomalies affected by race and developmental change) on neonates, preschoolers, young children, or adults. Subjectivity is involved in assessing some of the anomalies, but this is also true of neurological examinations and such widely used instruments as the Brazelton (1973). Training and calibration against experienced observers are highly desirable, but careful reading of the manual has been sufficient, as is seen in the many high values for inter-observer agreement that have been reported (see Krouse and Kaufman, 1982, p. 255).

As many as 93 anomalies have been measured (Tennes and Blackard, 1980), but by far the majority of studies has used the subset of 18 selected by Goldfarb and Botstein (1967) from Down's original set of 21. The subset is used because the total or total weighted score for this subset has yielded theoretically valuable discrimination or correlations in a large number of studies. The total or weighted scores are highly correlated, but the latter yield greater validity.

Whatever the merits of assessing a wide variety of possible anomalies, an investigator should *at least* assess the set that has been used most frequently, and provide data that permits calibration and comparison of results across studies. The set of 18 shown in Table 4.1 should be the core set, although there is a clear need for research on additional anomalies.

Krouse and Kaufman (1982) provide a useful critique of the measurement procedures for each anomaly, noting differences in assessment across studies, and the need for use of common criteria such as cutoff points for considering head circumference out of normal range, and procedures for measuring hypertelorism. They also point out that two anomalies are considered to be under genetic control in the sense of showing family resemblance. It might be a mistake, however, to delete these items from the exam (adherent ear lobes, curved fifth finger) because there is no reason why a morphological feature may not show family resemblance and also be affected by a disorder of fetal development. In a study by Campbell, Geller, Small, Petti, and Ferris (1978), the incidence of curved fifth finger was similar in autistic children and their nonautistic siblings, and the incidence was higher than in samples in which both siblings were normal. On the other hand, the incidence of adherent ear lobes was 13% in the autistic children and 0% in both nonautistic siblings and in normal

TABLE 4.1
Anomalies and Scoring Weights by Body Areas[a]

Anomaly	*Weight*
Head	
Fine electric hair, omit in infancy until permanent hair growth ≥ 1 inch	
Very fine hair that will not comb down	2
Fine hair that is soon awry after combing	1
Two or more hair whorls	1[a]
Head circumference outside normal range:	
> 1.5 S.D.	2
> 1.0 ≤ 1.5 S.D.	1
Eyes	
Epicanthus:	
Where upper and lower lids join the nose, point of union is:	
Deeply covered	2
Partly covered	1
Hypertelorism, use separate norms for non-Caucasian samples:	
Approximate distance between tear ducts:	
> 1.5 S.D.	2
> 1.0 ≤ 1.5 S.D.	1

(*Continued*)

TABLE 4.1
(*continued*)

Anomaly	*Weight*
Ears	
Low-seated ears:	
Point where ear joins the head not in line with corner of eye and nose bridge:	
Lower by > 0.5 cm	2
Lower by ≤ 0.5 cm	1
Adherent ear lobes:	
Lower edge of ears extend:	
Upward and back toward crown of head	2
Straight back toward rear of neck	1
Malformed ears	1
Asymmetrical ears	1
Soft and pliable ears	1[a]
Mouth	
High-steepled palate:	
Roof of mouth:	
Definitely steepled	2
Flat and narrow at the top	1
Furrowed tongue (one with deep ridges)	1
Geographic tongue	1[a]
Hands	
Curved fifth finger:	
Markedly curved inward toward other fingers	2
Slightly curved inward toward other fingers	1
Single transverse palmar crease	1
Feet	
Third toe longer than second:	
Definitely longer than second toe	2
Appears equal in length to second toe	1
Partial syndactylia of two middle toes	1
Gap between first and second toes (≥½ of the width of the big toe)	1

[a]Two or more hair whorls, soft and pliable ears, and geographic tongue are given a weight of 1 in this table rather than the customary weight of 0. The latter weight was assigned because the items did not discriminate in the original Goldfarb and Botstein (1967) comparisons of schizophrenic and normal children which was the only previous study available at that time on which to base weights. Pending revision of weights to reflect the wide range of subsequent applications, use of the weight of 1 for these three anomalies will provide for more uniformity between studies using weights versus these based merely on the number of anomalies. The weighted score should be computed with these three items scored 0 when comparison is being made with previous studies using weights.

This table is revised from Waldrop and Halverson (1971) with permission of the authors and publisher, Brunner/Mazel.

controls. Thus, in this particular study, curved fifth finger shows evidence of genetic control over family resemblance, whereas adherent ear lobes only shows evidence of a deviation in fetal development in the affected individual.

It has been 19 years since an original effort at standardization by George M. Weller led to the first published report on behavior correlates of anomalies (Waldrop, Pedersen, and Bell, 1968) and a description of the anomalies. Later, Waldrop and Halverson (1971) published a more detailed description and norms. The more precise the measurement of each anomaly, the less the error in making comparisons between groups. The adoption of common standards and research procedures would make it possible to align findings from different studies with more confidence. Most investigators have used the set described in Waldrop and Halverson (1971), and many have made adjustments for racial differences (such as hypertelorism and electric hair) by simply omitting items from the examination when their samples were heterogeneous. Some investigators have also made adjustments for developmental differences by deleting anomalies in examinations for age periods when the percentage of children showing the anomaly is high (Jacklin, Maccoby, and Halverson, 1980). These omissions, when applied to all cases in a homogeneous sample, do not affect the validity of group comparisons or correlations within the study, and usually only result in negligible differences in total score or weighted total score that are the differentiating statistics in most studies. Scores for individual anomalies are seldom the basis of comparisons because many of the individual anomalies show such low frequencies in the sample sizes studied that they could not differentiate major subgroups. In data from Steg and Rapoport (1975), although the total count differentiated learning disabled or childhood schizophrenia groups, and 10 of the 18 anomalies showed differences in the same direction as the total score, only two showed significant differences. Furthermore, despite developmental changes in some individual anomalies the weighted total score shows remarkably high stability of individual differences. Two studies have reported test-retest correlations above .80 between the newborn period and ages 1 to 3 using different examiners at the earlier and later ages (Burg, Hart, Quinn, and Rapoport, 1978; Waldrop, Bell, McLaughlin, and Halverson, 1978). Waldrop and Halverson (1971) reported test-retest correlations above .70 for samples between age two and a half and seven years, again using different examiners. Because different examiners were used, these test-retest values contain effects of unreliability due to interobserver differences and thus underestimate long-term stability. Evidently, stability of individual differences exists despite changes in the form and frequency of several components in the set of 18 anomalies.

The long-term stability of the weighted total anomalies scores, as well as the findings from many validity studies, indicate that variations in application of the procedures for individual items has not seriously detracted from the power of the measure of anomalies. The long-term stability also has implications for longitudinal measurement strategy. Within the age-range of newborns to early school-age children, the examination for anomalies could be administered at any time with considerable confidence that a stable congenital contributor has been indexed.

RESEARCH ON COGNITION AND ATTENTION

Tables 4.2, 4.3, and 4.4 summarize research on intelligence, school performance, and distractibility. The column involving anomalies differences or correlations briefly lists results from each study. To save space, statements concerning anomalies have been deleted from the summary of most findings. Either the total or weighted score may have been used. Except where indicated, all results were reported by the investigator as statistically significant. The symbols M and F are used for males and females and NA is used to indicate that information is not available in the published report.

The column "Aggregation and Basis" provides the data basis for the particular finding listed, following Epstein's (1980) thesis that inadequate sampling of behavior accounts for many inconsistencies in findings from a wide range of research areas. Adequate aggregation does not guarantee inter-observer agreement. There may have been inadequate training or instructions in reporting the behavior observed. Data on the problem of inter-observer agreement is not furnished in the table but is reported in the text, where there is information indicating failure to achieve customary standards.

It is assumed that the highest level of aggregation is achieved in the case of teachers who are interacting with a child in several settings and with other children over a period of one month or more (indicated by the number 1). Other levels are given numbers up to 7, as indicated in Tables 4.2, 4.3 and 4.4. In general, relatively high levels of aggregation are represented in most of the studies in Table 4.3 and 4.4, whereas only a moderate level characterizes the studies in Table 4.2, all of which used a single administration of a standardized IQ test. Aggregation basis is used in the context of other indicators of the value of a study. For example, if findings from a study lacking adequate behavior aggregation are essentially negative, whereas others with adequate levels of aggregation are positive, data from the latter are accorded more confidence.

The column "confound" provides an estimate of the extent to which the individual evaluating minor physical anomalies may have been influenced by knowledge of the behavior in question, or vice versa. Where the child's behavior, or the nature of the clinical service or treatment facility that provided access to the children reveals the dependent variable to the examiner, the term *probable* is listed under the column, unless the investigators specify that different individuals assessed the anomalies and the behavior. The study by Steg and Rapaport (1975) in Table 4.2 is an example of the referral source possibly influencing the assessment of anomalies. The original study by Waldrop, Pedersen and Bell

TABLE 4.2
Relations Between Anomalies and Intelligence

	Sex and N	*Age in Years*	*SES*	*Anomalies Correlation With IQ*	*Aggregation and Basis*	*Confound*
Oettinger et al. (1979)	M 92;F 67	NA	NA	n.s.	Standardized test (4)	None
Marcus, Hans et al. (1985)	M 46;F 54	8–15	M	n.s.	Standardized test (4)	None
Quinn & Rapoport (1974)	M 76	6–12	M	n.s.	Standardized test (4)	None
Quinn, Renfield et al. (1977)	123; Sex: NA	1		n.s.	Standardized test (4)	None
Rapoport, Quinn, & Lambrecht (1974)	M 76	6–12	M	n.s.	Standardized test (4)	None
Rosenberg & Weller (1973)	M 53;F 46	6–8	M	−.18 ($p < .05$)	Standardized test (4)	None
Steg & Rapoport (1975)						
Learning disabled	M 23	4–12	M	n.s.	Standardized test (4)	Unlikely
Child clinic	M 26			n.s.		
Tignor (1975)	M 46;F 47	7–8	M	−.29	Standardized test (4)	None
Waldrop, Bell, & Goering (1976)	F 93	7–12	LM	−.39	Standardized test (4)	None
Waldrop & Halverson (1971): Stability Study	M 35;F 27	7–8	M	M + F − .41	Standardized test (4)	None

TABLE 4.3
Relations Between Anomalies and School Performance

	Sex and N	*Age in Years*	*SES*	*Anomalies Difference or Correlation With IQ*	*Aggregation and Basis*	*Confound*
Halverson & Victor (1976)	M 50;F 50	7–11	M	M only r − .25 with achievement test; F − .20 n.s.	Standardized tests (4)	None
Oettinger et al. (1979)						
Learning disabled	A 41, Sex: NA	NA	NA	A > B anomalies; means NA	Special school placement (3)	NA
Controls	B 41					
Rosenberg & Weller (1973)	M 53;F 46	6–8	NA	9/11 with high anomalies retained in grade	Teachers' judgments (1)	None
Steg & Rapoport (1976)						
Learning disabled	A 23 all M	4–12	M	AB 4.24 vs. CD 2.73 anomalies	Special school or residential treatment placement (3)	Probable
Autistic, psychotic	B 28					
Child clinic	C 26					
Pediatric controls	D 31					
Tignor (1975)	M 46;F 47	7–8	M	r n.s. with achievement if − r with IQ partialled out	Standardized tests (4)	None
von Hilsheimer & Kurko (1979)						
Learning disabled	A 70 Sex: NA	14–16	M & U	A + B + C = 93%	Special or residential school placement (3)	Probable
Special education	B 32	7–12	M & U	≥ 3 anomalies; D = 62%		
Autistic	C 10	5–6	M & U			
Controls	D 648	13–15	M & U			
Waldrop, Bell, & Goering (1976)	F 93	7–12	LM	r n.s. with math or verbal achievement	Standardized tests (4)	None

[a]Except where indicated, all correlations, mean or percentage differences listed in this column are significant at or beyond the .05 level. For the Rosenberg and Weller study (1973) the entry indicates that nine out of the 11 children with five anomalies or more were retained in grade. The rest of the table in the original could not be reported for space reasons. The entry for the Steg & Rapoport study (1975) indicates that groups A and B were not significantly different in mean number of anomalies but were significantly different from the C and D groups. The entry for the von Hilsheimer & Kurko study (1979) indicates that groups A, B, and C were not significantly different with respect to percent of cases having three or more anomalies, but the three groups combined showed 93% and this was significantly different from the percent of 62% for the D group.

TABLE 4.4

Correlations Between Anomalies and Attention

	Sex and N	Age in Years	SES	Anomalies Correlation With IQ	Aggregation and Basis	Confound
Fogel (1985)	M 57;F 64	10–13	NA	M only high vs low anomalies = 30% vs 7% distractible children	Borderline: 1 day of study (6)	Probable
Halverson & Victor (1976)	M 50;F 50	7–11	M	M only r .35 with distractibility	Standardized checklist (4)	None
O'Donnell, O'Neill, & Staley (1979)						
Original study	A M 47;F 39	2–6	M	A B & C pooled r = M .44, F .18 n.s.	Teacher rating based on 1 month (2)	None
Replication study 1	B M 29;F 23	2–6	M			None
Replication study 2	C M 33;F 32	2–6	M			None
Schexnider et al. (1981)	M 20	1	M	Slower response decrement to repeated stimulus & failure to dishabituate to novelty	Insufficient (5)	None
Waldrop, Bell, McLaughlin, & Halverson (1978)	M 23	3	M	r .57 with short attention span factor	6 observations over 1 month (2)	None
Subsequent analysis of females in above study (see text)	F 25	3	M	r .35 with short attention span factor	6 observations over 1 month (2)	None
Waldrop, Pedersen, & Bell (1968)	M 43;F 31	2–3	M	M + F .51 with frenetic behavior	6 teacher ratings over 1 month (2)	None
Waldrop & Halverson (1971) Stability study	M 35;F 27	7–8	M	M + F .46 with frenetic behavior	Insufficient (20 minute observation) (7)	None

[a]Except where indicated, all correlations, mean or percent differences in this column are significant beyond the .05 level. The entry for Fogel indicates that, for males only, the high anomaly group contained 30% distractible children in comparison with 7% for the low anomaly group. Quantitative data for the study by Schexnider et al. (1981) were too complex to report in the limited space of this table. The entries for Waldrop, Pedersen, and Bell (1968) and for Waldrop and Halverson (1971) indicate that the difference between correlations for males and females are not significant so that average r's could be computed, using the z-transformation.

(1968) is unlikely to involve confound even though the same individual examined the children for anomalies and made ratings of their behavior because the nature of the relation between anomalies and behavior was not known until after the data had been gathered. No confound is attributed to findings from the Rapoport, Quinn, and Lamprecht (1974) and Sandberg, Wieselberg, and Shaffer (1980) studies because the child's behavior was assessed by school personnel, the anomalies by the investigators, and the procedures of the study would not necessarily give the investigators information on the nature of the questionnaire data before the examination for anomalies.

Intelligence

A review of 10 studies listed under this heading in Table 4.2 indicates that there is no clear relation of anomaly scores to IQ, that correlation values will be negative, if any, and range from −.18 to −.41 (Rosenberg and Weller, 1973; Waldrop, Bell, and Goering, 1976; Waldrop and Halverson, 1971–stability study). Restricted range cannot account for the differences between studies reporting or not reporting a relation. Oettinger, Evans, and Harris (1979) provide the only clear example of restricted range, because all children in their sample had average IQ or above, but Marcus, Hans, Byhouwer, and Norem (1985), Quinn, Renfield, Burg, and Rapoport (1977), and Steg and Rapoport (1975) all failed to obtain significant relations of anomalies to IQ, yet used samples with quite adequate range. Krouse and Kaufman (1982) commented that Quinn and Rapoport (1974) and Rapoport, Quinn and Lamprecht (1974) restricted their samples to those with IQs above 80. This hardly constitutes a restriction in range that would materially affect relations to the anomaly score. Nor would behavior aggregation or confound differences explain the variable results, because all studies used standardized tests with known test-retest stability or internal consistency, and none is likely to involve a confound, given the descriptions of procedures offered. In most studies individuals administering the test were not the same as those assessing the anomalies, or the investigators specifically state that the two procedures were independent (Rosenberg and Weller, 1973). Nonetheless, lacking any information on whether routine precautions were observed, and only having a description of data gathering procedures on which to form a judgement, the indication of whether a confound existed must be considered as an inference.

School Performance. Five out of the seven studies of school performance listed in Table 4.3, whether of achievement tests, grade retention, or the existence of learning disability, indicate that higher scores for minor physical anomalies are associated with less adequate school performance. This conclusion applies to males in both of the studies that analyzed their data separately or had all male samples. Results for females are variable, with only one study showing the relation. The findings for males, and those that did not separate their data for the sexes, hold over a range of aggregation levels and across studies with or without confounds. Krouse and Kaufman's (1982) conclusion that there is no consistent relation between anomalies and achievement appears to be unwarranted. Their erroneous conclusions are possibly due to: (1) a failure to distinguish between relations of anomalies to IQ versus to achievement, and (2) an inadequate literature review. Three of the studies listed under this heading in Table 4.3 were omitted from their review, despite having been published two to six years earlier.

Tignor's (1975) findings deserve attention on methodological grounds. If the other studies controlled for IQ deficit associated with high anomaly scores, would their findings evaporate? This is unlikely, because Table 4.2 testifies that most studies show no consistent relation between the anomaly scores and IQ. One further point on the findings; the study by Rosenberg and Weller produced particularly dramatic results, considering the presumed subjectivity of teachers' judgements that a child should repeat a grade. Separate analyses for the sexes were not reported, however, nine out of the 15 children who had to repeat the first grade, out of a total sample of 99 first graders in a single elementary school, had total weighted anomaly scores of five or more; not one of the 26 children with total weighted anomaly scores of zero or one was asked to repeat the grade. Head Start evaluation research looked toward IQ as an objective indication of intervention effectiveness, but the later follow-up indicators, such as placement in a special education classroom or grade retention, proved to be better indicators of the effectiveness of the intervention (Lazar and Darlington, 1982). Apparently, the sustained day-by-day contact of school teachers with high anomaly children can lead to actions that have more significance than objective tests.

Distractibility

Given that academic achievement is associated with anomalies in most studies and IQ is not, the characteristics of the high anomaly child that lead to problems in academic performance, such as grade retention, must be identified. The processes of attention lie at the heart of the young child's information-processing system, and two important aspects of this system that are usually found to be negatively correlated are ability to sustain attention and distractibility. The preschool and early school-age children from whom most of the findings in Table 4.4 have been obtained are in a setting that stresses the information-processing system. The classroom situation demands attention, but there are other children around and there is nothing quite as enticing as the activities of other children.

In the three samples reported by O'Donnell, O'Neill and Staley (1979), males show a significant positive correlation between the anomaly score and distractibility, as rated by teachers, whereas females show nonsignificant positive correlations. There are two differences between these studies and those by Waldrop and colleagues listed in Table 4.4, in which both males and females show significant positive correlations between distractibility and anomaly scores. Consider that samples used in the O'Donnell et al. studies were much more heterogeneous with respect to age (26 to 68 months) than the samples used by Waldrop et al. (24 to 32 months). However, it is difficult to see how this heterogeneity could have produced the differences in results. There were no sex differences in means or variances in the O'Donnell data, as might be expected if females are overcoming distractibility earlier than males. Findings of Victor and Halverson (1975) on grade one to five children do not lead us to expect much developmental change in distractibility. Victor and Halverson suggested that variation in this dimension of individual differences is substantially created and maintained by congenital factors, less so by developmental progression or socialization.

There is also a second difference between the two sets of studies. In the four studies by Waldrop et al., distractibility was measured by a factor based on a variety of direct observation measures as well as by teachers' ratings over a 1-month period. As a result, in this study more facets of distractibility may have been measured than the single teachers' rating based on the past 2 months of the childrens' preschool behavior, used in the study by O'Donnell et al.

The stability study on seven- and eight-year-olds reported by Waldrop and Halverson (1971) was based on a very brief period of observation. Consequently, positive correlations between distractibility and anomaly counts in both the male and female children would not be given credence but for their similarity to the earlier preschool findings.

The study in Table 4.4 by Waldrop, Bell, McLaughlin, and Halverson (1978) reported a finding for males only of a predictive relation (with few false positives but considerable false negatives) between anomalies assessed in the newborn period and fast moving, impulsive, and distractible play at age three years in a preschool setting. A similar though weaker relation for females was overlooked in the data analysis at that time. The subsequent analysis in Table 4.4 for the Waldrop et al. study just cited revealed a correlation of $-.35$ ($p < .02$) between a weighted score for anomalies in the newborn period and a summary score in the early preschool period for a factor termed *Short Attention Span.* This factor was based on observation counts on six occasions over a 1-month period in which the preschoolers attended in groups of five. The observation measures making up the factor were: number of play bouts (a bout was coded for any activity lasting 10 or more seconds); number of different play categories; time spent in gross motor activity; time spent exploring (total time for all activities in which less than 10 seconds were spent on the activity), and duration of play bout at the third quartile when lengths of play bouts for an individual were rank ordered.

To summarize results in Table 4.4, it appears that anomalies are positively related to distractibility in both males and females in studies where there is a high level of behavior aggregation, although in some studies the relation found in females is weaker or in the same direction but nonsignificant. These findings can, in turn provide an explanation for results that emerged in Tables 4.2 and 4.3. There is a negative relation between anomalies and achievement in males, but no consistent relation between anomalies and IQ (for either males or females). Whatever the child's IQ, poor school performance could be expected of a high anomaly male on most tasks that demand sustained attention and ability to follow directions. In addition, Victor and Halverson (1975) found that distractibility is correlated negatively in both males and females with overall achievement scores (males $-.39$; females $-.48$, $p < .05$ for females), which is consistent with the previous interpretation.

Higher or more consistent negative relations between anomalies and achievement in males may be partially a function of another correlate of anomalies, whose consideration takes us outside the focal interest of this chapter and the volume. High anomaly males are more active, whereas high anomaly females are *less* active (Waldrop and Halverson, 1971, replication study). The combination of high distractibility and activity in the male (Halverson and Victor, 1976) may lead to more consistent impairment on school tasks that require both attention and remaining quiet in one's seat. The high anomaly female is less active than other children, showing inhibition and overcontrol (Waldrop, Bell, and Goering, 1976) that impair relations with peers but not school performance. Thus she may show less adequate achievement solely because of high distractibility.

One study has extended the hypotheses from the studies by Waldrop et al., to one-year-olds, and attempted to define the attention deficit experimentally in high anomaly males (Schexnider, Bell, Shebilske, and Quinn, 1981). Caution is in order because of insufficient aggregation basis. It was found that high anomaly males who were tested immediately on arrival for study habituated slowly in total fixation time on repeated presentations of geometric forms, whereas high anomaly males who were tested after a pediatric examination habituated rapidly. Whether tested immediately or after other procedures, the high anomaly males showed less dishabituation than low anomaly males. The authors point out that the slow response decrement (e.g., slow waning of attention) in high anomaly males tested immediately is in line with a general finding of slow response decrement where there is cerebral pathology (traumatized, premature, hydrocephalic, or anencephalic infants), whereas the failure to dishabituate (e.g., failure to show renewed interest when novel stimuli appear) indicates inadequate processing of the input, despite the greater time spent attending. Furthermore, it was suggested that high anomaly infants shift from slower to overly rapid response decrement when task demand is increased or when the infant is fatigued. This hypothesis is consistent with the common observation that hyperactive children, who usually also have a deficit in attention, are increasingly restless and ineffective in test procedures as an evaluation session proceeds. Very rapid habituation may have begun, along with inadequate processing of input.

The foregoing findings indicate that formation of a risk group for problems of attention is possible as early as the first year, using not only the anomaly scores but also indicators of information-processing deficits. The results of Schexnider et al., provide a link to the work of Bornstein and Rose, in other chapters of this volume, which show continuity between encoding of visual stimuli in early infancy and intellectual and language development in childhood.

HYPOTHESES ON CAUSATION

Diet, hazardous chemicals, complications of pregnancy, and genetic defects may induce abnormal central nervous system structures underlying the individual differences in behavior that we have reviewed. In the discussion to follow, it is assumed that these causal factors disrupt normal fetal development, and that the effects persist without further maintenance from these sources. Once the underlying structures are affected, they persist in producing deviant behavior. The form of this deviant behavior will change as the organism develops, depending on what growth function is involved at any later time. This change in the normal ongoing growth process leads to the appearance of discontinuity of function despite stability of individual differences. A good example of this stability, despite apparent discontinuity, can be seen at the level of the visible defects in physical structures that we use to index the underlying damage to the central nervous system. Epicanthus and steepled palate are discriminative for the underlying damage at a time when there is normal change in the structure of the eye and the oral cavity. Despite this change in discriminative value, the overall index of anomalies shows very high stability of individual differences because it reflects the underlying overall damage to the organism.

Diet

In keeping with current national emphasis on prevention of cancer and cardiovascular disorder through diet, and with the recognition of the importance of diet for the outcome of pregnancy, one of the major hypotheses advanced to explain the existence of minor physical anomalies is that they are produced by highly processed foods characteristic of industrialized societies. Von Hilsheimer and Kurko (1979) brought the hypotheses of W. A. Price to the attention of investigators in this field. Price's research largely involved anomalies of the head that could be observed in skulls, making it possible to compare anomalies that existed before and after introduction of highly processed foods to a society, and in some cases after reintroduction of a preindustrial diet. The natural experiments were produced by war or economic changes that affected the society. In 10 societies, skulls of individuals living in the period before the introduction of "foods of commerce" showed few anomalies of the face, palate and teeth, whereas those living in the period after their introduction showed an increase. The rather innovative research by Price warrants much more attention than it has received.

Hazardous Chemicals

Despite rapid advances in the field of behavioral toxicology, the methods used to track the toxic effects of chemicals have not as yet been applied to the appearance of minor physical anomalies. In testimony before Congress, Goodstein (1985) pointed out that there may be as many as 50,000 chemicals in common use, and 1,000 new chemicals are being introduced each year. He summarized the serious consequences of exposure to some of these chemicals for impaired functioning of the peripheral and central nervous system and noted that the developing fetus is not protected against toxic chemicals. In fact, the fetus and young child are much more vulnerable to neurotoxicity than the adult. The serious consequences of neurotoxicity apparently can be seen in children if their mothers were exposed during pregnancy. It is possible that some of the effects noted by Price were due to the presence of toxic chemicals in foods coming from industrialized societies. The use of insecticides in mass production of foodstuffs could have led to contamination of societies that had previously had no exposure to insecticides, and therefore no consequent defects of the head.

Complications of Pregnancy and Delivery

As reported by Waldrop and Halverson (1971: study of children with speech and hearing deficits), severe complications of pregnancy, such as rubella, clearly produce a large number of minor physical anomalies, as well as some major anomalies and deficiencies in speech and hearing. Wouldn't this finding lead us to expect a relation between the number of anomalies and less severe pregnancy and birth complications (PBCs)?

It is most likely that complications during the first trimester would produce anomalies because the anomalies are formed during this period. However, complications in later pregnancy and delivery may show an association because the insult to fetal development during the first trimester could also affect later fetal development and birth. It is surprising that only two studies have reported significant relations between anomalies and PBCs (Rapoport, Quinn, and Lambrecht, 1974; Quinn and Rapoport, 1974). Both studies involved maternal report rather than actual search of medical records, but this may be an advantage because a symptom such as first trimester bleeding may be more reliably reported by the mother than by hurried medical staff. Frequently, these notes are sketchy and illegible, and they often lack information on early pregnancy. Despite this consideration of completeness and adequacy of records, it would be expected that something more than negative results or nonsignificant trends would emerge from other studies, some by the same authors on other populations using actual searches of medical records (Campbell et al. 1978; Lerer, 1977; Oettinger, Evans and Harris, 1979; Quinn, Renfield, Burg and Rapoport, 1977; Rapoport, Pandoni, Renfield, Lake and Ziegler, 1977; Steg and Rapoport, 1975).

So far there has been no report of a positive result from efforts to trace out relations of PBCs to single anomalies, probably because the frequencies of many anomalies is very low in an unselected population, as is the frequency of PBC's (25%), and because most studies of anomalies have used small samples. Nonetheless, there have been efforts. Lerer (1977) did not find a relation of single transverse palmar creases to maternal infections even in a sample of 182 hyperactives.

One study used a larger sample, selected for primary toxins presumed to have deleterious effects on fetal development, and studied 93 minor physical anomalies, but emerged with no evidence of relations to anomalies. Tennes and Blackard (1980) reviewed other studies of the fetal alcohol syndrome but found no effects on anomalies from marijuana, nicotine, caffeine, and alcohol usage during pregnancy in their sample of 278 lower-middle to middle-class mother–infant dyads, despite the fact that the sample included five women whose peak consumption of alcohol was 11 to 40 drinks in an eight-hour period (!) and who averaged three ounces or more of daily alcohol consumption during the pregnancy. The authors speculate that nonlinear or threshold effects may account for differences between their studies and others.

The evidence for the relation of PBCs to anomalies is far from compelling. Except in very severe disorders such as rubella and clinical fetal alcohol syndrome, what is the source of the anomalies that we see in less extreme samples? Defects controlled by genetic processes are a likely source.

Genetic Transmission of Chromosome Defects

Studies of twins and adoption are usually carried out after research has shown that some characteristics run in family lines. Evidence of psychopathology in family lines is necessary but not sufficient evidence of genetic determination. Research on the minor physical anomalies has reached the stage of family lines, but studies of adoption and twins could not be located. Steg and Rapoport (1975) have reported case history evidence of paternal antisocial behavior in families of children from a residential treatment center who had high anomaly counts, and of parental psychopathology in the few children with high anomaly scores in a sample receiving outpatient psychiatric treatment.

It is only possible at present to point to relevant findings that involve a more discriminative genetic approach than family lines. Minor physical anomalies show a strong and consistent relation to attention deficit disorder (current diagnostic definition of hyperactivity). Therefore it is worth noting that Alberts-Corush, Firestone, and Goodman (1986) reported evidence of more problems of attention in biological parents of children with attention-deficit disorder than in adoptive parents. Anomalies can be evaluated at any age up to twelve, and probably beyond, and thus it would be inexpensive but potentially worthwhile to examine children and parents in other adoption studies still in a data collection phase. Both twin and adoption designs need to be employed to evaluate possible origins of minor physical anomalies and related behaviors.

Sexual Differentiation of the Fetus

Four puzzling problems emerge from the review of findings and the foregoing hypotheses on causation. First of all, why are high anomaly counts not specific to one form of psychopathology such as attention-deficit disorder? Second, why are the measures that show correlations with anomalies also the measures that usually also show sex differences? In other words, why is the high anomaly male hypermasculine? Third, if viral insults such as rubella in the first trimester clearly produce large numbers of minor physical anomalies (as well as major ones), why do complications of pregnancy and delivery of a less severe nature fail to show associations with high anomaly counts? Fourth, why are the anomaly behavior relations much more consistent for males than for females?

Halverson (1981) offers an explanation for these puzzling findings. The hypothesis is based on neuroembryological studies in man and other mammals that indicate the brain is female in early fetal development. The brain becomes masculinized, and follows a different template for development in males, following secretion of androgen by the testes. Halverson assumes that anomalies are an indication that noxious or teratogenic events have occurred during embryogenesis, and that these events stress the fetus. The result is an increase in secretion of androgen by the male fetus. The present authors would add that genetic defects may also be causing stress on the fetus. Presumably, the heightened secretions result in an exaggeration of activity, aggression, and impulsivity that are basic to sexual differentiation in males. This would explain why the behavior dimensions that usually show sex differences are also the ones that show a high correlation with anomalies, why results for females differ from those for males, and why results are usually more consistent for males. The female fetus is not subject to the effects of androgen.

Following Halverson's hypothesis further, consider that anomalies show relations to many other forms of psychopathology than attention deficit disorder, such as autism, learning disability, retardation, and speech and hearing deficits, because action through the mechanism of fetal androgen secretion is only one of several channels through which the genetic damage, noxious agents, or teratogens exert effects. In the case of females and the other disorders, different brain structures may be affected, with different consequences for development.

The need for adoption and twin studies of anomalies and PBCs has already been discussed. Halverson points out that twin studies can determine whether there is more concordance of anomaly counts within monozygotic than within fraternal twins, whether the heritability is the same for males and females, and whether there is concordance of fraternal twins without heritability, as would be expected if problems in the course of the pregnancy are producing the concordance.

CONCLUSION

Minor physical anomalies serve as markers of disorders in embryonic development that have far-reaching consequences because the anomalies of the head, hands, and feet develop from the same embryological layer as the central nervous system and at the same time that sexual differentiation of the embryo occurs. Although they constitute biological contributors, they do not imply predestination of behavior because most of the behavioral outcomes are modifiable with appropriate education or therapy. These markers serve as a means of locating risk groups early in life, and of studying developmental pathways, optimal timing and nature of intervention. Most of the anomalies are only detectable by the trained eye, and labelling for the purpose of research on a risk group need not have negative consequences (Bell and Pearl, 1982).

Most investigators have used a set of 18 anomalies since the first published report of quantitative research on this set (Waldrop, Pedersen, and Bell, 1968), and a manual of standards and procedures is available. Neither variability in adherence to the manual, or developmental variability in the presence or absence of individual anomalies, has prevented the anomalies from showing validity. This is because the total score, rather than the scores for individual items, has been the primary measure of value. The total number of anomalies shows high stability from the newborn period to age seven years, affording considerable confidence that a stable congenital contributor has been indexed. This fact makes it possible to add an examination for anomalies to an ongoing study so as to analyze its relations retroactively. We also need application to larger samples to permit analysis of effects on behavior of individual anomalies. Behavioral effects of those that emerge at the same time could be studied as a group.

Findings have been summarized for anomaly relations to intelligence, school achievement, and distractibility. Special attention was given to two methodological issues, whether results are based on adequate behavior aggregation and whether the individual evaluating minor physical anomalies may have been influenced by knowledge of the behavior in question. The review indicates that high anomaly scores are associated in males with less adequate school performance, one of the most clear results involving grade retention, but that there is no clear relation to intelligence. Anomalies are associated with distractibility in both males and females, but with high levels of activity in males and low levels in females. It is assumed that high levels of activity in males potentiate the negative effects of distractibility on school performance. The conclusions on intelligence, school achievement, and distractibility can be asserted without qualification relative to problems of behavior aggregation or confound.

The fact that there are differences as well as similarities between correlates of anomalies for males and females is expected from the hypothesis that genetic defects or complications of pregnancy produce anomalies in males by stressing the embryo at the time sexual differentiation is occurring, increasing the secretion of androgen from the testes. Androgen triggers the differentiation. For this reason the behaviors that show high correlations with anomalies in males are also the measures that usually show normal sex differences: activity, aggressiveness, and impulsivity. The disorders of embryonic development exaggerate the female counterparts of activity and impulsivity, producing low activity and inhibition, but the mechanism must be different because the female embryo is not subject to the effects of androgen. Increased distractibility associated with anomalies in both sexes must also be produced by some other process, so that there may be several ways in which anomalies are produced.

Viral insults such as rubella produce both major and minor physical anomalies, and thus there is little question that this is one causal route for the anomalies. Studies of skull formation in societies before and after exposure to highly processed foods has yielded some very suggestive relations. Behavior toxicology indicates that toxic chemicals could be a contributor, and possibly through diets that have been contaminated by insecticide residues. There seems little doubt that severe insults to the embryo are related to complications and this consideration leads to the further expectation that there should be a relation of the less severe complications to minor physical anomalies. If there is a linear relation between insults, complications, and anomalies we should have uncovered ample evidence of the sequence in the nine studies conducted. Yet, this has not occurred, and the results of studies on the fetal alcohol syndrome and other substance abuse in mothers point to the possibility that there may be nonlinear or threshold relationships between amounts of toxin and anomalies. This is one of the areas in which research is most needed. A very useful collaboration could be developed between investigators interested in congenital contributors to development and those interested in the rapidly developing new field of behavior toxicology.

Research is also needed in the area of genetic transmission of chromosome defects. Case history evidence indicates psychopathology in parents of children with high anomaly counts, but twin and adoption studies are needed to sort out genetic and environmental transmission effects. Genetic transmission of chromosome breakdowns in embryonic development may produce anomalies without detectable complications of pregnancy and this would explain the failure to find consistent evidence of relations between complications and anomalies. The brief, ten-minute anomaly exam could be added to any current assessment in a twin or adoption study and would permit analysis of congenital contributors to all measures being obtained currently or gathered in the past.

From the findings on complex patterns or clinical syndromes it is evident that high anomaly counts are a relatively nonspecific biological contributor, but not completely nonspecific. Children being seen in general clinics for behavior disorders do not show high anomaly counts (Steg and Rapoport, 1975, and see Table 4.3). This finding, and the fact that normal children show much lower scores than those with clinical syndromes, makes it possible to use anomaly scores as general indicators of risk, though they need to be supplemented with other risk bases. For example, it has been possible to identify a potential risk group for attention-deficit disorder, as early as age one year, by selecting male infants with high anomaly scores and deficits in information processing. High anomaly males habituate more slowly when first exposed to a visual attention task, but more rapidly when heavy task demand is put on them, and fail to dishabituate within normal time limits regardless of task demand.

Whether the aberrant developmental process starts in embryo due to a genetic chromosome breakdown or the effects of a teratogen, the behavioral correlates in later development provide an instructive exercise in the complexity of human development and individual differences. On the one hand, we have apparent discontinuity between the action of viruses or genetic abnormalities in embryonic development, then the appearance of anomalies visible to the trained observer from the newborn period on, but with some of these anomalies even disappearing later on. The foregoing statement hardly seems continuous with the appearance of deficits in information processing by the first year, aggressive play or inhibited quiet play, depending on sex, by the second or third year, then low academic achievement emerging in males in the early elementary grades. There are even some discontinuities for both sexes, such as the disappearance in adults of impulsivity as a correlate of anomalies (Paulhus and Martin, 1986).

The apparent discontinuity between viral insults to the fetus and frenetic or inhibited play is less of a surprise if we know that some of the features of frenetic play are also features that differentiate the sexes, and that this sexual differentiation may have been occurring during the same time as the viral insults. Also, the convergence then divergence of the sexes over time seems less of a discontinuity if we assume that each is, in part, following a program for development that diverges increasingly from the first trimester of pregnancy. Each sex has its own continuity. If we make an assumption concerning the direction of sex differences, that it is in the direction of less controlled behavior for males and more controlled behavior for females, then an insult to the fetus might exaggerate both, and drive the sexes farther apart. This concept of control reduces apparent discontinuities in the relation between early deficits of attention and later activity, aggressive, impulsive, distractible play, then poor school achievement.

We may fill in the gaps between the appearance of different manifestations at different times with empirical knowledge, or concepts that guide our research. In either event, the appearance of discontinuities is reduced, and the understanding of continuities between events with different manifestations is increased. One further means of reducing the appearance of discontinuity is to understand that in most developmental studies the periods between observations are large, considering the rate of growth. If we only observe tadpoles and polywogs initially, then come back when they have become toads and frogs, the discrepancy is striking, but if we had observed the early forms daily during their very rapid growth we might not have seen any discontinuity at all, merely ever so gradual changes in form.

In summary, if we really thoroughly understand the process of development, and if intervals between our observations were adjusted to the rate of growth in a given period of study, much of what we see as discontinuity would be seen as continuity. However, discontinuities will remain on account of nodal or transition points in development at which reorganization of behavior occur.

REFERENCES

Alberts-Corush, J., Firestone, P., and Goodman, J. (1986). Attention and impulsivity characteristics of the biological and adoptive parents of hyperactive and normal control children. *American Journal of Orthopsychiatry, 56,* 413–423.

Bell, R. Q. (1986). Age-specific manifestations in changing psychosocial risk. In D. C. Farran and J. D. McKinney (Eds.), *The concept of risk in intellectual and psychosocial development.* New York: Academic Press.

Bell, R. Q., and Hertz, T. W. (1976). Toward more comparability and generalizability of developmental research. *Child Development, 47,* 6–13.

Bell, R. Q., and Pearl, D. (1982). Implications for early identification of changing risk status in seven categories of risk. *Journal of Prevention in Human Services, 1,* 45–59.

Brazelton, T. B. (1973). Neonatal Behavioral Assessment Scale. (Clinics in Developmental Medicine, No. 50). London: Heineman Medical Books.

Burg, C., Hart, D., Quinn, P., and Rapoport, J. (1978). Newborn minor physical anomalies and prediction of infant behavior. *Journal of Autism and Childhood Schizophrenia, 8,* 427–439.

Campbell, M., Geller, B., Small, A. M., Petti, T. A., and Ferris, S. H. (1978). Minor physical anomalies in young psychotic children. *American Journal of Psychiatry, 135,* 573–575.

Down, J. L. (1866). Observations on an ethnic classification of idiots. *London Hospital Clinical Lecturer and Reports, 3,* 259–262.

Epstein, S. (1980). The stability of behavior: II. Implication for psychological research. *American Psychologist, 35,* 790–806.

Fogel, C. A., Mednick, S. A., and Michelsen, N. (1985). Hyperactive behavior and minor physical anomalies. *Acta Psychiatrica Scandanavica, 72,* 551–556.

Goldfarb, W., and Botstein, A. (1967). Physical stigmata in schizophrenic children. Unpublished manuscript, Henry Ittleson Center for Child Research, Brooklyn, NY.

Goodstein, L. D. (1985, October 8). Testimony on behavioral effects of exposure to neurotopins before the U.S. House of Representatives, on behalf of the American Psychological Association.

Halverson, C. F. (1981, April 2). Minor physical anomalies and sex differences in behavior. Paper presented at the Biennial Meeting of the Society for Research in Child Development, Boston, MA.

Halverson, C. F., and Victor, J. B. (1976). Minor physical anomalies and problem behavior in elementary school children. *Child Development, 47,* 281–285.

Jacklin, C. N., Maccoby, E. E., and Halverson, C. F. (1980). Minor physical anomalies and preschool behavior. *Journal of Pediatric Psychology, 5,* 199–205.

Krouse, J. P., and Kaufman, J. M. (1982). Minor physical anomalies in exceptional children: A review and critique of research. *Journal of Abnormal Child Psychology, 10,* 247–264.

Lazar, I., and Darlington, R. (1982). Lasting effects of early education: A report from the consortium for longitudinal studies. *Monographs of Society for Research in Child Development, 47,* Nos. 2-3.

Lerer, R. J. (1977). Do hyperactive children tend to have abnormal palmar creases? Report of a suggestive association. *Clinical Pediatrics, 16,* 645–647.

Marcus, J., Hans, S. L., Byhouwer, B., and Norem, J. (1985). Relationships among neurological functioning, I.Q., and physical anomalies. *Schizophrenia Bulletin, 11,* 101–106.

O'Donnell, J. P., O'Neil, S. O., and Staley, A. (1979). Congenital correlates of distractibility. *Journal of Abnormal Child Psychology, 7,* 465–470.

Oettinger, L., Evans, H., and Harris, S. (1979). Minor physical anomalies: A review with special reference to family incidence. *Learning Disabilities: An Audio Journal for Continuing Education.* New York: Grune and Stratton.

Paulhus, D. L., and Martin, C. L. (1986). Predicting adult temperament from minor physical anomalies. *Journal of Personality and Social Psychology, 50,* 1235–1239.

Quinn, P., Renfield, M., Burg, C., and Rapoport, J. (1977). Minor physical anomalies: A newborn screening and one year follow-up. *Journal of Child Psychiatry, 16,* 662–669.

Quinn, P., and Rapoport, J. (1974). Minor physical anomalies and neurological status in hyperactive boys. *Pediatrics, 53,* 742–747.

Rapoport, J., and Quinn, P. (1975). Minor physical anomalies (stigmata) and early development deviation: A major biologic subgroup of "hyperactive children." *International Journal of Mental Health, 4,* 29–44.

Rapoport, J., Quinn, P., and Lamprecht, F. (1974). Minor physical anomalies and plasma dopamine-beta-hydroxylase activity in hyperactive boys. *American Journal of Psychiatry, 131,* 387–390.

Rapoport, J. L., Pandoni, C., Renfield, M., Lake, C. R., and Ziegler, M. G. (1977). Newborn dopamine-beta-hydroxylase, minor physical anomalies, and infant temperament. *American Journal of Psychiatry, 136,* 676–679.

Rosenberg, J. B., and Weller, G. M. (1973). Minor physical anomalies and academic performance in young school-children. *Developmental Medicine and Child Neurology, 15,* 131–135.

Sandburg, S. T., Wieselberg, M., and Shaffer, D. (1980). Hyperkinetic and conduct problems in a primary school population: Some epidemiological considerations. *Journal of Child Psychology and Psychiatry and Applied Disciplines, 21,* 293–311.

Schexnider, V. Y. R., Bell, R. Q., Shebilske, W. L., and Quinn, P. (1981). Habituation of visual attention in infants with minor physical anomalies. *Child Development, 52,* 812–818.

Steg, J. P., and Rapoport, J. L. (1975). Minor physical anomalies in normal, neurotic, learning disabled and severely disturbed children. *Journal of Autism and Childhood Schizophrenia, 5,* 299–307.

Tennes, K., and Blackard, C. (1980). Maternal alcohol consumption, birth weight, and minor physical anomalies. *American Journal of Obstetrics and Gynecology, 138,* 774–780.

Tignor, B. S. (1975). The relationship between minor physical anomalies and measures of attention and school achievement in primary school children. *Dissertation Abstracts,* (35 8-B), 4200.

Victor, J. B., and Halverson, C. F. (1975). Distractibility and hypersensitivity. *Journal of Abnormal Child Psychology, 3,* 83–94.

von Hilsheimer, G., and Kurko, V. (1979). Minor physical anomalies in exceptional children. *Journal of Learning Disabilities 12,* 462–469.

Waldrop, M., Pedersen, F., and Bell, R. Q. (1968). Minor physical anomalies and behavior in preschool children. *Child Development, 39,* 391–400.

Waldrop, M., and Halverson, C. F. (1971). Minor physical anomalies and hyperactive behavior in children. In J. Hellmuth (Ed.), *Exceptional infant* (Vol. 2). New York: Brunner/Mazel.

Waldrop, M., Bell, R. Q., and Goering, J. D. (1976). Minor physical anomalies and inhibited behavior in elementary school girls. *Journal of Child Psychology and Psychiatry, 17,* 113–122.

Waldrop, M., Bell, R. Q., McLaughlin, B., and Halverson, C. F. (1978). Newborn minor physical anomalies predict short attention span, peer aggression, and impulsivity at age 3. *Science, 199,* 563–565.

PART I

Section 3: Traditional Infant Tests

5 A Reconceptualization of Prediction from Infant Test Scores

Linda S. Siegel
Department of Special Education,
Ontario Institute for Studies in Education

INTRODUCTION

The purpose of this chapter is to examine the relation between scores on infant tests and scores on tests administered at some later point in development. The expectation that infant tests would be predictive of later development stems from the hypothesis that there are continuities in mental development. Theories of cognitive development assume that there is a common substrate to the diverse behaviors that we call cognitive development (e.g., Bruner, 1966; Piaget, 1960). Processes such as problem solving, understanding of causal relationships, and exploration of novelty are assumed to be fundamental aspects of cognitive development and independent of any particular behavioral manifestation. Infant tests, in particular the Bayley Scales of Infant Development (1969), measure a variety of cognitive, motor, and language functions. Therefore, it is reasonable to assume that stability in cognitive function may be manifest in significant relations between scores on infant tests and tests later in development.

In spite of theoretical expectations of stability in functioning between infancy and later periods, it is a common statement that scores on infant tests do not predict subsequent cognitive functioning. For example, in a recent article in *Child Development,* Bornstein and Sigman (1986) have stated "correlations between traditional developmental measures administered in the first year of life and childhood intelligence tests have regularly proven uniformly low." McCall (1979) stated that "after nearly one-half century of data collection and analysis, the results unequivocally show that scores on instruments of infant mental performance assessed during the first 18 months of life do not predict later IQ to any practical extent'' (p. 707). La Buda, De Fries, Plomin, and Fulker (1986) noted that ''the meager long term predictiveness of IQ scores in the first two years of life is greatly enhanced during the next two years'' (p. 1142).

Although this generalization is a common one, it is incorrect and does not adequately represent the evidence. In this chapter, I (1) present evidence to show that there is a strong relation between infant test scores and later test scores in early and middle childhood; (2) examine certain methodological and statistical aspects of studies of this relation; (3) demonstrate that the correlation coefficient, the statistic most commonly used to examine this relation, is inadequate and often misleading, and (4) suggest alternate methods of conceptualizing and analyzing this relation.

For the purposes of this discussion I confine my comments to infant tests administered during the first year of life. Correlations between tests given at eighteen and twenty-four months and later scores are often higher and may account for 50%-60% of variance. But what is at issue here is the relation between measures taken in the first year of life (time 1) and some later point in development (time 2).

CORRELATIONS BETWEEN INFANT TEST SCORES AND LATER SCORES

A number of studies have demonstrated statistically significant correlations between infant test scores obtained in the first year of life and later test scores. The following are examples of such studies. Wilson (1978) reported correlations ranging from .26 and .37 between the Bayley MDI administered at three months and the Stanford-Binet Form L-M at three years, the Wechsler Preschool and Primary Scale of Intelligence (WPPSI) at four, five, and six years, and the McCarthy Scales of Children's Abilities (MSCA) at four years. He also reported correlations between the six-month Bayley scores and the later scales from .16 to .31, and correlations between the nine-month Bayley scores and the later scales ranged from .25 to .36. Correlations ranging from .24 to .43 were found between the twelve-month Bayley scores and the Stanford-Binet, WPPSI, and MSCA.

In a study of the development of fullterm and preterm children, I have found significant correlations between Bayley scores and later test scores (Siegel, 1979, 1981, 1982, 1983a, b, 1985a, b). For example, the correlations between the Bayley Mental Scales at four to twelve months and the Reynell Developmental Language Scales (RDLS) at two years ranged from .26 to .46. At three years, these correlations ranged from .19 to .37, and at four years from .17 to .37. The correlations between the Bayley Psychomotor Scales at four to twelve months and RDLS at two years ranged from .37 to .55, at three years from .31 to .44, and at four years from .25 to .44. The correlations between the Bayley MDI and PDI (four to twelve months) and the Stanford-Binet at three years ranged from .27 to .45.

These significant relations have been found when attempts have been made to predict test scores even later in development. The correlations between the Bayley MDI scores at four to twelve months and the WISC-R Full Scale IQ at six years ranged from .23 to .48 (Siegel, 1985a). Both Wilson and I havc found significant correlations between first-year Bayley scores and five- and six-year IQ scores; these correlations are shown in Table 5.1. I have also found significant correlations between Bayley MDI scores and WISC-R intelligence test scores administered at eight years. These correlations were .44 at four and twelve months and .45 at eight months. It is quite remarkable that significant relations exist between the Bayley Scale scores in infancy and test scores even eight years later.

Similar patterns of correlations were found between scores on the Bayley Scales and measures of achievement at six years (Siegel 1985a). For example, the correlation between the Bayley administered at four, eight, and twelve months and achievement scores at age six years ranged from .19 to .57, all of which are statistically significant. In addition, there were statistically significant relations between Bayley scores in infancy and the Wide Range Achievement Test (WRAT scores), a measure of reading, spelling, and arithmetic, at seven and eight years. These relations are shown in Table 5.2.

For a group of children born prematurely, significant correlations of the Bayley MDI administered at four to twelve months and the McCarthy General Cognitive Index (GCI) ranged from .39 to .46 and for the Bayley PDI and the McCarthy GCI from .28 to .68 (Siegel, 1983a).

The Bayley scores were also significantly correlated with certain language (PPVT, NSST) and visual motor (VMI) tests at five years (Siegel, 1983b). The

TABLE 5.1
Prediction of 5- and 6-Year IQ Scores from Bayley Scores

Age of Bayley (months)	*Age (years)*	
	5	*6*
3[a]	.37	.34
4 MDI	.28	.23
PDI	.34	.42
6[a]	.29	.31
8 MDI	.30	.27
PDI	.40	.42
9[a]	.36	.34
12	.40	.48
	.28	.42

[a]These data are taken from "Synchronies in Mental Development" by R. S. Wilson, 1978, *Science,* 202, pp. 939–948.

TABLE 5.2
Correlations Between the Bayley Scales and WRAT at 7 and 8 Years

	7 Years			*8 Years*		
	Reading	*Spelling*	*Arithmetic*	*Reading*	*Spelling*	*Arithmetic*
			4 month			
PDI	.30*	.35**	.28*	.37**	.36**	.30*
			8 month			
PDI	.26*	.31*	ns	.45***	.42***	.38**
			12 month			
MDI	ns	ns	ns	.25*	.29*	.26*
PDI	ns	.26*	ns	.30*	.25*	.37**
			18 month			
MDI	.43***	.41***	.32**	.59***	.53***	.47***
			24 month			
MDI	.33**	.31*	ns	.45***	.45***	ns
PDI	ns	ns	ns	.47***	.27*	ns

*$p < .05$
**$p < .01$
***$p < .001$

Peabody Picture Vocabulary Test (PPVT) provides a measure of the child's vocabulary by having the child point to one of four pictures that depicts a particular word. The Northwestern Syntax Screening Test (NSST) is designed to provide measures of sentence comprehension and the production of correct syntax. The ITPA Grammatic Closure measures the child's production of certain morphological features of English. The Beery Developmental Test of Visual-Motor Integration measures the child's ability to copy increasingly complex shapes. Bayley scores in the first twelve months (and also later) correlated significantly with all of these tests. In some cases even higher correlations were found at six years (Siegel, 1985a, b). These tests measure specific behavior that are quite different in form from the type of functions measured in infant tests. In spite of this difference in surfact structure, there were statistically significant relationships.

Other studies have also found evidence of stability. Wachs (1975) found a significant correlation (.52) between the object permanence subscale of the Infant Psychological Development Scales of Uzgiris and Hunt (1975) at twelve months and the Stanford-Binet at thirty-one months. Roe (1977) found significant correlations between the Gesell scale at seven, nine, and fifteen months and five-year scores on the ITPA visual motor subtests. Moreover, Berk (1979) found that eight-month Bayley scores predict children who will be rated as suspect on a neurological exam at one to seven years. A number of other studies have reported significant correlations between infant tests and later scores (e.g., Cohen and Parmelee, 1983; Gannon, 1968; Goeffeney, Henderson, and Butler, 1971; Ireton, Thwing, and Graven, 1970).

Even subsets of items are often predictive of later test scores. Using the Kohen-Raz (1967) system, which separates the Bayley MDI scores into more homogeneous subsets, significant correlations have been found between these subscales and later Reynell and Stanford-Binet test scores (e.g., Siegel, 1979, 1981, 1982).

All of the previous correlations might more appropriately be described as moderate; however, they indicate some statistically significant relation and cannot be ignored. These correlations provide some evidence of stability. However, I present evidence that the story is more complicated.

INCONSISTENCIES AMONG STUDIES

There have been studies that have *not* found a relation between infant and later test scores. As McCall (1979, p. 712) noted, studies that have found little relations have used "samples of essentially normal infants. However, one of the original purposes of creating the infant tests was to reveal infants who might have severe pathologies." The use of samples of normal infants would seem to defeat the purpose of using infant tests. The infant tests were not designed to predict precise IQ scores but to detect infants who were having problems or who would subsequently experience difficulty. Infant tests were intended, and should be used to predict problems, not to precisely determine a score on an IQ test.

The exact score on an IQ test is not important; scores on IQ tests do not provide a precise estimate of performance or achievement. The range in which the score falls is more important than the exact score. It would be important to know that a child is functioning below average (or perhaps above average for some purposes), but the exact score does not provide useful information for educational purposes.

METHODOLOGICAL AND STATISTICAL CONSIDERATIONS

Statistical Issues

There are several reasons for the alleged failure in some studies of infant tests to predict scores on later tests. But these reasons are not, as many have argued, due to the inadequacy of infant tests. I believe that the problem lies with the use of the correlation coefficient, a statistic that is very subject to the nature of the distribution and, in addition, does not provide useful information about an individual case. Restricted range, use of the correlation, and failure to examine individual patterns are at least a few of the reasons for the apparent lack of predictability of infant tests. Many studies use a restricted range of scores. For example, many studies use only children whose scores are in the normal range at infancy (time 1). These children are still in the normal range later in development (time 2). Although the magnitude of the correlations is low, this is actually a very good prediction.

For example, Lewis and Brooks-Gunn (1981) reported a nonsignificant correlation between the Bayley scores in the first year and scores on the Bayley at two years. However, the mean scores at three months in the Bayley for their Sample 2 was 126.9 (SD = 15.44) and twenty-four months 152.0 (SD = 6.74). Obviously, with such high scores and such a narrow range, it is unlikely that there will be significant correlations. Furthermore, it could be said that the actual prediction was quite good if outcome within a range was used. It appears that all the children who had above average scores at time 1 also had above average scores at time 2. If this is the case, the prediction is perfect. It should be noted that the scores were not as high for their Sample 1 but on the twenty-four-month MDI, M = 126.42, and SD = 18.90 so that virtually all the two-year-old children had scores at least one standard deviation above the mean. Lewis and Brooks-Gunn also reported that Escalona Corman Scales, based on Piagetian theory, did not predict; however, it is important to note that one range of scores was 0-4, too small for a meaningful parametric statistical analysis.

The Correlation Coefficient: Is It Useful?

The previous discussion is based on findings using the correlation coefficient, often the only statistic to investigate the relation between infant test scores and later scores. This statistic is susceptible to the problem of restriction of range, in that lack of heterogeneity in the distribution of scores can result in a low correlation. For example, let us imagine that the following distribution of scores is obtained on time 1 and time 2 for five subjects—subject 1, 120 and 128; subject 2, 122 and 120; subject 3, 124 and 126; subject 4, 126 and 122; subject 5, 128 and 124. The correlation between these two sets of scores is −.33. Yet, all of these scores are actually within a narrow range, and the 10 scores would indicate that all these individuals were in the above-average range at both time 1 and time 2. In a sense, this is perfect prediction for an individual, but the correlation is not statistically significant. The correlation by itself would not allow the determination of any relation for an individual case.

The correlation does not provide information about individual patterns; however, this is not the only problem. Consider the following case of scores for individuals at time 1 and time 2: Subject 1, 110 and 120; subject 2, 112 and 122; subject 3, 114 and 124; subject 4, 116 and 126; subject 5, 118 and 128. The correlation between these two sets of scores is +1.00. However, without knowing the mean and standard deviation of each distribution, we cannot predict the score of an individual. The correlation coefficient is, therefore, not useful in an individual case. In subsequent sections of this chapter, I propose some alternative statistical analyses.

ALTERNATIVE APPROACHES

An alternative way of examining the stability issue is to compare the scores at time 1 of children who are showing delay at time 2 and those who are not showing delay at time 2. This type of comparison allows a test of the hypothesis that early low scores (less than 85, 90, or whatever) predict low scores later on. When this type of analysis is conducted, significant differences emerge even very early in development between the children who will subsequently show delay and those who will not (Siegel, 1979, 1981, 1982, 1983a, b). Often, there is relatively little overlap in scores at time 1 between groups who are differentiated at time 2 into below average and average functioning. Therefore, we can say that scores at time 1 (infancy) *do* predict the individuals who will develop problems.

Surface Versus Deep Structure

It is often claimed that there is little conceptual relation between behaviors measured in infancy and those later on. For example, Bornstein and Sigman (1986) asserted that there is a "lack of stability from traditional infant developmental scales to childhood intelligence tests" and that this constitutes evidence against stability of developmental status. This conclusion is based on a comparison of the surface features or the responses that do not resemble each other. As McCall, Eichorn, and Hogarty (1977) said, "individual differences in the 'deep structure' of behaviors remain stable while its surface grammar changes from age to age." Although the surface factors are different, the basic processes are the same and show some continuity. To illustrate this continuity in "deep structure," let us consider some evidence. For example, I have found that the correlation between the Beery Developmental Test of Visual Motor Integration (VMI), a measure of eye-hand coordination, administered at six years and the Psychomotor (PDI) scale of the Bayley administered at four months is .41 ($p <$ .001). The Bayley motor scale measures developmental milestones such as grasping and reaching. The Beery VMI measures the ability to preserve spatial and size relation when copying shapes. Obviously these abilities are quite different on the surface. It is reasonable to ask why a significant relation should hold between them. One possibility is that they both are reflections of the maturation of the nervous system in regard to the level of development of fine motor coordination, the PDI at time 1 and the Beery VMI at time 2. A child who shows a delay at time 1 because of the relatively slow maturation of that function will presumably show a delay at time 2 if there is a continuity (which there appears to be). Obviously we cannot reasonably ask a four- or twelve-month-old baby to copy shapes. Instead, the motor system is developing rapidly in the first year of life and if we measure its functioning, we have a set of behaviors, which although not resembling the to-be-predicted-behaviors, is, in fact, predictive. Furthermore, I have shown that if we limit our assessment to some items on the Bayley MDI that measure the child's manipulative skill at four months (Kohen-Raz, 1967), the correlation between these few items and scores on the Beery VMI at five years is .40 ($p < .01$) (Siegel, 1983).

A RECONCEPTUALIZATION

A Categorical System

I would like to suggest a reconceptualization of prediction. I believe that we are really interested in predicting ranges as opposed to exact scores. The correlation is a misleading statistic and assumes a level of precision of measurement that is not really intended by the psychological test. It is not really important to know whether a child will score 100 or 115, 105 or 120 on an IQ test. However, the difference between 80 and 95 and 100 is more critical. Typically, children who score 90 or below need special help in school (of course, children with higher scores may also). Presumably, we want to identify these children. When using the correlation, we are assuming an interval scale, that is, equal steps between each adjacent score. In reality we do not want to predict a child's exact score but how likely that child is to obtain a score in the below-average range where the child will need intervention or remediation. For example, I have shown that low (<85) Bayley scores at two years could be predicted by low Bayley scores (<85) at four, eight, twelve (and 18) months. For 71%-84% of the sample, it could be predicted whether they would show delay or have scores in the normal range. A similar type of analysis has been used by Aylward, Gustafson, Verhulst, and Colliver (1987), and they have reasonably good detection of subsequent developmental problems using this method. Hinde and Dennis (1986) proposed a similar type of categorization analysis. They note that relations between variables may occur only in part of a distribution; for example, individuals with low scores on one variable may have low scores on the other, but there may be no relationship for average or high scores. Such appears to be the case for infant tests. As Cairns (1986) noted, to study development faithfully, we need analyses at the individual level and a description of the process of development at the individual level.

The type of analysis that is most meaningful allows the determination of prediction of accuracy for the individual child. The type of analysis involves the "truth table" outlined in Figure 5.1. Children are classified into one of the

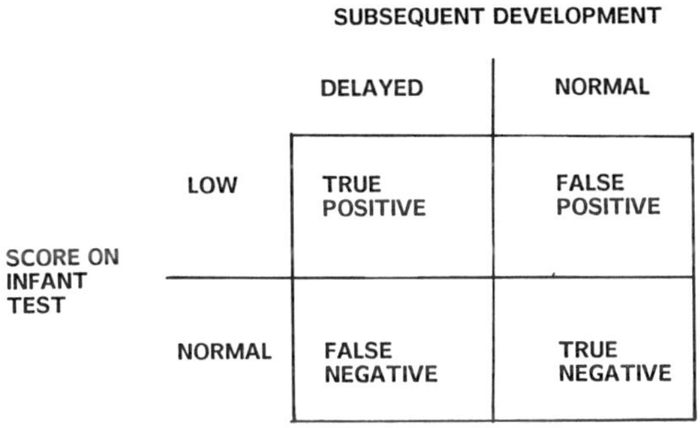

FIGURE 5.1. The classification system used to relate developmental outcome to scores on infant tests.

following categories: *true negatives* who have a score in the normal range in childhood and had a normal average score in infancy; *false negatives* who have a low score in childhood but who had an average score in infancy; *true positives* who were selected as having low scores in both infancy and childhood; and *false positives* who had low scores in infancy but not in childhood. This type of prediction also allows for a statement about the individual child; correlations, on the other hand, are based on group data and cannot tell us about an individual child. An example of the usefulness of this technique is shown in Table 5.3. These data are taken from a longitudinal study described earlier (e.g., Siegel, 1979). The relationship between low scores on the Bayley in infancy (≤85) and the absence or presence of a reading disability is shown in Table 5.3. As can be seen from the data presented in this table, a low Bayley score in infancy was predictive of a reading disability at eight years of age. Similarly, a Bayley score in the normal range (<85) indicated that the child was not likely to have a

TABLE 5.3
Ability of the Bayley to Detect a Reading Disability at 8 Years[a]

Time of Bayley Testing[b] (months)	*True Negative (Not Reading Disabled)*	*False Negative (Reading Disability not predicted)*	*True Positive (Reading Disabled)*	*False Positive (Incorrect Prediction of Reading Disability)*	*% Correct Prediction*
4	35	5	3	5	79.2
8	48	3	4	8	82.5
12	49	2	4	8	84.1

[a]Numbers represent individual cases
[b]Scores used were corrected MDI for prematurity for preterm infants

reading disability. Although there were some false positives and false negatives, the percentage was small and the overall prediction was quite good. In this case, the Bayley score was quite predictive of a reading disability.

Developmental Lag Model

In addition to the use of a categorical system, we need to consider what is the course of developmental change. Evidence is accumulating that the developmental lag model may be useful when measuring the relation between behaviors at two points in time. The developmental lag model assumes that in some individuals development of certain abilities is significantly slower than normal and that this slow development is representative of atypical functioning in this area throughout development. That is, the underlying structure remains lagging throughout development. Therefore, developmental difficulties at a later time may be predicted from atypical or slow development detected at an earlier time. However, the model goes further. The most accurate prediction of problems at time 2 will come from functions showing the fastest rate of development; in other words, those reaching ascendancy at time 1. Children who show slower than normal development at time 1 are the ones who will show problems at time 2 if the underlying structure of the process in question is the same and remains lagging. It is important to note that the deep structure, rather than the surface structure, of the behaviors needs to be the same. Behaviors that seem different on the surface may actually represent the same process. Because of the overwhelmingly large changes in development in what the child is capable of from birth to two years or six years or thirteen years or twenty years, we would not expect that it is even possible to measure behaviors that are similar at time 1 and time 2. However, if we ignore the surface structure and consider the possible underlying structure that is being measured, we may begin to understand continuity.

Tests of Specific Abilities

To examine questions of stability, we need to consider the use of more specific tests rather than global scores. That is, a more domain specific assessment of cognitive processes may be appropriate. For example, consider the case of language development. Although many tests purport to evaluate language development, they often measure different aspects of language. In my studies I have used separate measures of receptive and expressive language development. I have reported in a number of studies that in the first year of development the PDI scale of the Bayley administered in the first year of life is more highly correlated than the Bayley MDI with *expressive* language development at two years (Siegel, 1981), three years (Siegel, 1979), and four years (Siegel, 1982). In addition, Ramey, Campbell, and Nicholson (1973) found that the Bayley PDI was more highly correlated with the Illinois Test of Psycholinguistic Ability (ITPA) a measure of language functioning than was the Bayley MDI. Berk (1979) also found that the motor scale is a more accurate predictor of subsequent development than the mental scale. It may appear puzzling that a measure of motor and perceptual skills is more highly correlated with expressive language than the presumably more highly related cognitive skills measured by MDI. However, Baldwin (1897) and Lenneberg (1967) proposed that language and motor development are closely related because of a large maturational, as opposed to experiential, component of early language that is also reflected in early motor development. Both expressive language and motor skills may be manifestations of the levels and rate of development of the brain and nervous system and hence relations between these apparently different functions will be found. It is interesting to note that I did not find higher correlations of motor as opposed to mental development with language comprehension as frequently. Language comprehension may be more related to specific environmental experiences, for example, parental labelling of objects and events. In contrast, in early expressive language development the syntax (but not the content) of early utterances seems relatively consistent across individuals and perhaps even languages (Brown, 1973).

In summary, studies concerned with prediction of subsequent cognitive and language functioning from infant tests must be concerned with the following theoretical and methodological issues:

(1) Functions measured at time 1 and time 2 may not have the same surface structure but should be chosen to represent different developmental manifestations of the same underlying process.
(2) The correlation is sensitive to restriction of range. If the correlation is used at all, care should be taken to ensure that there is sufficient range.
(3) Assumptions should not be made about the precision of measurement of tests at time 1 or time 2. Specifically, considerations should be given to the idea that ordinal scores dominate most measurements of psychological processes.
(4) As a consequence of number 3, alternate data analysis techniques should be considered. Specifically, it is important to compare the mean scores at time 1 of the children who show problems at time 2 compared to those who do not. In addition, contingency analyses using cutoff scores at time 1 (average versus below average) and time 2 (problem versus no problem) have been shown to constitute a worthwhile approach.

ISSUES IN PREDICTION

Considering the evidence that there is significant continuity in development and that prediction of later cognitive functioning from scores on infant tests is possible, why has the generalization that infant test scores do not predict subsequent development been so widely accepted? I believe there are several reasons. First, there has not been a critical or thorough perusal of original sources. The consequence of failing to note methodological problems with studies of prediction and ignored positive instances has resulted in the persistence of the generalization of no prediction from infant tests.

In addition, there appears to be an implicit assumption by some scientists that prediction implies a genetic or at least biological determination of development. One reason for not accepting the evidence of prediction appears to be political; general determinism of intelligence is repugnant to some scientists. However, because we cannot conclude anything about genetic determination from these data, it is a false concern. The continuities noted are just as likely to result from environmental factors. As a matter of fact, I have found that a false negative (children who were apparently normal in infancy but delayed at a later time) came from environments that provide less stimulation and developmental opportunities than the true negatives, and, conversely, false positives (children who were delayed in infancy but functioning in the normal range at time 2) came from more stimulating homes than the true positives (children who were delayed at both points in time) (Siegel, 1979, 1981). Significant relations between development at two points in time do not imply that this relationship is a genetic one. There is simply no validation for a genetic or biological determination of behaviors on the basis of prediction.

The final problem is a difficult and subtle one. If we can, in fact, predict with some reasonable degree of certainty which infants are likely to develop problems, then this fact may have implications for screening, labelling, and treating developmental problems. The ethical issues introduced by screening devices are considerable: Do we have a right to label infants? Do we tell parents that their child has a low score and, if so, how do we tell them? Do we have an obligation to provide treatment? These very significant ethical issues make dealing with prediction and with data about good predictability difficult.

It is important to note that using infant tests to predict within the normal range is not using them for the purpose for which they were developed. They were designed to and do, in fact, predict developmental difficulties. It could be argued that infant tests are not necessary for this purpose and that an experienced clinician could do as well or better. This may be true, but it has never been tested. So, in the absence of evidence that some other system might be better than infant tests, it seems appropriate to use them, not to predict some IQ test score, but to determine which children are experiencing delayed development and are likely to show subsequent developmental problems.

It is appropriate to ask why attempts to predict subsequent developmental problems are important. This endeavour would be a worthwhile one if some kind of remedial help were available to young infants. There is evidence that programs are available that are helpful to the development of young infants (Scarr-Salapatek and Williams, 1973).

In spite of a widely held misconception, infant tests predict later test scores and can detect which children are likely to show problems. Although infant tests are not a perfect measuring tool, there is at least some continuity in the development of mental and perceptual motor functioning from infancy to early and middle childhood.

CONCLUSIONS

In this chapter I have examined the evidence for the widespread belief that traditional infant test scores obtained in the first year of life do not predict subsequent test scores obtained in childhood. Contrary to this belief, many studies have found a significant relation between infant test scores and test scores obtained later in childhood. In samples with sufficient heterogeneity and, consequently, where attenuation of correlations due to restricted range was not an issue, significant correlations have been obtained between scores on the Bayley Scales of Infant Development in the first year and mental test scores at two, three, four, five, six, seven, and eight years. An alternative way of examining the continuity issue is to compare the scores at time 1 of children who show delay at time 2 and those who do not show delay at time 2. This comparison allows a test of the hypothesis that low scores (less than 85 or 90 or some other arbitrary level) predict low scores later on. When this type of analysis is conducted, significant differences emerge very early in development between the children who will subsequently show delay and those who will not. Often, there is relatively little overlap in scores at time 1 between groups who are delayed at time 2 and those who are not. Therefore, we can say that scores in infancy *do* predict the individuals who will develop problems. In addition, children who show delays in childhood have been found to have significantly lower infant test scores than those who do not show such delays. Low infant test scores are highly predictive of low score on language, cognitive, perceptual, and visual motor tests in childhood.

I have suggested a reconceptualization of prediction. I believe that we are really interested in predicting ranges rather than exact scores. The correlation is a misleading statistic and assumes a level of precision of measurement that is not really intended by the psychological test. Is it really important to know whether a child will score 100 or 115, 105 or 120 on an IQ test? However, the difference between 80 and 95 or 85 and 100 is more critical. Typically, children whose scores are 90 or below need special help in school (of course, children with higher scores may also). Presumably, we want to identify these children. When using the correlation, we are assuming an interval scale; that is, equal steps between each adjacent score. In reality, we do not want to predict a child's exact score, but instead to predict how likely that child is to obtain a score on the below average range where the child will need some intervention or remediation. For example, I have shown that low (<85) Bayley scores at two years could be predicted by low Bayley scores (<85) at four, eight, twelve (and eighteen) months. For 71%-84% of the sample, it could be predicted whether they would show delay or have scores in the normal range. This type of prediction also allows for a statement about the individual child; correlations, on the other hand, are based on group data and cannot tell us about an individual child. Infant test scores predict subsequent test scores, and there appears to be significant stability in individual differences in intellectual functioning from infancy to childhood.

ACKNOWLEDGMENTS

The preparation of this chapter was supported by a grant from the Natural Sciences and Engineering Research Council of Canada and funds provided by OISE Small Scale Research Grant. The author wishes to thank Letty Guirnela and Susan Hall for secretarial assistance.

REFERENCES

Aylward, G. P., Gustafson, N., Verhulst, S. J., and Colliver, J. A. (1987). Consistency of diagnosis of cognitive, motor, and neurologic function over the first three years. *Journal of Pediatric Psychology, 12,* 77–95.

Baldwin, J. M. (1897). *Mental development in the child and the race.* New York: Mcmillan.

Bayley, N. (1969). *Bayley Scales of Infant Development.* New York: The Psychological Corporation.

Berk, R. A. (1979). The discriminate efficiency of the Bayley Scales of Infant Development. *Journal of Abnormal Child Psychology, 7,* 113–119.

Bornstein, M. H., and Sigman, M. D. (1986). Continuity in mental development from infancy. *Child Development, 57,* 251–274.

Brown, R. (1973). *A first language: The early stages.* Cambridge, MA: Harvard University Press.

Bruner, J. S. (1966). *Studies in cognitive growth.* New York: Wiley.

Cairns, R. B. (1986). Phenomena lost: Issues in the study of development. In J. Valsinger (Ed.), *The individual subject and scientific psychology,* (pp. 97–111). New York: Plenum.

Cohen, S. E., and Parmelee, A. H. (1983). Prediction of five-year Stanford Binet scores in preterm infants. *Child Development, 54,* 1242–1253.

Gannon, D. R. (1968). Relationships between 8 months performance on the Bayley scales of infant development at 48 months intelligence and concept formation scores. *Psychological Reports, 23,* 1199–1205.

Goeffeney, B., Henderson, N. B., and Butler, B. V. (1971). Negro-White male-female eight-month development scores compared with seven-year WISC and Bender test scores. *Child Development, 42,* 595–604.

Hinde, R. A., and Dennis, A. (1986). Categorizing individuals: An alternative to linear analysis. *International Journal of Behavioral Development, 9,* 105–119.

Ireton, H., Thwing, E., and Graven, H. (1970). Infant mental development and neurological status and intelligence at age four. *Child Development, 41,* 937–946.

Kohen-Raz, R. (1967). Scalogram analysis of some developmental sequences of infant behaviors as measured by the Bayley Infant Scale of Mental Development. *Genetic Psychology Monographs, 76,* 3–21.

La Buda, M. C., De Fries, J. C., Plomin, R., and Fulker, D. W. (1986). Longitudinal stability of cognitive ability from infancy to early childhood: Genetic and environmental etiologies. *Child Development, 57,* 1142–1150.

Lenneberg, E. (1967). *Biological foundations of language.* New York: Wiley.

Lewis, M., and Brooks-Gunn, J. (1981). Visual attention at three months as a predictor of cognitive functioning at two years of age. *Intelligence, 5,* 131–140.

McCall, R. B. (1979). The development of intellectual functioning and the prediction of later IQ. In J. D. Osofsky (Ed.), *Handbook of infant development* (pp. 707–741). New York: Wiley.

McCall, T. B., Eichorn, D. H., and Hogarty, P. S. (1977). Transition in early mental development. *Monographs of the Society of Research in Child Development, 42* (3), Serial No. 171.

Piaget, J. (1960). *Psychology of intelligence.* Patterson, NJ: Littlefield Adams.

Ramey, C. T., Campbell, F. A., and Nicholson, J. E. (1973). The predictive power of the Bayley scales of infant development and the Stanford-Binet intelligence test in a relatively constant environment. *Child Development, 44,* 790–795.

Roe, K. V. (1977). Correlations between Gesell scores in infancy and performance and non-verbal tests in early childhood. *Perceptual and Motor Skills, 45,* 1131–1134.

Scarr-Salapatek, S., and Williams, M. L. (1973). The effects of stimulation on low-birth-weight infants. *Child Development, 44,* 94–101.

Siegel, L. S. (1979). Infant perceptual, cognitive, and motor behaviours as predictors of subsequent cognitive and language development. *Canadian Journal of Psychology, 33,* 382–395.

Siegel, L. S. (1981). Infant tests as predictors of cognitive and language development at two years. *Child Development, 52,* 545–557.

Siegel, L. S. (1982). Early cognitive and environmental correlates of language development at 4 years. *International Journal of Behavioral Development, 5,* 433–444.

Siegel, L. S. (1983a). Correction of prematurity and its consequences for the assessment of the very low birthweight infant. *Child Development, 54,* 1176–1188.

Siegel, L. S. (1983b). Predicting possible learning disabilities in preterm and fullterm infants. In T. Field and A. Sostek (Eds.), *Infants born at risk: Physiological, psychological, perceptual processes,* (pp. 295–315). New York: Grune & Stratton.

Siegel, L. S. (1985a). Biological and environmental variables as predictors of intellectual functioning at 6 years. In S. Harel and N. Anastasiow (Eds.), *The at-risk infant: Psycho/socio/medical aspects* (pp. 65–73). Baltimore, MD: Brooks.

Siegel, L. S. (1985b). A risk index to predict learning problems in preterm and fullterm children. In W. K. Frankenburg, R. N. Emde, and J. W. Sullivan (Eds.), *Early identification of children at risk: An international perspective* (pp. 231–244). New York: Plenum.

Uzgiris, I., and Hunt, McV. (1975). *Assessment in infancy: Ordinal scales of psychological development.* Urbana, IL: University of Illinois Press.

Wachs, T. D. (1975). Relation of Infants' performance on Piaget scales between twelve and twenty-four months and their Stanford-Binet performance at thirty-one months. *Child Development, 46,* 929–935.

Wilson, R. S. (1978). Synchronies in mental development: An epigenetic perspective. *Science, 202,* 939–948.

6 Differentiating the Risk for High-Risk Preterm Infai

Jane V. Hunt
University of California, Berkeley

Bruce A. B. Cooper
University of California, San Francisco

INTRODUCTION

In this chapter we consider issues of stability and continuity in mental development as they apply to a population of preterm infants evaluated from two to eight years of age. On the basis of neonatal criteria, all were initially designated as at risk for developmental problems and were evaluted repeatedly in a longitudinal study (Hunt, 1981, 1983, 1986; Hunt and Rhodes, 1977). Evaluations always included a standard intelligence test, providing IQ comparisons across ages. At eight years of age, the majority of children had normal IQs, but individual differences within the normal-IQ group were apparent, including a range of dysfunctions in specific intellectual and academic abilities.

We have been interested in defining some of the more obvious dysfunctions as outcome categories within the normal-IQ group at eight years (Hunt, Cooper, and Tooley, 1988). We have also examined the longitudinal data for predictors of the outcomes, both to confirm the descriptive evidence for qualitative differences at two through six years, and also to predict categorical outcomes from information available in infancy. The categorical approach to outcome status is seen as a logical method for approximating prediction for the individual because each child is assigned to a specific outcome category. Predicting outcome for the individual from infancy or early childhood has been an important, but elusive goal of high-risk studies.

The examination of longitudinal data for the normal-IQ portion of the high-risk sample is seen as directly relevant for the study of normal populations. The emphasis on mild disabilities or unusual discrepancies in tested abilities has special advantages, including relative ease of definition. Characteristics can be defined from established parameters of familiar standard tests administered in childhood. Furthermore, the model defines patterns of ability in an exaggerated form, but in terms of functional differences that can be found in normal distributions (for example, relative language ability). Because of the exaggeration, we would expect that the precursors of functional differences might be more readily traced in the antecedent data. The major drawback in studying specific dysfunctions prospectively is their anticipated low incidence in unselected populations, and so the method of choice is to investigate a population at risk for a high incidence of such problems. We anticipated that our preterm infants of very low birth weight, as well as other categories of preterm infants who required neonatal intensive care, would provide such a population at school age, based on the results of tests and clinical ratings at younger ages (Hunt, 1981; Hunt, Tooley, and Harvin, 1982).

Longitudinal data were examined retrospectively for indicators of continuity in the behavioral antecedents of the outcomes defined at 8 years (Hunt, Cooper, and Tooley, unpublished). We have been interested in three aspects of cross-age continuity—*functional continuity,* which refers to behavioral distinctions among the outcome groups at younger ages that approximate the qualitative differences at older ages; *developmental continuity,* or, developmental shifts in the qualitative characteristics that, nevertheless, distinguish among the outcome groups at younger ages; and, *continuity of change,* or, a predictable and regularized trajectory of the rate of development (such as rate of physical growth or mental development) that forces outcome groups further apart across succeeding ages.

We did not want to prejudge the issue of functional continuity in our search for predictors of specific mental traits. Therefore, we did not construct a priori predictors composed of test items with similar functional content (for example, language items) to predict dysfunction (for example, language disability). Rather, we have taken the position that behavioral predictors may take a different form at younger ages. We hypothesized that, as an alternative to functional continuity, lags might be found in those mental abilities that are typically being incorporated at a younger age, and that such lags might be relevant predictors of future dysfunction. This perspective is similar to Kagan's original discussion of *heterotypic* continuity (Kagan, 1971). We have examined the longitudinal data in order to provide information on the relative importance of functional and developmental continuity.

Finally, we have been interested in the association between neonatal illnesses and stresses encountered by high-risk preterm infants and long-term deficits in mental abilities. Interactions between the early risk conditions and subsequent opportunities for "self-righting" effects from the environment (Gorski, Davison, and Brazelton, 1979; Sameroff and Chandler, 1975; Werner and Smith, 1982) have also been of special interest. Such effects may also influence continuity of development, albeit continuity that is represented by a developmental trajectory rather than a static state. For example, there may be ages when environmental input is especially important in generating long-lasting effects (see discussion by Emde and Harmon, 1984).

BACKGROUND

A longitudinal study of preterm infants was established in 1965, simultaneously with the introduction of a neonatal intensive care hospital nursery. The purpose of the study was to monitor the development of the recipients of this novel approach to newborn care. A major research program in neonatal pulmonary disease was implemented, with both clinical and laboratory components. Clinical emphasis was directed towards very small preterm infants, and particularly those who developed hyaline membrane disease and associated complications of the newborn. The follow-up clinic, which provided a variety of developmental evaluations at successive ages, was nested in the larger research program. Mental development was evaluated with standard tests at each age, beginning at 6 months. The established testing protocol was essentially constant from 1965 through 1978. It called for annual evaluations from twelve months through six years and at eight and eleven years.

The numbers of infants enrolled in follow-up each year increased as survival rates increased. Considerable effort was made to enroll and continue to follow children in certain key categories, including all infants born at our hospital (inborn) with birthweights below 1750 grams, outborn infants (born elsewhere and transferred in the first hours of life) with birthweights below 1000 grams, and larger preterm infants, inborn and outborn, with hyaline membrane disease who received certain innovative treatments instituted in 1969.

Follow-up assessments included medical histories, social histories, measurements of physical growth and physiological status, tests of sensory and neurological function, mental development, and, at school age, academic achievement. The array of objective evaluations was augmented by information provided by parents and children over the years, enhanced by the continuous participation of a team of interdisciplinary investigators. Extensive neonatal information pertaining to illnesses, treatments, and measures of physiological and neurological status has been incorporated into data available for longitudinal analyses. As noted, the major focus of the longitudinal study was to examine the long-term consequences of neonatal status. The research question at each age of evaluation was to determine the kinds of developmental problems noted.

We had previously reported that most of the children, including those of very low birthweight (VLBW, at or below 1500 grams), had IQs within the normal range on standardized tests at four to six years of age (Hunt, Tooley, and Harvin, 1982). However, from a clinical perspective many of these children were considered suspect, with indications of specific disabilities such as language dysfunction or visual motor integration problems suggesting possible difficulties in future intellectual and academic achievement. The test battery administered at four to six years included the Stanford-Binet Intelligence Scale, Form L-M (Terman and Merrill, 1973), the Goodenough-Harris Draw a Person Test (Harris, 1963), and the Developmental Test of Visual Motor Integration (Beery, 1967). Evidence for specific problems came primarily from ratings made by examiners after the administration of these tests, but ratings were often by the same examiner across ages and thus could not provide independent data at each age. In contrast, test scores and subscores at eight years of age provided objective data to investigate specific intellectual differences in the normal-IQ population. Furthermore, concurrent assessments of academic achievement at eight years were available to evaluate the educational importance of specific differences.

STUDY 1: OUTCOME OF VERY LOW BIRTHWEIGHT INFANTS

Defining Problems at Eight Years

At eight years of age, the protocol of mental testing provided a number of subscales and other standard scores used to study specific functional deficits and to characterize academic achievement. Scores, rather than clinical ratings and interview material, were chosen for this purpose because of their objectivity and replicability. For example, information on school failure or success, although highly relevant to educational and social adjustment, was not generally useful in defining academic achievement because children were located in a broad variety of educational settings. Achievement scores were therefore the measurements selected to define learning problems.

The protocol at eight years included the Wechsler Intelligence Scale for children, Revised (WISC-R) (Wechsler, 1974); the Bender Gestalt Test for Young Children, a test of visual-motor integration (Koppitz, 1963, 1975); and the Wide Range Achievement Test (WRAT), which measures performance in word recognition, spelling, and arithmetic (Jastak and Jastak, 1978). The WISC-R provided a Verbal IQ (VIQ) and Performance IQ (PIQ) in addition to the Full-Scale IQ.

Two outcomes were defined by WISC-R Full-Scale IQ alone. These were the *Low IQ* group, with IQs from 70 to 84 (that is, from one to two standard deviations below average), and the *Very Low IQ* group, with IQs below 70. The remaining children had IQs at or above 85, and therefore within the normal range or higher. (Whereas Wechsler (1974) included scores from 80 to 84 as "low normal," we have adhered to the SD definition as a better correlate of educational interventions.)

Extreme discrepancies between PIQ and VIQ (15 or more points) in normal-

IQ children defined two outcome groups: *Low Verbal* and *Low Performance*. A third special deficit group, *Low Visual Motor*, was composed of children with unusually low Bender scores in relation to normal IQ, and who did not have the PIQ/VIQ discrepancies. The remaining children, with normal IQs and none of the three identified score deficits, made up the nondiscrepant (*Standard/Normal*) outcome group. Thus, each child was assigned to a single outcome category.

Incidence of Specific Outcomes

We examined outcomes for 108 VLBW children (Hunt, Cooper, and Tooley, 1988). The proportions in each outcome category are shown in Table 6.1. Most of the children had IQs at or above 85 at age eight years, making the determination of specific disabilities of special interest. Table 6.1 also indicates the proportion of each outcome group with learning disabilities (LD) as defined by the California Administrative Code (1986), that is, with WRAT standard scores one and one-half standard deviations below IQ. Eighteen children were identified as LD (16.7%). Approximately 10% of the Normal/Standard (nondiscrepant) group had learning disabilities, suggesting that this group might be examined further. The importance of two functional problems, Low Performance and Low Visual-Motor, was suggested by the high incidence of LD in those outcomes. The Low Verbal outcome group had only one child with learning disabilities as defined by discrepancy scores, perhaps because the group had a lower average IQ than the other normal-IQ categories.

We noted a sex difference, with learning disabilities more common in males (22%) than in females (12%), an expected and well-established finding. However, we also located the children with achievement scores comparably higher than their IQs, the overachievers (unpublished data). They came largely from the ranks of children with low-normal (85–99), low, and very low IQs, as would be expected, and were predominantly girls. The sex difference in the two extremes of relative achievement strongly suggested some sex-related cultural difference in educational attainment. The LD group was too small for further differentiation.

TABLE 6.1
Outcome at 8 Years for 108 Children with Very Low Birthweight: Proportion with Learning Disabilities (LD) in Each Outcome

	Normal/ Standard	*Low Visual-Motor*	*Low Performance*	*Low Verbal*	*Low IQ*	*Very Low IQ*	*Total*
N	39	23	13	13	15	5	108
%	36.1	21.3	12.0	12.0	13.9	4.6	100
% LD in each outcome:	10.3	34.8	30.8	7.7	6.7	0.0	16.7

Varying the Likelihood of Outcomes

Two major variables were examined for their influence on the outcomes of the 108 VLBW children tested at eight years (Hunt, Cooper, and Tooley, 1988). Parent education level, averaged for both parents (where applicable), was used as a marker variable to examine general effects of family status. Neonatal illness ratings were used to characterize the overall neonatal status of each infant, while subsuming specific illnesses and complications. The variables were dichotomized into high and low parent education and high and low neonatal illness, and the dichotomies were examined for their effects on outcomes. The outcomes were combined for this analysis into: (1) Normal (n = 35), which included all children in the Normal/Standard outcome group, less four children with learning disabilities (see Table 6.1); (2) Mild Disabilities (n = 53), which included the four Normal/Standard children with learning disabilities and all children in the Low Verbal, Low Performance, and Low Visual-Motor groups; and (3) Moderate to Severe Disabilities (n = 20), which included all children with IQs below 85.

The results of these comparisons indicated an interaction between parent education and neonatal illness. The major effect of neonatal illness was to influence the proportion of children in the Normal outcome group, which varied from 44% in the low illness category to 18% in the high illness category. Parent education level did not influence the likelihood of normal outcome but clearly influenced the severity of problems. The most serious problems (moderate to severe category) were encountered by 30% of the children with low parent education (high school graduates or less) and by 10% of those with high parent education. In the worst case (the combination of high neonatal illness and low parent education), the likelihood of falling in the moderate to severe category rose to 54.5%.

STUDY 2: RETROSPECTIVE COMPARISONS OF OUTCOME GROUPS

We have been interested in tracing the earlier characteristics of children with different outcomes at eight years. To accomplish this task we examined longitudinal data for 314 children tested at eight years of age, including 108 with very low birthweight (from Study 1, previously described), and 206 additional preterm infants enrolled and followed in different categories considered medically at risk during neonatal life (Hunt, Cooper, and Tooley, unpublished). The group was enlarged for this study to increase the numbers of children in each outcome category. Neonatal status was not an issue in the analysis. The proportions in each outcome category at eight years were similar to those presented in Table 6.1 for the VLBW population, and included 259 (82.5%) with IQs at or above 85—

Normal/Standard, n = 158; Low Verbal, n = 35; Low Performance, n = 34; Low Visual-Motor, n = 32. In addition, there was 14.3% with Low IQ (IQ 70–84), and 3.2% with Very Low IQ (IQ below 70).

IQ Comparisons

The testing protocol included the Cattell Infant Intelligence Scale (Cattell, 1940) at six, twelve, and twenty-four months and the Stanford-Binet L-M at three through six years of age. In Figure 6.1, average IQs at each younger age and WISC-R Full Scale IQs at eight years are depicted by outcome groups. All scores through six years of age were adjusted for prematurity. In addition, Cattell IQs were adjusted by ten points (see scale in Figure 6.1) to allow for differences in normative values between the Cattell test and the 1972 revision of the Stanford-Binet L-M. The proportion of children tested at each younger age averaged 67.8% and ranged from 50.6% at six months to 83.8% at four years. IQ increases from two through five years were a general trend for groups with individual IQs above 85 at eight years (Groups 1-4). A relative deceleration in rate of IQ gain between two and three years was evident for groups 5 and 6 (Low and Very Low IQ). For the Very Low IQ group, the deceleration continued for an additional year until the average mental age equalled three years (see Hunt, 1986). Of the four outcome groups with normal IQs at eight years, only the Low Verbal group

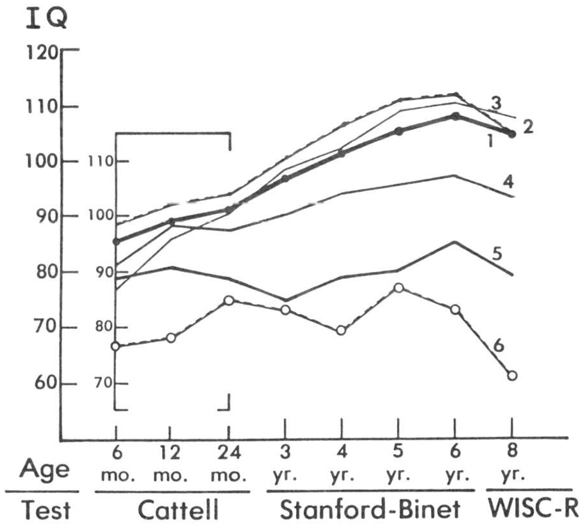

FIGURE 6.1. IQ comparisons from 6 months to 8 years for six outcome groups identified at 8 years: (1) Normal/Standard, (2) Low Visual-Motor, (3) Low Performance, (4) Low Verbal, (5) Low IQ, (6) Very Low IQ.

(group 4) showed any marked difference in average scores at younger ages, with a slower average rise in IQ from two through six years. Differences between Low Verbal and Standard groups were statistically significant at five and six years. A very slight decrease in IQ between the 1972 Stanford-Binet L-M and WISC-R is expected (Wechsler, 1974). A larger decrease at eight years was noted for groups 5 and 6 (Low and Very Low IQ).

Test Item Comparisons

The Cattell and Stanford-Binet L-M do not generate subscale scores, but individual items were examined at each age (two through six years) for differences among the normal-IQ outcome groups defined at eight years (Hunt, Cooper, and Tooley, unpublished). Items were examined by locating "hard" and "easy" items for each of the three outcome groups with score discrepancies at eight years. That is, percents passing each item were examined in reference to the Normal/Standard (nondiscrepant) outcome group. Figure 6.2 shows one such comparison, that of the Normal and Low Verbal groups at age three years. In this figure, items for the Normal group were realigned according to percents passing so that the variations of the Low Verbal group would be readily apparent. The highest and lowest quartiles of discrepancies between the groups are indicated (that is, the seven most discrepant item comparisons in each direction). Absolute values were not used because of the IQ differences between outcome groups. In this instance, the Low Verbal group had a lower average IQ at three years (See

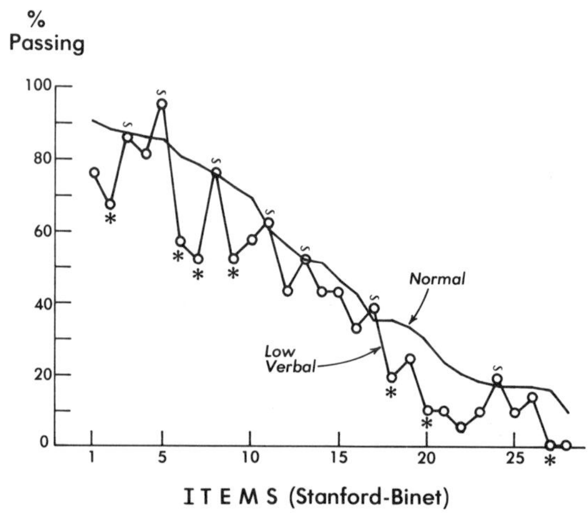

FIGURE 6.2. Percents passing Stanford-Binet L-M test items at 3 years: Comparison of Normal/Standard and Low Verbal outcome groups identified at 8 years. "Hard" (*) and "Easy" (~) items are indicated, determined by difference scores between groups.

Figure 6.1), so, necessarily, most item percents fell below those of the Normal group.

The hard items for the Low Verbal group were examined for item content. At three years, five of seven items had important language content and a sixth item tested auditory memory. In contrast, the quartile of easy items (relative to the Normal group) included five items requiring virtually no language comprehension or construction: draws a vertical line, strings beads, copies a circle, remembers and points to a picture, and completes a two-piece puzzle. A sixth item required both visual and auditory short-term memory. These six items might be successfully completed by a child with no understanding of English. In contrast, the hard items were largely dependent on specific language comprehension and use.

The functional similarity between the hard items for the Low Verbal group and the language deficit encountered at age eight years was apparent. The same functional relation was also noted for the Low Performance outcome group at age three years. In fact, a number of items bore an inverse relation, in that specific hard and easy items were reversed for Low Verbal and Low Performance groups. The Low Visual-Motor group showed no special functional characteristics in Stanford-Binet item performance at three years (or indeed, at any age). Hard items for the Low Visual-Motor group at three years included three items also difficult for Low Verbal children and three others also difficult for the Low Performance group. The increment of difference from the Normal percent passing for these items was small. The likelihood is that Stanford-Binet performance at this age was essentially unrelated to later Bender performance.

The pattern for hard and easy items noted at three years was noted at all ages for the Low Performance group, with best abilities in verbal tasks and most difficulties with the nonverbal items. The Low Verbal group revealed an inverse pattern at three, five, and six years, but hard items for this group were equivocal at two years, most being the same as for the Low Performance group. In general, for these two normal-IQ outcome groups, specific discrepancies in mental abilities were present from two to three years onward, which distinguished qualitative performance from that of the Normal/Standard group. The Low Visual-Motor group showed consistency across ages in that hard and easy items were about evenly divided between verbal and performance tasks. No special item content was noted to distinguish that group at the younger ages, despite the distinct visual-motor deficit at 8 years as compared to the Normal/Standard group.

Roles of Neonatal Illness and Parent Education

The roles of neonatal illness and parent education in the mental development of the high-risk population were explored by examining the relative importance of each to IQ across all ages, as well as the interaction of the two variables at each age. Data for the entire population of 314 children in all outcome groups were included, except for 35 children (11.1%) for whom parent education values were

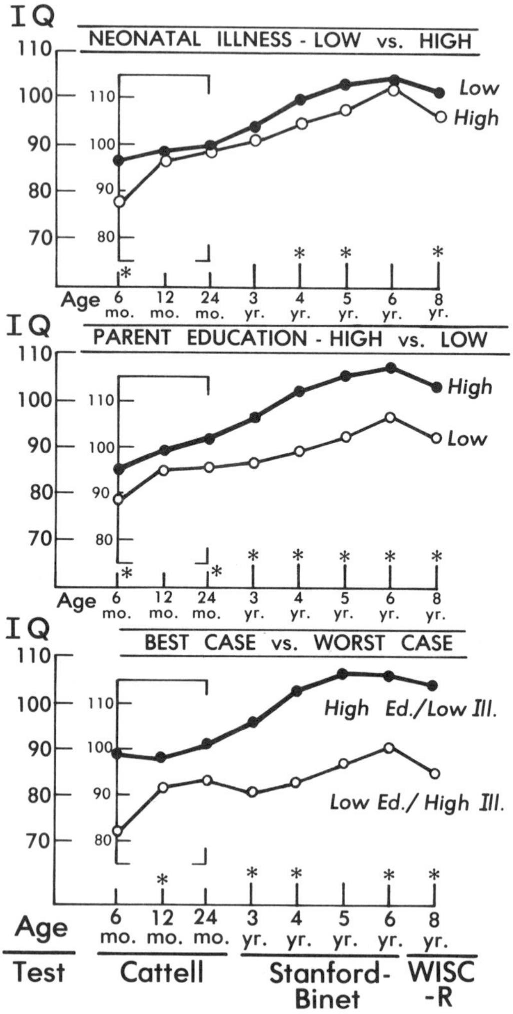

FIGURE 6.3. IQ comparisons for high-risk preterm infants across ages: Top) by severity of neonatal illness (low versus high), Middle) by averaged parent education level (high versus low), and Bottom) by "Best Case" (high parent education and low neonatal illness) versus "Worst Case" (low parent education and high neonatal illness). Significance (*) is indicated for $p < .05$ or less.

not available. As was done for the VLBW population (see Study 1), the neonatal illness and family education variables were dichotomized. Children were categorized according to the dichotomies and average IQs were compared. Figure 6.3 indicates the IQs obtained at each age for three comparisons: top—IQ according to low and high neonatal illness; middle—according to high and low averaged parent education; and, bottom—a comparison of "best case" and "worst case"; that is, children with low neonatal illness and high parent education versus those with high neonatal illness and low parent education. Statistical significance between groups is indicated in Figure 6.3. (For the third comparison, best and worst case, significant interactions are indicated, and in each instance the comparisons shown were those controlling the interaction.)

The comparisons in Figure 6.3 indicated the continuing importance of neo natal illness to IQ for the high-risk group, well beyond infancy and even to eight years of age. Furthermore, as expected, the even greater influence of family milieu, as represented by parent education, was evident. The difference between the best case and the worst case was compelling in terms of IQ differences, and the interaction between the two variables was evident beginning at twelve months of age. The change in developmental rates between twenty-four months and three years was most apparent in the last comparison. Slowly increasing average IQs were found for all comparison groups in Figure 6.3 from three through six years.

STUDY 3: PREDICTORS OF OUTCOME AT 8 YEARS

We considered Stanford-Binet items as potential behavioral predictors of the categorical outcomes identified at eight years (Hunt, Cooper, and Tooley, unpublished). We were particularly interested in whether specific items or item sets could estimate prospectively the probability that otherwise normal children would display deficits in verbal, performance, or visual-motor ability compared to one another and compared to children in the normal-IQ range who had no similar deficits.

The typical statistical method for prediction is some form of linear regression. In this situation, however, where the task was to predict categorical outcomes from dichotomous items, linear regression was considered inappropriate. (Our criterion was the probability that children would or would not display deficits, not the relative extent of their deficits). We chose logistic regression as our statistical method because the interpretation of its results is familiar. It is analogous to linear regression, yet it is designed to predict probabilities for categorical criterion variables (Aldrich and Nelson, 1984; Harrell, 1986).

Through a series of analyses, we examined data for the 259 normal-IQ children in Study 2 to identify at each age the items providing significant and unique contributions to the prediction of outcome. The potentially predictive items in these analyses were submitted in small sets because our sample sizes were relatively small. Items were identified that consistently predicted outcomes through straight (five items at a time), forward, and backward stepwise regression (ten items at a time). Those identified from the small sets that were consistently predictive in the three analytic stages were then combined in a straight regression to determine if their unique contributions were maintained. Items failing that test were excluded from final analysis. Thus, the primary task was to identify empirical predictors, and only then to inspect the qualitative content of the items.

The comparison of each discrepancy group with the nondiscrepant (Standard) group supported the evidence for functional continuity described in Study 2. Nine predictors discriminated the Low Performance group, and all were included in hard (6) or easy (3) items in Study 2. Five of the six hard predictors were exclusively performance tasks, and two of three easy predictors were clearly verbal ones. Seven predictors discriminated the Low Verbal group, and 6 had been described as hard items in Study 2. By contrast, 14 individual items predicted membership in the Low Visual-Motor outcome group. Although 13 of 14 predictors were also included as hard or easy items, no coherent pattern, according to the item content, was apparent. These results provide important support for functional continuity in the Verbal/Performance discrepancies. The computational selection procedure included only those few items at each age that had unique contributions, or in other words, the predictors were not intercorrelated.

The results were strikingly clear when we compared Low Verbal with Low Performance outcome. The content of eight out of nine predictive items across assessments from three through six years was consistent with the functional deficits at eight years. Even at three years of age each group was strong in the area of the other group's weakness.

The comparison of the Low Verbal and Low Visual-Motor groups did not reveal any qualitative pattern in predictors. The Low Visual-Motor group outperformed the Low Verbal group in all of eight predictive items scattered across the four assessments, and content was varied. The predictors thus reflected the consistency of the overall IQ difference between the two groups (see Figure 6.1).

In all, this statistical strategy gave results that conformed with our examination of hard and easy items, even though the number of predictive items identified was necessarily smaller. Qualitative characteristics of predictors were consistent with the patterns of strengths and weaknesses described for outcome groups from two through six years.

DISCUSSION

The use of standard intelligence test scores as either predictors or outcome measurements continues to attract interest, even as theoretical concerns have shifted to focus more closely on specific abilities and their origins in infancy (see Bornstein and Rose, chapters 8 and 9 in this volume). Ambivalence about the value of a summary score such as the IQ has been apparent among investigators, and especially for infant tests, where poor predictive validity has long been established (Bayley, 1933, 1949). Nevertheless, the infant test score continues to be at least a referent in many studies of cognitive development, as does the IQ at older ages. This is a recognition of the robust statistical properties of the measurements.

Major longitudinal studies of high-risk infants, such as the one reported here, have usually incorporated standardized intelligence tests in the protocol of evaluations. This is true because of the general acceptance of test scores for reporting current status of the child, and also because most long-term studies entered uncharted developmental territory with few theoretical guidelines to determine the selection of specific cognitive tasks across ages. In the studies described here, we subsequently utilized the standard test data for our own purposes, to examine the continuity of specific deficits in mental development.

A Focus on Individual Differences

Our studies have focused on specific behavioral typologies in describing intellectual status at 8 years. This categorical approach to the data was developed in an effort to approximate prediction for the individual and thus bring diagnostic concerns of the clinician and theoretical interest of cognitive psychology closer together. The categories that were created were, admittedly, largely opportunistic, determined by the protocol of tests and measurements given and limited by the numbers of children available. As anticipated, most children had IQs in the normal range at eight years and so major emphasis was given to subdividing that large subgroup into more specific categories based on functional discrepancies.

Two of the outcome categories we defined were selected to approximate common clinical problems noted at four to six years, namely language disability and visual-motor integration disability. The way in which language disability was defined by test score discrepancy (VIQ versus PIQ) led to the identification of a third outcome type called "performance disability," to include children with the inverse association between VIQ and PIQ.

Evidence for Functional Continuity

The behavioral consistency of both the Low Language and the Low Performance groups from two through six years was compelling. The large discrepancy in abilities at eight years for both groups was foreshadowed by the qualitative characteristics of hard and easy test items at younger ages. Surprisingly, the Low Performance group showed more consistent definition at the younger ages than the Low Language group, despite the predominant emphasis on language tasks in the Stanford-Binet L-M. Best item predictors for these outcome groups, derived statistically, added weight to the argument for specific functional continuity. In contrast, there was no apparent commonality in the abilities tapped by the Bender visual-motor test at eight years and the Cattell and Stanford-Binet L-M at two through six years, and thus no evidence for either functional or developmental continuity in the Low Visual-Motor group. Indeed, even scores from the Test of Visual Motor Integration (Beery Test) given at four, five, and six years did not correlate very highly with Bender scores at eight years for the combined groups with normal IQs (.22, .28, .30; $p < .01$). The question remains, what does the Bender score discrepancy mean as defined for our outcome group, and what were its antecedents? The relatively high incidence of learning disabilities in the Low Visual-Motor outcome group (see Table 6.1) indicated that the low Bender score was associated with some genuine intellectual dysfunction.

Specific item analysis to compare outcome groups was not attempted for the Cattell tests given at six and twelve months. The infant tests were scheduled according to chronological age rather than age adjusted for prematurity, thus the range of adjusted ages and, therefore, of relevant specific items was very broad during the first year. No assumption could be made that gestational age and outcome were independent. An analysis of test items by adjusted ages will be possible for VLBW infants born after 1979 in our study.

Evidence for IQ Stability and Change

One hypothesis not well-supported by the data proposed that outcome categories with significant differences in IQ at eight years would show different IQ trajectories across age. According to the hypothesis, although groups might be similar in average IQ during infancy, IQ divergence would increase across ages in a predictable way, thus fulfilling our definition of continuity in developmental rates. Such a possibility had clinical appeal because individual *changes* in IQ might prove to be predictive when actual IQ levels were not. In fact, for those groups significantly different from the Normal/Standard outcome at any age (groups 4, 5, and 6 in Figure 6.1), only the Very Low IQ group (group 6) showed such a trend, whereas all other groups were remarkably similar in IQ trajectory from three through eight years. Differences in IQ level were already established at or before three years and important shifts in IQ level appeared to take place between two and three years. Some evidence for group differences suggesting continuity in developmental rates was found when the influence of parent education level was considered (Figure 6.3, middle). In this instance the groups diverged in IQ across ages from one through four years, and the difference remained constant thereafter.

The consistent, slow rise in IQs across ages two through six years (Figure 6.1) was not readily explained. The finding was not the result of prematurity artifact ("catch up") because all IQs had been systematically adjusted for prematurity. Overall, the population was predominantly middle-class, as exemplified by the fact that the average parent education level was above high school graduate. Although we surmised that the improvement in IQ was the result of resiliency, that is, continuing recovery from neonatal events, we noted that there was a similar rise in the scores of children who did and did not experience considerable neonatal illness (Figure 6.3, top). Inflation in Stanford-Binet performance at five and six years was a general finding, and between-age IQ correlations from four through eight years were consistent and high ($r = .80$ in each comparison for the normal-IQ children).

Neonatal illness exerted a highly significant influence on scores at six months ($p < .002$, Figure 6.3, top). By age 2 years, the influence of parent education level on scores became highly significant ($p < .003$, Figure 6.3, middle). The shift in relative importance of the two variables during infancy suggested that, during the first two years of life both the initial developmental insult and processes of recovery were influencing developmental test scores, but in opposing ways, resulting in what Fischer and colleagues have described as first-order discontinuities (Fischer, Pipp, and Bullock, 1984). Individually, such discontinuities are typically noted as idiosyncratic changes in developmental rates.

Long-term Prediction

We determined that the likelihood of an outcome at eight years was altered for VLBW infants according to dichotomized levels of neonatal illness and averaged parent education. Neonatal illness influenced the likelihood of normal outcome, whereas parent education influenced the probable severity of the intellectual deficit (Hunt, Cooper, and Tooley, 1988). These changes in probability, applicable to the individual infant, represent one aspect of continuity, namely predictability. We can predict that identified infants are likely to have different outcomes eight years later, based on (in this instance) two pieces of information available very early in life. The way in which this differentiation comes about may not be known, but some underlying regulation of development is assumed. In other words, neonatal illness (and presumed damage to the central nervous system) continues to exert a long-lasting effect even into childhood, but that effect is, itself, regulated by unspecified familial constants.

The IQ comparisons in Figure 6.3 are relevant to long-term prediction of categories in that the most severe problem categories had been defined by IQ levels. The advantage of categorizing outcomes, even by IQ levels, is evident when we compare Figure 6.3, bottom ("best case" versus "worst case") with the probability data determined for the same dichotomies. In Figure 6.3, the average IQ of the "worst case" subgroup at age eight is approximately 85. However, when working directly with categories we determined that the likelihood of having IQ below 85 in this subgroup was 54.5%. The possibility of improving prediction for the individual is greater when we take the latter approach to analysis. For example, the general associations of neonatal illness and parent education with Low and Very Low IQ categories can be refined and recombined to give a higher likelihood of membership in these categories. In this way we can work to determine precise predictors of long-term deficits.

CONCLUSIONS

The following conclusions may be drawn from the work presented in this chapter:

- Useful outcome categories can be determined from standard test scores at eight years that correspond, in some degree, to recognized clinical entities of intellectual dysfunction or unusual ability patterns.
- The incidence of the unusual outcomes was considerably greater for children from a high-risk preterm infant population than expected by normative data.
- The outcome categories proved useful for retrospective studies of mental abilities at younger ages, by both descriptive and statistical methods.
- Results supported an hypothesis of functional continuity in mental development, meaning that specific ability patterns were apparent, in kind, at younger ages. For children with discrepancies in Verbal and Performance IQ, the outcome group with relatively poorer ability in performance skills showed that ability pattern from age two years; the outcome group with lesser ability in verbal skills showed that contrast by three years.
- Children with relatively poorer ability in visual-motor integration skills were not identified in the retrospective studies.
- No evidence was found for an hypothesis of developmental continuity across ages two through eight years, defined as developmentally appropriate qualitative changes in behavioral characteristics that, nevertheless, distinguished outcome groups.
- Little evidence was found for continuity in developmental rates across ages, defined as steady changes in trajectory (such as changes in IQ) that forced groups further and further apart across ages. The exception was found for level of parent education, which was associated with increasing IQ discrepancies from one through four years.
- The use of categorical outcome data permitted the determination of likelihoods for certain outcomes, analagous to the prediction of individual differences.

ACKNOWLEDGMENTS

Preparation of this chapter was supported in part by SCOR Grant HL-27356, and by HD 17669 to the Cardiovascular Research Institute, University of California, San Francisco. We wish to acknowledge the assistance and support of Dr. William H. Tooley, co-investigator and Director of the Neonatal Follow-up Study at the University of California, San Francisco.

REFERENCES

Aldrich, J. H., and Nelson, F. D. (1984). *Linear Probability, Logit, and Probit Models.* Sage University Paper Series on Quanitative Applications in the Social Sciences, Series #07-045. Beverly Hills: Sage Publications.

Bayley, N. (1933). Mental growth during the first three years. A developmental study of 61 children by repeated tests. *Genetic Psychology Monographs, 14,* 1–92.

Bayley, N. (1949). Consistency and variability in the growth of intelligence from birth to eighteen years. *Journal of Genetic Psychology, 75,* 165–196.

Beery, K. E. (1967). *Developmental test of visual-motor integration.* Chicago: Follett Educational Corporation.

California Administrative Code, Title V, Section 3030(a-j). (1986). Revised by Special Education Policy Statement SE-15.

Cattell, P. (1940). *The measurement of intelligence of infants and young children.* New York: The Psychological Corporation.

Emde, R. N., and Harmon, R. J. (1984). Entering a new era in the search for developmental discontinuities. In R. N. Emde and R. J. Harmon (Eds.), *Continuities and discontinuities in development* (1–11). New York: Plenum.

Fisher, K. W., Pipp, S. L., and Bullock, D. (1984). Detecting developmental discontinuities. In R. N. Emde and R. J. Harmon (Eds.), *Continuities and discontinuities in development* (95–121). New York: Plenum.

Gorski, P. A., Davison, M. F., and Brazelton, T. B. (1979). Stages of behavioral organization in the high-risk neonate: Theoretical and clinical considerations. *Seminars in Perinatology, 3,* 51–72.

Harrell, F. E., Jr. (1986). The logist procedure. In SAS Institute, Inc., *SUGI supplemental library user's guide, version 5 edition,* Cary, N.C.: SAS Institute, Inc.

Harris, D. B. (1963). *Children's drawings as measures of intellectual maturity: A revision and extension of the Goodenough Draw-a-Man Test.* New York: Harcourt, Brace and World.

Hunt, J. V. (1981). Predicting intellectual disorders in childhood for preterm infants with birthweights below 1501 grams. In S. L. Friedman and M. Sigman (Eds.), *Preterm birth and psychological development* (329–351). New York: Academic Press.

Hunt, J. V. (1983). Environmental risks in fetal and neonatal life as bilogical determinants of infant intelligence. In M. Lewis (Ed.), *Origins of Intelligence* (2nd ed.). New York: Plenum.

Hunt, J. V. (1986). Developmental risk in infants. In B. K. Keogh (Ed.), *Advances in special education, vol. 5, Developmental problems in infancy and the preschool years* (25–59). Greenwich, CT: JAI Press.

Hunt, J. V., Cooper, B. A. B., and Tooley, W. H. (1988). *Continuity of differences in specific mental abilities: A retrospective study of longitudinal data.* Submitted for review.

Hunt, J. V., Cooper, B. A. B., and Tooley, W. H. (1988). Outcome of very-low-birth-weight infants at 8 and 11 years: Role of neonatal illness and family status. *Pediatrics, 82,* 596–603.

Hunt, J. V., and Rhodes, L. (1977). Mental development of preterm infants during the first year. *Child Development, 48,* 204–210.

Hunt, J. V., Tooley, W. H., and Harvin, D. (1982). Learning disabilities in children with birth weights ≤ 1500 grams. In T. K. Oliver and T. H. Kirschbaum (Eds.), *Seminars in Perinatology,* vol. 5 (pp. 280–287). New York: Grune and Stratton.

Jastak, J. F., and Jastak, S. (1978). *The wide range achievement test.* Wilmington, DE: Jastak Associates, Inc.

Kagan, J. (1971). *Change and continuity in infancy.* New York: Wiley.

Koppitz, E. M. (1963). *The Bender gestalt test for young children.* New York: Grune and Stratton.

Koppitz, E. M. (1975). *The Bender gestalt test for young children, vol. II, research and application, 1963–1973.* New York: Grune and Stratton.

Sameroff, A. J., and Chandler, M. J. (1975). Reproductive risk and the continuum of caretaking casualty. In F. D. Horowitz (Ed.), *Review of child development research* (*vol. 4*). Chicago: University of Chicago Press.

Terman, L. M., and Merrill, M. A. (1973). *Stanford-Binet intelligence scale: Manual for the third revision, Form L-M.* Boston: Houghton Mifflin.

Wechsler, D. (1974). *Wechsler intelligence scale for children - revised.* New York: The Psychological Corporation.

Werner, E. E., and Smith, R. S. (1982). *Vulnerable, but invincible: A longitudinal study of resilient children and youth.* New York: McGraw-Hill.

7 Transformations and Continuities: Intellectual Functioning in Infancy and Beyond

Ina C. Užgiris
Clark University

INTRODUCTION

In most general terms, the issue of continuity in development pertains to the question of connections between functioning in the early years and later. Psychologists have debated this issue for many years, and although it has not been resolved, many aspects have been clarified in recent discussions (e.g., Emmerich, 1968; Kagan, 1980; Lerner, 1984; McCall, 1977). Maybe the most important clarification is the understanding that the issue of continuity cannot be adequately settled simply on the basis of empirical data. This does not mean that empirical data are irrelevant, but that specific findings gain meaning and relevance within a particular conceptualization of this issue. One aim of the present chapter is to indicate the severe lack of data relevant to many aspects of this debate.

A simple approach to the question of continuity has been to identify some theories of development with a continuity position and to interpret others as taking a discontinuity stance. From this standpoint, theories viewing development in more quantitative terms are considered to be continuity theories and those viewing development in terms of stages with qualitative transitions are considered to hold a discontinuity position. Piaget's theory of intellectual development usually serves as a prime example of a discontinuity theory. However, such wholesale relegation of theories to either a continuity or a discontinuity position is unwarranted, because most theories recognize both types of change in relation to different aspects of functioning. Thus, it is more productive to discuss the continuity issue in relation to specific dimensions of human functioning than in relation to development in general.

The period of infancy has been a special focus of this debate. On the one hand, the discontinuity view seems to apply particularly well to the transition from infancy to childhood. Infants' limited skills in the spheres of physical mobility, organization of activity, and communication with others make it clear to observers that this first period of life is separate and distinct. The restriction of infant functioning largely to the here and now suggests that infants lack not only knowledge and skills, but also rely on different processes in their activities. On the other hand, the experiences of infancy have been proposed to have substantial and enduring effects on later functioning, implying an underlying connection between the apparently disparate activities during infancy and later periods. In this manner, the issue of continuity has been linked with the nature-nurture controversy. Although the ties between these two debates are not specifically examined in this chapter, at times both controversies become intertwined in the interpretation of data.

Development entails change by definition, and thus, the issue of continuity forces an examination of the nature of developmental change. Changes that involve integration of existing modes into evolving modes of functioning may be more easily reconciled with a continuity position than changes that emerge through differentiation and transformation. Moreover, psychologists seem more interested in understanding changes as they occur during individual lifetimes, but developmental theory, particularly with respect to descriptions of developmental change, is more focused on generalized patterns and universal tendencies. An examination of the issue of continuity highlights the need to integrate the individual perspective into developmental theory (Valsiner, 1986).

In this chapter, the continuity issue is addressed through an examination of research on infant development guided by Piaget's theory or using assessment procedures based on his work. Piaget's theory describes development in terms of a sequence of qualitative transformations for a generalized person and does not give much consideration to individual variation around the generalized pattern. At first view, research with a Piagetian orientation should provide the clearest evidence for the case of discontinuity in intellectual development. However, although there is ample support for the occurrence of qualitative transformations, there is also evidence for the persistence of certain kinds of individual inclinations. Therefore, it is necessary to first consider some theoretical aspects of the continuity issue.

The first aim of the present chapter is to examine the ways in which the continuity position is expressed within developmental theory in order to underscore that the continuity issue can be most fruitfully pursued with respect to specific aspects of functioning rather than the course of development as a whole. The data reviewed all pertain to intellectual functioning in the period of infancy and illustrate the meagerness of empirical research on certain aspects of the continuity question. Therefore, this chapter also suggests some directions for future studies. And finally, it raises the question of the unit of study to be adopted in research on continuities in development in view of the interactive nature of human functioning.

THE MEANINGS OF CONTINUITY

Previous discussions of the continuity issue have clarified that it may pertain to the kinds of change observed in the course of development, to the relations posited between functioning during different periods, or to the continuance of individual differences over time. To facilitate communication, several terms have been proposed for these different meanings of continuity. In this chapter, the term *continuity* is used to refer to the persistence of functions or processes at some measurable level during ontogenesis (cf. Kagan, 1980), and the term *constancy* to denote unchanging behavioral patterns or some underlying elements producing those behavior patterns. In keeping with earlier proposals (Emmerich, 1964; McCall, 1977), the term *stability* is used to describe the maintenance of individual differences among a group of individuals over time. Sequential invariance of achievements claimed by constructivist theories is discussed as a distinct position and is termed *continuance of functioning*.

Continuity

Theories that tend to describe human behavior in terms of traitlike characteristics appear to favor the continuity position. The same dispositions are noted at different periods in life and are assumed to be due to the same underlying processes. For example, although sociability may have different behavioral manifestations at different ages and may vary in the frequency of specific modes of expression or the choice of partners, it is a trait that can be observed from infancy to old age and can be assumed to fulfill similar human needs throughout the lifetime. Intelligence has often been conceived in a similar way. Even though the manifestations of intelligence vary greatly from age to age and even from situation to situation, an underlying disposition is thought to tie together all the various manifestations. Thus, continuity is posited for the disposition and, sometimes, for its strength. Current information-processing perspectives on intelligence include many features of this framework (e.g., Siegler, 1986), although the underlying processes providing for continuity are described differently.

As Werner (1957) pointed out, the continuity debate within these types of theories centers on the smoothness of change over time. If change is incremental and gradual, the growth function can be described as continuous; if there are abrupt changes, discontinuity in growth is assumed. However, in both cases, the dimension along which change takes place remains the same during growth. It is clear that the smoothness of observed change depends a great deal on how data are presented (McCall, 1981; Wohlwill, 1973). An aggregate growth curve for a group of individuals or for several adjacent time periods may appear smooth, although the individual growth curves may include abrupt changes or gaps. Consequently, the continuity portrayed in quantitative growth curves may, to a large extent, be a matter of treatment of data.

As the previous discussion suggests, even these theories include aspects of continuity and discontinuity in conceptualizing change during ontogenesis. Although the underlying dimension, function, or process is said to remain the same, its behavioral manifestations, quantitative values, and even relations to other dimensions (Emmerich, 1968) may change with development. Thus, description of behavioral change in terms of continuity or discontinuity is to some extent a matter of focus on a particular type of change.

When behavioral manifestations of a specific characteristic at two periods are markedly different and a continuity position is espoused, constancy of some underlying element or process is often assumed in order to sustain the continuity conception. For example, although the temperamental trait of "moodiness" is demonstrated through different actions by infants, children, and adults, who may rely on different perceptual, memory, and cognitive processes for their disparate actions, continuity may be posited on the basis of the constancy of some presumed genetic predisposition enduring throughout life. For intellectual activities as well, a continuity position often becomes linked with the assumption of a genetic predisposition toward a given level of competence, which remains constant throughout ontogenesis. However, because genetic determinants are expressed only in interaction with a concrete situation and their activation need not begin at birth or extend throughout all developmental periods, the summoning of genetic determinants is only another way for positing continuity through an underlying constancy.

In contrast, constructivist theories of development have been viewed as holding a discontinuity position, because they posit a reorganization of underlying processes in the course of transition to each new developmental level. The transitions are qualitative and discontinuous in that the emerging functioning cannot be reduced to the previous form of functioning. Yet, even these theories posit the continuance of certain aspects of functioning. As Werner (1957) pointed out, quantitative and continuous change often characterize the perfection of a new function once it has emerged. More importantly, in Piaget's (1975/1985) theory, the structural reorganizations characterizing each stage in development are the outcomes of the continuous functioning of assimilation, accommodation, and equilibration, the invariants that make development possible. Thus, constructivist theories recognize continuance of other aspects while emphasizing transformation of the interrelations of functions within a totality.

There is also another conception of continuity embodied in the sequential assumptions of constructivist theories. Continuance inheres in the posited linkage between earlier and later structures, such that the emergence of later structures is, in part, dependent on the presence of the earlier ones. The transformations that accompany the sequential emergence of new structural organizations have led to the view that these theories hold a discontinuity position. The discontinuity inheres, however, in the organization of cognitive processes at different developmental levels, whereas connectedness resides in their sequential interdependence (cf. Rutter, 1984).

Several conceptual analyses of the various relations between the achievements forming a developmental sequence have been offered (e.g., Flavell, 1972; Kagan, 1980; Strauss, 1982; Užgiris, 1987). The most important distinction that has been drawn is between sequences in which new achievements add to or replace previous achievements and those in which new achievements are in some way derived from earlier ones. In this latter case, sequential continuity is most clearly demonstrated. An even further distinction has been suggested by Campbell and Richie (1983). They differentiate between prerequisites and precursors in sequential relations. Achievements that come to be integrated as components of higher-level functioning or mediate the attainment of such functioning are considered prerequisites; only those achievements that become modified in the transition to higher levels of functioning are considered precursors. Campbell and Richie argued for using precursor relations to define sequential continuity and thereby to trace unified domains of functioning.

An example of precursor-type continuity might be development in the understanding of logical relations as proposed by Piaget (1970/1972). In the sensorimotor period, relations of order, inclusion, or substitution are understood in terms of actions on concrete objects (Forman, 1982; Langer, 1980, 1986). This understanding is transformed to a symbolic understanding of such relations as a direct modification of the earlier understanding. In contrast, in the realm of causal functioning, specific goal-related means may come to substitute for generalized action procedures with development, making the generalized action procedures a link in the sequential development of causal understanding, but not a precursor of higher-level understanding. These examples demonstrate that identification of sequential continuities is to a large extent a theoretical endeavor.

In the discussion so far, the issue of continuity has been taken up with respect to the types of change occurring in the course of development. Change may be viewed in quantitative or qualitative terms, and the structural interconnections between the various facets of functioning may or may not be considered, but in all cases the focus is on some domain of functioning over the course of development. In the limit, persistence of a characteristic without change may yield constancy in that aspect of functioning. Thus, such considerations may be said to pertain to developmental continuity. Even more often, the general issue of continuity is related to the maintenance of individual differences during ontogenesis.

Stability

The comparison of individuals requires some quantifiable measure. When change with development is conceived in quantitative terms, that quantification may also serve as the basis for individual comparison. For example, if vocabulary growth is quantified in terms of the number of different words that are correctly used in conversation, then that number can also serve as a measure of an individual's standing in relation to others. In contrast, when developmental change is viewed as qualitative, the level achieved by an individual is only a coarse indication of the individual's standing when compared to others. It has been suggested (Hunt, 1976, 1980) that time taken to achieve a given level might be a more quantitative measure of progress along a developmental sequence. In either case, it is important to note that synchronous comparison of individuals and comparison of their relative standing over time deal with rather different questions.

A comparison of individuals at a given time requires only a means to determine their relative standing in some realm of functioning, but a comparison of individuals across time also requires a metric for change within that realm of functioning. Assessment of the stability of individuals' standings over time has typically relied on the correlation of standings at time 1 with standings at time 2. As has been pointedly shown in previous discussions of this matter (Emmerich, 1964; McCall, 1977), a high correlation merely indicates stability of relative ranks among the individuals being compared and does not show anything about consistency or change in the overall level of achievement for the group as a whole. In a developmental context, where change in the level of achievement is expected, a high correlation and, hence, high stability indicates the maintenance of rates of change for that group of individuals rather than a continuity in their measured achievement. Nevertheless, stability in rankings often has been taken as the measure of developmental continuity.

An implicit mechanism allowing such a conflation of stability and continuity seems to be the assumption that rate of change and the level achieved must be strongly related. It is an assumption inherent in such measures as the IQ, because children who have achieved at a more rapid rate up to a given time period and, thus, have attained a higher IQ, are expected to maintain that same rate of achievement throughout development, retaining the higher IQ at maturity. In fact, individual rates of achievement may vary in keeping with developmental spurts and pauses due to both inherent factors and environmental opportunities. This flux in the actual rate of progress along various dimensions of functioning must advise caution in making inferences about continuity in level of functioning from rates of achievement measured at a particular developmental period.

Nonetheless, in the context of empirical studies, the issue of continuity often takes the form of stability in the rates of progress during ontogenesis. With the issue presented in this form, it might be argued that constructivist theories have no inherent reason to opt for a position of continuity. Description of development in terms of periods of transformation and periods of consolidation suggests that individual rates of change should not remain stable, but vary in the course of development; however, a constructivist theory such as Piaget's does not consider individual rates of change. It could be argued that because of prerequisite and precursor relations among achievements and because of the continuous action of the accommodation–assimilation–equilibration process complex, the relative positions of individuals might be maintained at least during periods of within-stage functioning. But because of the grounding of progress in interaction with the world, an equivalent case could be made for instability. There seems particularly little reason to expect a relation between rates of progress and the level of development that is ultimately achieved (Užgiris, 1976), but if development does occur, the form of the subsequent level of functioning is theoretically invariant.

If the issue of stability is phrased in terms of stability of rates of progress, the constructivist theories may be aligned with a position of discontinuity, because they do not require that an individual's rate of progress at one period be closely related to the rate of progress at another period. Those factors that contribute to developmental progress (biological endowment, experience, self-regulation) may operate in a similar manner at all developmental periods, but there is nothing in the theory that inherently requires that comparable rates of progress be maintained from period to period. In regard to rates of progress, to the extent that behavioral or information-processing theories rely on genetic or maturational factors as the determining mechanism, they seem more closely aligned to the continuity position.

Predictability

Correlation between the standings of individuals at time 1 and time 2 is not only used for examining the maintenance of rates of progress; it often represents an attempt to predict individual standing at time 2 or at maturity. Prediction of an individual's level of functioning in some domain is an understandable goal and a highly important consideration for many practical decisions. Practical decisions, however, require predictability for individuals, not groups. at least within tolerable ranges of false positives and negatives. At the same time, predictability does not depend on continuity in any function that is being assessed.

For purposes of predictability, it does not matter if it is difficult to construct a link between an earlier measurement and a later one. If the Apgar score predicted the level of intellectual functioning at maturity with considerable accuracy, for many purposes it would not be important that a connection between physiological status soon after birth and problem solving in adulthood were difficult to trace. In predictability, the correlation with outcome at time 2 is of critical importance, and understanding the links between the indicator measure and outcome can be left for future studies. This being the case, predictability cannot be taken as evidence for continuity in the function under investigation.

When samples of infants being assessed include physically handicapped or impaired individuals, and a higher correlation between their cognitive performance early and at some later age is obtained, that predictability alone does not serve as evidence for continuity in cognitive functioning. The impairment or some aspect related to the impairment may be the constant factor allowing for predictability. Thus, although for practical purposes it is very important to determine what can be expected for children with impairments, results for these children do not establish developmental continuity for them or samples composed of different types of individuals. Even when longitudinal studies demonstrate that predictability includes stability of individual functioning, it is necessary to show the persistence of some process or function over time to claim continuity. Ultimately, such linkage can be made only conceptually.

LONGITUDINAL STUDIES FROM A PIAGETIAN APPROACH

The possibility of finding better infant measures has been raised because the magnitude of correlations between performance on standardized infant tests and IQ scores obtained in childhood has not been impressive. One new measure utilized in several studies has been the various assessment scales derived from descriptions of infant achievements found in Piaget's work (Casati and Lézine, 1968; Užgiris and Hunt, 1975). Although one can have many misgivings about the use of these kinds of assessment scales in the manner of psychometric tests, some sample results are presented in order to concretely illustrate the conceptual considerations that have been raised in the previous section. In addition, the results from some other studies with a more constructivist orientation are given, because they highlight different aspects of the continuity issue.

Possibly because questions such as the cohesiveness of stages and the invariance of sequences have been more central to constructivist theories, very few longitudinal studies examining the developmental patterns of individual subjects have been carried out. There are a few studies focused on individual transitions during the period of sensorimotor functioning, but studies of transition from the sensorimotor period to other periods are almost nonexistant. It seems that the assumption of necessary links between earlier and later achievements has diverted interest away from studying how individuals actually construct these links.

The great majority of studies concerned with the invariance of sequential progression has applied scaling procedures to cross-sectional data even when examining transitions in the sensorimotor period. The Piagetian sequence of six sensorimotor stages has generally been found to be invariant among various groups of infants (for review, see Užgiris, 1983). Sequential invariance has also been demonstrated for separate domains of functioning in various populations (e.g., Cicchetti and Mans-Wagener, 1987; Hunt, 1987; Kahn, 1987; Užgiris, 1987). However, the demonstration that groups of infants follow the same sequence in the course of development does not indicate anything about their individual rates of progress or the stability of individual rankings within some comparison group.

There are a few studies that have used Piagetian assessment scales to obtain data comparable to those usually obtained with psychometric tests. The findings from these studies regarding predictability of later scores from assessments during infancy are also quite comparable. They show that individual standings have some stability during infancy and correlate with childhood psychometric test performance to a moderate degree. An example of such data is presented in Table 7.1, taken from a longitudinal study by Wachs (1975), showing the correlations between Užgiris-Hunt Scale performance during the second year of life and Stanford-Binet scores at 31 months.

The data in Table 7.1 have the fairly typical pattern of positive, slight, but increasing correlation to later performance across the second year of life. As the significance of correlation coefficients is so dependent on sample size, the absolute magnitude of these correlations may be more relevant than their significance in making comparisons with other studies. The differential pattern of correlation for individual scales demonstrates two aspects of development that are not empha-

TABLE 7.1
Product-Moment Correlations Between Užgiris-Hunt Scale Scores at Five Age Levels (in Months) and the Stanford-Binet at 31 Months

	Age (in months)				
Scale	*12 (N = 21)*	*15 (N = 20)*	*18 (N = 22)*	*21 (N = 20)*	*24 (N = 17)*
Object Permanence	.52**	.40*	.36*	.42*	.56*
Means-Ends	.06	.55**	.38*	.24	.04
Vocal Imitation	.02	.23	.48*	.46*	.52*
Gestural Imitation	−.12	.17	.41*	.14	.54*
Causality	.11	.24	.45*	.48*	.44*
Relations in Space	−.05	.23	.49**	.21	.64**
Schemes	.32	.43*	.66**	.12	.46*

*$p < .05$
**$p < .01$

Note. From "Relations of infants' performance on Piaget scales between twelve and twenty-four months and their Stanford-Binet performance at thirty-one months" by T. D. Wachs, 1975, *Child Development, 46,* p. 932. Copyright 1975 by the University of Chicago Press. Adapted by permission.

sized in discussions of findings with psychometric tests. First, the differential correlations suggest that the interrelations between domains of functioning change during infancy. These changing relations between various domains of functioning need to be considered rather than hidden by averaging into a single score. There is ample evidence from Piagetian studies that functioning is restructured several times during the sensorimotor period (e.g., Curcio and Houlihan, 1987; Dunst and Rheingrover, 1983; Rensen, Kerssier, Molenaar, and Oppenheimer, 1987; Užgiris, 1983; Wachs and Hubert, 1981). Moreover, these results indicate that predictability of later scores may vary depending on the domain of functioning assessed at the earlier time. As shown in Table 7.1, achievement on the Object Permanence scale is more predictive of Stanford-Binet IQ in the third year of life than achievement on the other scales, except toward the very end of the sensorimotor period.

Similar data for infants with Down's syndrome are presented in Table 7.2 (Cicchetti and Mans-Wagener, 1987). In this study, the criterion score was obtained at 24 months on the same Piagetian assessment instrument as at all previous testings. For these infants, their relative standing on the Užgiris-Hunt Scales became quite stable during the second year of life, which may reflect some characteristic of this population. In agreement with data shown in Table 7.1, these results indicate that relative standings in Object Permanence and Vocal Imitation have greater stability during the second year than standings in other domains of functioning.

My longitudinal study of 12 infants (Užgiris, 1987) provides data on the relations between sensorimotor functioning during the first two years of life and performance at twenty-four months on Piagetian as well as (for ten of the infants) on standard psychometric tests. Although correlations derived from such a small sample have to be treated with great caution, their general agreement with results from other studies gives them at least suggestive value. As shown in Table 7.3, these results indicate that prediction of infant standing at twenty-four months on both psychometric and Piagetian measures is similar, although it might be argued that a Piagetian assessment should possess greater continuance than a psychometric test with earlier measures.

Moreover, the data in Table 7.3 show that predictability from different times of assessment is also not equivalent. If development proceeds through spurts and plateaus, it may be expected that predictability from periods of transformation and periods of relative consolidation would differ. Age is obviously not a very good indicator of a phase in individual development; some infants of the same age may be in transition, whereas others may be in a period of consolidation. Nevertheless, possibly because this small sample of infants was relatively homogeneous, it is clear that prediction from assessments at 9 or 20 months is much better than prediction from assessments at twelve or fifteen months. Such findings illustrate that in reaching conclusions regarding stability and predictability

TABLE 7.2
Rank-Order Correlations Between Uẑgiris-Hunt Scale Scores at Different Ages and the Score at 24 Months for Infants with Down Syndrome

	Age (in months)				
Scale	*5*	*9*	*13*	*16*	*19*
Object Permanence	.20	.34**	.41**	.44**	.60**
Means-Ends	.12	.25	.59**	.49**	.44**
Vocal Imitation	.29*	.30*	.23	.44**	.51**
Gestural Imitation	.08	.19	.44**	.17	.64**
Causality	.30*	.04	.27*	.12	.60**
Relations in Space	.04	.12	−.01	.12	.26*
Schemes was not administered					

*$p < .05$
**$p < .01$
Note. From "Sequences, stages, and structures in the organization of cognitive development in infants with Down Sydrome" by D. Cicchetti and L. Mans-Wagener. In I. Č. Uẑgiris and J. McV. Hunt (Eds.), *Infant performance and experience: New findings with the Ordinal Scales* (p. 296), 1987, Urbana: University of Illinois Press. Copyright 1987 by the Board of Trustees of the University of Illinois. Adapted by permission. $N = 43$ at all ages.

of infant performance it may be necessary to consider the phase within a developmental sequence from which prediction to later standings is made.

To illustrate stability of individual standings during the sensorimotor period, the intercorrelations between rankings on the Uẑgiris-Hunt Scales for my longitudinal sample at selected ages are shown in Table 7.4. These data illustrate that there is no clear increase or decrease in the stability of individual standings across age. In fact, some more distant assessments show greater stability than

TABLE 7.3
Rank-Order Correlations Between Uẑgiris-Hunt Scale Scores at Different Ages with the Uẑgiris-Hunt Total Score, Bayley MDI, and the Stanford-Binet at 24 Months

	Age (in months)					
	4	*9*	*12*	*15*	*18*	*20*
24-month Scores						
Uẑgiris-Hunt	.51	.54*	.30	.56*	.41	.57*
Bayley MDI	.12	.67*	.15	.46	.46	.60*
Stanford-Binet	.40	.68*	.21	.03	.66*	.65*

*$p < .05$
Note. N = 10

TABLE 7.4
Intercorrelations of Rankings on the Užgiris-Hunt Scale for Selected Observations During the First Two Years

Age (in months)	Age (in months) 4	9	12	18	22	24
4	–	.41	.71*	.19	.47	.51*
9		–	.29	.40	.79*	.54*
12			–	.41	.24	.30
18				–	.36	.41
22					–	.78*

*$p < .05$
Note. N = 12

others closer in time, suggesting that there are reorganizations in sensorimotor functioning. Although the nature of these reorganizations and the best methods to study them are open to discussion (cf. Curcio and Houlihan, 1987; Dunst, Brassell, and Rheingrover, 1981; Dunst and Rheingrover, 1983; Užgiris, 1983; Wachs and Hubert, 1981), their existence is recognized in research from quite varied orientations (McCall, Eichorn, and Hogarty, 1977; Trevarthen and Hubley, 1978). The presence of periods of transition can be expected to influence the stability of standings during infancy and childhood as well.

From a Piagetian perspective, once a level of functioning is attained, it is expected to be maintained. A few studies have attempted to evaluate this expectation by examining the performance of infants in longitudinal studies. They show that there is some back-tracking, some of it probably due to errors of measurement, and, more importantly, that the back-tracking is unevenly distributed across ages and domains (Užgiris, 1987). The data from my longitudinal study are given in Table 7.5. For each session, the level attained in a given domain was compared to the highest level attained in the previous session for each infant, and the number of instances of advancement or decline for all the infants were noted. The overall percentage of decline was not very high in view of the density of observations, but as is evident in Table 7.5, declines were relatively more prevalent at eight, thirteen, fifteen to seventeen, and twenty to twenty-one months. In conjunction with other evidence, these data may be taken to indicate that, during periods of reorganization, intellectual functioning does not progress at a stable, constant rate. They suggest that individual rates of progress may be expected to vary over the course of reorganizations and consolidations in development.

Moreover, for an individual, the periods of reorganization in different domains need not coincide. The view that intellectual functioning comprises several distinct domains (e.g., Fischer, 1980; Gardner, 1985) has recently gained prominence. In the Piagetian assessment scales, various domains of functioning

TABLE 7.5
Mean Percentage of Decline for All Užgiris-Hunt Scales across Sessions 1 Month Apart

Month of Age	*Mean Percentage of Change*	*Mean Percentage of Decline*
5	48.7	2.3
6	44.9	5.8
7	50.0	4.7
8	59.7	8.4
9	45.1	4.7
10	38.1	5.8
11	33.4	1.1
12	42.7	4.6
13	35.4	11.8
14	27.1	4.6
15	42.8	13.1
16	58.1	20.1
17	32.9	12.9
18	38.6	11.4
19	37.3	6.4
20	39.9	11.6
21	25.7	11.6
22	30.9	10.3
23	27.1	8.1
24	20.3	7.1

Note. $N = 12$

are evaluated separately, which allows an examination of the rates of progress in different domains. Any variation of developmental rates across domains is particularly evident when different populations are compared. Table 7.6 presents a comparison of developmental progress in the Cicchetti and Mans-Wagener's (1987) sample of infants with Down's syndrome and the infants in my longitudinal sample. As can be readily seen, progress in vocal imitation is particularly slow in infants with Down's syndrome. Progress in means-ends coordination is slow initially, but becomes more rapid in the second year. A delay in vocal imitation development among infants with Down's syndrome or mental retardation has been noted in other studies as well (Kahn, 1987). Consequently, conclusions concerning stability in particular populations can be influenced by selective focus on specific domains of functioning.

If intellectual functioning encompasses several different domains, it seems important to consider not only what domains are included in infant assessments, but also what domains constitute the later assessments. It has been customary to use psychometric test scores as the measure of later functioning. Although for certain purposes their use may be justified, there are certainly other measures of

TABLE 7.6
Comparison of Achievement on Different Užgiris-Hunt Scales by Normal Infants and Infants with Down's Syndrome

	Percentage of Total Steps Achieved						
Age	*Object Permanence*	*Means-Ends*	*Vocal Imitation*	*Gestural Imitation*	*Causality*	*Relations in Space*	*Schemes*
5 mo.							
Normal	24	29	49	0	42	36	32
Down	16	24	20	0	33	33	–
9 mo.							
Normal	55	54	57	48	56	54	63
Down	32	49	26	16	52	50	–
13 mo.							
Normal	66	70	73	59	61	79	87
Down	49	68	36	45	62	67	–
19 mo.							
Normal	92	86	96	83	76	91	93
Down	81	80	53	61	77	91	–
24 mo.							
Normal	98	95	99	96	92	95	99
Down	95	86	60	71	85	98	–

Note. The data for normal infants (N = 12) are from "The study of sequential order in cognitive development" by I. Č. Užgiris and the data for infants with Down's Syndrome (N = 43) are from "Sequences, stages, and structures in the organization of cognitive development in infants with Down Syndrome" by D. Cicchetti and L. Mans-Wagener. In I. C. Užgiris and J. McV. Hunt (Eds.), *Infant performance and experience: New findings with the Ordinal Scales* (p. 148 and p. 295), 1987, Urbana, IL: University of Illinois Press. Copyright 1987 by the Board of Trustees of the University of Illinois. Adapted by permission.

intellectual functioning that might be equally valuable. It is noteworthy that there are practically no studies relating sensorimotor functioning in infancy to Piagetian measures of intellectual achievement in childhood. In one sense, such studies might be deemed uninteresting, because all normally developing children are expected to achieve conservation and hierarchical classification skills sooner or later. The goal has been prediction of the ultimate level of functioning, so individual differences that do not correlate with ultimate level have been generally deemed unimportant (Užgiris, 1976). On the other hand, lack of such studies leaves a gap in understanding how the links between achievements at earlier and later levels are constructed by individual children.

One specific domain to which sensorimotor functioning has been related is language acquisition. Although there has been some disagreement as to which domains of sensorimotor functioning are more closely linked to attainment of language skills (see Bates and Snyder, 1987, for review), most studies have found some prerequisite relations between specific sensorimotor achievements and particular aspects of language acquisition (e.g., Bates, Benigni, Bretherton, Camaioni, and Volterra, 1979; Cipriani and Bruni, 1986; Corrigan, 1978; Kahn, 1984; Miller, Chapman, Branston and Reichle, 1980). An example of correlational data between sensorimotor achievement at different ages and language proficiency at two years in a sample of full-term and preterm infants (Siegel, 1981) is shown in Table 7.7. The correlations are not high, but they are fairly similar to the ones obtained for standard infant tests.

Some other studies have searched for relations between sensorimotor functioning and representational development as manifest in symbolic play and communication ability (e.g., Kruper, 1988; Nicolich, 1977; Sexton, 1983; Sigman and Ungerer, 1984; Sugarman-Bell, 1978). They have also found specific relations between particular sensorimotor achievements and aspects of symbolic functioning, but not global similarities in rates of development in different domains. These types of results suggest that examination of specific links between conceptually related achievements may be more productive than the search for stability in rates of progress across developmental transitions.

In summary, the findings from studies using Piagetian assessment scales

TABLE 7.7
Correlations Between Uẑgiris-Hunt Scale Scores at Different Age Levels and Reynell Language Scale Scores at 2 Years

	Age (in months)			
Scale	*4*	*8*	*12*	*18*
	Comprehension			
Object Permanence	.26*	.27**	.39**	.39**
Means-Ends	.40**	.42**	.41**	.14
Vocal Imitation	.22*	.35**	.01	.15
Gestural Imitation	.22*	.21*	.33**	.23*
Relations in Space	.34**	.35**	.22*	.18
Schemes	.33**	.27**	.22*	.32**
	Expression			
Object Permanence	.07	.14	.30**	.37**
Means-Ends	.35**	.40**	.40**	.23*
Vocal Imitation	.26**	.27**	.05	.13
Gestural Imitation	.17	.17	.31**	.31**
Relations in Space	.37**	.27**	.18	.30**
Schemes	.37**	.19	.41**	.31**

*$p < .05$
**$p < .01$

Note. From "Infant tests as predictors of cognitive and language development at two years" by L. S. Siegel, 1981, *Child Development, 52,* p. 552. Copyright 1981 by the University of Chicago Press. Adapted by permission. N = c.67 full term and c.70 pre-term.

support the conclusion that infant achievements are to some extent predictive of intellectual standing in childhood. They also indicate that other characteristics of developmental change in infancy are important to consider in relating empirical evidence to the issue of continuity in intellectual development. In particular, the occurrence of reorganizations among the various processes constituting intellectual functioning in different domains has to be recognized in such discussions.

CONCLUSIONS

Although the issue of continuity in intellectual development is ultimately a theoretical one, the available empirical studies are also limited by failure to take into account many aspects of the continuity question. Several of these have been raised throughout this chapter. In the concluding section, some considerations that might inform future research on continuity are presented and discussed.

One aspect of the continuity issue that has not been given much consideration is the choice of a criterion measure to which early intellectual functioning is related. In most studies, IQ scores have been accepted as criterion measures, even though their validity as measures of many facets of intellectual functioning can be questioned. The matter of criterion is raised not to suggest that there is one best measure to which early functioning should be related, but to urge serious reflection on what constitutes mature, high-level intellectual functioning in its full complexity. Such explication would also facilitate conceptual delineation of dimensions of functioning that might be expected to be continually manifest throughout development. At least, a choice of IQ as the criterion measure needs to be justified rather than automatically accepted.

As the possibility of alternate criterion measures implies, continuity of intellectual functioning in different domains might differ and has to be examined. The infant measures derived from Piaget's work allow assessment of functioning in several domains. Studies using these measures have shown that there tends to be considerable variation in level of functioning across domains throughout infancy. Similar discrepancies in level of achievement across domains have been found throughout childhood. Consequently, it seems doubtful that averaging of achievement levels in disparate areas provides the best representation of an individual's intellectual ability.

Moreover, a delineation of several domains of functioning need not imply their isolation from each other. Constructivist theories such as Piaget's call attention to the integration of different aspects of functioning into a structured whole at each stage of development (Piaget, 1968/1970). This theoretical assumption has often been translated into the empirical expectation of high correlations between attainments in different domains of functioning. At base, however, this assumption only suggests that the various systems of functioning are interconnected and support each other (Turiel and Davidson, 1986). Consequently, the relations between achievements in different domains may change in the course of development and there may be alternate ways to support hierarchically higher levels of functioning.

The structured aspect of intellectual functioning is quite important for the issue of continuity. One conception of continuity postulates that certain processes or functions are maintained throughout development, although their expression, efficiency, or scope of application changes. Research concerned with a specific process (or domain) may uncover continuity of that process, but fail to note certain qualitative transformations due to the integration of that process into a system composed of several different processes. For example, the interesting studies showing that attentional processes may reflect aspects of intellectual ability throughout infancy and childhood (Bornstein, chapter 8 in this volume; Bornstein and Sigman, 1986), have not, so far, addressed the question of the relation of attentional processes to other cognitive functions such as representation, memory, or reasoning, at different periods in development. Stability with respect to an element of a system may not necessarily indicate stability of the system as a whole.

A developmental perspective on the issue of continuity also suggests that it is important to consider the phase in development when an individual's achievement is assessed. If there are phases of transformation and of consolidation in development, assessments of level of functioning as well as the links between different achievements can be expected to differ depending on the phase in which they are made. This matter is of particular importance when individuals are compared to each other, because matching on chronological age does not assure a match in terms of developmental phase. Some of the variability attributed to inadequacy of infant assessment procedures may be due to the more frequent reorganizations of intellectual functioning during the early years and, hence, a greater likelihood of individual variation in terms of developmental phase at assessment.

However, it should not be concluded that because phases of consolidation provide a more stable picture of intellectual achievement, they also give the best prediction of ultimate level of functioning. Transitional phases are periods of the most rapid advancement and may represent times of the most intense utilization of environmental opportunities available to an individual. Consequently, measures of reorganization during transitional phases may be sensitive to some individual differences that are less reflected in measures of consolidated achievement.

Comparison of individuals has been most often made in terms of rate of progress in achieving given levels of functioning, on the assumption that the rate of progress is correlated with the highest level ultimately achieved. There seems to be empirical evidence that infants with various severe impairments progress more slowly and attain a lower level of functioning at maturity. However, it can be questioned whether this assumption holds equally well for all subgroups of infants. Because of the interactive nature of development, severe impairments may act to restrict the plasticity of development; they may limit the individual's ability to influence the environment to provide the most suitable opportunities and may dampen the impact of opportunities that are created. Infants without severe impairments, however, may have much greater flexibility in their course toward mature functioning.

Ways of characterizing individual differences other than rates of progress need to be considered. Individuals differ in how quickly they extend new achievements to different realms of functioning and how broadly they eventually apply them. The extensity of application of cognitive functions may provide one measure of individual difference. The interlinkage of different functions and their substitutability may provide another. In addition, the ability to utilize various aids to organize a higher level of functioning may give another measure of an individual's intellectual resources. This notion is related to utilization of scaffolding in Bruner's (1978) terminology and to Vygotsky's (1978) idea of the zone of proximal development. It is being explored for assessing the potential of very premature infants (Als, chapter 1 in this volume), but it merits wider investigation.

Individual differences have appeared to be most tractable when conceived in terms of constant characteristics. However, because infants and children are open, developing systems, conception of their characteristics as reflections of constant dispositions or traits may not have been the most productive. Continuity may exist in the sequential and integrative linkage of achievements and in the types of opportunities that individuals shape for their own development, whereas discontinuity may be present in the emergence of new skills and in the rate of their attainment throughout the course of development. Intellectual development from infancy weaves aspects of discontinuity and continuity into a fabric that continues to change throughout a human life.

ACKNOWLEDGMENTS

The research of many investigators with the Ordinal Scales has made the writing of this chapter possible. I am especially grateful to F. Serafica for conducting the psychometric testing of ten of the infants in my longitudinal study. Kathy Sutton deserves thanks for her expert secretarial assistance.

REFERENCES

Bates, E., Benigni, L., Bretherton, I., Camaioni, L., and Volterra, V. (1979). *The emergence of symbols: Cognition and communication in infancy*. New York: Academic Press.

Bates, E., and Snyder, L. (1987). The cognitive hypothesis in language development. In I. C. Užgiris and J. McV. Hunt (Eds.), *Infant performance and experience* (pp. 168–204). Urbana, IL: University of Illinois Press.

Bornstein, M. H., and Sigman, M. D. (1986). Continuity in mental development from infancy. *Child Development, 57,* 251–274.

Bruner, J. S. (1978). Learning how to do things with words. In J. S. Bruner and A. Garton (Eds.), *Human growth and development* (pp. 277–285). Oxford: Clarendon Press.

Campbell, R. L., and Richie, D. M. (1983). Problems in the theory of developmental sequences: Prerequisites and precursors. *Human Development, 26,* 156–172.

Casati, I., and Lézine, I. (1968). *Les étapes de l'intelligence sensorimotrice.* Paris: Les Editions du Centre de Psychologie Appliquée.

Cicchetti, D., and Mans-Wagener, L. (1987). Sequences, stages, and structures in the organization of cognitive development in infants with Down syndrome. In I. C. Užgiris and J. McV. Hunt (Eds.), *Infant performance and experience* (pp. 281–310). Urbana, IL: University of Illinois Press.

Cipriani, P., and Bruni, G. (1986). Relations between sensorimotor attainments and development of language comprehension in retarded children. *Italian Journal of Neurological Sciences, 5,* 133–141.

Corrigan, R. (1978). Language development as related to stage 6 object permanence development. *Journal of Child Language, 5,* 173–189.

Curcio, F., and Houlihan, J. (1987). Varieties of organization between domains of sensorimotor intelligence in normal and atypical populations. In I. C. Užgiris and J. McV. Hunt (Eds.), *Infant performance and experience* (pp. 98–130). Urbana, IL: University of Illinois Press.

Dunst, C. J., Brassell, W. R., and Rheingrover, R. M. (1981). Structural and organizational features of sensorimotor intelligence among retarded infants and toddlers. *British Journal of Educational Psychology, 51,* 133–143.

Dunst, C. J., and Rheingrover, R. M. (1983). Structural characteristics of sensorimotor development among Down's syndrome infants. *Journal of Mental Deficiency Research, 27,* 11–22.

Emmerich, W. (1964). Continuity and stability in early social development. *Child Development, 35,* 311–332.

Emmerich, W. (1968). Personality development and concepts of structure. *Child Development, 39,* 671–690.

Fischer, K. W. (1980). A theory of cognitive development: The control and construction of hierarchies of skills. *Psychological Review, 87,* 477–531.

Flavell, J. H. (1972). An analysis of cognitive developmental sequences. *Genetic Psychology Monographs, 86,* 279–350.

Forman, G. E. (Ed.). (1982). *Action and thought.* New York: Academic Press.

Gardner, H. (1985). *Frames of mind.* New York: Basic Books.

Hunt, J. McV. (1976). The utility of ordinal scales inspired by Piaget's observations. *Merrill-Palmer Quarterly, 22,* 31–46.

Hunt, J. McV. (1980). *Early psychological development and experience.* Worcester, MA: Clark University Press.

Hunt, J. McV. (1987). The effects of differing kinds of experience in early rearing conditions. In I. C. Užgiris and J. McV. Hunt (Eds.), *Infant performance and experience* (pp. 39–97). Urbana, IL: University of Illinois Press.

Kagan, J. (1980). Perspectives on continuity. In O. G. Brim, Jr. and J. Kagan (Eds.), *Continuity and change in human development* (pp. 26–74). Cambridge, MA: Harvard University Press.

Kahn, J. V. (1984). Cognitive training and initial use of referential speech. *Topics in Language Disorders, 5,* 14–28.

Kahn, J. V. (1987). Uses of the Scales with mentally retarded populations. In I. C. Užgiris and J. McV. Hunt (Eds.), *Infant performance and experience* (pp. 252–280). Urbana, IL: University of Illinois Press.

Kruper, J. C. (1988). *Infants' interactions within the family triad.* Unpublished doctoral dissertation, Clark University, Worcester, MA.

Langer, J. (1980). *The origins of logic: Six to twelve months.* New York: Academic Press.
Langer, J. (1986). *The origins of logic: One to two years.* New York: Academic Press.
Lerner, R. M. (1984). *On the nature of human plasticity.* New York: Cambridge University Press.
McCall, R. B. (1977). Challenges to a science of developmental psychology. *Child Development, 48,* 333–344.
McCall, R. B. (1981). Nature-nurture and the two realms of development: A proposed integration with respect to mental development. *Child Development, 52,* 1–12.
McCall, R. B., Eichorn, D. H., and Hogarty, P. S. (1977). Transitions in early mental development. *Monographs of the Society for Research in Child Development, 42* (3), Serial No. 171.
Miller, J., Chapman, R., Branston, M., and Reichle, J. (1980). Language comprehension in sensorimotor stages V and VI. *Journal of Speech and Hearing Research, 23,* 284–311.
Nicolich, L. McC. (1977). Beyond sensorimotor intelligence: Assessment of symbolic maturity through analysis of pretend play. *Merrill-Palmer Quarterly, 23,* 89–99.
Piaget, J. (1970). *Structuralism* (C. Maschler, Trans.). New York: Basic Books. (Original work published 1968)
Piaget, J. (1972). *The principles of genetic epistemology* (W. Mays, Trans.). New York: Basic Books. (Original work published 1970)
Piaget, J. (1985). *The equilibration of cognitive structures* (T. Brown and K. J. Thampy, Trans.). Chicago: University of Chicago Press. (Original work published 1975)
Rensen, F. S. X., Kerssier, I., Molenaar, P. C. M., and Oppenheimer, L. (1987). Sensorimotorische ontwikkeling: Een vergelijkende strukturele analyse van normaal begaafde en diep geestelijk gehandikapte kinderen [Sensori-motor development: A comparative structural analysis of mentally normal and profoundly mentally handicapped children]. *RUIT, 50,* 5–16.
Rutter, M. (1984). Continuities and discontinuities in socioemotional development: Empirical and conceptual perspectives. In R. N. Emde and R. J. Harmon (Eds.), *Continuities and discontinuities in development* (pp. 41–68). New York: Plenum.
Sexton, M. E. (1983). The development of understanding of causality in infancy. *Infant Behavior and Development, 6,* 201–210.
Siegel, L. S. (1981). Infant tests as predictors of cognitive and language development at two years. *Child Development, 52,* 545–557.
Siegler, R. S. (1986). *Children's thinking.* Englewood Cliffs, NJ: Prentice-Hall.
Sigman, M., and Ungerer, J. A. (1984). Cognitive and language skills in autistic, mentally retarded and normal children. *Developmental Psychology, 20,* 293–302.
Strauss, S. (1982). Ancestral and descendant behaviors: The case of U-shaped behavioral growth. In T. G. Bever (Ed.), *Regressions in mental development.* Hillsdale, NJ: Lawrence Erlbaum Associates.
Sugarman-Bell, S. (1978). Some organizational aspects of pre-verbal communication. In I. Markova (Ed.), *The social context of language.* New York: Wiley.
Turiel, E., and Davidson, P. (1986). Heterogeneity, inconsistency, and asynchrony in the development of cognitive structures. In I. Levin (Ed.), *Stage and structure: Reopening the debate* (pp. 106–143). Norwood, NJ: Ablex.
Trevarthen, C., and Hubley, P. (1978). Secondary intersubjectivity: Confidence, confiding, and acts of meaning in the first year. In A. Lock (Ed.), *Action, gesture and symbol* (pp. 183–229). New York: Academic Press.
Užgiris, I. C. (1976). Infant development from a Piagetian approach: Introduction to a symposium. *Merrill-Palmer Quarterly, 22,* 3–10.
Užgiris, I. C. (1983). Organization of sensorimotor intelligence. In M. Lewis (Ed.), *Origins of intelligence* (2nd ed., pp. 135–189). New York: Plenum.
Užgiris, I. C. (1987). The study of sequential order in cognitive development. In I. Č. Užgiris and J. McV. Hunt (Eds.), *Infant performance and experience* (pp. 131–167). Urbana, IL: University of Illinois Press.

Užgiris, I. C., and Hunt, J. McV. (1975). *Assessment in infancy.* Urbana, IL: University of Illinois Press.

Valsiner, J. (1986). Between groups and individuals. In J. Valsiner (Ed.), *The individual subject and scientific psychology* (pp. 113–151). New York: Plenum.

Vygotsky, L. S. (1978). *Mind in society.* Cambridge, MA: Harvard University Press.

Wachs, T. D. (1975). Relation of infants' performance on Piaget scales between twelve and twenty-four months and their Stanford-Binet performance at thirty-one months. *Child Development, 46,* 929–935.

Wachs, T. D., and Hubert N. C. (1981). Changes in the structure of cognitive-intellectual performance during the second year of life. *Infant Behavior and Development, 4,* 151–161.

Werner, H. (1957). The concept of development from a comparative and organismic point of view. In D. B. Harris (Ed.), *The concept of development* (pp. 125–148). Minneapolis: University of Minnesota Press.

Wohlwill, J. F. (1973). *The study of behavioral development.* New York: Academic Press.

PART I

Section 4: Information Processing Capacities

8 Stability in Early Mental Development: From Attention and Information Processing in Infancy to Language and Cognition in Childhood

Marc H. Bornstein
National Institute of Child Health and Human Development
and
New York University

INTRODUCTION

The question of stability in development generally, and in mental development specifically, is traditional in developmental study. Stability in development describes consistency in the relative ranks of individuals in a group with respect to status or performance over time. On this construal, stability in mental development means that those individuals who perform well at one time can be expected to perform well again at a later time, and those individuals who perform poorly at first can be expected to perform poorly again later. By contrast, instability implies fluctuation in the relative performance of individuals over time.

Opinions about whether development may be characterized as stable or unstable have seemed to fluctuate historically based on philosophy, on the results of the freshest longitudinal measures, or on predilections for interpreting shared variance in performance across time (see Brim and Kagan, 1980; Emde and Harmon, 1984; McCall, 1981; Wohlwill, 1973). The main focus of this chapter is to evaluate new data and theory on stability in mental development based on the predictive validity of information-processing measures made near the beginning of postnatal life to normative indices of mental development and performance in childhood.

Contemporary opinion about whether there is stability in mental development has been largely informed by longitudinal studies based on infant tests essentially derived from the original Binet mental development scales, first formulated around the turn of the century (e.g., Binet and Simon, 1905). These traditional infant tests have included the Gesell Developmental Schedules (Gesell and Armatruda, 1947), the Griffiths Mental Development Test (Griffiths, 1954), and the Bayley Scales of Infant Development (Bayley, 1969). Bayley's classic longitudinal results, shown in Figure 8.1, represent the common finding. They indicated a lack of stability, that is a weak crossage correlation, in cognitive development between the first years of life and young adulthood. Bayley reported these data in 1949 on a cohort of 27 children that she followed from three months to eighteen years of age. She administered her own test in infancy and later correlated the children's performance as infants with their performance on a standardized intelligence test at eighteen years. As shown in Figure 8.1, the predictive correlation from infancy to maturity hovers around zero.

Bayley's finding, which has been replicated many times (see Fagan and Singer, 1983; Honzik, 1986; Kopp and McCall, 1980), had a profound impact on broader psychological theorizing, in the sense that it gave rise to several general conclusions about both the nature and development of the human mind. At the risk of simplifying, one view holds that there is no general intelligence factor in infancy and no stability of general intelligence from infancy to childhood. A second view purports that, although there may be such a thing as a general intelligence factor, it is not stable, at least during the early part of the lifespan. These two interpretations of mental development radically differ from one another (as, for example, on the question of the existence of general intelligence at all), but both evolved from data (based on traditional infant tests) that do not support the construct of stability in early mental development.

Conviction favoring instability in mental development has enjoyed wide endorsement since the time of Bayley's first reports. However, evaluation pro-

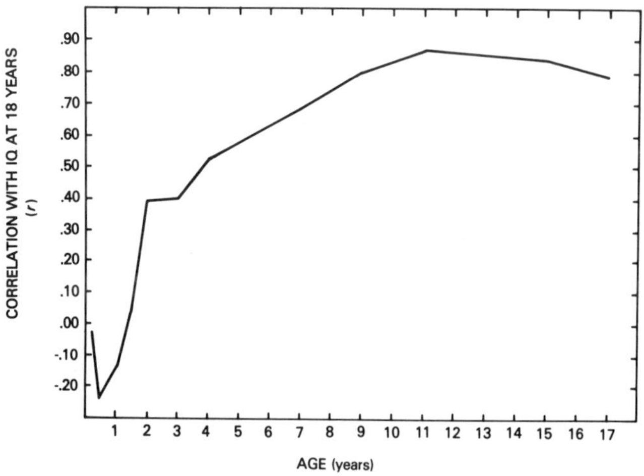

FIGURE 8.1. Correlations of intelligence test scores ($N = 27$) at each age with intelligence test scores at 18 years (after Bayley, 1949, Table 6).

cedures on which such findings were based have also been recognized by numerous researchers to be problematic. For example, in some studies nonrepresentative sampling may have resulted in substantial attenuation of predictive correlations (e.g., Bayley, 1949; Rose, Slater, and Perry, 1986). Additionally, task analysis shows that some items on some traditional infant tests draw on infants' motor skills or on their affective expressiveness (e.g., Haviland, 1983). There is little a priori reason to expect that these aspects of performance early in life necessarily relate to later cognitive performance. McCall (1981) has reviewed other criticisms.

Findings of instability based on traditional infant tests raise the question of whether a theory of stability in mental development is faulty, or more simply whether the measures so far applied are inappropriate or invalid. If stability in mental development from infancy is to be fully understood, and a fair test of a stability hypothesis to be conducted, alternative infant measures are clearly needed. To meet prior cirticisms, these measures should be, at least, nonmotor and independent of affect. Moreover, as contemporary task analysis suggests that performance on traditional intelligence tests also reflects information-processing skills (e.g., Hunt, 1978, 1983; Hunt, Lunneborg, and Lewis, 1975), infant tests hypothesized to link to intelligence-test performance in childhood ought likewise to tap information processing by design.

Several such infant measures have been discussed in the literature from time to time; the one I explore in depth in this chapter is *habituation.* I first define and illustrate habituation in infancy and discuss its theoretical underpinnings. I also evaluate the psychometric adequacy of habituation, including assessments of individual differences and reliability and stability. In addition, I review extant studies of the concurrent validity of habituation in infancy and, importantly, the predictive validity of habituation for children's cognitive and verbal proficiency. Finally, I raise several cautionary arguments pertinent to the validity of habituation as predictive of later intelligence specifically and of stability in development generally.

HABITUATION: AN ATTENTION MEASURE OF INFORMATION PROCESSING IN INFANCY

What is habituation? Imagine an infant sitting in a little seat facing a blank screen. A stimulus or pair of stimuli is projected onto the screen. A camera looks through a hole in the screen to record the infant's face and particularly the pattern of the infant's looking. When a stimulus is switched on, typically the infant will visually orient and attend to the stimulus. If the stimulus is then made available continuously or is presented repeatedly, the infant's visual attending to the stimulus will wane. In the literature of infancy, this decrement in observed behavior has been termed *habituation*. Habituation has been inferred to reflect, at least in part, the infant's increasing knowledge of the stimulus.

Operationalization

Several regimens have been developed to assess infant habituation in the laboratory (for a review see Bornstein, 1985a). Historically, two procedures have been especially popular. In the fixed-trials procedure, a stimulus is presented to the infant for a set number of discrete exposure periods each of predetermined duration. In the infant-control procedure, a stimulus is presented to the infant for as long as the infant looks, and presentations continue until the infant reaches a predetermined habituation criterion (commonly, two or three consecutive looks each less than 50% of the mean of the infant's initial two or three looks).

The fixed-trials procedure was the first to be introduced and is still often used even though its sensitivity to individual differences has been questioned. For example, it has been argued that with this method infants' looking may be influenced more by fixed experimental parameters (e.g., trial length, number of trials) than by the infants' own volitional processing of stimulation. Thus, infants who happen not to be looking at the location of the stimulus at its onset have their inspection times artificially truncated, just as they do if they are still looking at the stimulus at its offset. The infant-control procedure, which is of more recent vintage, confers control of stimulus presentation to the infant (i.e., the stimulus remains available to view until the infant looks away from it) thereby rectifying insensitivities of the fixed-trials procedure. These distinctions aside, the two procedures yield data that support broadly similar conclusions about the psychometric adequacy and validity of habituation, and the robustness of these two procedures speaks positively for both individual-difference and information-processing assumptions underlying the technique.

The two habituation procedures yield quantitative and qualitative data that are commonly taken to represent infants' processing of the habituation stimulus, or at least some information in it. Quantitative data assess duration and magnitude aspects of attention decrement as, for example, total looking time, number of looks, and amount of habituation for the fixed-trials procedure, and total looking as well as trials through criterion and decrement and slope of decline for the infant-control procedure. Habituation has also been described qualitatively, being characterized by linear or exponential decrease, by increase-decrease, or by fluctuating patterns.

Theory

With continuous or repeated presentation of a stimulus, infants' looking declines from its initial level; at least, that is the observed behavior. As I have suggested, much more is commonly inferred.

Our best theoretical understanding of the processes underlying habituation, although still imperfect, derives from the Russian physiologist Sokolov. Sokolov (1958/1963, 1969) placed an "information acquisition" interpretation on habituation, strongly grounding it in neurological function. In brief, he suggested that a novel stimulus initially provokes an orienting response from an organism. With repeated exposure to the same stimulus, a neuronal model (specifically a cortical representation) of the stimulus is constructed that continuously increases in fidelity until it preserves intensity, quality, and duration information about the stimulus. Subsequent stimulation is compared in memory with this neuronal model. An orienting response is either elicited or actively inhibited depending on whether a match or mismatch occurs.

The essence of habituation in human infants is therefore hypothesized to reflect reciprocal processes consisting of mental construction and comparison. Constructor processes are believed to comprise the infant's acquisition of information about the stimulus toward the development of a neural trace, memory model, or schema that is increasingly faithful to the stimulus. Complementary comparator processes are thought to be involved in judging subsequent incoming stimulation against the mental representation. To the extent that new stimulation and representation do not match, looking is maintained, presumably exciting the constructor to model a more faithful or more articulated representation until stimulation and representation match. Many models of habituation processes have been proposed (see Bornstein, 1985a; Lewis and Baldini, 1979). Whichever model best characterizes habituation, all imply that habituation entails feedback loops in the nervous system built up from experience and intended to guide future action.

Much is still unknown about how habituation is regulated. Whether the hypothetical constructor functions actively or passively is unknown. Whether constructor processes begin at the introduction of the stimulus or later, and whether its processes are incremental or all-or-none (independent of when they actually begin) are unknown. Furthermore, whether the mental representation in the preverbal infant is imaginal, symbolic, or propositional is unknown. How the comparator knows that the current representation differs from the habituation stimulus, and how it knows the state of maturity of the representation, are unknown. Similarly, why looking stops—whether on account of economy of energy expenditure or the desire for additional stimulus seeking on the part of the organism—is not known. Habituation appears to be "noumenal" in Kant's terminology—an unknown, perhaps unknowable, yet logically necessary mental operation.

However primitive our neurological and even theoretical understanding of habituation may be, it has been construed as the partial analog in adults of construction of and comparison with some kind of internal representation of external information. This introduction to a theory of habituation is not inconsequential because, as I show later in this chapter, habituation in infancy links to language and cognitive skills in childhood, and it seems necessary to evaluate at some point exactly *what* about habituation connects with *what* of later cognitive competencies. Moreover, habituation certainly may encompass factors other than cognitive ones, such as motivation, and I return to this issue at a later point.

Implications

If it is appropriate to place an information-processing interpretation on habituation, this would suggest, at the least, three simple predictions: First, other things being equal, older and more developed or more mature babies ought to habituate more efficiently than younger and less developed and less mature babies; second, simpler stimuli ought to provoke more rapid habituation than more complex stimuli in babies of a given age; and, third, infants habituated to a stimulus should later be able to distinguish a novel stimulus in comparison with their internal representation of the familiar stimulus.

The evidence supporting each of these predictions is compelling and helps to validate the information-processing interpretation of habituation. I now turn to evaluate some of that evidence. In one of the very first studies of habituation in human infants to be published in the English language, Fantz (1964) demonstrated the expected age-related change in information processing. Using a fixed-trials procedure, Fantz showed pairs of patterns over ten successive trials to babies ranging in age from one to six months. On each trial, one member of the stimulus pair remained the same and the other varied. Fantz found that one- to two-month-olds looked equally at the constant and variable patterns over trials, whereas older infants showed steadily decreasing amounts of looking at the constant pattern relative to the variable one with four- to six-month-olds looking the least at the constant pattern. In short, older babies habituated more efficiently than younger babies. Bornstein, Pêcheux, and Lécuyer (1988) obtained similar results using the infant-control procedure. They recorded total accumulated looking time in infants at three and at five months of age and over weekly habituation sessions for infants between two and seven months of age. As they aged across the first year, infants required less and less cumulative exposure time to reach a constant habituation criterion.

The second prediction of an information-processing interpretation of habituation, the influence of stimulus complexity, was first examined by Caron and Caron (1969) not long after Fantz's original study. They compared fixed trials habituation in three groups of three-and-one-half-month-old babies. They showed a variety of stimuli to the babies on trials one to four, to which all groups maintained a high level of attention. On trials five to nine, each group saw a new but repeated stimulus; these stimuli represented three levels of complexity. The group that was shown a 2 X 2 checkerboard habituated most quickly; the group that was shown a 12 X 12 checkerboard habituated less quickly; and the group that was shown a 24 X 24 checkerboard habituated least quickly of all. Linear trend analysis substantiated the control that stimulus complexity exercised over habituation. Results from my laboratory show that the infant-control procedure gives equally strong evidence of stimulus influence; for example, five-month-olds who habituate to a single form require significantly fewer trials to reach criterion than do five-month-olds who habituate to multiple forms.

The Carons' data also speak to the third prediction derived from an information-processing interpretation of habituation, namely, the recovery of attention to novelty from familiarity. After habituation to repeated stimulation on trials five to nine in the study mentioned earlier, babies were exposed to heterogeneous stimulation across trials ten to twelve: Babies looked more at this novel stimulation than they had at the repeated stimulus. The infants' discriminative response to a stimulus change provides clear and converging support for a representation-making interpretation of the foregoing habituation. Indeed, the consensus that decrement and recovery of attention involve stimulus information processing provides the basis for the widespread use of these measures as techniques to study perception and cognition in infancy (see Salapatek and Cohen, 1987).

In overview, studies of age, stimulus control, and discrimination strengthen the conviction that habituation in infancy taps information processing. On this basis, habituation presents itself as a serious candidate in the search for a nonmotor, affectively neutral, information-processing behavior in infancy with potential predictive validity for childhood cognitive functioning. Habituation is the decrement of attention infants manifest to an aspect of the environment that is unchanging. The recovery of attention infants demonstrate to an aspect of the environment that is novel (following habituation) constitutes a second nonmotor, affectively neutral, information-processing behavior whose predictive validity has also been thought to be worthy of exploration in this connection (e.g., Bornstein and Sigman, 1986; Fagan and Singer, 1983). A third candidate infant measure is cross-modal transfer (Rose, chapter 9 in this volume).

PSYCHOMETRIC ADEQUACY OF HABITUATION IN INFANCY

Before we can see whether habituation performance in infancy predicts measures of mental performance in childhood, habituation needs to satisfy two criteria of psychometric adequacy. First, habituation must demonstrate sensitivity to individual differences among infants. Second, habituation must show short-term reliability. Although a psychological phenomenon may possess momentary psychometric integrity, its utility as a meaningful construct rests on its replicability across occasions spaced reasonably close together in time. Satisfaction of these two criteria, individual differences and reliability (if not long-term stability), is basic to validating the meaningfulness of habituation and prerequisite to evaluating its concurrent and predictive validity in relation to criterion variables of cognitive development. In the following sections, habituation data that bear on each of these two issues of psychometric adequacy are discussed.

Individual Differences

Several researchers have investigated individual differences in habituation using fixed-trials and infant-control procedures with infants in the middle of the first year of life. Stimuli have usually been faces or geometric patterns. DeLoache (1976), for example, found trials to criterion to be a well-distributed habituation variable in a sample of four-month-olds. Bornstein and Ruddy (1984) studied both four-month-old singletons and twins, and found good distributions, reflecting substantial individual differences, for several different habituation variables. Normally, duration and magnitude variables in the infant-control habituation paradigm show a considerable range of individual differences (e.g., Bornstein and Benasich, 1986; Colombo, Mitchell, O'Brien, and Horowitz, 1987). These results indicate that habituation constitutes a good variable in correlational studies.

Beside these quantitative differences, habituation procedures normally yield qualitatively distinct patterns. McCall and Kagan (1970), who used the fixed-trials procedure, identified (at least) three types of infants, including rapid, slow, and idiosyncratic habituators. Bornstein and Benasich (1986), who used the infant-control procedure, identified three patterns that are conceptually parallel to those of McCall and Kagan: a rapid linear or exponential decrease, an increase-decrease, and a fluctuating pattern (see Figure 8.2).

The qualitative and quantitative perspectives on habituation correspond. Infants who habituate linearly or exponentially require significantly fewer exposures to the stimulus than infants who follow increase-decrease or fluctuating patterns. Research also shows that the first group accumulates half the time in reaching criterion as the latter two (Bornstein and Benasich, 1986). These data indicate that habituation is adequately sensitive to individual differences.

Reliability and Stability

Several studies of the short-term reliability and long-term stability of duration and magnitude measures of habituation in infancy have been published. Figure 8.3 summarizes those results. For example, Bornstein and Benasich (1986) assessed the short-term reliability of habituation in infants in two evaluations that

FIGURE 8.2. Results of two infant-control habituation sessions for three infants. These babies illustrate three main patterns of habituation and the short-term reliability of habituation patterns. The infant at the top showed an exponential decrease from his baseline to a 50% habituation criterion in two sessions; the infant in the middle first looked more, than rapidly habituated to criterion both times; and, the infant at the bottom showed a fluctuating looking-time function in each session before reaching the habituation criterion (after Bornstein and Benasich, 1986).

HABITUATION AT 5 MONTHS
INDIVIDUAL DIFFERENCES AND RELIABILITY

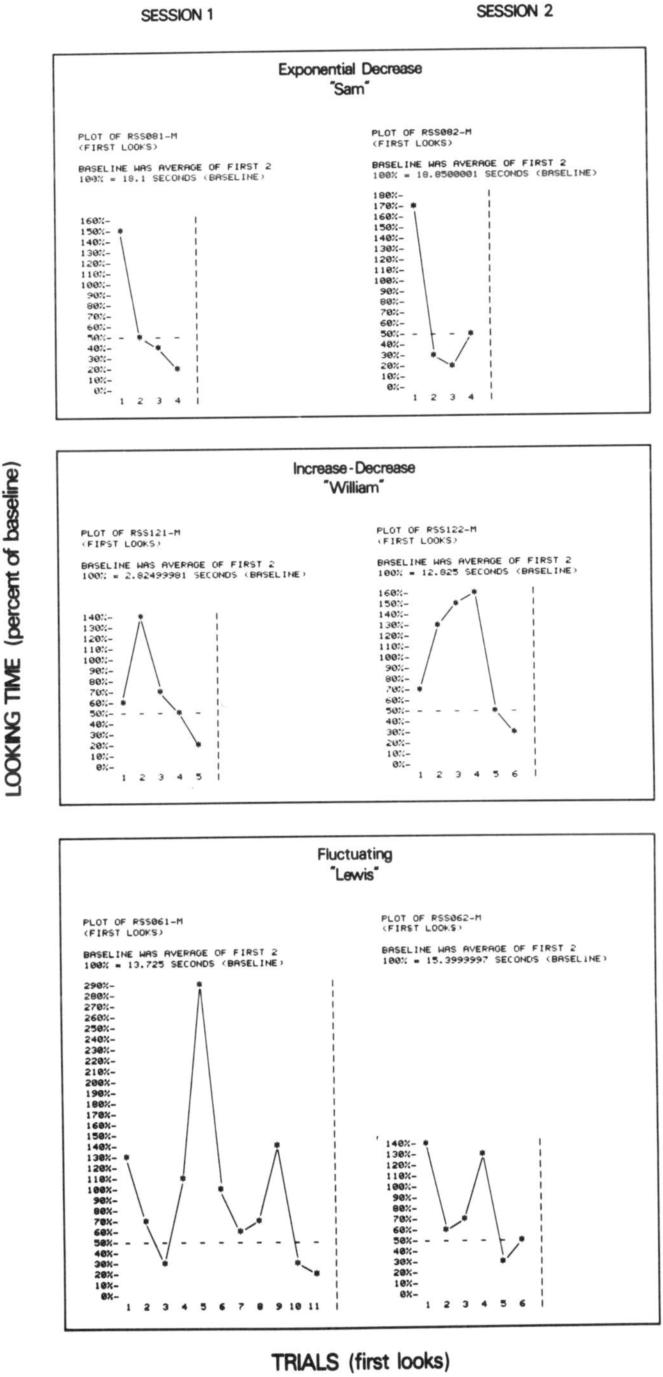

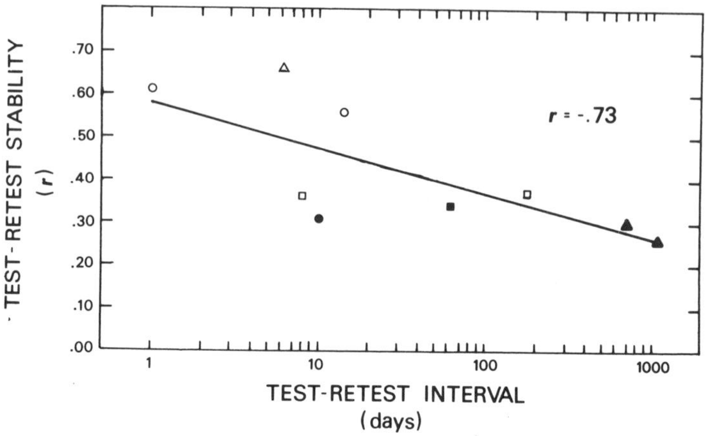

FIGURE 8.3. Test-retest stability (*r*) of measures of habituation duration and magnitude for infants first tested in the first six months of life as a function of test-retest interval (days). (○ = Pêcheux and Lécuyer, 1983; ● = Bornstein and Benasich, 1986; □ = Colombo et al., 1987; ■ = Bornstein et al., 1988; △ = Rose et al., 1986; ▲ = Miller et al., 1979.)

took place ten days apart. In this study, several indexes of habituation showed significant, if medium effect size, stability. Notably, a factor composed of the babies' baseline levels of looking, slopes, and decrements (considered as indicator variables) resulted in a statistically significant, if again medium, effect size of short-term reliability. Figure 8.3 bears out the Guttman (1966) "simplex" with respect to correlation in development testing: Pairs of tests administered closer together in time tend to yield higher stability estimates. As may be seen, day-to-day and week-to-week reliability of habituation measures has reached effect sizes of close to .70. Of course, estimates of stability can be expected to vary depending on data collection procedures, age and state of the child, nature of the stimuli, and other factors.

Qualitative measures of habituation are also reasonably stable over the short term, as the data from Bornstein and Benasich (1986) presented in Figure 8.2 illustrate. A nominal scale metric showed that habituation pattern is statistically stable over ten days. Figure 8.2 displays examples of stable patterns, characteristic of more than two-thirds of infants studied. Similarly, Colombo et al. (1987) recently found significant repeatability of these same habituation patterns in babies between three and nine months of age.

In overview, there is clear evidence for individual differences in quantitative measures as well as corresponding qualitative patterns of habituation in infants. Furthermore, habituation is a reasonably stable (although less than perfect) measure of infant functioning at least over the short term. These findings, which demonstrate the robustness of habituation, further strengthen the rationale for investigating habituation in infancy in relation to later aspects of cognitive development.

VALIDITY OF HABITUATION FOR INFANT AND CHILD COGNITION

Given the information-processing implications of habituation, and the evidence for individual differences and stability of habituation, it is desirable to examine the concurrent validity of habituation in early infancy, as well as the degree of predictive validity habituation in infancy harbors for children's later cognitive functioning. Relatively greater decrements, quicker decays, or lesser amounts of cumulative looking are generally interpreted as more efficient styles of information processing in habituation. Relatedly, relatively greater amounts of looking at novel stimuli, or reciprocally lesser amounts of looking at familiar stimuli, are generally interpreted as more efficient information processing in recovery designs. In this section, I review extant studies of concurrent validity and of predictive validity of habituation and recovery in infancy for cognitive performance in infancy and childhood.

Concurrent Validity

Infants and young children who habituate efficiently tend to prefer complexity (Greenberg, O'Donnell, and Crawford, 1973), to show advanced sensorimotor development (Johnson and Brody, 1977), to explore their environment more rapidly (Fenson, Sapper, and Minner, 1974; Messer, Kagan, and McCall, 1970; Pêcheux and Lécuyer, 1983), to play in relatively sophisticated ways (Kagan, 1971; Riksen-Walraven, 1978), to problem solve quickly and to attain concepts efficiently (Lewis, Goldberg, and Campbell, 1969), and to excel at oddity identification, picture matching, and block configuration in traditional tests of intelligence (Miller, Spiridigliozzi, Ryan, Callan, and McLaughlin, 1980).[1] Similar associations obtain between recovery and diverse cognitive skills (see Fagan and Singer, 1983, for a review). Moreover, infants who might be expected to differ in intelligence later in life show commensurate individual differences in decrement as well as recovery of attention. Perinatal risk adversely affects decrement (Friedman, 1975; Lewis et al., 1969; Sigman, Kopp, Littman, and Parmelee, 1977) and recovery (Caron and Caron, 1981; Rose, 1980; Rose, Gottfried, and Bridger, 1979; Sigman, 1977; Sigman and Parmelee, 1974; Siqueland, 1981). Similarly, trisomy-21 is associated with less efficient habituation (Barnet,

[1]Madison, Madison, and Adubato (1986) reported that fetal habituation rate predicts postnatal responsiveness to the environment, and in specific the Mental Development Index of the Bayley (Bayley, 1969).

Ohlrich, and Shanks, 1971; Cohen, 1981) and recovery (Cohen, 1981; Miranda and Fantz, 1974).

Predictive Validity

Habituation in infancy has been shown to predict cognitive performance in the same children years later. Table 8.1 contains representative data from several separate longitudinal studies conducted in my laboratory, linking measures of habituation in the first six months of life with various cognitive outcome measures evaluated between one and four years of age in the same children. Habituation in infancy gauged quantitatively (or qualitatively) predicts Bayley performance, language production and comprehension, play sophistication, and representational competence (a latent variable constructed of language comprehension and play sophistication) at one year, verbal competence at two years, and full-scale intelligence-test performance at four years. For example, Tamis-LeMonda and I measured habituation baseline, slope, and decrement at five months in relation to language comprehension and play sophistication at thirteen months in a sample of 37 children. We also assessed mothers' encouraging attention at both ages. We then used structural equation modeling to examine the unique contribution of infant habituation to toddler cognitive abilities. A latent

TABLE 8.1
Representative Predictive Correlations from Habituation in Infancy

To	*Age (months)*	*r*
Bayley Scale Score[a]	12	.46
Productive Vocabulary[b]	12	.52
Bates Language Comprehension[c]	13	.35
Belsky Play Competence[d]	13	.36
Representational Competence[e]	13	.57
Reynell Language Score[f]	24	.55
Wechsler Test Score[g]	48	.54

[a]Bayley Scales of Infant Development (Bayley, 1969).

[b]Maternal estimate (Bornstein and Ruddy, 1984).

[c]Maternal Language Interview (Bates, Bretherton, and Snyder, 1988).

[d]Manual for the Assessment of Performance, Competence, and Executive Capacity in Infant Play (Belsky and Most, 1981; Belsky, Hrncir, and Vondra, 1983).

[e]Latent variable of language comprehension (*c*) and play sophistication (*d*) (Tamis-LeMonda and Bornstein, 1989).

[f]Reynell Developmental Language Scales (Reynell, 1981).

[g]Wechsler Preschool and Primary Scale of Intelligence (Wechsler, 1963).

variable of habituation (constructed of the three indicator variables) significantly predicted a latent variable of representational competence (constructed of the two indicator variables of language comprehension and play sophistication) after the influences of both five- and thirteen month maternal encouraging attention were partialled (see Table 8.1). This finding indicates a substantial direct tie between early habituation and later cognitive development (Tamis-LeMonda and Bornstein, 1989). The median of the predictive correlations in Table 8.1 reaches the .50 region.

Table 8.2 summarizes the corpus of longitudinal investigations that have evaluated the predictive validity of decrement as well as recovery of attention in infancy in relation to a variety of measures of children's later mental performance. The top half of the table lists measures of decrement, and the bottom half contains intramodal and intermodal measures of recovery. Investigators are listed at the left. Next, the measures used and the ages of the subjects are listed at both the infancy and the childhood assessments. Note that infants' ages range from one and one-half to seven months, and children's ages range from two to eight years. At the far right, the longitudinal correlation between measures in infancy and childhood for each sample is presented. The median predictive correlation for measures of decrement is .49; for measures of recovery it is .46; and across all the studies listed in Table 8.2 it is .46.

As Table 8.2 attests, a significant if moderate degree of predictive validity holds between measures of attention in the infant's first six months of life and measures of cognitive competence beginning in the second year of childhood. This relation obtains across different laboratories, across different populations of both normal and at-risk infants, across different measures in infancy, across different modalities including the visual and auditory, and for (at least) a small variety of different outcomes in childhood. Although not large in absolute terms, in a climate of belief in instability, these correlations suggest a meaningful degree of stability in individual mental development.

COMMENT, CAVEAT, AND QUALIFICATION

Before reaching any final resolution about stability in mental development from infancy, these predictive validity data of decrement and recovery of attention warrant cautionary consideration and comment.

First, it is important to remember that the infant and child measures that connect over time may still not be the most sensitive or appropriate for questions about the stability of cognition in early life. It is necessary to consider obtained validity assessments in light of the reliability of the measures of habituation. If assessments of habituation itself could be refined to improve habituation's short-term reliability, the predictive validity of habituation could be expected to increase commensurately. Applying the formula for attenuation of correlation rela-

TABLE 8.2
Two Measures of Attention in the First Half-Year of Life
in Relation to Several Measures of Cognitive Competence
in the Second Year of Childhood and Later: Longitudinal Studies

		Infancy		Childhood		
Authors[a]*, Year*	*N*	*Measure*	*Age (months)*	*Measure*	*Age (years)*	*Correlation*[b]
		Decrement: Habituation and Fixation Time				
Bornstein, 1984, 1985a	20	Amount	4	WPPSI (N = 14)	4	.54
Bornstein, 1985b	18	Index[c]	5	RDLS-R	2	.55
Lewis and Brooks-Gunn, 1981	22	Amount	3	Bayley	2	.61
Miller et al., 1979	29	Amount	2–4	Language Comprehension	3.3	.39
Rose, Slater, and Perry, 1986	21	Index[f]	1.5–6.5	WPPSI (N = 16)	4.5	.63
				BAS (N = 16)	4.5	.77
Sigman, 1983	96[d]	Fixation time[e]	(Term)	Stanford-Binet	5	.29
Sigman, Cohen, Beckwith, and Parmelee, 1986	58[d]	Amount	4	Stanford-Binet	5	.44
				WISC-R (N = 56)	8	.28
	96[d]	Fixation time[e]	(Term)	WISC-R (N = 91)	8	.36

		Recovery: Novelty Preference, Response to Novelty, and Recognition Memory				
Bornstein, 1984	20	Recognition memory	4	WPPSI (N = 14)	4	.54
Caron, Caron, and Glass, 1983	31	Response to novelty	5–6	Stanford-Binet	3	.42
Fagan and McGrath, 1981	35	Novelty preference	7	Language scales	3.8	.41
	19	Novelty preference	5	PPVT	4.3	.33
	20	Novelty preference	4–5	Language scales	6.5	.66
	19	Novelty preference	5	Language scales	7.5	.46
Lewis and Brooks-Gunn, 1981	22	Response to novelty	3	Bayley	2	.52
	57	Response to novelty	3	Bayley	2	.40
O'Connor, Cohen, and Parmelee, 1984	28[d]	Auditory response to novelty	4	Stanford-Binet	5	.60
Rose and Wallace, 1985	35[d]	Novelty preference	6	Stanford-Binet (N = 14)	2.8	.66
				Stanford-Binet (N = 17)	3.3	.45
				WISC-R (N = 19)	6	.56
Yarrow, Klein, Lomonaco, and Morgan, 1975	39	Novelty preference	6	Stanford-Binet	3.6	.35

[a]Authors are listed in alphabetical order.

[b]All correlations are absolute values and significant at $p < .05$; direction and nature of the correlation depend on the measures.

[c]Latent variable of baseline, slope, and amount.

[d]Sample consists of or includes preterm infants; testing carried out at corrected age.

[e]One trial or first trial.

[f]Mean of total fixation time, duration of first fixation, average fixation duration, and average trial duration.

tive to reliability (Cohen and Cohen, 1983) yields a potential predictive relation of .70 between the infant and child measures. Relatedly, the outcome measures of childhood mental functioning that have been examined thus far are restricted to crystallized intelligence (that is, acquired information and knowledge), whereas assessments of fluid intelligence might yield more apt associations with infant competencies (Cattell, 1971). In this connection, many new domains of children's skills and talents await exploration as criterion measures of infant habituation (Feldman and Adams, chapter 15 in this volume; Gardner, 1984). This brief clearly argues for more refined testing of infants, and for the application of a multifactor model of intelligence, in assessing prediction of cognitive development from infancy. In short, the predictive relations obtained so far may represent only a lower-bound of existing stability.

Existing studies of the predictive validity of infant measures focus on the first six months of life. It is possible that the predictive validity of decrement and recovery will differ for older infants because infants' skills change with age. For example, habituation in the twelve-month infant promises to be very different from habituation in the six-month infant, and if so the nature of prediction from habituation can be expected to vary with infant age.

Inspection of these predictive data reveals that verbal ability and psychometrically measured intelligence (which is itself largely verbal in nature) are the forms of childhood cognition most often reported in outcome studies. Why is language competence so frequently the criterion variable? Some investigators may have limited themselves to testing verbal intelligence; others may have reported associations with language because, of several abilities actually assessed, language was the only criterion measure to show a significant relation with their infant information-processing measure. Without detailed knowledge of how many measures were employed in different studies, and of how many of these measures were independent, it is difficult to certify that the general pattern of findings does not reflect a Type I error. However, the consistency and similarity of results across studies tend to rebut the critique that these are random effects.

Three separate reports substantiate a special relation between infant attention and childhood language ability. Bornstein (1985b) reported that habituation predicted children's intelligence-test performance but not their visual discrimination-learning, and Rose, Slater, and Perry (1986) observed that habituation predicted the verbal components of children's intelligence consistently better than the performance components. In a similar vein, Fagan (1984) found that recovery predicted children's PPVT scores, but not their recognition memory. However, the issue of predictive specificity is still open. Recently, Bornstein and Tamis-LeMonda (1987a) found that habituation in the middle of the first year of life predicted play sophistication, in addition to language comprehension, at the beginning of the second year.

The infant-to-child stability implicitly assumes that consistency resides in or is carried by the individual. The models that would account for such developmental stability are all too often left inexplicit. Two kinds of models can be proposed to explain stability in the infant. One posits that a single unmeasured or latent variable (perhaps Spearman's *g*) equally determines variance in attention in infancy and variance in intelligence in childhood. A second model posits that attention is a measured variable that stands for unmeasured cognitive ability in infancy, that Wechsler performance (for example) is a measured variable that stands for unmeasured cognitive ability in childhood, and that estimation of the correlation between the two latent unmeasured variables characterizes the stability of cognitive development. In this model, infant cognitive ability is conceived of as part of childhood cognitive ability and stands to it in the form of a part-whole relation.[2] These are just two of many possible models that could be invoked to account for the observed stability correlation between infant attention and childhood mental performance. Identifying the model that best accounts for stability of this sort poses a serious challenge to future investigators of cognitive development.

Moreover, it is necessary to consider alternative, perhaps supplementary, interpretations of the longitudinal association between attention in infancy and intelligence in childhood. In particular, it is plausible that the predictive association between infancy and childhood is not direct (as implied thus far), but is carried by a different variable that shares variance with both infancy and childhood measures. One such possible "third" variable is *in* the infant; another is *in* the infant's supportive environment.

Could observed developmental consistency in the individual be sustained by some other unchanging aspect of the child, like motivation? Many experts include motivation in their overarching constructs of intelligence (e.g., Scarr, 1981; Wechsler, 1963, 1974, 1981). On this account, measures of attention could reflect, at least in part, the infant's motivation to explore new environments, and intelligence-test performance could reflect, at least in part, the child's motivation to explore new testing materials and tasks as well as to perform well during testing. Through shared variance with motivation, attention in infancy and intelligence in childhood could bear a relation to one another over time. A more indirect influence would be in the ways motivation modifies learning

[2]If attention in infancy correlates with intelligence-test performance in childhood $r = .46$, the measured variable of attention in infancy stands in relation to the latent variable of infant cognitive ability as $\sqrt{.45}$ (the reliability of the habituation), and the measured variable of intelligence-test performance stands in relation to the latent variable of childhood cognitive ability as $\sqrt{.96}$ (the reliability of the Wechsler test), then, from the usual assumptions of path analysis, the correlation between the latent variables for infant and cognitive ability can be estimated as the correlation between the observed measures divided by the product of the relations of the observed measures to their latent variables; that estimated longitudinal correlation is .70.

throughout childhood, so that the infant who preferred novel stimulation would learn more in early life and would consequently score higher in childhood on tests of intelligence.

The evidence for motivation playing a critical role in the predictive correlation between information processing in infancy and childhood cognitive functioning is difficult to evaluate because of known difficulties associated with assessing motivation, especially in infancy. Nonetheless, the argument for motivation as a mediating variable loses force in light of the fact that many other aspects of infant performance have shown low or erratic predictive validity for later intelligence-test performance. There is little reason that other kinds of performance, such as on the Bayley Scales, should not share variance with motivation the same way as habituation. In addition, however integrated the constructs of motivation and cognition are, exceptions clearly show that the two may possess a high degree of independence: Children who are overachievers or underachievers plainly demonstrate that motivation and cognition are separable constructs. Furthermore, IQ does not perfectly predict school achievement.

The convergence of decrement and recovery data on stability in mental development seemingly places great weight on "little shoulders." However, it is important to remember that infants do not grow up in a vacuum, but under the tutelage of their caretakers. It seems plausible that, at least in some measure, caretakers could provide continuing external support for assessed individual stability between infancy and childhood. Specifically, mothers' consistent and systematic activities with their offspring could maintain individual differences in habituation in infancy and in intelligence-test performance in childhood. The question here is whether habituation in mid-infancy predicts childhood cognition over and above the continuing influential contributions of caretaking. Unfortunately, data pertinent to this question are meager on two counts. First, the developmental literature has only recently taken significant strides toward specification and operationalization of parental activities that promote cognitive development. Second, studies of caretaker influences on the development of cognition that include measures of habituation are very scarce. With this in mind, it is unnecessary to underscore the tentativeness of the following results.

Coordinate with one study of the predictive validity of infant habituation, I simultaneously conducted home observations of participating mothers and their babies (Bornstein, 1985b). In particular, I assessed maternal *didactics,* that is, how frequently mothers encouraged their infants to attend to properties, objects, and events in the environment. Mothers showed a wide distribution in their didactic organization of interaction. Importantly, these maternal activities influenced the development of cognition in children. Mothers' didactically encouraging attention in their infants exercised a significant influence from four months to one year and then to four years on children's verbal and cognitive performance; again, the predictive correlations reached the .50 region. These results, and those of related studies, therefore indicate a clear role for caretaker didactics in early cognitive growth. Ancillary studies demonstrate that maternal didactic activities are individually stable over the short-term (Bornstein and Tamis-LeMonda, 1987b) as well as the long-term (Bornstein, 1985b) in infancy.

Regression analyses applied to data in this study compare the short-term predictive validity of infant habituation and maternal didactics at four months: Each predicted a significant and independent proportion of variance in toddlers' verbal proficiency at twelve months (28% and 31%, respectively), and together the two predicted a significant proportion (45%) of the variance. A path analysis summarizes findings of longer-term relations, even if it oversimplifies infant and maternal contributions to childhood cognitive competence (Figure 8.4). This multivariate correlational technique shows path coefficients (unidirectional partial correlations). They give evidence of direct effects of each independent variable on the dependent variable, such that a unit change in habituation or in encouraging attention yields a change in productive vocabulary or in Wechsler performance in proportion to the coefficient. This path analysis may best be thought of as a descriptive clarification of direct linear relations among key variables. In this model, mother and infant variables at two time periods are shown as successive predictors of one cognitive index in childhood, Wechsler test performance.

In answer to our question, the regression and path analyses together demonstrate that infant information processing (habituation) links both to verbal proficiency at one year and to intelligence test performance at four years, and does so essentially independent of mothers' didactic encouragement (which, as can be seen, is also a good predictor). A replication study between five and thirteen months confirmed these results (Tamis-LeMonda and Bornstein, 1989). Maternal encouraging attention in infancy predicted toddlers' representational compe-

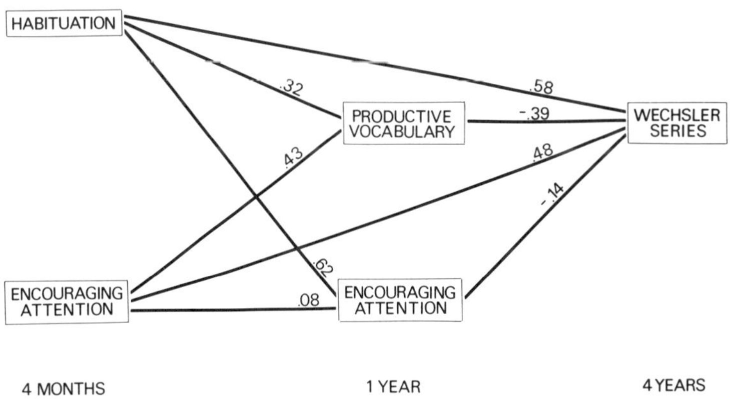

FIGURE 8.4. Unrestricted path model (and β-weights) among variables assessed to predict cognitive development between infancy and childhood (from Bornstein, 1985b).

tence, but so did habituation efficiency, and partial correlations showed that both mother and infant were independently influential. Clearly, the two principals in development—infant and caretaker—jointly contribute to cognitive growth in the child. From early life, however, there seems to be a considerable degree of stability in the infant.

CONCLUSIONS

In reflecting on her original longitudinal research, Bayley (1949, p. 167) speculated that "it may be that although we have not yet found the right tests, further search will reveal some infant behaviors which are characteristic of underlying intellectual functions, whose nature is such that they can be used for purposes of predicting the quality of intelligence at later ages." Overall, the data I present in this chapter point to a significant degree of predictability in intellectual development if information-processing measures of decrement and recovery of attention are evaluated early in life. Moreover, this developmental stability seems to be sustained independent of continuing caretaker input past the middle of the first year of life.

Assessments of the status of the infant at the beginning of life and of the prediction of childhood cognitive skills from infancy are of abiding theoretical and practical interest to students of human development. They not only inform about the course of normative development, but they open potentially significant avenues for increasingly accurate and early diagnosis of at-risk status and for the design of appropriate compensatory measures for different populations of babies. Clearly, the hypothesized relations and supporting data presented here warrant serious consideration, close scrutiny, and additional cross comparison. At the same time, this pattern of data impresses us as sufficiently robust to lend some scientific credence to Milton's adage in *Paradise Regained* that: "The childhood shows the man."

ACKNOWLEDGMENTS

Portions of this chapter appear in *Human Development*. Supported by research grants (HD20559 and HD20807) and a Research Career Development Award (HD00521) from the National Institute of Child Health and Human Development. This chapter was partially completed during my tenure as Professeur Invité at the Laboratoire de Psychologie du Développement et de l'Éducation de l'Enfant, Sorbonne, Paris. I thank H. Bornstein, R. Bradley, D. Feldman, J. Suwalsky, and B. Wright for comments and assistance. Request reprints from Marc H. Bornstein, Section on Child and Family Research, National Institute of Child

Health and Human Development, Building 31—Room B2B15, 9000 Rockville Pike, Bethesda, MD 20892.

REFERENCES

Barnet, A. B., Ohlrich, E. S., and Shanks, B. L. (1971). EEG evoked responses to repetitive auditory stimulation in normal and Down's syndrome infant. *Developmental Medicine and Child Neurology, 13,* 321–329.

Bates, E., Bretherton, I., and Snyder, L. (1988). *From first words to grammar.* New York: Cambridge University Press.

Bayley, N. (1949). Consistency and variability in the growth of intelligence from birth to eighteen years. *Journal of Genetic Psychology, 75,* 165–196.

Bayley, N. (1969). *Bayley scales of infant development.* New York: The Psychological Corporation.

Belsky, J., Hrncir, E., and Vondra, J. (1983). *Manual for the assessment of performance, competence, and executive capacity in infant play.* Unpublished manuscript, The Pennsylvania State University.

Belsky, J., and Most, R. K. (1981). From exploration to play: A cross-sectional study of infant free play behavior. *Developmental Psychology, 17,* 630–639.

Binet, A., and Simon, T. (1905). Méthodes nouvelles pour le diagnostic du niveau intellectuel des normaux. *L'Année Psychologique, 11,* 191–244.

Bornstein, M. H. (1984). *Infant attention and caregiver stimulation: Two contributions to early cognitive development.* Paper presented at the International Conference on Infant Studies, New York City.

Bornstein, M. H. (1985a). Habituation of attention as a measure of visual information processing in human infants: Summary, systematization, and synthesis. In G. Gottlieb and N. A. Krasnegor (Eds.), *Measurement of audition and vision in the first year of postnatal life: A methodological overview* (pp. 253–300). Norwood, NJ: Ablex.

Bornstein, M. H. (1985b). How infant and mother jointly contribute to developing cognitive competence in the child. *Proceedings of the National Academy of Sciences* (*U.S.A.*), *82,* 7470–7473.

Bornstein, M. H., and Benasich, A. A. (1986). Infant habituation: Assessments of individual differences and short-term reliability at five months. *Child Development, 57,* 87–99.

Bornstein, M. H., Pêcheux, M. -G., and Lécuyer, R. (1988). Visual habituation in human infants: Development and rearing circumstances. *Psychological Research, 50,* 130–133.

Bornstein, M. H., and Ruddy, M. (1984). Infant attention and maternal stimulation: Prediction of cognitive and linguistic development in singletons and twins. In H. Bouma and D. Bouwhuis (Eds.), *Attention and performance X* (pp. 433–445). London: Lawrence Erlbaum Associates.

Bornstein, M. H., and Sigman, M. D. (1986). Continuity in mental development from infancy. *Child Development, 57,* 251–274.

Bornstein, M. H., and Tamis-LeMonda, C. S. (1987a). *Habituation performance at 5 months predicts play performance at 13 months.* Unpublished manuscript, National Institute of Child Health and Human Development.

Bornstein, M. H., and Tamis-LeMonda, C. S. (1987b). *Stability and continuity in maternal activities towards firstborn infants still in the first six months of life.* Unpublished manuscript, National Institute of Child Health and Human Development.

Brim Jr., O. F., and Kagan, J. (Eds.). (1980). *Continuity and change in human development.* Cambridge, MA: Harvard University Press.

Caron, A. J., and Caron, R. F. (1969). Degree of stimulus complexity and habituation of visual fixation in infants. *Psychonomic Science, 14,* 78–79.

Caron, A. J., and Caron, R. F. (1981). Processing of relational information as an index of infant risk. In S. L. Friedman and M. Sigman (Eds.), *Preterm birth and psychological development* (pp. 219–240). New York: Plenum.

Caron, A. J., Caron, R. F., and Glass, P. (1983). Responsiveness to relational information as a measure of cognitive functioning in nonsuspect infants. In T. Field and A. Sostek (Eds.), *Infants born at risk: Physiological, perceptual, and cognitive processes* (pp. 181–209). New York: Grune and Stratton.

Cattell, R. (1971). *Abilities: Their structure, growth, and action.* Boston, MA: Houghton Mifflin.

Cohen, J., and Cohen, P. (1983). *Applied multiple regression/correlation analysis for the behavioral sciences.* Hillsdale, NJ: Lawrence Erlbaum Associates.

Cohen, L. B. (1981). Examination of habituation as a measure of aberrant infant development. In S. L. Friedman and M. Sigman (Eds.), *Preterm birth and psychological development* (pp. 241–253). New York: Academic Press.

Colombo, J., Mitchell, D. W., O'Brien, M., and Horowitz, F. D. (1987). The stability of visual habituation during the first year of life. *Child Development, 58,* 474–487.

DeLoache, J. S. (1976). Rate of habituation and visual memory in infants. *Child Development, 47,* 145–154.

Emde, R. N., and Harmon, R. J. (Eds.). (1984). *Continuities and discontinuities in development.* New York: Plenum.

Fagan, J. F. (1984). The relationship of novelty preferences during infancy to later intelligence and later recognition memory. *Intelligence, 8,* 339–346.

Fagan, J. F., and McGrath, S. K. (1981). Infant recognition memory and later intelligence. *Intelligence, 5,* 121–130.

Fagan, J. F., and Singer, L. T. (1983). Infant recognition memory as a measure of intelligence. In L. P. Lipsitt (Ed.), *Advances in infancy research* (Vol. 2, pp. 31–78). Norwood, NJ: Ablex.

Fantz, R. L. (1964). Visual experience in infants: Decreased attention to familiar patterns relative to novel ones. *Science, 146,* 668–670.

Fenson, L., Sapper, V., and Minner, D. G. (1974). Attention and manipulative play in the 1-year-old child. *Child Development, 45,* 757–764.

Friedman, S. (1975). Infant habituation: Process, problems, and possibilities. In N. Ellis (Ed.), *Aberrant development in infancy: Human and animal studies* (pp. 217–239). New York: Halsted.

Gardner, H. (1984). *Frames of mind: The theory of multiple intelligences.* New York: Basic Books.

Gesell, A. L., and Armatruda, C. S. (1947). *Developmental diagnosis: Normal and abnormal child development, clinical methods, and practical applications.* New York: Harper.

Greenberg, D. J., O'Donnell, W. J., and Crawford, D. (1973). Complexity levels, habituation, and individual differences in early infancy. *Child Development, 44,* 569–574.

Griffiths, R. (1954). *The abilities of babies.* New York: McGraw-Hill.

Guttman, L. (1966). Order analysis of correlation matrices. In R. B. Catell (Ed.), *Handbook of multivariate experimental psychology.* Chicago, IL: Rand McNally.

Haviland, J. (1983). Looking smart: The relationship between affect and intelligence in infancy. In M. Lewis (Ed.), *Origins of intelligence: Infancy and early childhood* (pp. 423–449). New York: Plenum.

Honzik, M. P. (1986). The role of the family in the development of mental abilities: A 50-year study. In N. Datan, A. L. Greene, and H. W. Reese (Eds.), *Life-span developmental psychology: Intergenerational relations* (pp. 185–210). Hillsdale, NJ: Lawrence Erlbaum Associates.

Hunt, E. B. (1978). Mechanics of verbal ability. *Psychological Review, 85,* 109–130.

Hunt, E. B. (1983). On the nature of intelligence. *Science. 219,* 141–146.

Hunt, E. B., Lunneborg, C., and Lewis, J. (1975). What does it mean to be high verbal? *Cognitive Psychology, 7,* 194–227.

Johnson, D., and Brody, N. (1977). Visual habituation, sensorimotor development, and tempo of play in one-year-old infants. *Child Development, 48,* 315–319.

Kagan, J. (1971). *Change and continuity in infancy.* New York: Wiley.

Kopp, C. B., and McCall, R. B. (1980). Stability and instability in mental performance among normal, at-risk, and handicapped infants and children. In P. B. Baltes and O. G. Brim (Eds.), *Life-span development and behavior* (Vol. 4, pp. 33–61). New York: Academic Press.

Lewis, M., and Baldini, N. (1979). Attentional processes and individual differences. In G. A. Hale and M. Lewis (Eds.), *Attention and cognitive development* (pp. 135–172). New York: Plenum.

Lewis, M., and Brooks-Gunn, J. (1981). Visual attention at three months as a predictor of cognitive functioning at two years of age. *Intelligence, 5,* 131–140.

Lewis, M., Goldberg, S., and Campbell, H. (1969). A developmental study of information processing within the first three years of life: Response decrement to a redundant signal. *Monographs of the Society for Research in Child Development, 39* (9), Serial No. 133.

Madison, L. S., Madison, J. K., and Adubato, S. A. (1986). Infant behavior and development in relation to fetal movement and habituation. *Child Development, 57,* 1475–1482.

McCall, R. B. (1981). Early predictors of later I.Q.: The search continues. *Intelligence, 5,* 141–147.

McCall, R. B., and Kagan, J. (1970). Individual differences in the infant's distribution of attention to stimulus discrepancy. *Development Psychology, 2,* 159–170.

Messer, S. B., Kagan, J., and McCall, R. B. (1970). Fixation time and tempo of play in infants. *Development Psychology, 3,* 406.

Miller, D. J., Ryan, E. B., Aberger, E., McGuire, M. D., Short, E. J., and Kenny, D. A. (1979). Relationships between assessments of habituation and cognitive performance in the early years of life. *International Journal of Behavioral Development, 2,* 159–170.

Miller, D., Spiridigliozzi, G., Ryan, E. B., Callan, M. P., and McLaughlin, J. E. (1980). Habituation and cognitive performance: Relationships between measures at four years of age and earlier assessments. *International Journal of Behavioral Development, 3,* 131–146.

Miranda, S. B., and Fantz, R. L. (1974). Recognition memory in Down's syndrome and normal infants. *Child Development, 45,* 651–660.

O'Connor, M. J., Cohen, S., and Parmelee, A. H. (1984). Infant auditory discrimination in preterm and full-term infants as a predictor of 5-year intelligence. *Developmental Psychology, 20,* 159–170.

Pêcheux, M. G., and Lécuyer, R.(1983). Habituation rate and free exploration tempo in 4-month-old infants. *International Journal of Behavioral Development, 6,* 37–50.

Reynell, J. (1981). *Reynell developmental language scales (rev. ed.).* Windsor, England: NFER-Nelson.

Riksen-Walraven, J. M. (1978). Effects of caregiver behavior on habituation rate and self-efficacy in infants. *International Journal of Behavioral Development, 1,* 105–130.

Rose, D. H., Slater, A., and Perry, H. (1986). Prediction of childhood intelligence from habituation in early infancy. *Intelligence, 10,* 251–263.

Rose, S. A. (1980). Enhancing visual recognition memory in infants. *Developmental Psychology, 16,* 85–92.

Rose, S. A., Gottfried, A., and Bridger, W. (1979). Effects of haptic cues on visual recognition memory in full-term and preterm infants. *Infant Behavior and Development, 2,* 55–67.

Rose, S. A., and Wallace, I. F. (1985). Visual recognition memory: A predictor of later cognitive functioning in preterms. *Child Development, 56,* 843–852.

Salapatek, P., and Cohen, L. (Eds.). (1987). *Handbook of infant perception* (Vols. 1–2). Orlando, FL: Academic Press.

Scarr, S. (1981). Testing *for* children: Assessment and the many determinants of intellectual competence. *American Psychologist, 36,* 1159–1166.

Sigman, M. D. (1977). Early development of preterm and full-term infants: Exploratory behavior in eight-month-olds. *Child Development, 47,* 606–612.

Sigman, M. D. (1983). Individual differences in infant attention: Relations to birth status and intelligence at five years. In T. Field and A. Sostek (Eds.), *Infants born at risk: Physiological, perceptual, and cognitive processes* (pp. 271–293). New York: Grune and Stratton.

Sigman, M. D., Cohen, S. E., Beckwith, L., and Parmelee, A. H. (1986). Infant attention in relation to intellectual abilities in childhood. *Developmental Psychology, 22,* 788–792.

Sigman, M. D., Kopp, C. B., Littman, B., and Parmelee, A. H. (1977). Infant visual attentiveness in relation to birth condition. *Developmental Psychology, 13,* 431–437.

Sigman, M. D., and Parmelee, A. H. (1974). Visual preferences of four-month-old premature and full-term infants. *Child Development, 45,* 959–965.

Siqueland, E. R. (1981). Studies of visual recognition memory in preterm infants: Differences in development as a function of perinatal morbidity factors. In S. L. Friedman and M. Sigman (Eds.), *Preterm birth and psychological development* (pp. 271–288). New York: Academic Press.

Sokolov, Y. N. (1958/1963). [*Perception and the conditioned reflex*] (S. W. Waydenfeld, Trans.). New York: Macmillan.

Sokolov, Y. N. (1969). The modeling properties of the nervous system. In M. Cole and F. Maltzman (Eds.), *A handbook of contemporary Soviet psychology* (pp. 671–704). New York: Basic Books.

Tamis-LeMonda, C. S., and Bornstein, M. H. (1989). Infant habituation and maternal encouragement of attention at 5 months in relation to the development of language, play, and representational competence at 13 months. *Child Development.*

Wechsler, D. (1963). *Wechsler preschool and primary scale of intelligence.* New York: The Psychological Corporation.

Wechsler, D. (1974). *Wechsler intelligence scale for children-revised.* New York: The Psychological Corporation.

Wechsler, D. (1981). *Wechsler adult intelligence scale-revised.* New York: The Psychological Corporation.

Wohlwill, J. (1973). *The study of behavioral development.* New York: Academic Press.

Yarrow, L. J., Klein, R. P., Lomonoco, S., and Morgan, G. A. (1975). Cognitive and motivational development in early childhood. In B. X. Friedlander, G. M. Sterritt, and G. E. Kirk (Eds.), *Exceptional infant* (Vol. 3, pp. 491–502). New York: Brunner/Mazel.

9 Measuring Infant Intelligence: New Perspectives

Susan A. Rose
Department of Pediatrics,
Albert Einstein College of Medicine

INTRODUCTION

Infant intelligence—an oxymoron? Until recently, one would have thought so. After all, at the turn of the century William James, in an unforgetable, and now classic phrase, characterized the infant's world as a ''blooming, buzzing confusion.'' For the past 20 or 30 years, however, evidence has been accumulating that challenges that view. Indeed, this volume attests to the strength of that challenge.

The new evidence for stabilities in development, and more specifically for stabilities in cognitive development beginning quite early in infancy, has generated considerable interest and excitement on at least two fronts. Thc first has to do with the very nature of the competencies now being shown to exist in infancy. Such competencies seem to be, in at least rudimentary form, similar to or analogs of adult information-processing skills. Demonstrations of infants' capacity for discrimination, memory, categorization, abstraction, and the like are increasingly common (for reviews, see Olson and Sherman, 1983; Rose and Ruff, 1987; Rovee-Collier and Gekoski, 1979). Examination of encoding and retrieval skills occupies a central role in studies of the infant mind. By contrast, the infant research that predominated in the first half of the 20th century had quite a different focus. Then, interest centered far more on charting the development of behaviors such as reaching, grasping, orienting, and the like; sensory-motor behaviors that have enormous significance for infant competence, but have frequently seemed to have only limited significance for later cognition (Bayley, 1970; Hunt, 1981; Kopp and McCall, 1982).

The very character of the more recent work on infant development has changed, and, as Feldman and Adams (chapter 15 in this volume) observe, ''has been done to illuminate universal qualities of the mind, what there is in the beginning for most children.'' The very idea that universal qualities of the mind can be identified and measured in the early months of life is, I think, one of the most exciting developments in the field of psychology. And the initial success of psychologists at this enterprise is certainly quite encouraging. As the field itself matures, there will no doubt emerge a clearer understanding and appreciation of the differences between infant and adult cognition, but the early excitement certainly lies in demonstrating the considerable, and largely unexpected, power of the infant mind.

The second basis for the excitement has to do with the fact that these early competencies are proving to have a measurable relation to later intelligence. Infants who perform well on various measures of information processing during the first few months of life tend to perform proficiently on traditional assessments of cognitive competence in later childhood, between two and eight years of age (e.g., Bornstein and Sigman, 1986; Fagan and Singer, 1983). Such relations imply that individual differences in early cognitive abilities are meaningful, not only in and of themselves, but also because they tap a quality of mind that endures, or at least has some lawful relation to later qualities of mind. For the past 50 years, the prevailing view had been that the capabilities and characteristics of infancy bear little, if any, identifiable relation to later cognition, intelligence, or mental activity (e.g., Kopp and McCall, 1982), although there are exceptions (e.g., Siegel, 1983, chapter 5 in this volume). These new studies certainly signal a major turnaround.

The studies linking early competencies to later intelligence have, for the most part, used measures of habituation or recognition memory—generally visual habituation or visual recognition memory. The processes involved in both can be conceptualized as basic to the acquisition of new information and to the ability to deal with novelty, abilities similar to those singled out by Sternberg as integral components of individual differences throughout the entire life span (Berg and Sternberg, 1985). Habituation is commonly assessed by the decrement in response that occurs to an unchanging stimulus and the recovery (dishabituation) of attention to stimulus change (Bornstein, chapter 8 in this volume). Recognition memory, on the other hand, is assessed by the differential preference for novel as opposed to familiar stimuli that occurs following a period of familiarization. (In this paradigm, the initial familiarization period is preset in duration so, unlike habituation, no waning of attention to the stimulus need occur.) Measures of habituation are taken as presumptive evidence of how fast and completely the infant encodes the stimulus and constructs an engram or trace of it. Measures of dishabituation, and of recognition memory, are taken as presumptive evidence of the accuracy or completeness of the engram and the ability to distinguish the memory trace of the old from the new.

If individual differences in habituation and visual recognition are to be meaningfully related to later cognition, then measures of these processes would be expected to exhibit the following four psychometric properties: (1) stability, (2) reliability, (3) concurrent validity, and (4) predictive validity. In this chapter, I present data from our laboratory bearing on each of these points.

These data are collected from several studies, all of which have assessed recognition memory using the paired-comparison paradigm. In this paradigm, a target is exposed for a brief period of familiarization and then withdrawn to be replaced in the test phase with two stimuli: the previously exposed (familiar) stimulus now paired with a novel one. Typically infants attend more to the novel member of the test pair, although a systematic preference in either direction can be used as evidence of recognition memory (e.g., Rose, Gottfried, Melloy-Carminar, and Bridger, 1982). In some of our work, the stimulus is presented tactually during familiarization and visually during test in order to assess tactual-visual cross-modal transfer.

STABILITY

Measures of infant attention have traditionally been used in studies concerned with group performance. As these measures begin to be used to assess individual, rather than group differences, the issue of stability assumes greater importance. Stability refers to the tendency of individuals to maintain their relative standing when retested after a relatively long stretch of time. Depending on the continuity in absolute level over time, stability can reflect the degree to which the quality being measured is an enduring or ephemeral one. What can be regarded as a long stretch of time for the purpose of establishing stability depends on the theoretical conceptualization of the quality being measured. In adults, a test-retest period of at least six months is often required to establish the stability of a characteristic (Nunnally, 1978). In infants, no comparable time period has been established, although a far shorter period would seem appropriate during a time of such rapid maturation. To date, assessments of stability for infant attention measures have been relatively rare.

The data we have bearing on the issue of stability are drawn from a longitudinal study, still underway. The overall purpose of this study is to examine the development and interrelation of various early information-processing measures and the usefulness of such measures for predicting cognitive functioning in later childhood. Performance is being assessed for a cohort of 46 fullterm and 63 high-risk preterm infants (birthweight < 1500 grams). Recruitment for the longitudinal study was initially targeted to the infant's 7-month birthday, but then extended both downwards and upwards in order to obtain data at three time points: six, seven, and eight months. Because the six- and eight-month testing sessions were introduced only after testing was well underway (particularly preterm recruitment, which had begun a few months before fullterm recruitment) some, but not all, subjects were seen at all three ages.

Our first examination of issues of stability was carried out using a group of 30 fullterms from this larger cohort, all of whom were tested at six, seven, and eight months of age (Rose and Feldman, 1987). At each session, these infants received at least one (of two) series of paired-comparison problems. There were six problems of visual recognition memory in this first series: three used Abstract Patterns as stimuli, and three used photos of Faces. Each problem consisted of a familiarization phase, in which the infant saw two identical stimulus targets. The familiarization phase for each problem lasted until the infant had looked at the target for a preset amount of time—5 seconds, for Abstract Patterns, 20 seconds, for Faces. Immediately following each familiarization was a 10-second test in which one of the familiar targets was presented alongside the novel member of the pair. In order to minimize procedural variation, trials were given in a fixed order (with Abstract Pattern and Face problems alternating), and the familiar and novel members of each pair were held constant across infants and sessions.

Novelty percentages were computed for each of the six problems by dividing the time spent looking at the novel stimulus on the test by the total time spent looking at both stimuli, and then multiplying by 100. Scores were aggregated into means for each type of problem, and also into a single Picture Recognition summary score representing performance across all six problems. To evaluate the stability of these novelty scores, correlations were computed between scores at six and seven months, seven and eight months, and six and eight months.

For the composites of six problems, infants showed moderate stability in mean novelty scores between assessements 1 and 2 months apart. Scores obtained at six months correlated .30 with scores at seven months, and .30 with scores obtained at eight months; scores at seven and eight months were even more highly correlated, .51. Stability levels were lower for aggregates composed of only three scores (i.e., for those consisting solely of Abstract Patterns or solely of Faces).

Stability coefficients were also computed using subjects from the entire cohort, and including data obtained on a second series of five problems. The first series consisted of the three Abstract Pattern and three Face problems previously mentioned. The second series, which was administered immediately after the first, consisted of three additional problems of visual recognition memory (these used three-dimensional geometric forms) and two problems of cross-modal transfer. In the cross-modal tasks, tactual-to-visual transfer was assessed by an adaptation of the paired-comparison paradigm: the target stimulus was presented tactually for familiarization and then visually for the test, where it was paired with a novel visual stimulus. Again, trials were given in a fixed order, and the novel and familiar stimuli were held constant. The familiarization was 20 seconds for Geometric Form problems and 60 seconds for Cross-Modal problems. Correlations were similar for males and females, and for preterms and fullterms, so the data could be combined across these variables. As a result, each stability coefficient could be based on a substantial sample size (*N*s were in the 40s and 50s).

Cross-age correlations were computed separately for each of the four types of problems, and for three successively broader summary scores. The first summary score, *Picture Recognition,* was an aggregate consisting of the six problems involving visual recognition of two-dimensional stimuli—Abstract Patterns and Faces. The second summary score, *Visual Recognition,* included all nine problems of visual recogniton memory—Abstract Patterns, Faces, and Geometric Forms. The third summary score, *General Recognition,* aggregated all eleven problems (now including the two Cross-Modal).

Here again, there was moderate stability between assessments 1 and 2 months apart: in general, cross-age correlations of .30 to .50 were found for the three summary scores, that is for the composites of six to eleven problems (Rose, Feldman, and Wallace, 1988b). The stability coefficients were more variable, and generally lower, for the four specific types of problem (each of which included only two or three components). The cross-age correlations achieved reasonable (and similar) stability for the aggregates of six, nine, or eleven problems.

Aggregate novelty scores had been formed here by averaging over novelty percentages for individual problems. Such scores are commonly formed in this way because it is generally assumed that increasingly higher novelty scores correspond to increasingly better recognition memory. However, we found stability coefficients of similar magnitude for summary scores created by dichotomizing the data (Rose and Feldman, 1987). These alternative summary scores were constructed by counting the number of problems on which a subject showed a clear novelty response (here designated as $\geq 56\%$, a value selected as criterion because it was close to both the mean and median of all problems). Summary scores based on these counts also yielded cross-age correlations in the .30s. The similarity of stability coefficients computed from continuous and dichotomous scores suggests that, once a clear novelty preference has been established, variation in the actual magnitude of that preference may be of little consequence. In general, greater degrees of novelty preference have been thought to reflect increasingly better recognition. However, we see here that when variations in response magnitude are ignored, by treating scores on each problem in a binary fashion (as indicating the presence or absence of recognition), the cross-age correlations are relatively unchanged. Therefore, what is stable across age may be the very tendency to exhibit a novelty preference over a variety of problems rather than the actual magnitude of that preference. The possibility deserves further exploration, as it bears on the meaning of the infant's behavior.

Stability across these three ages was also found for another measure derived from the paired-comparison tasks—namely exposure time. Exposure-time scores, reflecting the time required to accumulate a preset amount of looking to the familiar stimulus, were examined for the 30 fullterms from the first study (Rose and Feldman, 1987). The cross-age correlations for these scores ranged from .32 to .38; all were significant.

We think that the exposure-time scores may prove important as a measure of the infant's capacity to sustain attention; infants with shorter exposure times are those who look at the stimulus more steadily (i.e., they have fewer pauses) than those with longer exposure times. It would seem probable that the stability of these differences in concentrated versus dispersed looking patterns represent a difference among infants that is related to their ability to sustain visual attention.

The two measures, exposure-time and novelty scores, were not related to one another (correlations between the two were low and nonsignificant), indicating that each taps somewhat independent aspects of the infant's attention (Rose and Feldman, 1987). Moreover, neither novelty nor exposure-time scores were correlated significantly with concurrent 7-month Bayley MDI or PDI, indicating that these measures, and their stabilities, are not simply a reflection of individual differences in overall developmental level. The novelty scores, which have more frequently been studied, are traditionally interpreted as a measure of recognition memory, and as such seem to reflect a capacity unrelated to the aspect of attention tapped by exposure-time scores.

INTERNAL CONSISTENCY

When composite scores are made up of items which measure the same ability or trait, the reliability of these scores can be estimated by assessing their internal consistency with an index such as Chronbach's alpha coefficient. To the extent that problems subsumed in the various summary scores share substantial common variance, alpha coefficients of reasonable magnitude would be expected. However, reliability of the novelty scores, as estimated by Chronbach's alpha, was surprisingly poor (Rose et al., 1988b). Alpha coefficients were computed in our longitudinal study at each of three ages (i.e., six, seven, and eight months) for composites ranging upwards to 11 problems. None of the values exceeded .24. The median was only .19. These low alphas are largely due to the low (close to zero) intercorrelations among problem scores. The picture improves somewhat if the four means (one for each type of problem) are used as components of the larger composites, but even here the maximum alpha never exceeded .47. Apparently, more variance is unique to each problem than is shared among problems. And indeed, cross-age correlations that involve identical problems proved to be consistently higher than those involving different problems.

It is puzzling that there is so little variance shared across problems. Similar problems are commonly used in infant studies. All problems involved age-appropriate discriminations, and therefore might have been expected to share more variance than they did. Possibly the problems are more dissimilar than they appear, even those ostensibly of the same type (e.g., Faces). If this is the case, the variance shared among problems might be improved by increasing the similarity of stimuli. Yet it should be noted that even with a homogeneous set of letterlike stimuli, Colombo (1987) found that the correlations between problems was low, averaging only .24 for seven-month-olds. Moment-to-moment fluctuations in attention may attenuate internal consistency because each individual problem samples such a small fraction of infant behavior. If the vagaries in infant attention could be better controlled, it is possible that error variance would be reduced and the proportion of shared variance increased.

In view of the high degree of prediction possible from these infancy measures (discussed later), it is surprising that their internal consistency was so low. Measures that are unreliable cannot correlate highly with anything else, so we are forced to conclude that internal consistency indices may be a poor way to estimate reliability for these types of measures. The stability coefficients, which indicate that infants are fairly consistent in their recognition abilities even over fairly lengthy periods (one or two months), suggest that reliability could be better estimated here with test-retest methods. This suggestion presupposes that cross-age correlations would be considerably enhanced if the test-retest interval were reduced to but a few days.

CONCURRENT VALIDITY

The term *concurrent validity* is often used to refer to the relation between a measure and a criterion. We are somewhat hampered, however, in selecting a criterion that will earmark in infancy those individuals who will show later cognitive deficits. We have dealt with this problem here by considering instead the performance of infants who are thought to be at-risk for such deficits.

In a series of earlier studies, we found evidence for the concurrent validity of measures of visual recognition memory and cross-modal transfer: Groups expected to have a higher rate of cognitive deficits or difficulty later in life often performed poorly on such measures during the first year of life. The risk groups we have used have been preterms. We selected preterm infants for study because they represent a larger population who are at risk for cognitive impairment but whose cognitive difficulties often elude detection before school age (e.g., Drillen, Thompson, and Burgoyne, 1980; Frances-Williams and Davies, 1974, but see Field, Dempsey, and Shuman, 1983; Siegel, 1983, chapter 5 in this volume). In five separate studies, six- and twelve-month-old preterms were found to perform poorly on information-processing tasks relative to fullterms, generally showing no evidence of recognition memory on problems that elicited significant novelty scores in fullterms (Rose, 1980, 1983; Rose, Feldman, McCarton, and Wolfson, 1988a; Rose, Gottfried, and Bridger, 1978, 1979).

It should be pointed out that, in all our studies, preterms are tested at their "corrected age" (i.e., age estimated from their expected date of birth). This point is important for two reasons. Not only do such measures show promise for detecting cognitive difficulties that have previously been undetected, but these deficits cannot readily be dismissed on maturational grounds. The fact that they are evident even though prematures have been given time to catch up suggests a reflection of important differences in emerging cognitive functioning that exist despite longer postnatal experience.

In one of our early studies, 6-month-old fullterm and preterm infants were tested for visual recognition memory of various two-dimensional patterns (Rose, 1980). (The preterm groups used in the study had mean gestational ages of approximately 33 weeks, and mean birthweights of around 1630 grams.) Infants were given three problems; the first used Abstract Patterns as stimuli; the second used different configurations of circular elements; and the third used photos of faces. Each problem consisted of a familiarization phase, in which the infant saw two identical stimulus targets. As is customary in our studies, the familiarization phase lasted until the infant had looked at the target for a preset amount of time, in this case, 5, 10, and 20 seconds, respectively. Immediately following each familiarization was a ten-second test in which one of the familiar targets was paired with a novel stimulus. Preterm infants failed to differentiate between novel and familiar test stimuli on any of the problems, whereas fullterm infants showed a significant novelty preference on Abstract Patterns and Faces (69% and 65%, respectively). (The ten seconds of study time used in the second problem appears to have been too brief for even fullterms to process these stimuli.) Similarly poor performance was found for a second group of preterms (Rose, 1980, Study 2). Of particular interest, however, is the fact that the performance of preterm infants improved dramatically when familiarization times were substantially increased. This improvement suggested that the preterms were unable to encode the information as quickly as the fullterms. Their success with longer familiarization times indicates that they were able to store and retrieve the information and to make the visual discriminations involved. The difference in performance with relatively short and long familiarization times suggests that preterms have a pronounced deficit in the speed with which they process information about their visual world.

Similar results were obtained in a study that used parametric variations in familiarization time (Rose, 1983). This study investigated the effects of increasing familiarization time on the visual recognition memory of 6- and 12-month-old fullterm and preterm infants. (Both preterm groups had mean gestational ages of approximately 34.5 weeks and mean birthweights slightly greater than 1800 grams.) Infants were given trials in which they viewed a three-dimensional object for either 10, 15, 20, or 30 seconds of familiarization and were then tested for visual recognition memory using the paired-comparison technique (members of a pair differed from one another primarily in terms of shape).

Variations in familiarization time were systematically related to age for both groups; however, at both ages, preterms required considerably more familiarization time than their fullterm counterparts. At six months of age, fullterms achieved significant scores with only 15 seconds of familiarization, whereas the scores for preterms exceeded chance only after 30 seconds; at twelve months of age, fullterms achieved significant scores with as little as 10 seconds of familiarization (the briefest familiarization time used), whereas preterms required 20 seconds. Thus, although older infants required less familiarization time than younger infants, at both ages preterms required considerably longer familiarization time than fullterms. Overall, the pattern of results replicates the earlier findings of developmental lags in visual information processing of six-month-old preterms and extends these findings to twelve-month-olds. These findings suggest that there are persistent differences between preterms and fullterms throughout at least the first year of life in this very fundamental aspect of cognition.

Not only do preterms show developmental lags in the ability to process exclusively visual information, but they often seem to have greater difficulty than fullterms in intersensory functioning. In a study of cross-modal transfer, we investigated infants' ability to recognize an object visually when the information about it had been initially obtained in a different modality. To do this, we modified the procedure used for studying visual recognition memory. In adapting this paradigm, the stimuli were presented either tactually or orally during familiarization and visually during test. When the stimuli are presented in different modalities during familiarization and test, the occurrence of recognition memory demonstrates cross-modal transfer (i.e., indicates that the infant visually recognizes stimuli never seen, but only felt or mouthed).

In one cross-modal study (Rose, Gottfried, and Bridger, 1978), 12-month-old fullterm and preterm infants (mean gestational age 32.6 weeks, mean birthweight around 1650 grams) received three cross-modal tasks (one oral-visual, two tactual-visual). There were two groups of fullterms in this study, one middle-class, the other of low SES background. Each cross-modal task consisted of a 30-second familiarization period during which one stimulus from a pair was presented, and a 20-second visual recognition test, during which both members of the pair, the familiar and novel, were presented visually. (Members of a pair differed from one another primarily in terms of shape.) In the oral-visual task, the stimulus was placed in the infant's mouth for familiarization, whereas in the tactual-visual tasks it was placed in the infant's hand. In each case, the experimenter shielded the object from the infant's view.

On these problems, preterms (and the low-SES fullterms) showed less cross-modal transfer at twelve months of age than middle-class fullterms. In fact, the preterms performed at chance level on all three cross-modal problems, whereas the middle-class fullterms looked significantly longer at the novel stimulus throughout (novelty percentages ranged from 57% to 67%). These results suggest that, whereas twelve-month-old middle-class fullterms gain knowledge about the shape of an object by feeling it and mouthing it, and can make this information available to the visual modality, preterms have difficulty doing so.

We have also found that preterms have more difficulty than fullterms in another aspect of intersensory functioning, namely, extracting visual information from objects that are explored in a multimodal fashion, those that the infant actively looks at, touches, and manipulates (Rose, Gottfried, and Bridger, 1979). Contrary to our expectations, manipulation turned out to impede, rather than facilitate subsequent visual recognition for both groups. However, the effect was more marked among the preterms. At 6 months of age, fullterms showed evidence of visual recognition memory when familiarization was exclusively visual, but performance dropped to chance in conditions where manipulation had been permitted during familiarization; at twelve months, fullterms showed evidence of recognition in all conditions, although novelty scores were somewhat attenuated in conditions where manipulation had been permitted during familiarization. Preterms, on the other hand, showed no evidence of memory in any of the conditions at six months, and at twelve months showed memory only in the visual conditions. At twelve months, the performance of the preterms was strikingly similar to that of the younger preterms. Both groups showed evidence of memory in the visual conditions but not in conditions involving manipulation. In this study then, preterms again showed lags in the ability to process exclusively visual information and also in the ability to deal with haptic and visual cues simultaneously.

We have replicated this finding of poor performance among preterms in an ongoing longitudinal study (Rose et al., 1988a), which compares the performance of fullterms with preterms at particularly high risk (< 1500 grams). At seven months of age, preterms not only showed less differential attentiveness to novelty than fullterms (particularly on Abstract Pattern and Face problems), but also required longer exposure times to accrue the preset amounts of looking at the familiarization stimulus. These longer exposure times were primarily due to longer pauses between fixations, although the two groups also differed during familiarization in the duration of fixation and the frequency in shifts of gaze. For the preterms, novelty and exposure-time scores were related to several medical risk factors. Novelty scores were particularly compromised in preterms who had suffered RDS postnatally, especially in those who had required prolonged mechanical ventilation. In general, high-risk preterms exhibited deficits in visual recognition memory and in the ability to recruit, sustain, and shift attention.

PREDICTIVE VALIDITY

We have now completed three studies on the predictive validity of infant information-processing measures. The first two were somewhat serendipitous; they came into being because some of the preterm infants who had participated in two of our earlier cross-sectional studies (Rose, 1980; Rose, et al., 1978) also turned out to be participants in a longitudinal project being carried out by other investigators at the Kennedy Center of Albert Einstein College of Medicine. The availability of data from that project enabled us to examine, in at least a preliminary way, the predictive validity of the earlier measures. The third study is a report on the infants in our ongoing investigation of high-risk preterms (birthweight < 1500 grams) and fullterms. From its outset, this latter study was designed to be longitudinal.

The first study (Rose and Wallace, 1985a) reported data for 35 preterms who had participated in a study of visual recognition memory when the infants were 6 months of age (Rose, 1980), and had been seen for developmental assessment through six years of age. A single novelty score was computed for each infant by averaging across the three or four visual problems given at six months; these scores were then correlated with performance on standard psychometric assessments administered at various ages. The Bayley Scales of Infant Development (Bayley, 1969) had been administered at six, twelve, and twenty-four months, the Stanford-Binet Intelligence Test, Form L-M (Terman & Merrill, 1973) at 34 and 40 months, and the Wechsler Intelligence Scale for Children-Revised (WISC-R; Wechsler, 1974) at 6 years. The first three assessments were administered at the child's "corrected" age (i.e., age from expected date of birth). The 34- and 40-month, as well as the six-year assessment, were given at the child's chronological age. Although 34- and 40-month scores were corrected for prematurity, the six-year scores were not.

The most notable finding was the consistent relation between 6-month visual recognition memory and childhood cognitive status. Infant novelty scores correlated significantly with measures of cognitive outcome at 24, 34, 40 months and six years, with correlations ranging from .53 to .66. The strong positive relation between six-month visual novelty scores and later outcome contrasts sharply with the failure of the Mental Developmental Index (MDI) of the early Bayley scores (at either six or twelve months) to predict such outcomes. The failure of Bayley MDI scores obtained before age 2 years to predict later cognitive status in the present study is in keeping with the findings of many other investigators (e.g., Bayley, 1970; Hunt, 1981; Kopp and McCall, 1982; but see Siegel, chapter 5 in this volume). Also consistent with other studies were the strong correlations (.32 to .68) between parental education and cognitive outcome beginning at about two years of age (e.g., Cohen and Parmelee, 1983; Fagan and McGrath, 1981).

Multiple correlations indicated that visual recognition memory and parental education, taken together, correlated strongly with cognitive outcome at 24 months and six years; R = .60 to .70. In other words, 36% – 50% of the variance in these outcomes (or 28% – 43% of the adjusted variance) could be predicted from knowledge of these two variables alone. (It should be pointed out that visual recognition memory and parental education did not correlate with one another, $r = .07$.) Although these two predictors contributed about equally and significantly to six-year verbal IQ, visual novelty scores tended to contribute somewhat more to 24-month Bayley mental scores, six-year Full Scale IQ, and six-year performance IQ: the independent contribution from novelty scores was significant (amounting to 20%–28% of the variance in 2- and 6-year outcome) and generally even stronger than that from parental education.

In a second study (Rose and Wallace, 1985b), fullterms and preterms who had received tasks of cross-modal transfer and intra-modal transfer (visual recognition memory) at 12 months of age (Gottfried et al., 1977; Rose et al., 1978) were tested in standard psychometric tests at older ages: fullterms at 24 months, and preterms at 24, 34, 40 months and six years. A single cross-modal score was computed for each infant by averaging across the three problems administered at 12 months, and a single visual intra-modal score was similarly computed.

Both 12-month measures showed strong and consistent correlations with later outcome. For fullterms, cross-modal and intra-modal functioning correlated .49 and .39, respectively, with 24-month Bayley MDI scores; for preterms, these 12-month measures related not only to 24-month Bayley MDI scores but to each subsequent measure of cognitive outcome through six years (*r*s ranged from .38 to .64). As was the case in the previous study, these early information-processing measures were unrelated to contemporaneous Bayley scores, and the latter failed to predict subsequent cognition. Unlike early Bayley scores, the cross-modal and intra-modal measures seem to tap aspects of information processing shared with later measures of cognition. Here, too, the information-processing measures added unique variance to the multiple correlations, over and above that contributed by parental education (which again proved to be a significant predictor of cognitive outcome beginning at two years). Multiple correlations, using all three measures, ranged from $R = .63$ to .75, indicating that between 41% and 56% of the variance in cognitive outcome (or 33% to 48% of the adjusted variance) can be accounted for just from knowledge of these three variables. Overall, the results of the present study extend those of the previous one to older infants, to fullterms as well as preterms, and to cross-modal as well as intra-modal visual functioning. It is worth noting that, in both studies, the relations between the early information-processing measures and later outcomes were linear, and not carried by the consistency of low-scoring children alone.

As noted earlier, in our current longitudinal study of perceptual–cognitive development, a fairly large sample of fullterm and high-risk preterms (< 1500 grams birthweight) were tested at six, seven, and eight months on a battery of problems: nine assessed visual recognition memory (three each using Abstract Patterns, Faces, and Geometric Forms as stimuli), and two assessed tactual-visual cross-modal transfer. The inclusion of four such sets of problems allowed us to examine predictive validity for measures that consisted of specific types of problems and for composites encompassing more varied types of problems (Rose et al., 1988b). Data could be combined across age to create an assessment of early information processing consisting of upwards to 33 problems because the same battery of problems was administered at each age. Developmental testing has been completed through age three years, and three-year Stanford-Binet scores served as the outcome measure in this first report.

Scores obtained at each age—six, seven, and eight months—were significantly related to three-year IQ scores. Although some specific types of problems were significantly correlated with outcome (in particular, Abstract Patterns and Faces at all three ages, and Geometric Forms at seven months), correlations were generally increased when the individual measures were aggregated into larger composites. For the three summary scores, comprising six, nine or eleven problems, correlations ranged from .37 to .63, and clustered between .50 and .60. These predictive relations were similar at each age (i.e., similar correlations were obtained whether the information-processing measures were administered when the infant was six, seven, or eight months of age). Moreover, data from the various ages often added unique (nonredundant) variance. In these cases, combining data across two or three ages led to multiple correlations as high as .72. In other words, fully half the variance in three-year IQ could be accounted for by cross-age clusters that combined data from 12 to 33 problems.

The predictive relations between infancy measures at six, seven, and eight months and later IQ were similar in three major respects. First, all the predictive findings were independent of the infant's risk status, i.e., they held for full terms and preterms alike. Second, the absolute magnitudes of the raw correlations were similar at all three ages. This was true not only for the three summary scores, but also for each of the smaller composites representing the four types of problems. Third, the amount of variance in three-year IQ predicted by the four sets of problems taken together was similar at each of the three ages. The similarity of predictive relations for each age underscores the replicability of these findings. It should also be noted that cutoffs established for predicting children at risk for mental retardation (IQ < 70) and for learning problems (IQ < 85) showed reasonable sensitivity and specificity.

Overall, then, the results of these studies, and other recent studies (see Bornstein and Sigman, 1986; Fagan and Singer, 1983) suggest that cognitive abilities can be assessed in infancy, and that individual differences in such cognitive abilities show far greater consistency than previously thought.

CONCLUSIONS

Sufficient information on the psychometric properties of the infant measures currently in use and on their relation to later cognition is much needed. Many studies to date have used small samples, relatively restricted IQ ranges, and infant measures of unknown reliability. In fact, few have even examined issues of long-term stability, short-term test-retest reliability, or internal consistency. A greater body of research is needed to elucidate the strengths and weaknesses of the various infant measures used in individual-difference research and to delineate the limitations in predicting from infancy to later childhood.

Additionally, there are new directions in which we should begin to move. We need studies aimed at achieving a better understanding of the nature of early cognition, its growth, and the qualities of mind that form the basis for the observed stabilities. In this regard, the measures of cognition used to assess infant functioning, and those used to assess outcome, both require closer examination.

Many of the infant prediction studies to date have used a single type of outcome measure, namely, a traditional intelligence test, such as the Stanford-Binet, the WPPSI, or the WISC-R. These tests consist of a variety of tasks, each of which tap different functions, such as digit span, short-term memory, verbal comprehension, vocabulary, the perception and manipulation of geometric patterns, deductive reasoning, and general information. The intelligence quotient, commonly referred to as IQ, is a weighted composite of scores on these separate tasks. IQ has traditionally had such a strong hold on our thinking about intelligence because, as Feldman and Adams (chapter 15 in this volume) suggest, "an IQ estimate is believed to be an indication of a child's overall power of mind." As a psychometric measure, IQ provides a quantitative perspective on the nature of intellectual growth that allows for a meaningful comparison of individual children (Siegler and Richards, 1982). To many researchers IQ has seemed to be the logical choice for a global estimate of general intelligence and mental prowess: It has high reliability and high stability; moreover, it stands as one of the most robust predictors of the child's success in school. No other measure of cognition has been so widely accepted or validated. IQ scores allow intelligence to be tested as a set of quantifiable dimensions along which people can be ordered (Siegler and Richards, 1982).

Nonetheless, traditional IQ tests have some drawbacks that limit their usefulness as outcome measures—at least as the sole measure of outcome. These drawbacks stem from several factors. First, standard IQ measures generally attempt to isolate rather global, structural constellations of individual differences in test performance. In such tests, intelligence is considered in terms of abilities—verbal ability, spatial ability and the like; the mental processes that contribute to, or account for, individual differences in these abilities are given little attention (Sternberg, 1985). Furthermore, although the tasks comprising an intelligence test were designed to measure different abilities, scores on the various components are nearly always positively correlated, sometimes substantially so. This suggests that a single ability, or small set of abilities, determines performance on what are ostensibly very different tasks (Hunt, 1983). It is, for example, unclear as to whether IQ is most appropriately represented by (1) a single consistent, general trait (Spearman, 1927); (2) a collection of multiple, clearly delineated components, such as those identifiable by factor analyses (e.g., Horn, 1980); or (3) a collection of loosely related skills which, despite having no defining attribute, have prototypical instances, a hierarchical organization, and a stable correlational structure (Neisser, 1979). (See Siegler and Richards, 1982, for a discussion.) There is a third drawback with traditional IQ tests because they fail to identify or specify anything about the individual's thought processes. As Hunt (1983, p. 141) pointed out, IQ is "a statistical abstraction rather than a measure of a definable cognitive ability." Sternberg (1977) observed that because of statistical limitations, factor analyses lack inferential power for distinguishing among theories and, because of psychological limitations, factors have no psychological reality as components of intelligence (i.e., structural factors do not identify processing components). Moreover, the factors identified in any analysis can depend heavily on methodological assumptions, the nature and number of the particular items involved, and the particular subject population tested (Siegler and Richards, 1982, p. 904).

It is for these reasons that cognitive theorists have increasingly questioned the value of IQ as an adequate representation of the concept of intelligence (e.g., Hunt, 1983; Sternberg, 1985). These theorists seek to identify and understand the nature of the processes that enter into an individual's performance on various intellectual tasks. Alternative conceptualizations of intelligence have recently been proposed, such as Gardner's theory of multiple intelligences (1985) and Sternberg's componential theory of intelligence (1977, 1985). These alternative approaches often begin with a theory of cognition, or the process of cognition, and then go on to identify those aspects of individual mental performance that should be important on theoretical grounds (Hunt, 1983). In other words, this approach is characterized by experimental efforts to identify and analyze the specific thought processes that characterize intelligence: memory strategies, inferential abilities, symbol manipulation, capacity factors, the representation of information, problem-solving strategies, and so forth. In contrast to traditional intelligence tests, which reflect a person's knowledge of the world along with a more basic set of skills for information processing, information-processing theorists seek to identify and study the basic processing skills in relative isolation (Cooper and Regan, 1982). From this perspective, differences among individuals are viewed in terms of differences in capacity (e.g., rate of encoding), strategies, knowledge base, or the like.

In this respect, it is noteworthy that the infant measures that have proven to be most strongly related to later cognition all tap encoding or memorial processes. Of course, the problem is to identify more precisely the nature of the infant's information-processing system. Are there separate memory storage systems analogous to the working memory and long-term memory found in studies of adults? How does information get in and out of long-term memory? In what form is information stored—is it represented in images, in amodal codes? How is it retrieved? Are the processes of memorial organization, storage, and retrieval fundamentally the same across age? Or, is it that skillful execution of one process at an early age lays the foundation for skillful execution of a different one at a later age? We need to identify the range of processes that are available and to better understand their developmental course.

In our own work we have identified two aspects of information processing that seem to be independent of one another: recognition memory and attention during familiarization (Rose and Feldman, 1987). Each also seems to be relatively stable, at least across a two-month span, and independent of concurrent sensory-motor development, as assessed by the Bayley Mental Developmental Index. Also, we have found evidence that infants at risk for cognitive impairment differ from normal infants in at least one specifiable aspect of the recognition process, namely, the speed of encoding (Rose, 1980, 1983). In these latter studies, the retrieval of already encoded information did not seem to be affected by risk. Thus, differences in processing ability may be of more importance than differences in storage capacity and/or retrieval strategies. As this research proceeds, clearer pictures of the nature of early information-processing skills and of the nature of these newly discovered stabilities in cognition should emerge. Of course, questions remain as to whether infant attentional measures will eventually lead to the development of better operational measures of abstraction, reasoning or problem solving than is currently provided by traditional cognitive tests.

ACKNOWLEDGMENTS

Support for this work was provided by a Behavioral Sciences Research Grant from the March of Dimes Birth Defects Foundation and by Grant HD 13810 from the NIH. The author would like to express her appreciation to Judith F. Feldman, Frances Goldenberg, Patricia Melloy-Carminar, Johanna Wolfson, and Ina F. Wallace for their contributions to the work discussed in this chapter.

REFERENCES

Bayley, N. (1969). *Bayley scales of infant development.* New York: The Psychological Corporation.

Bayley, N. (1970). Development of mental abilities. In P. H. Mussen (Ed.), *Carmichael's manual of child psychology.* (Vol. 1, pp. 1163–1210). New York: Wiley.

Berg, C. A., and Sternberg, R. J. (1985). Response to novelty: Continuity versus discontinuity in the developmental course of intelligence. In H. W. Reese (Ed.), *Child Development and Behavior* (Vol. 19, pp. 1–47). New York: Academic Press.

Bornstein, M. H., and Sigman, M. D. (1986). Continuity in mental development from infancy. *Child Development, 57,* 251–274.

Cohen, S. E., and Parmelee, A. H. (1983). Prediction of five-year Stanford-Binet scores in preterm infants. *Child Development, 54,* 1242–1253.

Cooper, L. A., and Regan, D. T. (1982). Attention, perception and intelligence. In R. J. Sternberg (Ed.), *Handbook of human intelligence* (pp. 123–169). New York: Cambridge University Press.
Drillien, C. M., Thompson, A. J. M., and Burgoyne, K. (1980). Low birthweight children at early school age: A longitudinal study. *Developmental Medicine and Child Neurology, 22,* 26–47.
Colombo, J. (1987, April). *The psychometrics of infant visual behavior*. Paper presented at the Society for Research in Child Development, Baltimore, MD.
Fagan, J. F., and McGrath, S. K. (1981). Infant recognition memory and later intelligence. *Intelligence, 5,* 121–130.
Fagan, J. F., and Singer, L. T. (1983). Infant recognition memory as a measure of intelligence. In L. P. Lipsitt (Ed.), *Advances in infancy research* (Vol. 2, pp. 31–78). Norwalk, NJ: Ablex.
Field, T., Dempsey, J., and Shuman, H. H. (1983). Five-year follow-up of preterm respiratory distress syndrome and post-term postmaturity syndrome infants. In T. Field and A. Sostek, (Eds.), *Infants born at risk: Physiological, perceptual and cognitive processes* (pp. 317–335). New York: Grune & Stratton.
Frances-Williams, J., and Davies, P. A. (1974). Very low birthweight and later intelligence. *Developmental Medicine and Child Neurology, 16,* 709–728.
Gardner, H. (1985). *The mind's new science*. New York: Basic Books.
Gottfried, A. W., Rose, S. A., and Bridger, W. H. (1977). Cross-modal transfer in human infants. *Child Development. 48,* 118–123.
Horn, J. L. (1980). Concepts of intellect in relation to learning and adult development. *Intelligence, 4,* 285–317.
Hunt, E. (1983). On the nature of intelligence. *Science, 219,* 141–146.
Hunt, J. V. (1981). Predicting intellectual disorders in childhood for preterm infants with birthweights below 1501 gm. In S. L. Friedman and M. Sigman (Eds.), *Preterm birth and psychological development* (pp. 329–350). New York: Academic Press.
Kopp, C. B., and McCall, R. B. (1982). Predicting later mental performance for normal, at-risk, and handicapped infants. In P. B. Bates and O. G. Brim (Eds.), *Life-span development and behavior* (Vol. 4, pp. 33–61). New York: Academic Press.
Neisser, V. (1979). The concept of intelligence. *Intelligence, 3,* 217–227.
Nunnally, J. C. (1978). *Psychometric Theory* (2nd ed.). New York: McGraw-Hill.
Olson, G. M., and Sherman, T. (1983). Attention, learning and memory in infants. In M. M. Haith and J. J. Campos (Eds.), P. H. Mussen (Series Ed.), *Handbook of child psychology: Vol. 2. Infancy and developmental psychobiology* (pp. 1001–1080). New York: Wiley.
Rose, S. A. (1980). Enhancing visual recognition memory in preterm infants. *Developmental Psychology, 16,* 85–92.
Rose, S. A. (1983). Differential rates of visual information processing in fullterm and preterm infants. *Child Development, 54,* 1189–1198.
Rose, S. A., and Feldman, J. F. (1987). Infant visual attention: Stability of individual differences from six to eight months. *Developmental Psychology, 23,* 490–498.
Rose, S. A., Feldman, J. F., McCarton, C. M., and Wolfson, J. (1988-a). Information processing in seven-month-old infants as a function of risk status. *Child Development. 59,* 589–603.
Rose, S. A., Feldman, J. F. and Wallace, I. F. (1988 b). Individual differences in infant information processing: Reliability, stability and prediction. *Child Development, 59,* 1177–1197.
Rose, S. A., Gottfried, A. W., and Bridger, W. H. (1978). Cross-modal transfer in infants: Relationship to prematurity and socio-economic background. *Developmental Psychology, 14,* 643–652.
Rose, S. A., Gottfried, A. W., and Bridger, W. H. (1979). Effects of haptic cues on visual recognition memory in fullterms and preterms. *Infant Behavior and Development, 2,* 55–67.
Rose, S. A., Gottfried, A. W., Melloy-Carminar, P. M., and Bridger, W. H. (1982). Familiarity and novelty preferences in infant recognition memory: Implications for information processing. *Developmental Psychology, 18,* 704–713.

Rose, S. A., and Ruff, H. A. (1987). Cross-modal abilities in human infants. In J. D. Osofsky, (Ed.), *Handbook of Infant Development* (Vol. 2, pp. 318–362). New York: Wiley.

Rose, S. A., and Wallace, I.F. (1985a). Cross-modal and intra-modal transfer as predictors of mental development in fullterm and preterm infants. *Developmental Psychology, 21,* 949–962.

Rose, S. A., and Wallace, I. F. (1985b). Visual recognition memory: A predictor of later cognitive functioning in preterms. *Child Development, 56,* 843–852.

Rovee-Collier, C. K., and Gekoski, M. J. (1979). The economics of infancy: A review of conjugate reinforcement. In H. W. Reese and L. P. Lipsitt (Eds.), *Advances in child development* (Vol. 13, pp. 195–255). New York: Academic Press.

Siegel, L. S. (1983). Correction for prematurity and its consequences for the assessment of the very low birth weight infant. *Child Development, 54,* 1176–1188.

Siegler, R. S., and Richards, D. D. (1982). The development of intelligence. In R. J. Sternberg (Ed.), *Handbook of human intelligence* (pp. 897–971). New York: Cambridge University Press.

Spearman, C. (1927). *The abilities of man.* London: Macmillan.

Sternberg, R. J. (1977). *Intelligence, information processing, and analogical reasoning: The componential analysis of human abilities.* Hillsdale, NJ: Lawrence Erlbaum Associates.

Sternberg, R. J. (1985). *Beyond IQ: A triarchic theory of human intelligence.* New York: Cambridge University Press.

Terman, L. M., and Merrill, M. A. (1973). *Stanford-Binet Intelligence Scale, Form L-M.* Boston: Houghton Mifflin.

Wechsler, D. (1974). *Wechsler Intelligence Scale for Children-Revised.* New York: The Psychological Corporation.

PART I

Section 5: Experience

10 The Use of the HOME Inventory in Longitudinal Studies of Child Development

Robert H. Bradley
Center for Research on Teaching & Learning, University of Arkansas at Little Rock

INTRODUCTION

The decade of the 1960s was a watershed period in child development research. Few times in recent history have witnessed such a reshaping of our thinking about human development. One idea that emerged during this fertile period became particularly significant for longitudinal studies mounted in subsequent years: The idea that the early environment played a critical role in cognitive development and achievement (Bloom, 1964; Caldwell, 1968; Hunt, 1961).

As the 1960s shone a spotlight on the role of the home environment in children's early development, the 1970s helped to redefine our understanding of how specific environmental factors impinge on development throughout childhood (Bell, 1969; Bronfenbrenner, 1979; Sameroff and Chandler, 1975). Out of the cataclysm of activity and research of the 1960s and early 1970s two very critical ideas emerged. First, infants are competent, viable organisms who undergo qualitative changes in all spheres of development in the early months and years of life. Second, individual patterns of development for children result from a series of specific transactions between infant and environment, each shaping the other as the child displays increasingly complex and differentiated sets of capabilities and behaviors.

It was against this backdrop of child development research that we began a longitudinal study of the relation between home environment and child development during infancy (Caldwell, Elardo, and Elardo, 1972). The study commenced in Little Rock, Arkansas in 1970. Initial findings from the study (Elardo, Bradley, and Caldwell, 1975; Bradley and Caldwell, 1976) prompted its continuation: to examine the relation of environment and development through later periods of childhood. As new ideas about the relation of environment and development emerged in the 1970s and early 1980s, we undertook additional studies—some cross-sectional, some longitudinal—in an effort to further explore what is now often characterized as a complex and dynamic set of relationships (Ramey and Baker-Ward, 1982; Belsky, 1983).

This chapter presents findings from these studies that seem particularly pertinent to the issues of stability and continuity in human development during the first eleven years of life. The chapter begins by describing the HOME Inventory, a measure of environmental quality, that has been a center piece in our studies of children's development. It continues by presenting the general pattern of relations between those aspects of the home environment indexed by HOME and children's mental development during the preschool years. This is followed by a discussion of variations in the general pattern across several demographic groups. The chapter then focuses on research dealing directly with the effect of consistency in environments on mental development. An attempt is made to delineate the relative contributions of early and contemporaneous environments on mental test scores. The latter sections of the chapter discuss the relation of environment and development during the school years. The chapter concludes with a consideration of future needs of research on the relation of environment and development for young children.

THE HOME INVENTORY

One of the principle measures used in all our investigations is the HOME Inventory. It is an observation/interview technique that requires a visit to the home of a target child while both the child and primary caregiver are present. HOME (Home Observation for the Measurement of the Environment) is designed to assess the quality and quantity of cognitive, social, and emotional support available to a child in the family environment. It measures specific transactions between caregiver and child, various objects and events that might stimulate the child, and a variety of experiences provided in the home or by family members that offer opportunities for growth and development. The inventory takes about one hour to administer. As a technique for measuring the quality of the environment, its power or intensity of focus is probably best characterized as midrange. That is, it provides a more detailed and comprehensive mapping of the environment than common structural and status measures—and even most interview measures. However, it provides a less detailed portrait than some time-sampling and event-sampling techniques. Its kind of like a road map, something more than a general set of directions, something less than detailed plats for each block.

There are now three published versions of the HOME Inventory; a fourth is in production. The HOME Inventory used with families of infants (birth to age three) contains 45 items clustered into six subscales: (1) Parental Responsivity; (2) Acceptance of Child; (3) Organization of the Environment; (4) Play Materials; (5) Parental Involvement with Child; and (6) Variety of Experience. The Inventory used with families of preschoolers (ages 3 to 6) contains 55 items clustered into eight subscales: (1) Learning Materials; (2) Stimulation of Communicative Competence; (3) Physical Environment; (4) Parental Nurturance and Responsivity; (5) Academic Stimulation; (6) Modeling and Encouragement of Social Maturity; (7) Variety in Experience; and (8) Acceptance of Child. The Inventory used with families of elementary school children (ages 6 to 10) contains 59 items clustered into eight subscales: (1) Parental Responsivity; (2) Encouragement of Maturity; (3) Emotional Climate of Family; (4) Materials and Experiences; (5) Provision for Active Stimulation; (6) Family Participation; (7) Paternal Involvement; and (8) Physical Environment. Items for all three versions are scored in binary (yes-no) fashion. The version currently under construction is designed for use with families of adolescents (ages ten to fifteen years).

Caldwell and Bradley (1984) presented psychometric information for the Infant, Preschool, and Elementary versions of the Inventory. Inter-observer agreement for the three versions ranges from 90% to 95% (See Elardo & Bradley, 1981, for a review of research on the Inventory). Internal consistency estimates (alpha coefficients) for the three instruments are .89, .93, and .90, respectively. A combination of content analysis, item analyses, and factor analysis was used to cluster items on each version into the subscales identified in the previous paragraph. Alphas for the subscales range from .44 to .89, largely dependent on the number of items in the subscale. Low to moderate correlations were observed between subscales (.00 to .60) with a median of around .30. HOME is moderately correlated with sociodemographic indices (.20 to .60).

When viewed from an ecological or general systems perspective, both stability and continuity in development are best understood against a backdrop of the context in which development occurs. Phenotypic variations in human characteristics result from the interplay of genes and environments over time. Even in cases where genes exercise considerable control over the rate and form of changes in characteristics, the environment may serve as a trigger for genetically controlled change or as a guide to the specific amount or form of the change. At extreme levels, environments may substantially alter the rate or form of the change. In sum, stability and continuity in development are best comprehended (and mapped) in relation to *stabilities* and *continuities* in the environment—points made by Hunt (1961) and Bloom (1964) a quarter century ago.

THE LITTLE ROCK LONGITUDINAL STUDY

Recruitment of participants for the Little Rock Longitudinal Study began in November 1970. Well-baby clinics, birth records from hospitals, and personal contacts in the community all served as sources of infants. Children were drawn from both middle-class and lower-class backgrounds. However, a disproportionate number were from poor families because that was the focus of the study. A total of 174 participants were recruited; but only about half were used in the analyses reported later because the others were involved in early intervention programs at our center.

Children were administered the Bayley Scales of Infant Development up to age 24 months, the Stanford-Binet Intelligence Test at 36 and 54 months of age, and the Science Research Associates Achievement Test battery in school at age six to seven years and again at age ten to eleven years. Families were administered the infant version of HOME when the child was six, twelve, and twenty-four months old, the Preschool version when the child was three and four and a half years old, and the Elementary version when the child was ten years old. Attrition resulted in the loss of all but 42 children by the 10-year assessment point. These 42 children were rated using the Classroom Behavior Inventory (Schaefer and Aaronson, 1977) at age ten to eleven years. The CBI consists of 18 items clustered into three bipolar subscales: task orientation versus distractability, consideration versus hostility, and introversion versus extraversion. Teachers rate the child on a four-point scale for each item. They were also asked to appraise the child's overall adjustment using the same four-point format.

Early analyses of data from the Little Rock Longitudinal Study involved simple correlations between HOME and children's mental test scores in the first five years of life. Included in Table 10.1 are correlations between HOME scores at six,

TABLE 10.1
Correlations between 6-, 12-, and 24-month HOME Scores and Mental Test Scores Gathered at 1, 3, and 4½ Years

	Time of HOME Assessment						
	6-Months			*12-Months*		*24-Months*	
HOME Subscales	*1-yr. MDI*[b]	*3-yr. IQ*	*4½-yr. IQ*	*1-yr. MDI*	*3-yr. IQ*	*3-yr. IQ*	*4½-yr. IQ*
Responsivity	.09	.25*	.27	.15	.39*	.49*	.50*
Acceptance	.13	.24*	.10	.01	.24*	.41*	.28*
Organization	.20	.40*	.31*	.20	.39*	.41*	.33*
Toys	.05	.41*	.44*	.28*	.56*	.64*	.56*
Involvement	.08	.33*	.28*	.28*	.47*	.55*	.55*
Variety	.27*	.31*	.30*	.05	.28*	.50*	.39*
Total Score	.16	.50*	.44*	.30*	.58*	.71*	.57*
Multiple Correlation[a]	.30	.54*	.50	.40	.59*	.72*	.63*

*$p < .05$
[a]This represents the multiple correlation of all six HOME subscales.
[b]MDI = Mental Development Index from Bayley Scales

twelve, and twenty-four months and the following measures of mental development: 12-month Bayley MDI, 36-month and 54-month Stanford-Binet IQ.

The results reveal several things about the relation between children's home environments during infancy and their mental development during early childhood:

(1) There is only a *low* correlation between the home environment and mental test scores in the first year of life (never greater than .40).

(2) There is a *moderate* correlation between specific aspects of the home environment (e.g., Parental Responsivity, Play Materials, Parental Involvement) in infancy and IQ during the preschool years. The correlation diminishes only slightly as the length of time between home environment and mental test assessments increases (See Table 10.1).

(3) There are clear differences in patterns of relationships between specific home environment factors and mental test scores. Relations differ both in strength and stability. For example, both the Play Materials and Parental Involvement subscales were correlated .5 to .6 with IQ at three and four and a half years, whereas Acceptance was correlated only around .3. Relatedly, twelve-month scores on the Variety of Stimulation subscale was correlated $< .3$ with three-year IQ, but twenty-four-month scores on the same subscale were correlated .5 with the three-year IQ score.

After examining the simple relationships between HOME and mental test scores in the first few years of life, we attempted to analyze data in such as way as to answer more truly developmental questions. That is, we looked at HOME in relation to changes in mental test performance across time. Attrition was such that we could only use data through the third year of life. Using these data, an attempt was made to mirror the approach used by McCall, Appelbaum, and Hogarty (1973) to analyze the Fels Longitudinal data. Limitations in the data prevented the use of cluster analysis to identify groups of children whose mental test scores increased, decreased, or remained stable. These designations were made on the basis of simple changes in mental test scores from six to thirty-six months. Constraints were imposed so as to reduce the effect of regression to the mean as a confounding factor in the analysis. The approach resulted in labeling 8 children as having an increasing mental test profile, 38 as stable, and 18 as decreasing.

Subscales from the HOME, measured when the child was 6 months old, were used in a multiple discriminant analysis to differentiate among the group that increased in mental test scores, the group that remained stable, and the group that decreased. The six HOME subscales provided significant discrimination among the groups ($p < .01$). Significant univariate effects were observed for Parental Involvement, Play Materials, and Organization. The overall "hit rate" for classification using HOME scores was modest (about 72%). Post hoc analyses revealed that about 30% to 40% of the misses occurred in homes that changed substantially between six and thirty-six months. These results, along with others to be reported later, lead to three assumptions:

(1) Differences in the early environment are associated with identifiable trajectories in mental test scores, trajectories that are somewhat *independent of initial developmental status*. Thus, differences in the quality of the early home environment can contribute to *discontinuity* in the rank order of mental test scores over the first three years of life.

(2) There is only *modest stability in the home environment* (stability coefficients for HOME subscales generally ranged from .40 to .70).

(3) Developmental studies should include measures of the home environment at multiple time points if reliable findings about environment/development relationships are to emerge.

HOME AND IQ IN DIFFERENT DEMOGRAPHIC GROUPS

The initial set of analyses involving HOME and mental test data established a base for more detailed studies of the relationship. Included were studies involving HOME, social status, and IQ for different demographic groups. These studies were important for two reasons: (1) to determine whether environmental process measures, like HOME, afforded a more detailed understanding of the relationship between environment and development than was possible with social status and family structure measures alone; and (2) to determine the extent to which the relationship between home environment and cognitive development varied as a function of such factors as gender and ethnicity.

The correlation between HOME and three-year IQ was somewhat higher than the correlation between SES and IQ. The descrepancy was greatest among Blacks (.58 versus .35, $p < .05$) The difference between Blacks and whites with regards the HOME-IQ correlation was small. However, unlike the case for Blacks, for whites the HOME-IQ relation was similar to the SES-IQ relation. These findings suggest that for some ethnic groups, SES may be a rather poor proxy for environmental quality.

Our findings also revealed some small gender differences in the relationship between HOME and IQ (correlations being higher for females). In our sample, the differences in correlations did not appear to reflect any differences in means or standard deviations between females and males.

Consortium Study

Unfortunately, data from our major longitudinal study provide only limited information about ethnic differences in the pattern of relations between home environment and cognitive development and the extent to which the quality of the environment is associated with continuity and discontinuity in mental test scores for different ethnic groups. For this reason, data from the Little Rock Longitudinal Study were pooled with data from five other sites into a single large data set: (1) Craig Ramey at Chapel Hill, North Carolina; (2) Linda Siegel at Hamilton, Ontario; (3) Kathy Barnard and her colleagues at Seattle, Washington; (4) Allen Gottfried at Fullerton, California; and (5) Dale Johnson at Houston, Texas. All the cooperating investigators had ongoing longitudinal studies at their respective sites, studies that included some common measurements (SES, HOME, Bayley, and IQ) at common time points. Some adjustments of data from some of the sites had to be made in order to "fit" the united data set (e.g., creation of a common metric for SES). However, these adjustments tended to be small and within limits acceptable for scientific analysis. The combined data set included nearly 1000 children (497 whites, 161 Blacks, 262 Mexican-Americans, 11 others).

An attempt was made to "equate" ethnic groups by matching them on the basis of twelve-month total HOME scores because there was a natural confound between ethnicity and social status. One hundred twelve exact matches between Black, white, and Mexican-American groups were obtained: 19 more within one point. Due to the fact that there were no upper middle-class Mexican-Americans in the study, ethnic comparisons are limited to lower-class and lower middle-class sectors.

Results are displayed in Table 10.2. Among white children, HOME showed only low correlations with twelve-month Bayley MDI (.30 or less). However, twelve-month HOME scores showed moderate relations with twenty-four-month MDI and thirty-six-month IQ (up to .50). Parental Responsivity, Play Materials, Parental Involvement, and Variety of Stimulation showed the strongest relationships. Of the twenty-four-month HOME scores, Parental Responsivity, Acceptance of Child, Play Materials, and Parental Involvement had the most pronounced relations with mental test scores (.40 to .60). Thirty-six-month HOME scores also showed moderate relations with twenty-four-month MDI and thirty-six-month IQ.

For Black children, the pattern of HOME-developmental quotient relations was somewhat different than for whites. HOME was not related to twelve-month MDI; and there were only low correlations (.20 to .30) with twenty-four-month MDI. However, HOME scores, especially twenty-four-month and thirty-six-month HOME scores, were moderately related to thirty-six-month IQ. All the subscales except Acceptance of Child were correlated with mental test scores (.30 to .50).

The pattern of correlations for Mexican-American children was quite different from that of either white or Black children. There were no significant correlations between HOME and twelve-month MDI. There were several low to moderate (.20 to .40) correlations with twenty-four-month MDI. Parental Responsivity at twelve months, Play Materials at twelve and twenty-four months, Parental Involvement at twelve and twenty-four months, Learning Stimulation and Pride

TABLE 10.2
Correlations Between HOME Subscales and Mental Test Scores from Consortium Study

	12-mo. MDI			*24-mo. MDI*			*36-mo. IQ*		
HOME Subscales	*W*	*B*	*MA*	*W*	*B*	*MA*	*W*	*B*	*MA*
12-month									
Responsivity	.11	.11	.09	.29	.15	.30	.33	.20	.05
Acceptance	−.02	−.20	.04	.16	−.11	.00	.15	.07	.02
Organization	.09	.13	.00	.08	.07	.24	.18	.37	.05
Play Materials	.32	.22	.05	.42	.23	.41	.32	.40	.21
Involvement	.12	.25	−.02	.43	.21	.34	.30	.32	.34
Variety	.16	.14	−.07	.32	.09	−.13	.37	.14	.11
Total	.23	.17	.03	.52	.19	.41	.47	.41	.22
24-month									
Responsivity	.14	.06	.07	.48	.25	.00	.49	.33	.05
Acceptance	.11	.05	−.12	.50	−.04	.10	.62	.22	−.12
Organization	.02	.19	.10	.13	.20	.05	.14	.32	.20
Play Materials	.32	.19	−.06	.52	.30	.43	.41	.45	.21
Involvement	.14	.08	−.12	.56	.29	.23	.40	.42	.06
Variety	.13	.19	.08	.23	.24	−.11	.10	.47	.01
Total	.22	.13	−.08	.62	.28	.24	.57	.49	.14
36-month									
Learning Stimulation	.06	.17	.02	.45	.28	.14	.35	.49	.15
Pride and Affection	−.06	.16	−.04	.18	.36	−.05	.25	.53	.07
Total	.09	.25	.17	.46	.33	.05	.42	.50	.10

Note. W = white, B = black, MA = Mexican-American

and Affection at thirty-six months, were all related to twenty-four-month Bayley MDI. Strangely, only twelve-month Parental Involvement showed a correlation > .30 with thirty-six-month IQ. Play Materials at twelve and twenty-four months was marginal (.20).

The precise reasons for the observed ethnic differences in patterns of correlations between HOME and mental test scores are not clear. Part of the difference may relate to variations in both the stability and continuity of stimulation and support available to children from different ethnic groups in their homes. Black, white and Mexican-American families appear to differ in the amounts of stimulation and support they provide their children at different points in the life span. For example, Black parents seem to wait longer than white parents and Mexican-American parents to increase stimulation of development (i.e., there is discontinuity in the Play Materials and Parental Involvement scores for whites and Mexican-Americans from age one to age two years). There is also less stability in Parental Involvement between these two age points for Blacks than whites (.37 versus .53); and no stability at all for Mexican-American families (−.01). Using

Belsky's (1983) process model of parenting as a theoretical orientation, the consortium findings might suggest:

(1) Parent's individual propensities to provide stimulation and support to their children may interact with cultural styles about the timing and focus of those inputs such that there is less stability in the rank order of inputs over time for parents in some ethnic groups and less continuity in the level of inputs in some ethnic groups from one age point to another. As a result, there may be varying degrees of predictability of mental test scores in different ethnic groups.

Failure-to-Thrive Study

In addition to studies relating the home environment to children's mental development, we have also undertaken studies that have examined the relation between HOME and other aspects of development. One such study involved 23 children who had experienced growth retardation; specifically, nonorganic failure-to-thrive (NOFTT). NOFTT is a physical condition that entails instability in growth not known to have an organic basis. The 23 NOFTT children were matched to 23 normally growing children (i.e., children with reasonably stable patterns of growth) on the basis of sex, age, race, maternal education, family income, and household crowding (Casey, Bradley, and Wortham, 1984).

Partial results from the study are presented in Table 10.3. Families of NOFTT children scored significantly lower on three of the six HOME subscales: Responsivity, Acceptance, and Organization. No difference between groups was observed on the Coddington Life Events Scale.

A multiple discriminant analysis using the six HOME subscales to differentiate between NOFTT and control groups resulted in 72% correct predictions. A

TABLE 10.3
HOME Inventory and Coddington Life Events Scores for Failure-to-Thrive and Matched Controls

	NOFTT		*Control*		
	M	*SD*	*M*	*D*	*Significance*
Coddington Life Events	93.9	58.4	123.8	111.8	NS
HOME Inventory					
I. Responsivity	7.7	2.3	8.9	1.9	$p < .03$
II. Acceptance	5.1	1.6	6.2	1.1	$p < .01$
III. Organization	4.7	1.2	5.3	0.7	$p < .02$
IV. Play Materials	6.0	2.4	6.5	1.8	NS
V. Involvement	3.7	2.2	3.9	1.8	NS
VI. Variety	2.1	1.3	2.3	1.4	NS
Total HOME	29.2	7.7	33.0	6.1	$p < .04$

second discriminant function analysis was performed in an effort to better identify some of the misclassified cases. Specifically, more stringent criteria for assignment of classification were used. This analysis resulted in none of the controls being classified as NOFTT and only four of 23 NOFTT's being classified as controls. Three of the four who were misclassified had low scores on both Variety of Stimulation and Parental Involvement.

These findings were in general agreement with other studies of maltreated children. They suggest several things with respect to stability in development:

(1) The kinds of factors tapped by HOME may be related to a broad array of developmental outcomes.
(2) Low levels of specific kinds of support may cause a slow-down or disruption in the normal rate of development.
(3) Certain developmental outcomes, especially adverse developmental outcomes, may be associated with more than one set or pattern of environmental inputs. One pattern may be predominant; but there may be second or third sets that result in similar outcomes for smaller numbers of children. These findings imply that certain types of longitudinal studies may need to consider a stage-oriented approach to data analysis: first, analyses aimed at identifying the most common pattern of environment/development relations, followed by other analyses aimed at identifying secondary or tertiary patterns that apply to some misclassified or aberrant cases.

DELINEATING THE RELATION OF EARLY HOME TO 3-YEAR IQ

Advances in theory pertaining to environment/development relations in the early 1970s led us to look beyond basically simple correlations and regression models in an effort to further delineate the relation between environment and development during infancy. These efforts focused us more directly on the stability issue—or, more specifically, on the issue of consistencies in the environment and how they relate to development.

Panel Analysis

One analysis, involving the use of cross-lag panel analysis, attempted to examine "bi-directional" effects between parent and child. This technique, although the subject of deserved crititism (Rogosa, 1980), was suggestive of child as well as adult effects in the first two years of life (see Figure 10.1).

Early versus Later Environments

Next, we examined the question of whether correlations between early HOME scores and later IQ represent the unique contribution of the early environment, or

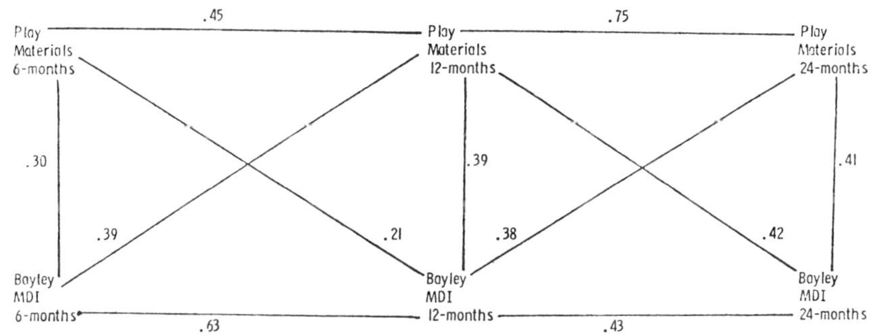

FIGURE 10.1.

whether they result from the fact that early environment tends to be highly correlated with later environment. With our limited data set, a series of partial correlations was performed to investigate the issue. Specifically, six-month HOME scores were correlated with three-year IQ, controlling for twelve-month HOMES scores. Then twelve-month HOMES scores were correlated with three-year IQ, controlling for six-month HOME scores. A similar set of partial correlations was done examining twelve-month versus twenty-four-month HOME scores. Separate analyses were done for males and females and for Blacks and whites. If the partial correlation between earlier environment and later IQ with later environment controlled is significant, it would provide evidence of the unique contribution of the early environment to mental development. By contrast, if the partial correlation is not significant, it suggests that the relation of early environment to later IQ is mediated through the relation with later environment—in essence, the stability of the home environment.

For females, no significant residual correlations between six-month HOME scores and IQ were observed with twelve-month HOME scores partialled out. By contrast, a significant partial correlation between twelve-month HOME scores and IQ was observed when twenty-four-month HOME was controlled. All twenty-four-month HOME subscales revealed significant partial correlations with IQ when twelve-month HOME scores were controlled.

For males, three of the six HOME subscales (Organization of the Environment, Provision of Appropriate Play Materials, and Parental Involvement) measured at six months showed significant partials with IQ when twelve-month HOME scores were controlled. Almost the same picture emerged when partial correlations between twelve-month HOME scores and IQ were calculated, regardless of whether six-month or twenty-four-month HOME scores were partialled out of the relation.

For Blacks, a rather inconsistent pattern of partial correlations was obtained. At six months, only Organization of the Environment showed a significant partial correlation with twelve-month HOME controlled. By comparison, correlations between three twelve-month HOME subscale scores and IQ were noted with six-month HOME scores partialled out (Acceptance of Child, Provision of

Appropriate Play Materials, and Variety of Daily Stimulation). Among the partial correlations between twelve-month HOME subscales and IQ with twenty-four-month HOME subscale scores controlled, only one subscale, Variety of Stimulation, reached significance, and that was negative ($r = -.38$). By contrast, four of the six subscales at twenty-four months showed significant partial correlations and the total HOME score had a very strong partial correlation ($r = .54$).

For whites, the pattern of partial correlations is a bit more consistent. With twelve-month HOME scores partialled out, the correlation between two subscales at six months and later IQ was significant (Provision of Appropriate Play Materials, Variety of Stimulation). A very strong partial correlation was observed between twelve-month scores on Acceptance of Child and IQ with six-month scores controlled ($r = .47$). A significant partial was also obtained for Provision of Appropriate Play Materials. Twelve-month HOME scores from two subscales (Acceptance of Child and Parental Involvement) showed significant partial correlations with twenty-four-month scores controlled. All partials except two (Acceptance of Child and Provision of Appropriate Play Materials) were significant when twenty-four-month HOME scores were correlated with three-year IQ. Interestingly, six-month total HOME scores and twenty-four-month total HOME scores both had significant partials with IQ when twelve-month HOME scores were controlled; but, the reverse was not true.

The stability of the six HOME factors varied considerably across the four subgoups (BM, WM, BF, WF). For Black males, there was littls evidence for consistency for the HOME scores across the three time-points studied. Most coefficients were in the .20–.40 range. For Black females there was little consistency from six to twelve months, slightly more from twelve to twenty-four months. The correlation between twelve-month and twenty-four-month total scores was .66. For white males, there was modest consistency across the three periods (a number of coefficients in the .30–.60 range). The greatest consistency observed was for white females. The correlation between six- and twelve-month total scores was .76; between twelve- and twenty-four-month scores the correlation was .87.

Findings from the partial correlation analyses seem to suggest the following:

(1) Stability in some aspects of the home environment appears related to mental development during the first three years of life.

(2) Mental development also seems related to the level of stimulation and support available in the environment at specific points in the life span, irrespective of the level of stimulation and support at other points in the life span.

Consortium Study

Extreme Scores

The combined data set that included data from the Little Rock Longitudinal Study plus data from the other five sites already described also made it possible to look at how interaction between environment and development contributes to intelligence. The large number of children in the consortium sample meant that there were significant numbers who had extreme scores on both early environmental and early developmental measures (either both low or both high). Tablc 10.4 displays the distribution of three-year IQ scores for three groups of children: (1) those at "double advantage" (one-year HOME and one-year Bayley scores > 1 SD above the mean); (2) those at "double disadvantage" (one-year HOME and one-year Bayley scores > 1 SD below the mean); (3) all other children. The third group had a distribution of three-year IQs that was nearly normal. Distributions of the two extreme groups were quite skewed, with means that differed substantially from the standardization group. In sum, children with extreme scores in the same direction on both early environmental and early developmental measures tended to have stable patterns of mental test scores. Stability in the rank order of mental test scores appears to be promoted not only by the general impact of extreme developmental or extreme environmental scores but by their interaction as well.

LISREL Analysis

The consortium data set also made it feasible to test more complex models of early environmental action using structural equations. The purpose of the LISREL analyses was not so much to establish whether early or later environ-

TABLE 10.4
Distribution of 36-month IQ Scores for Children who Scored in Extreme Ranges on both the HOME Inventory and Bayley Scales of Infant Development at 12 Months

	12-Month MDI and HOME Scores			
36-month IQ Standard Scores	*Both at least 1 SD below the Mean*	*No more than 1 extreme score in the same direction*	*Both at least 1 SD above the Mean*	*Total N*
−3.0 to −2.5	1	2		3
−2.5 to −2.0	1	7		8
−2.0 to −1.5	4	25		29
−1.5 to −1.0	5	41		46
−1.0 to −0.5	5	68		73
−0.5 to 0	9	115	1	125
0 to 0.5	1	95	5	101
0.5 to 1.0	1	77	5	83
1.0 to 1.5		63	7	70
1.5 to 2.0		21	7	28
2.0 to 2.5		2	1	3
2.5 to 3.0		1	1	1
3.0 to 3.5		2		2
TOTAL N	27	519	27	573

FIRST MODEL

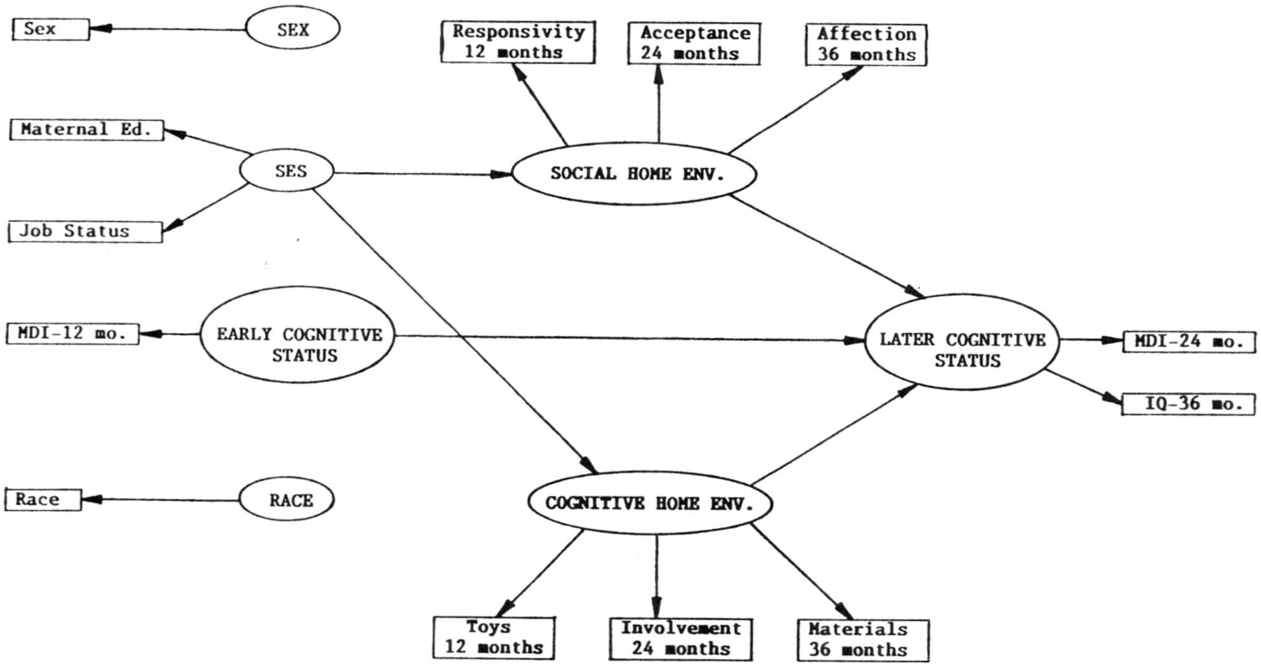

FIGURE 10.2.

FINAL MODEL

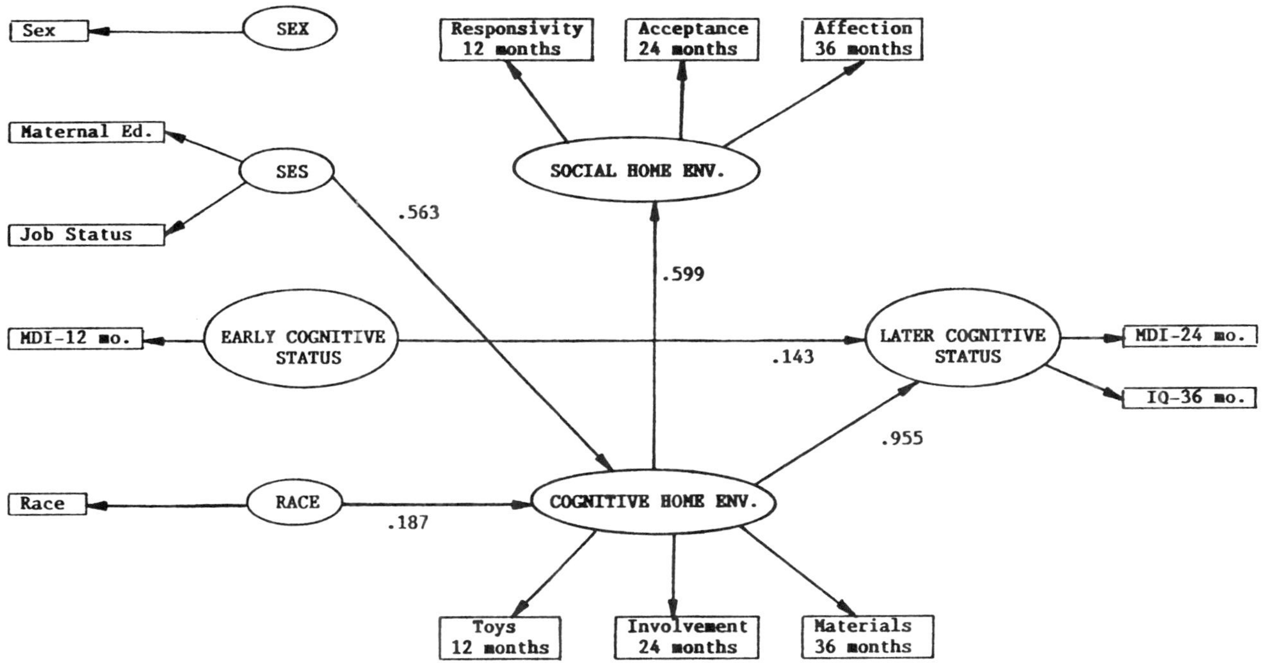

FIGURE 10.3.

mental factors contributed most to the rank order of mental test scores observed at age three or whether early developmental scores independent of environment were most responsible for later developmental status (i.e., there is stability in mental test scores independent of environmental quality), as to understand how those developmental and environmental factors interrelate in their effect on cognitive development at age three years. Specifically, Figures 10.2 and 10.3 show a first effort at using structural equations to test models of early development. The total sample was randomly split into two subsamples. One subsample was used to build a model, the second to cross-validate. We began with a simple five-variable model that included SES, twelve-month Bayley MDI, the social home environment, the cognitive home environment, and cognitive outcome score. Using both theory and information provided internal to LISREL we modified the model in a series of small steps to arrive at the final model depicted in Figure 10.3. The "goodness-of-fit index" for the initial subsample was modest (.86). On the cross-validation sample it was .83.

The results are interesting and revealing. Cognitive competence in late infancy appears most directly related to early cognitive status and the quality of the cognitive home environment. The effect of SES on cognitive performance appears mainly through the cognitive home environment. The social home environment appears to have little direct effect on cognitive performance. Instead, the social home environment seems to be influenced by the quality of the cognitive home environment; that is, parents who are interested in assisting their child's early development may tend to be more nurturant and responsive.

HOME ENVIRONMENT AND ACADEMIC ACHIEVEMENT

School Performance at Age Seven Years

As the children from the Little Rock Longitudinal Study reached 1st grade, we became interested in determining whether the rather substantial relationships observed between HOME and IQ during early childhood were mirrored in the relationship between HOME and academic performance. Only about 42 children could be obtained and tested at this point and IQ tests could not be given to the children due to lack of funds. Also of interest was whether any consistency in observed relationship was mediated through early IQ or through overall quality of the environment later in childhood.

Bivariate and partial correlational analyses were performed to determine the relation between early environmental scores and achievement test performance at the end of first grade. As Table 10.5 reveals, there were several significant correlations between twelve-month HOME scores and later achievement. In general, the partial correlations between twelve-month HOME scores and first-grade achievement with twelve-month MDI scores controlled were at essentially

TABLE 10.5
Correlations Between 12-month HOME Scores and First-Grade Achievement Controlling for 12-month MDI, 3-year IQ, 24-month HOME and 36-month HOME

	Achievement Scores		
HOME Subscales	*Reading*	*Language Arts*	*Mathematics*
Responsivity[a]	.30	.14	.01
MDI[b]	.25	.08	−.05
MDI + IQ[c]	.23	.01	−.14
Acceptance[a]	.19	.29	.31
MDI[b]	.20	.30	.33*
MDI + IQ[c]	.10	.24	.27
Organization[a]	.38*	.32*	.19
MDI[b]	.36*	.29	.17
MDI + IQ[c]	.14	.06	−.10
Toys[a]	.58**	.47**	.44**
MDI[b]	.56**	.44**	.42**
MDI + IQ[c]	.36*	.19	.17
Involvement[a]	.25	.20	.04
MDI[b]	.21	.16	.00
MDI + IQ[c]	.00	−.06	−.26
Variety[a]	.32*	.39*	.15
MDI[b]	.30	.37*	.12
MDI + IQ[c]	.32	.40*	.09
TOTAL[a]	.56**	.47**	.33*
MDI[b]	.54**	.44**	.30
MDI + IQ[c]	.34*	.20	.02
24 and 36 mo. HOME[d]	.17	.08	−.21

[a]Simple product-moment correlation between HOME score and Achievement score.

[b]Parital correlation between HOME and Achievement controlling for 12-month MDI.

[c]Parital correlation between HOME and Achievement controlling for MDI & 3-yr. IQ.

[d]Partial correlation between HOME and Achievement controlling for later HOME scores.

$*p < .05$.

$**p < .01$.

the same level as the simple bivariate correlations. However, when the effects of three-year IQ were partialed out, little significant residual relation remained between twelve-month HOME scores and first-grade achievement test scores. As Table 10.5 shows, only three significant partials were observed. Similarly, when twenty-four- and thirty-six-month HOME scores were partialled out, little residual relation remained.

TABLE 10.6
Correlations Between 24-month HOME Scores and First-Grade Achievement Scores Controlling for 12-month MDI, 3-year IQ, 24-month HOME and 36-month HOME
(N = 37)

	Achievement Scores		
HOME Subscales	*Reading*	*Language Arts*	*Mathematics*
Responsivity[a]	.30	.16	.27
MDI[b]	.27	.12	.24
MDI + IQ[c]	−.10	−.31	−.11
Acceptance[a]	.41**	.43**	.46**
MDI[b]	.39*	.42*	.45**
MDI + IQ[c]	.33*	.37*	.41*
Organization[a]	.35*	.31	.26
MDI[b]	.33*	.29	.24
MDI + IQ[c]	.13	.07	.02
Toys[a]	.55**	.53**	.49**
MDI[b]	.56**	.54**	.50**
MDI + IQ[c]	.22	.19	.16
Involvement[a]	.39*	.47**	.49**
MDI[b]	.39*	.47**	.49**
MDI + IQ[c]	.03	.16	.23
Variety[a]	.52**	.47**	.39*
MDI[b]	.51**	.45**	.37*
MDI + IQ[c]	.31	.23	.13
TOTAL[a]	.65**	.59**	.61**
MDI[b]	.64**	.58**	.60**
MDI + IQ[c]	.35*	.24	.32*
24 and 36 mo. HOME[d]	.30	.38*	.43**

[a]Simple product-moment correlation between HOME score and Achievement score.

[b]Parital correlation between HOME and Achievement controlling for 12-month MDI.

[c]Parital correlation between HOME and Achievement controlling for MDI & 3-yr. IQ.

[d]Partial correlation between HOME and Achievement controlling for later HOME scores.

*$p < .05$.

**$p < .01$.

When twenty-four-month HOME scores were correlated with first-grade achievement, many significant relations were observed. Partialing out twelve-month MDI from the twenty-four-month HOME/achievement relation revealed little change in the level of the correlation from that shown in simple correlations (see Table 10.6). However, partialing out three-year IQ resulted in little residual correlation. The subscale acceptance of the child did show a significant partial for all three achievement scores, as did the total HOME score. In the case of the twenty-four-month total HOME score, a significant residual correlation was observed when the thirty-six-month total HOME score was partialed out

School Performance at Age Eleven Years

The most recent follow-up of Little Rock children occurred when they were age eleven years. SRA achievement test scores were obtained from 42 children. In addition, the Classroom Behavior Inventory ratings were done by the teacher, and the elementary version of the HOME was administered in the home.

As Table 10.7 shows, there was general consistency in the pattern of correla-

TABLE 10.7
Correlations Between HOME Scores at 6 Months, 2 Years, 10 Years, and Classroom Behavior at Age 10 Years

HOME Scores	*Extraversion*	*Task Orientation*	*Consideration*	*Adjustment*	*SRA Composite*
6-Month					
Responsivity	−.02	.25	.38*	.17	.19
Acceptance	.10	.29*	.35*	.24	.15
Organization	−.13	.00	.02	.06	−.02
Toys	.17	.06	.22	.29*	.15
Involvement	.11	.13	.12	.31*	.15
Variety	−.19	.21	.32*	.24	−.04
Total	.07	.24	.38*	.33*	.19
2-Year					
Responsivity	.11	.01	.19	.23	.20
Acceptance	.08	−.09	−.14	.10	.07
Organization	.15	.28	.33*	.39*	.21
Toys	.01	.14	.19	.32*	.32*
Involvement	−.13	.26	.28	.22	.36*
Variety	.00	.35*	.39*	.36*	.17
Total	.05	.21	.30*	.38*	.33*
10-Year					
Responsivity	.07	.22	.29*	.45*	.22
Encourage Maturity	.13	.09	.21	.32*	.16
Climate	.21	.18	−.10	.02	.26
Materials	.12	.21	.22	.35*	.20
Act. Involvement	.01	.48*	.34*	.37*	.43*
Participation	.05	.43*	.37*	.48*	.32*
Paternal Involv.	.15	.15	.10	.09	−.01
Physical Environ.	.09	.10	.08	.36*	.16
Total	.15	.41*	.34*	.50*	.37*

*$p < .05$

tions obtained between HOME scores and SRA scores as compared to the achievement test results obtained when the children were age seven years—albeit most of the coefficients were a little lower. Correlations between six-month HOME subscale scores and fourth-grade SRA achievement test scores were not significant. A scattering of significant correlations was noted between HOME subscales and teacher's ratings of the child's school behavior (.29 to .38). Correlations between twenty-four-month HOME scores and school achievement were not much different. Provision of Appropriate Play Materials and Parental Involvement showed marginal relationships with SRA scores (.32 to .43). Organization of the Environment, Play Materials, and Variety of Stimulation showed significant correlations with school behavior (see Table 10.7).

Elementary HOME scores and SRA scores were available for 42 children. Significant correlations were observed for two HOME subscales (Provision for Active Stimulation and Family Participation in Developmentally Stimulating Experiences) and composite SRA score. Significant correlations were observed between six of the eight HOME subscales and teacher's ratings of overall school adjustment (r = .32 to .48).

Similar to what was done with the earlier achievement test and mental test scores, an attempt was made to determine whether the significant correlations obtained between HOME scores and cognitive scores were primarily a function of the fact that early HOME scores had unique predictive value for achievement at age 11 years. Using data from the Infant HOME, the Elementary HOME, fourth-grade SRA scores, and fourth-grade Classroom Behavior Inventory scores, three models of environmental action were examined with partial correlations: (1) the primacy of early experience, (2) the predominance of contemporary experience, and (3) the impact of stable environments. These analyses contribute to an understanding of how stability in environments contribute to stability in development.

The first two models were most directly testable. Evidence supporting the primacy of early experience occurred when partial correlations between Infant HOME and 11-year SRA were significant controlling for Elementary HOME and the stability of the environment between infancy and elementary school age. Evidence for the predominance of contemporary experience consisted of significant partial correlations between Elementary HOME and 11-year SRA with Infant HOME and the stability of the environment were controlled. Model 3 (the impact of stable environments) was more difficult to examine. It required that there be a reasonably high stability coefficient for the aspect of the environment being examined, plus neither of the partials for Models 1 and 2 could be significant—or at least they had to be markedly lower than the corresponding bivariate correlations.

Results provided some support for all three models. For example, the Availability of Appropriate Play Materials at age two years was significantly related to SRA scores despite the intervening environment. Variety of experience during infancy also showed some relation to later classroom behavior despite later experience, but the evidence was marginal. Model 2 (the predominance of contemporary experience) also received some support in the case of Provision for Active Involvement. Partial correlations between this subscale of the Elementary HOME and both achievement and classroom behavior were significant with early experience and the stability of experience controlled. A roughly similar picture emerged with respect to the subscale, Family Participation in Developmentally Stimulating Experiences.

Results favoring Model 3 (the importance of stability) are more equivocal. However, the environmental dimension, "parental involvement," shows some indications that stability is a significant factor. When the stability coefficient for Involvement was partialled from the relation between Parental Involvement in infancy and later behavior, all partials became nonsignificant. When the stability coefficient was partialled from the relation between Active Involvement at age ten years and contemporaneous behavior, some of the partials became nonsignificant and most others were markedly reduced in magnitude. Involvement is a dimension that McCall, Appelbaum, and Hogarty (1973) found to be related to increasing IQ profiles across the first seventeen years of life in the Fels longitudinal sample. Data from the Little Rock study suggests that the relation of Involvement to child competence is considerable at least partially because the dimension is stable and a child's experience with a supportive, encouraging—or nonsupportive—parent cumulates in its impact over time.

THE FUTURE

What is needed in the future if we are to arrive at a better understanding of the role of the home environment in developmental continuity and stability in development? First, home environment measures must be incorporated into studies that test broader ecological models of child development. In our current longitudinal study of 282 handicapped children, we have "HOME-like" measures of a child's educational as well as home environments. Also included are measures of parental attitude, parental coping, social and instrumental support, and life events. Moreover, there is need for a measure of the home environment that covers the entire childhood period. We intend to extend HOME upwards into adolescence. A prelimary form of the Adolescent HOME is already being field tested as part of our study of handicapped children. We have plans to restandardize the HOME, combining all forms into a single form applicable across childhood (like the Wechsler scales). A single form would have great value in longitudinal investigations where repeated assessments of the home environment are used. Common scales with common metrics and common meanings would greatly enhance interpretability of findings. Furthermore, there is need for a broader taxonomic scheme for the home environment.

Recently, we have begun to design a taxonomic scheme of the home environment. It is called a "Taxonomy of Environmental Functions," and is an attempt to organize information about the home environment. It grew out of frustration with most available research and theory as ways of integrating information about the relationship between home environment and child development. In brief, the taxonomy is organized around the principle that the environment performs several functions in the service of optimal growth and development: (1) sustenance, (2) stimulation, (3) support, (4) structure, and (5) surveillance. Each element of the environment can be described at two levels: its "structural properties" and its "dynamic properties." The result is a "box within a box" model of classification (see Figure 10.4), a two-stage system of taxonomic classification. The two stages are presented in Figure 10.5.

The purpose of this chapter is not to discuss the proposed taxonomic scheme in detail—indeed, the scheme needs much further work to become useful for

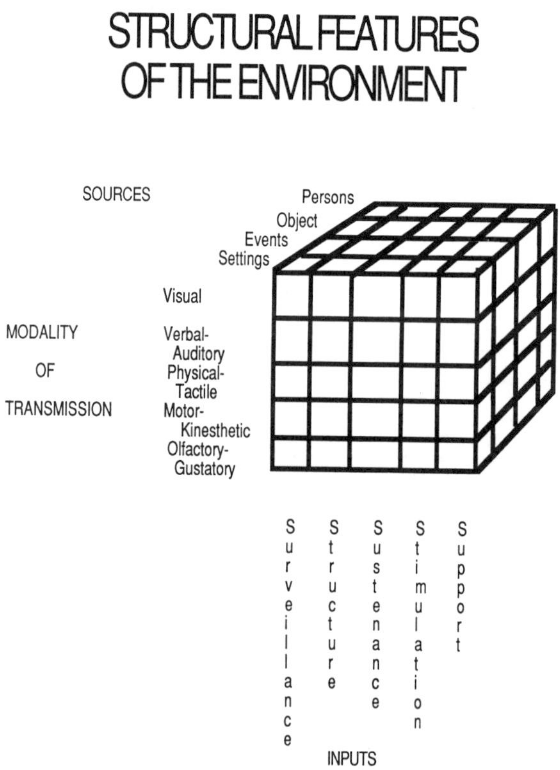

FIGURE 10.4.

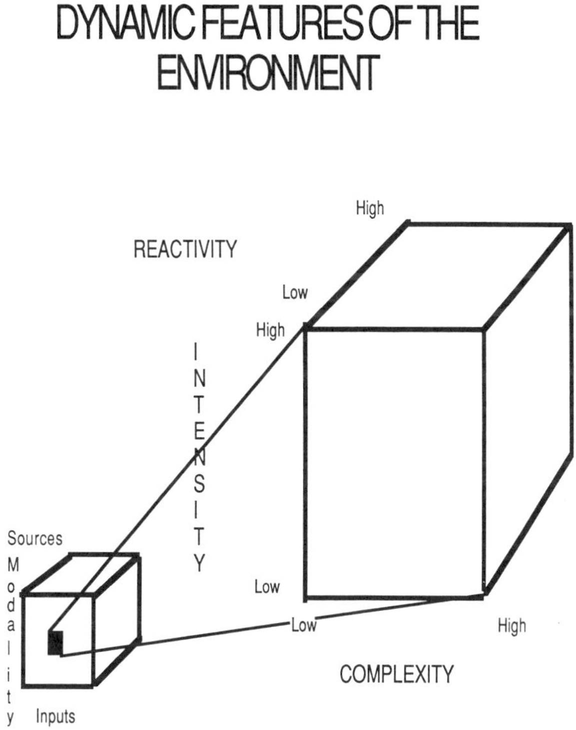

FIGURE 10.5.

research in child development. The scheme is introduced simply to illustrate the importance of a taxonomy for the home environment:

(1) It will help identify critical gaps in the current literature on environment/development relationships.
(2) It will help identify how the home environment "changes" (in "structure" or "dynamics") to support stability in development across the life span.
(3) It will help identify how "consistencies" or "inconsistencies" in the environment contribute to developmental stability and continuity.

CONCLUSIONS

The role played by home environment in higher order species is very hard to determine. Experience is so diverse, the processing of experience so elaborate, and the process of development within and across behavioral domains so diffuse and dynamic that consistent patterns of relationships between environment and development are hard to discern. Our findings indicate that stability in the environment is often alligned with stable patterns of development. They also indicate that extreme environmental conditions may tend to produce more than usually stable patterns of development if the environmental conditions mirror initial developmental status or more than usually unstable patterns of development if they are at opposite ends of the continuum of "desirability." Additionally, our findings indicate that some of the same environmental conditions associated with increases or decreases in one domain of development may also be associated with increases or decreases in other domains of development. Finally, although there is evidence that stable environments are often associated with identifiable patterns of development, there is also evidence of differences across age, gender, ethnic, and social class groups in terms of the particular relationships that apply ("specificities" of environmental effects to borrow the term of Wachs and Gruen, 1982) and evidence for the importance of particular environmental effects that seem unrelated to environmental stability.

Neither our approach to research nor any other is sufficient to reveal all the consistencies and specificities in the relationship. Sometimes an effect can occur under Condition A, sometimes under Condition B, and sometimes under Condition C. It doesn't mean that there is either no pattern or a large array of patterns—just multiple patterns. Revealing some of those multiple patterns is part of the challenge for future longitudinal studies.

REFERENCES

Bell, R. (1969). A reinterpretation of the direction of effects in studies of socialization. *Psychological Review, 75,* 81–95.

Belsky, J. (1984). The determinants of parenting: An ecological integration. *Child Development, 55,* 83–96.

Bloom, B. (1964). *Stability and change in human characteristics.* New York: Wiley.

Bradley, R., and Caldwell, B. (1976). The relationship of infants' home environment to mental test performance at fifty-four months: A follow-up study. *Child Development, 47,* 1172–1174.

Bradley, R., and Caldwell, B. (1980). Home environment, cognitive competence and IQ among males and females. *Child Development, 51,* 1140–1148.

Bradley, R., and Caldwell, B. (1982). The consistency of the home environment and its relation to child development. *International Journal of Behavioral Development, 5,* 445–465.

Bradley, R., and Caldwell, B. (1984). The relation of infants' home environments to achievement test performance in first grade: A follow-up study. *Child Development, 55,* 803–809.

Bronfenbrenner, U. (1979). *The ecology of human development.* Cambridge, MA: Harvard University Press.

Caldwell, B. (1968). On designing supplementary environments for early child development. *BAEYC Reports, 10,* 1–11.

Caldwell, B., Elardo, R., and Elardo, P. (1972). *The longitudinal observation and intervention study*. Paper presented at the Southeastern Conference on Human Development. Williamsburg, VA.

Caldwell, B., Freyer, M. Day care and early education. (1982). In B. Spodek (Ed.), *Handbook of research in early childhood education*. New York: Free Press.

Casey, P., Bradley, R., and Wortham, B. (1984). Social and non-social home environments of children with non-organic failure-to-thrive. *Pediatrics, 73,* 348–353.

Elardo, R., Bradley, R. (1981). Home Observation for Measurement of the Environment: A review of research. *Developmental Review, 1,* 113–145.

Elardo, R., Bradley, R., and Caldwell, B. (1975). The relation of infants' home environments to mental test performance from 6 to 36 months: A longitudinal analysis. *Child Development, 46,* 71–76.

Elardo, R., Bradley, R., and Caldwell, B. (1977). A longitudinal study of the relation of infants' home environment to language development at age three. *Child Development, 48,* 595–603.

Golden, M. and Birns, B. (1968). Social class and cognitive development in infancy. *Merrill-Palmer Quarterly, 14,* 139–160.

Hunt, J. (1961). *Intelligence and experience*. New York: Ronald Press.

McCall, R., Appelbaum, M., and Hogarty, P. (1973). Developmental change in mental performance. *Monographs of the Society for Research in Child Development, 38.*

Moore, T. (1968). Language and intelligence: A longitudinal study of the first eight years, Part II, Environmental correlates of mental growth. *Human Development, 11,* 1–24.

Ramey, C., and Baker-Ward, L. (1982). Psychosocial retardation and the early experience paradigm. In D. Bricker (Ed.), *Intervention with at-risk and handicapped infants* (pp. 269–290). Baltimore, MD: University Park Press.

Rogosa, D. (1980). A critique of cross-lagged correlation. *Psychological Bulletin, 88,* 245–258.

Sameroff, A., and Chandler, M. (1975). Reproductive risk and the continuum of caretaking casualty. In F. Horowitz (Ed.), *Review of child development research IV*. Chicago: University of Chicago Press.

Schaefer, E., and Aaronson, M. (1977). *Classroom Behavior Inventory*. Unpublished manuscript. University of North Carolina, Chapel Hill, NC.

Wachs, T., and Gruen, G. (1982). *Early experience and human development*. New York: Plenum.

11 Developmental Plasticity and Predictability: Consequences of Ecological Change

Craig T. Ramey
Marvin W. Lee
Margaret R. Burchinal
Frank Porter Graham Child Development Center

INTRODUCTION

A major issue in psychology has been the explanation of the processes that govern stability, continuity, and development. Various theories have been proposed to account for these phenomena. The theories typically echo the arguments heard in the traditional nature versus nurture debate. Proponents of stability and continuity often stress the constraining force of biological underpinnings or nature, whereas those who focus on plasticity point to the role of the environment or nurture in their discussion.

Closer examination of the terms *stability*, *continuity*, and *development* reveals that they are antithetical, and thus tend to confuse the debate when used in compound terms such as developmental continuity and developmental stability. Continuity is defined by *Webster's New Collegiate Dictionary* (1975) as "uninterrupted connection, persistence without essential change," whereas stability is "the strength to stand or endure or to resist change." In contrast, development is defined as "the process or result of unfolding, growth and differentiation." Therefore, development is not accurately described when using terms that do not allow for change in form or function. Instead, we suggest the use of the more neutral term *predictability* for describing the maintenance of relative standing on particular characteristics over time, and *plasticity* for describing change in characteristics over time. Predictability is the appropriate term for describing maintenance of rank because the word is not necessarily developmental in definition. Instead it refers to the ability "to declare in advance, especially to foretell on the basis of observation, experience or scientific reason." Thus predictability can denote both nondevelopmental phenomena in which absolute levels of a characteristic remain constant over time, as well as consistency in relative rank over time on a characteristic such as intelligence that becomes more differentiated. Similarly, the term *plasticity* is suggested for use in describing the ability of an individual to change in response to environmental imperatives. The definition of plasticity, "the capacity of organisms with the same genotype to vary in developmental pattern," captures this alterable aspect of development.

Developmental plasticity has been described by Nesselroade and Baltes (1979), who advocated the importance of identifying patterns of individual development. Their model emphasizes the individuality of growth and the individual's ability to respond to environmental demands. Thus, this approach allows both the form of the individual's developmental function and the parametric values of these functions to vary across individuals.

Other conceptions of the factors responsible for development have also highlighted the interaction between individuals and the conditions under which development takes place. For example, Cairns (1979) suggested that development is multiply determined by variables in the child and the child's environment and operates by general principles through which development occurs in a relatively similar manner across individuals. More recently, in his interactional model of development, Magnusson (1988, p. 55) posited that development occurs in the context of "consistent personality dispositions which direct behavior and thereby influence and determine, to some extent, the person's interaction with the environment."

Specific contextual and transactional influences on early development have been outlined in the general systems models developed by Ramey, MacPhee, and Yeates (1982) and Ramey, Bryant, Sparling, and Wasik (1984). These models, developed in the context of the creation and evaluation of early intervention programs, were designed to make more explicit the educationally alterable and unalterable factors that affect the growth and development of young children. Ramey et al. (1984), for example, used a biosocial systems model as an aid in understanding the development of low birthweight children and the environmental interventions that have been designed to enhance their development during the preschool years. Within this model interest is focused on four general levels of influence. These levels are: (1) the biological and social histories of the child and the caregivers, (2) the current status of individual family members (e.g., child and caregiver), (3) the transactions that can occur among individuals within the family and between individuals and forces outside the family, and (4) the consequent future status or potential outcomes of individual family members and their relationships.

In this model, development of young children and their families is assumed to both be a process characterized by reciprocal influence and mutual regulation, and the product of multiple biological and environmental causes. Therefore to understand development, with respect to educational intervention, it is necessary to describe how biological and social forces relate to one another within the historical present and to describe how specific alterations in various elements of the system may influence future performance of individuals. Consistent with the conceptualizations of Nesselroade and Baltes (1979), Cairns (1979), and Magnusson (1988), the model by Ramey and his colleagues implies that developmental patterns may vary across individuals as a function of differential experiences.

PREDICTABILITY AND PLASTICITY

Studies of development are usually concerned with either individual predictability or between-group plasticity. Examination of individual predictability reveals that it must also consider intraindividual variation across time. However, this is rarely done in actual practice in developmental psychology because to address this issue adequately requires large numbers of repeated observations per individual and scores in a metric that reflect the individual's actual level of development on this attribute (i.e., not relative rank such as IQ scores). High correlations are sometimes interpreted as indicative of intraindividual trait stability. Obviously, this is a potential fallacy because individual consistency, even of a very high level, does not imply any particular shape to the developmental function or even that different individuals exhibit the same pattern of development.

Between-group plasticity aggregates intraindividual differences to demonstrate changes in group performance across time. Between-group plasticity is determined by the comparison of group means and change is indicated by differences in the size of group means and/or the demonstration of different developmental functions among groups (e.g., linear, quadratic, cubic, etc.).

Examination of individual predictability and between-group plasticity rely on different analysis techniques and, as a result, different and apparently contradictory fundamental conclusions are frequently drawn regarding the malleability of development. The use of correlations in the examination of individual predictability of differences in intellectual development has sometimes led to conclusions of stability with an emphasis on heredity as a major determinant. Meanwhile, studies that focus on the ability of early intervention to change group levels of intellectual development and, thereby, demonstrate developmental plasticity often ignore the potential simultaneous existence of a high level of individual predictability across time.

Researchers have usually treated individual predictability and between-group plasticity as mutually exclusive. However, closer examination of the issues of development may provide a reconciliation of these two areas of research. A comprehensive study of development must be concerned with both whether the average developmental functions of two or more groups differ across time and whether the individual differences within the groups demonstrate individual predictability (i.e., whether relative ranks within the group are maintained).

One question that arises with respect to early education intervention programs is whether alterations in developmental functions of a trait such as intelligence also produce changes in the stability of individual predictability or in the relative importance of the familial determinants of individual differences. Such programs are frequently designed to produce average group gains in IQ for treated children relative to controls or, in other words, to alter the developmental function. However, intervention programs may also alter the stability or relative contribution of determinants of individual differences in IQ.

In the remainder of this chapter we examine the data from one such longitudinal program designed to test the efficacy of educational intervention to alter the intellectual development of disadvantaged children. That program is known as the Carolina Early Intervention Program, and it is concerned with the developmental functioning of young children at risk for developmental problems allegedly due to the poor economic and/or social situations of their families.

THE CAROLINA EARLY INTERVENTION PROGRAM

Participants

Between 1972 and 1980, six cohorts of high-risk children were recruited during the last trimester of their mother's pregnancy and randomly assigned to a treatment or control group. Randomization, within the limitations of sampling theory, enhances the initial statistical equivalence of groups (i.e., that pretreatment differences between the groups reflect only chance variation), thus potentially allowing subsequently observed group differences to be plausibly attributed to the treatment program. For the first four cohorts (known as the Abecedarian Project), the children were randomly assigned to a group that received a systematic educational daycare program beginning by three months of age or to a control group that received no systematic educational program. The same selection criteria were used for the fifth and sixth cohorts (known as Project CARE), but the children were randomly assigned to one of three conditions: (1) a systematic center-based educational program beginning before three months of age, (2) a home-based intervention program beginning before three months of age, or (3) a control group that received no systematic educational program. In this chapter, we do not discuss the home-based only intervention condition. Instead, we concentrate on the findings that compare the children who attended the Frank Porter Graham Child Development Center and their control counterparts. This is the sample that we refer to as the Carolina Early Intervention Program. Seventy children were enrolled in the intervention program and 76 in the control group.

Throughout this project, retention has been high. At fifty-four months of age, 87% of intervention children were activity enrolled (n = 61) and 89% of controls (n = 68).

Table 11.1 contains a summary of entry characteristics of the children's families. In general, the mothers tended to be young, Black, poor, single, and with less than a high-school education. Consistent with epidemiological data from Ramey, Stedman, Borders-Patterson, and Mengel (1978) their children were at high-risk for delayed intellectual development and poor readiness for public school.

Components of the Program

The Carolina Early Intervention Program is a multidisciplinary extra-familial support system designed to prevent intellectual underdevelopment in high-risk children. The program is composed of both intervention modalities and intervention content areas. The modalities of intervention are a developmental daycare beginning between six and twelve weeks of age, a toy lending library, a home visiting program, and parent group meetings. The program content is composed of a specific child-oriented curriculum, a parent problem-solving curriculum, and a somewhat informal network of family support resources. The program has been described more fully elsewhere (Ramey, Bryant, Campbell, Sparling, & Wasik, 1988) and is presented here only briefly.

The modalities of the intervention were conceptualized to enhance the child's intellectual functioning in the following ways: Developmental daycare was hypothesized to directly enhance the child's development by providing systematic and daily exposure to professional caregivers who were affectionate, involved, responsive, nonpunitive and who, through a planned environment and curricu-

TABLE 11.1
Entry Characteristics for Carolina Early Intervention Program Mothers and Infants with Complete Intellectual Data

	Control (N = 68)		*Intervention* (N = 61)	
	M	*sd*	*M*	*sd*
Maternal Characteristics				
WAIS Full Scale IQ	84.9	10.4	85.2	12.3
Age	20.9	5.7	20.0	4.2
Last Grade Completed	10.4	1.8	10.6	1.7
Percent Married	22		20	
Child Characteristics				
Percent Black	94		97	
Percent Female	49		43	

lum, provided a set of experiences that were safe, healthful, organized, varied, and developmentally appropriate. In addition, the toy lending library was hypothesized to increase both material and informational supports to the family and to facilitate positive social interactions with family caregivers. Also the home visiting program provided childrearing information and family supports that supposedly enhanced development by encouraging appropriate expectations and abilities of mothers and, perhaps, other family members. And finally, the Parent Group Program was hypothesized to increase the social supports available to families by linking parents who were facing similar issues with each other and with resource persons from the community. In summary, the CEIP was a multifaceted and intensive effort designed to affect positively some allegedly causal factors and thereby directly affect the intellectual development of these high-risk children.

TABLE 11.2
Themes and Skill Areas in the Carolina Early Intervention Program Education Curriculum

Broad Themes	*Specific Skill Area*
Cognitive and Fine Motor	1. Awareness of object permanence
	2. Awareness of positions in space
	3. Puzzle skills
	4. Sorting skills and
	5. Matching skills
	6. Awareness of cause and effect
	7. Sensory awareness
Social and Self	8. Awareness of self image
	9. Skills in sharing with an adult
	10. Skills in interacting with other children
	11. Skills in imitating gestures
	12. Self-help skills
	13. Awareness of needs and feelings
Motor	14. Rhythm skills
	15. Balance skills
	16. Skills in throwing/pushing/pulling
Language	17. Dialogue skills
	18. Skills in using books
	19. Skills in talking about picture-object pairs
	20. Skills in talking about concept pictures
	21. Skills in talking about action pictures
	22. Skills in talking about object pictures
	23. Skills in talking about relationship pictures

Program Content

Our infant and child curricula were devised by Sparling and Lewis (1979, 1981, 1984, 1985) and have had certain characteristics in common. They have been (1) divided into gamelike episodes, (2) applied in individualized and recurring cycles, and (3) integrated into all aspects of the child's day. The learning activities were developed to cover a full spectrum of developmental skill areas. The areas, organized into four broad themes, are presented in Table 11.2.

In summary, the child curriculum as it functioned in our intervention program might be described as: cyclic, gamelike, integral to daily activities of living, and covering 23 child development areas under four broad developmental categories.

INTELLECTUAL RESULTS AND THE ISSUES OF PREDICTABILITY AND PLASTICITY

The Carolina Early Intervention Program is a research-oriented endeavor. The main question concerns the efficacy of early intervention to prevent developmental problems. More specifically, we have focused on the efficacy of the intervention program to promote intellectual performance and to prevent intellectual delays and/or deficits.

We believe that standardized measures of intellectual functioning are a good way to determine the summative level of risk expressed in the treatment and control samples. Intellectual functioning is currently best assessed normatively using standardized IQ tests, the definitive diagnostic criteria of DSMIII for clinical level retardation.

In the Carolina Early Intervention Program standardized developmental tests have been administered at six-month intervals. The specific tests (e.g., Bayley Scales of Infant Development, McCarthy Scales of Children's Abilities, and Stanford-Binet Intelligence Scale) were chosen primarily on the basis of their psychometric adequacy.

The issues of individual predictability and between-group plasticity were examined empirically within the longitudinal samples to determine their relationship. Repeated measures of preschool cognitive performance were analyzed using three approaches to studying these developmental issues. First, the average preschool cognitive scores of the experimental and control children were compared to determine if the treatment produced evidence for intellectual plasticity. Moreover, correlations were computed to address the issue of predictability. And finally, developmental functions based on indices of both predictability and change were identified that describe different longitudinal patterns of preschool cognitive development within this sample.

Between-Group Plasticity

The eight cognitive scores collected during the preschool period were submitted to a repeated-measures multivariate analysis of variance (MANOVA) to identify intervention effects on preschool cognitive development. The groups differed significantly during the preschool period, $F(8,120) = 6.08$, $p < .0001$. Table 11.3 displays the means and standard deviations of the two groups at the eight assessment ages as well as the statistical comparisons of means at each age. These comparisons reveal that the intervention group significantly outscored the control group at each age, with the difference between the groups increasing across time. Because children were randomly assigned to a group, these results are consistent with the hypothesis that the intervention positively affected the cognitive development of these disadvantaged children. Thus, these data demonstrate intellectual plasticity due to environmental factors.

Individual Predictability

In contrast, these preschool cognitive scores can also be used to demonstrate developmental predictability. The across-time correlations among the eight as-

TABLE 11.3
Comparisons of Preschool Cognitive Scores by Group

Test		*Intervention*	*Control*	*F(1,127)*	*p*
Bayley					
MDI @ 6m	*M*	107.3	101.7	4.6	.03
	sd	15.3	14.1		
MDI @12m	*M*	112.8	105.8	7.2	.009
	sd	14.7	15.1		
MDI @18m	*M*	110.1	94.0	39.7	.0001
	sd	14.6	14.3		
Stanford-Binet					
IQ @24m	*M*	97.2	86.2	32.2	.0001
	sd	11.6	10.3		
IQ @36m	*M*	101.9	87.2	38.2	.0001
	sd	12.5	14.1		
McCarthy					
GCI @42m	*M*	103.0	94.4	17.5	.0001
	sd	10.2	12.7		
Stanford-Binet					
IQ @48m	*M*	101.1	91.0	21.7	.0001
	sd	11.0	13.4		
McCarthy					
GCI @54m	*M*	101.4	92.7	17.1	.0001
	sd	10.1	13.4		

TABLE 11.4
Across Time Correlations of Preschool Cognitive Scores
Within-Group Correlations

	Intervention							
	MDI6	*MDI12*	*MDI18*	*SB24*	*SB36*	*GCI42*	*SB48*	*GCI54*
Control								
MDI6	—	.49	.30	.25	.27	.18[a]	.13[a]	.16[a]
MDI12	.54	—	.63	.45	.47	.36	.29	.27
MDI18	.24	.49	—	.72	.59	.47	.35	.38
SB24	.45	.51	.63	—	.64	.58	.58	.44
SB36	.31	.30	.63	.69	—	.69	.66	.62
GCI42	.34	.37	.56	.68	.67	—	.63	.65
SB48	.36	.30	.58	.72	.76	.81	—	.61
GCI54	.26	.28	.52	.63	.65	.80	.82	—
Pooled Within-Group Correlations								
MDI6	—	.52	.27	.35	.29	.27	.26	.21
MDI12		—	.56	.48	.37	.36	.29	.27
MDI18			—	.67	.61	.52	.48	.46
SB24				—	.66	.62	.65	.54
SB36					—	.68	.72	.64
GCI42						—	.74	.75
SB48							—	.74
GCI54								—

[a]All correlations except these are significant at $p < .05$.

sessments of cognitive development were computed to index the predictability of the cognitive development of these children (see Table 11.4 for the correlation matrices of the two groups). Pooled within-treatment correlations were computed. Before pooling the correlations across groups, the two groups' estimated variances and covariances of the eight cognitive measure were compared simultaneously. The two groups did not significantly differ on the variances or covariances of these cognitive scores, chi-square = 36.25, $df = 36$, $p = .46$. The pooled within-group correlations, reported in Table 11.4, display the expected longitudinal characteristics of intellectual scores; that is, a simplex pattern with increased predictability as has been observed in most other studies of intellectual development across the preschool period. Thus, these correlations support the argument that increasing individual predictability characterizes the cognitive development of these disadvantaged children. Further evidence for individual predictability was observed when the correlations between maternal IQ and the child's preschool cognitive scores were examined. The resulting pattern of increasing associations after infancy was as expected. (see Table 11.5).

TABLE 11.5
Correlations of Maternal and Child Preschool Cognitive Scores

	MDI6	*MDI12*	*MDI18*	*SB24*	*SB36*	*GCI42*	*SB48*	*GCI54*
Intervention Maternal IQ	.12	.10	.08	.25*	.26*	.40**	.50***	.43***
Control Maternal IQ	.16	.17	.35**	.32**	.37**	.32**	.44**	.43***
Pooled Maternal IQ	.14	.13	.21*	.29**	.31***	.35***	.46***	.42***

*$p < .05$
**$p < .01$
***$p < .001$

The conclusions regarding individual predictability and between-group plasticity of intellectual development are not, however, contradictory. Methodologically, they simply reflect the results of different analysis methods. The first relied on comparisons of group level, whereas the second used correlations to assess individual differences. It is not surprising that the two methods support different conclusions because the correlations reflect the degree of covariance between the cognitive measures after removing the effect of the mean and variance of each measure. Thus, it appears that environmental factors such as early intervention daycare may change the level of cognitive performance on the average, but do not necessarily change the spread or scatter or the predictability of these scores across time.

Estimating Developmental Functions

An analysis was performed to identify types of growth curves that characterize the cognitive development of these children. A cluster analysis was performed on the children's eight preschool intellectual scores. These scores were standardized across groups to a mean of 0 and a standard deviation of 1. Thus, standardization eliminated test effects and the across-time variation of the tests around the group mean on the shape of the estimated developmental functions. The cluster analysis was based on both the child's mean level of preschool cognitive performance and on across-time patterns of variation. Children were assigned to clusters in a manner that minimized the sum of the squared distance between the average profile of a cluster and the individual profiles of the children comprising that cluster (i.e., Ward's, 1963 method of clustering was employed). The four-cluster solution was selected because it met two criteria. It accounted for the most variance (56%) with the fewest clusters among the solutions in which clusters all contained more than five children.

The developmental functions associated with these clusters were then compared to determine how the functions differed. A repeated-measures MANOVA was performed in which coefficients of polynomial growth curves were estimated for each cluster and compared across clusters. These coefficients reflect the degree to which the particular cluster's average performance across time differed from the sample's mean (the mean level), and the extent to which linear, quadratic, and cubic trends described that pattern of change that was observed within that cluster. The coefficients differed significantly among clusters, as one would expect because the cluster analysis grouped children such that the clusters

TABLE 11.6
Indices of Preschool Cognitive Developmental Functions for the Four Clusters

		Cluster			
		Above Average Stable	*Below Average Slowly Increasing*	*Above Average Increasing*	*Below Average Declining*
		1 (n = 59)	2 (n = 38)	3 (n = 18)	4 (n = 14)
Within Sample-Standardized Scores					
MDI6	*M*	0.46	−0.75	0.46	−0.49
	sd	(0.84)	(0.85)	(0.97)	(0.51)
MDI12	*M*	0.25	−0.73	1.05	−0.43
	sd	(0.66)	(1.05)	(0.55)	(0.91)
MDI18	*M*	0.24	−0.64	1.41	−1.12
	sd	(0.66)	(0.64)	(0.56)	(0.88)
SB24	*M*	0.28	−0.71	1.46	−1.16
	sd	(0.62)	(0.56)	(0.83)	(0.31)
SB36	*M*	0.31	−0.57	1.40	−1.55
	sd	(0.58)	(0.61)	(0.52)	(0.52)
GCI42	*M*	0.21	−0.32	1.33	−1.75
	sd	(0.64)	(0.64)	(0.52)	(0.52)
SB48	*M*	0.23	−0.35	1.39	−1.80
	sd	(0.55)	(0.53)	(0.74)	(0.43)
GCI54	*M*	0.26	−0.33	1.20	−1.74
	sd	(0.64)	(0.66)	(0.38)	(0.84)
Polynomial Coefficients					
Mean Level	*M*	0.79***	−1.55***	3.43***	−3.55***
	sd	(0.12)	(0.15)	(0.22)	(0.25)
Linear Trend	*M*	−0.12	0.47**	0.48*	−1.39***
	sd	(0.12)	(0.15)	(0.21)	(0.24)
Quadratic	*M*	0.09	0.05	−0.65***	0.33
	sd	(0.09)	(0.11)	(0.16)	(0.19)
Cubic	*M*	−0.08	−0.07	0.30*	0.12
	sd	(0.08)	(0.10)	(0.15)	(0.16)

*$p < .05$
**$p < .01$
***$p < .001$

showed maximally different developmental patterns. Table 11.6 displays the clusters' average level of cognitive performance, linear trend across time, quadratic change over time, and cubic trend development. Figure 11.1 shows these estimated developmental functions using the standardized scores.

These clusters reflect very different patterns of preschool cognitive development. The first and third clusters had mean scores that were above the entire sample's mean at all assessment occasions. The first cluster's developmental function was characterized by stable, slightly above average performance across time. The cluster was named "ABOVE AVERAGE, STABLE" to describe this trend. The third cluster was called "ABOVE AVERAGE, INCREASING" because its developmental function reflected positive linear, quadratic, and cubic growth. On the average, these children were scoring more than a standard deviation above the entire sample's mean on all postinfancy assessments. Conversely, the developmental functions of clusters 2 and 4 reflected cognitive performances that were below the entire sample's mean on all assessment occasions. Cluster 2 was named "BELOW AVERAGE, SLOWLY INCREASING" because it was characterized by a developmental function that was gradually linearly increasing across the preschool period. The function of cluster 4, named "BELOW AVERAGE, DECLINING", showed marked linear decline.

The developmental functions of the four clusters were examined descriptively with the original scores. Table 11.7 lists group means. These functions describe development in terms of the actual assessment. They reflect the differences among the clusters as well as other factors that, in general, may be influencial on

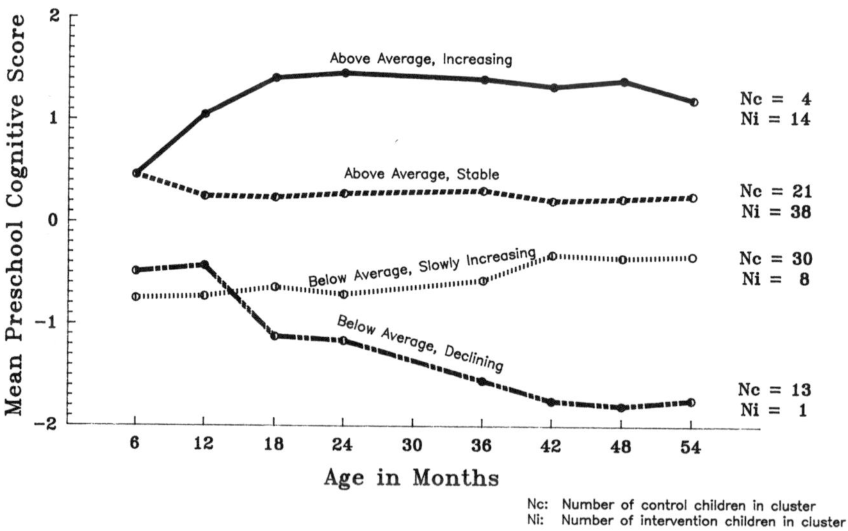

FIGURE 11.1. Mean standardized preschool cognitive scores for the four clusters of the Carolina Early Intervention Program.

TABLE 11.7
Preschool Cognitive Scores for the Four Clusters

		Cluster			
		Above Average Stable 1 (n = 59)	*Below Average Slowly Increasing* 2 (n = 38)	*Above Average Increasing* 3 (n = 18)	*Below Average Declining* 4 (n = 14)
MDI6	*M*	111.3	93.1	111.3	97.0
	sd	(12.7)	(12.7)	(14.6)	(7.7)
MDI12	*M*	112.9	98.0	125.1	102.6
	sd	(10.0)	(16.0)	(8.3)	(13.8)
MDI18	*M*	105.6	91.1	124.9	83.2
	sd	(10.9)	(10.5)	(9.2)	(14.2)
SB24	*M*	94.3	82.6	108.2	77.3
	sd	(7.3)	(6.7)	(9.8)	(3.7)
SB36	*M*	98.9	85.6	115.4	70.7
	sd	(8.8)	(9.3)	(7.8)	(7.9)
GCI42	*M*	101.1	94.6	114.9	76.9
	sd	(7.8)	(7.9)	(6.5)	(6.4)
SB48	*M*	98.8	91.2	114.3	71.9
	sd	(7.3)	(7.1)	(10.0)	(5.7)
GCI54	*M*	100.1	92.6	112.0	74.6
	sd	(8.1)	(8.4)	(4.9)	(10.6)

the cognitive development of these children. For example, the marked decline during late infancy may mirror the general trend of decreases associated with tests becoming more verbal that is typically observed in poverty children.

The last issue examined was whether measures of the child's biosocial ecology predicted cluster membership. A log-linear model was used to determine if the cluster membership could be predicted from the mother's IQ, a measure of the quality of the home environment (Caldwell and Bradley, 1978), and treatment condition. The quality of the home was represented by the mean of scores on the Home Observation for the Measurement of the Environment (HOME) from six, eighteen, thirty, forty-two, and fifty-four months of age, standardized to a mean of 0 and a standard deviation of 1. A log-linear analysis was used because the model included both a categorical predictor (treatment) and a categorical outcome (cluster membership). All interactions were dropped from the model. The resulting model indicated that cluster membership was significantly related to maternal IQ (chi-square = 8.15, df = 3, p = .04), to HOME (chi-square = 15.49, df = 3, p = .001), and to treatment (chi-square = 27.97, df = 3, $p < .0001$).

All three predictors were significant, thus the association between the clusters and each predictor was tested to identify which clusters differed on each predictor. All pairwise comparisons were performed when the univariate test indicated that the clusters differed significantly on a given predictor. Table 11.8 shows the estimated developmental functions (i.e., mean cognitive scores for each cluster and the average score on the three predictors for the four clusters as well as results of group comparisons).

A log-linear analysis revealed that the proportion of children who received the intervention was significantly greater in the clusters whose developmental functions were always above the mean (i.e., in the ABOVE AVERAGE, STABLE and the ABOVE AVERAGE, INCREASING clusters) than in the clusters whose functions were always below the mean (i.e., in the BELOW AVERAGE, SLOWLY INCREASING and BELOW AVERAGE, DECLINING clusters). In other words, all pairwise comparisons of either ABOVE AVERAGE cluster with the BELOW AVERAGE clusters were significant. However, neither the comparison of the two ABOVE AVERAGE clusters nor the comparison of the two BELOW AVERAGE clusters was significant.

Analyses of variance were performed on the two continuous predictors. The four clusters differed significantly on maternal IQ, $F(3,127) = 6.40$, $p = .0005$. Although the two clusters with relatively stable developmental functions (i.e., the ABOVE AVERAGE, STABLE and the BELOW AVERAGE, SLOWLY INCREASING clusters) did not significantly differ on mean maternal IQ, all other pairwise comparisons were significant. The ABOVE AVERAGE, INCREASING cluster had mothers with higher IQ scores on the average, whereas the BELOW AVERAGE, DECLINING cluster had mothers who performed significantly less well on IQ tests.

A similar pattern was observed in the analysis of the HOME mean scores. The four clusters differed significantly on the HOME, $F(3,127) = 7.92$, $p < .0001$. The two clusters with relatively stable developmental functions did not significantly differ; the ABOVE AVERAGE, STABLE and the BELOW AVERAGE, SLOWLY INCREASING clusters did not significantly differ on the HOME mean score. The cluster with a markedly increasing developmental function, the ABOVE AVERAGE, INCREASING cluster, showed significantly higher aver-

TABLE 11.8a
Source Table: Predicting Cluster Membership from Maternal IQ, HOME, and Treatment Group

Variable	*df*	*F*	*Contrasts*
Treatment	3	26.72[a]	(1 & 3) > (2 & 4)
HOME	3,125	10.56	3 > (1, 2, 4)
			(1 & 3) > 4
Maternal IQ	3,125	6.40	3 > (1 & 2) > 4

[a]Test is chi-square rather than *F*.

TABLE 11.8B
Means by Cluster on the Predictors

		Cluster			
		Above Average Stable 1 (*n* = 59)	*Below Average Slowly Increasing* 2 (*n* = 38)	*Above Average Increasing* 3 (*n* = 18)	*Below Average Declining* 4 (*n* = 14)
Treatment % Intervention		64%	21%	78%	7%
Maternal IQ	*M*	84.9	84.2	93.3	76.9
	sd	(11.4)	(8.0)	(12.5)	(11.0)
HOME	*M*	0.02	−0.25	0.76	−0.45
	sd	(0.70)	(0.84)	(0.38)	(0.65)

age HOME scores than all other clusters. The cluster with a decreasing developmental function had significantly lower average HOME scores than two of the three other clusters. In other words, the BELOW AVERAGE, DECLINING cluster's mean HOME score was significantly lower than the mean in either cluster with above-average levels of cognitive performance, but not than the other cluster with below-average mean levels of cognitive performance.

In summary, the developmental functions as identified by the cluster analysis varied on interesting aspects of the child's environment. Children in clusters characterized by cognitive developmental functions with above-average mean levels were most likely to have received the early intervention. In addition, the children whose cluster's cognitive functions showed either marked increases or decreases over time tended to differ from the other clusters on both HOME scores and maternal IQ. Children in the clusters characterized by marked increases in cognitive performance were most likely to have received the intervention, to have had mothers with significantly higher IQs, as well as home environments that, on the average, were rated as more stimulating. Children in clusters characterized by marked decreases in cognitive performance during the preschool years were least likely to have received the intervention, had mothers whose IQs tended to be lower, and had significantly lower average HOME scores.

CONCLUSION

These results reveal that altering the ecology of disadvantaged children through educational intervention changed the level of their cognitive performance on the average, but did not change the across time predictability of their intellectual development. Indeed, individual predictability or stability in the relative ranks of individuals was demonstrated, while change in group patterns or different developmental functions were observed as a product of environmental intervention, maternal IQ, and the quality of the home. Therefore, the phenomenon of a high level of individual predictability and between-group plasticity are not mutually exclusive. Furthermore, conclusions about the validity of the models of individual predictability and between-group plasticity can be made only when the appropriate techniques are applied (i.e., correlations do not test hypotheses of plasticity, and comparisons of group means do not provide evidence of predictability). In this longitudinal study one can identify both individual predictability and between-group plasticity when the same characteristic is examined across time in two separate analyses. Evidence for the existence of both individual predictability and between-group plasticity is also demonstrated in an examination of the relation between maternal IQ and child outcomes. Predictability across time is shown by the high correlation between these two variables in spite of the strong environmental impact on children's cognitive development that is demonstrated in the cluster analysis. This result also suggests that educational daycare can increase high-risk children's cognitive development independent of factors such as maternal IQ.

Various types of cognitive growth characterized the development of these children. The identified growth curves were shown to be associated with relevant aspects of the biosocial ecology of the children. Children showing markedly increasing developmental functions tended to have the most facilitative environments: early intervention, mothers with higher IQs, and more stimulating home environments.

Therefore we interpret these findings as supportive of the positions of Cairns (1979), Magnusson (1988), and Nesselroade and Baltes (1979) that highlight the plasticity of development, and characterize it as the interaction between the individual and the environment that produces meaningful developmental trajectories. These results also suggest the potential value of early screening for individual and environmental characteristics that may place children at risk for academic failure. Furthermore, they demonstrate the efficacy of early educational intervention in preventing the usually observed decline in high-risk children's intellectual development.

ACKNOWLEDGMENTS

This research has been supported by grants from the National Institute of Child Health and Human Development, the U.S. Department of Education, the Administration for Children, Youth, and Families, the Spencer Foundation, the Carnegie Foundation, the Department of Human Resources of the State of North

Carolina, and the Department of Social Services of Orange County, North Carolina. We wish to thank Marie Butts and Laura Caldwell for preparing the manuscript.

REFERENCES

Bayley, N. (1969). *Bayley scales of infant development.* New York: The Psychological Corporation.

Cairns, R. B. (1979). *Social development: The origins and plasticity of interchanges.* San Francisco: W. H. Freeman.

Caldwell, B. M., and Bradley, R. H. (1978). *Manual for the home observation for measurement of the environment.* Little Rock: University of Arkansas.

Magnusson, D. (1988). *Individual development from an interactional perspective: A longitudinal study.* Hillsdale, NJ: Lawrence Erlbaum Associates.

McCarthy, D. (1972). *McCarthy Scales of Children's Abilities.* New York: Psychological Corporation.

Nesselroade, J. R., and Baltes, P. B. (1979). *Longitudinal research in the study of behavior and development.* New York: Academic Press.

Ramey, C. T., Bryant, D. M., Campbell, F. A., J. J. Sparling, and Wasik, B. H. (1988). Early intervention for high-risk children: The Carolina Early Intervention Program. In R. Price (Ed.), *Fourteen ounces of Prevention* (pp. 32–43). American Psychological Association.

Ramey, C. T., Bryant, D. M., Sparling, J. J., and Wasik, B. H. (1984). A Biosocial systems perspective on environmental interventions for low birth weight infants. *Clinical Obstetrics and Gynecology, 27,* 672–692.

Ramey, C. T., MacPhee, D., and Yeates, K. O. (1982). Preventing developmental retardation: A general systems model. In L. A. Bond and J. M. Joffe (Eds.), *Facilitating infant and early childhood development* (pp. 343–401). Hanover, NH: University Press of New England.

Ramey, C. T., Stedman, D. J., Borders-Patterson, A., and Mengel, W. (1978). Predicting school failure from information available at birth. *American Journal of Mental Deficiency, 82.*

Sparling, J., and Lewis, I. (1979). *Learning games for the first three years: A guide to parent-child play.* New York: Walker.

Sparling, J., and Lewis, I. (1981). *Learning games for the first three years: A program for parent/center partnership.* New York: Walker Education Book Corporation.

Sparling, J., and Lewis, I. (1984). *Learning games for threes and fours: A guide to adult and child play.* New York: Walker and Company.

Sparling, J., and Lewis, I. (1985). *Partners for learning.* Winston-Salem, NC: Kaplan Press.

Terman, L. M., and Merrill, M. Q. (1972). *Stanford-Binet Intelligence Scale: 1972 Norms Edition.* Boston: Houghton Mifflin.

Ward, J. (1963). Hierarchical grouping to optimize an objective function. *Journal of the American Statistical Association, 58,* 236–244.

Webster's New Collegiate Dictionary. (1975). Springfield, MA: G & C Merriam Co..

12 Can Early Interaction Predict? How and How Much?

Roger Bakeman
Lauren B. Adamson
Josephine V. Brown
Melvin Eldridge
Georgia State University

INTRODUCTION

If a praying mantis possessed the mentality of a human, or alternatively, if human minds were encased in bodies like those possessed by a praying mantis, what sort of developmental psychology would these creatures develop? Would they devote entire conferences to questions of continuity of structure and function? Would they even be concerned with stability of individual differences? Given the dramatic physical changes insects experience, questions of continuity might seem inconsequential and notions of stability implausible.

We do know the following: For whatever reason—human bodies experienced as relatively continuous or humanlike minds seeking to impose order—continuity and stability have remained central themes and enduring concerns of developmental psychologists in modern times (Kagan, 1984). The present volume is an expression of that concern. A major purpose is to ask whether data from any of a variety of different domains predict developmental outcome, and to what extent, and then to reflect on what implications these results might have for questions of developmental process.

The purpose of this chapter is necessarily much narrower. We are primarily concerned here with questions about the prediction of individual differences in social and cognitive competence based on information about prior variations in only one domain—mother-infant interaction during the first months of life. The questions we ask are mainly about questions of predictability, defining predictability in a Pearson product-moment correlational sense.

Moreover, we focus primarily on the results of one study conducted in the

1970s by Bakeman and Brown (1980). This work was frankly exploratory. What we would like to do here is take advantage of the distance almost a decade can give and comment on both its promising and problematic aspects. Our intent is to focus attention on some basic issues that we think anyone considering studies of the effects of early social interaction on subsequent behavioral development should address.

The comments we make are of two general types. First, conceptual matters involved in attempting to forecast children's later levels of social and cognitive functioning from a viewing of early interactions are considered. Included are concerns about how the process of interaction during different periods of development is understood and how the possible mechanisms by which it might conceivably work its effects. In addition, more technical matters, such as the strength of the effects detected and the number of infants studied, are addressed.

BAKEMAN AND BROWN REVISITED

As a prelude to our revisitation of the Bakeman and Brown study, it may be helpful to review its major features. Twenty-one relatively healthy preterm and 22 fullterm infants, all born in circumstances regarded as disadvantaged, were followed from birth through age 4 years. Infants were observed interacting with their mothers just before hospital discharge and then one and three months thereafter. Preterm infants averaged 32 weeks gestational age at birth and spent about four weeks in the hospital. Thus at the time of these observation sessions the preterm infants were on average four weeks older chronologically than the full-term infants, but four weeks younger conceptionally.

The observation sessions included a feeding and lasted about 30 minutes. During that time, trained observers electronically recorded occurrences and durations for a relatively large number of ethologically inspired behavioral codes such as "mother looks at infant," and "infant burps." Various summary scores were derived from these behavioral records. The intent was to devise measures that would transcend frequencies for particular codes and thus the "behavior dialogic" measures included; for example, the proportion of time mothers and infants acted at the same time and an information–theory-based measure of how variable the interaction was overall. The observers also rated both the mothers' and the infants' responsiveness. Then, when the infants were nine months old and again when they were twenty months old, the mothers' verbal responsiveness was assessed with the HOME scale.

Both cognitive and social outcomes were assessed. Cognitive development was gauged with the Bayley MDI at twelve and twenty-four months and with the Stanford-Binet at thirty-six and forty-eight months (corrected ages). Social development was gauged during a three-week day camp conducted when, on average, the infants were 38 months old. The major measures were social competence, which was derived from staff ratings, and social participation (percentage of time actively involved with others), which was derived from coding videotapes.

None of the many scores derived from systematic coding of mother-infant interaction during the first few months of life—which included amounts of time devoted to specific activities like the mother stimulating her infant, as well as amounts of time devoted to maternal activity generally and to joint mother and infant coactivity—was associated with later cognitive or social competence. Ratings of maternal responsiveness made at the same time also failed to predict, although ratings of infant responsiveness were associated with social but not cognitive measures at age three. Knowing how responsive a baby was rated during social interactions in the first months of life let us account for 7.6% of the variance in later social competence and social participation.

In contrast to our difficulty making predictions based on measures derived from early social interaction, measures of maternal emotional and verbal responsiveness, assessed by the HOME when infants were nine and twenty months of age, correlated with three- and four-year Stanford-Binet scores (rs = .41 and .42, respectively). The mothers' twenty-month (but not her nine-month) responsiveness correlated with three-year social competence as well (r = .48), but not with social participation scores.

In sum, mothers and infants were observed during a feeding twice during the neonatal period and once shortly thereafter. Responsiveness was rated and over 100 particular behaviors were defined and their occurrences coded. A multitude of measures was derived from the coded data. Some reflected behavioral categories, others more abstract dialogic or information–theory-derived properties of the interaction. These measures revealed consistent differences between preterm and full-term infants (Brown and Bakeman, 1980), but did not predict the level of either social or cognitive functioning in early childhood.

HOW CAN INTERACTION PREDICT: CONCEPTS AND MECHANISM

The Bakeman and Brown study was designed over a decade ago. It and others like it raise the question, "Does the social interaction experienced by infants during their first six months of life have consequences for their social and mental development two to three years later?" The answer from the Bakeman and Brown study would seem to be no, but it would be wrong to regard the results of any one study, with its particular procedures and measures, as definitive. Has a definitive answer then emerged from the accumulated findings of several studies? We do not think so. In fact, we are beginning to think that the relatively undifferentiated way the question is typically framed may actually have impeded the desired accumulation.

For the sake of illustration, and recognizing that we are caricaturing our own earlier work, let us describe the sort of study we find problematic. It begins with only the most global concept of mother-infant interaction and proceeds to collect a staggering amount of data detailing various codable and countable events. Design details such as infants' age(s) and procedural details such as the observational setting are simply asserted without rationale. No discussion of mechanism or process justifies particular outcome measures. Many scores are derived and many correlations with later outcome are computed, or worse, a number of scores are dumped into a stepwise multiple regression. Significance may well be found but in the presence of so many chance-capitalizing statistics, and absent cross-validation, investigators may be sorely misrepresenting their evidence if they conclude that prediction has been demonstrated. With all the benefit that hindsight so generously confers, and in the interest of reducing the number of studies that resemble the caricature just described, we would urge others planning similar studies to reflect first on the three questions posed in the following paragraphs.

Are Important Aspects of Interaction Identified?

To our 1980s' ears, *interaction* sounds like a fuzzy buzzword, a term with too many possible meanings to be very useful. Bakeman and Brown may have had in mind particular aspects of interaction that they thought theoretically important, but their prose mentioned only undifferentiated interaction. The problem is that amorphous notions of interaction result in a multitude of operations—from counting smiles to the information-theory measure Bakeman and Brown derived. Such operations are rarely comparable and as a result the sort of accumulation of scientific results we would like to see suffers.

We recommend that the phrase *social interaction* be banished and that researchers use more specific terms instead, terms that reflect their thinking with greater precision. Too many diverse notions can huddle under an umbrella term as undifferentiated as social interaction. In addition, we recommend that investigators should feel constrained *not* to develop new procedures when satisfactory ones already exist for defining and assessing those specific aspects of interaction. Consider, for example, the order and renewed vitality acceptance of consensual Brazelton clusters has brought to studies of neonatal individuality, an acceptance that has required both conceptual and operational agreement (Lester, 1984).

Certainly candidates for specific terms, now often collapsed into the category *social interaction,* are not lacking. For example, both Linn and Horowitz (1983) and Belsky, Taylor, and Rovine (1984) identified and assessed specific aspects of interaction in ways that are useful and instructive. The approach taken by these two teams of investigators was quite different. The aspect of interaction important to Linn and Horowitz was maternal *contingent responsiveness.* They viewed this as an environmental variable, an aspect of an infant's experience that might ultimately affect outcome and more immediately might be associated with individual behavioral variability.

Following Emde (1978), Linn and Horowitz (1983) chose to view variability of Brazelton scores not as a psychometric nuisance, but as an index of a newborn's adaptability, a neonatal characteristic that might pull greater responsiveness from the environment. The methodological challenge then was to measure environmental responsiveness. Like Bakeman and Brown, Linn and Horowitz began by recording the occurrences of a number of discrete behavioral events such as mothers' touching or talking to their infants and infants' vocalizing or looking at their mothers. Infants who experienced greater maternal responsiveness to their actions in the time intervals just after they acted, as compared with before, were categorized as having responsive mothers. Not all infants fit the predicted pattern, but there was a statistically significant tendency for newborns whose Brazelton scores indicated greater variability to experience more contingent responsiveness.

This correlational study raises a number of intriguing causal questions, but for present purposes we want to focus on the merits of Linn and Horowitz's approach to mother-infant interaction. They identified a single aspect of interaction—contingent responsiveness—that has considerable theoretical interest (e.g., Lewis and Goldberg, 1969; Watson, 1972). They then proceeded to measure it in an elegant and compelling way.

Others who share Linn and Horowitz's concern with contingent responsiveness should use the term explicitly rather than let it implicitly huddle under the term *interaction*. Of course, operational definitions need not be identical. For example, rating scales, which are considerably less labor intensive than Linn and Horowitz's microanalytically based lagged conditional probability profiles, could be used instead. In fact, Bakeman and Brown used rating scales to assess maternal responsiveness to infants' cues, which seems conceptually quite similar to contingent responsiveness as used by Linn and Horowitz. The point is, common conceptual definitions for specific terms like contingent responsiveness, explicitly stated, should greatly increase comparability among studies.

Belsky and his associates (Belsky, Taylor, and Rovine, 1984) took a somewhat different approach. The aspect of interaction they identified was *reciprocal interaction,* a term that includes, but is somewhat broader than contingent responsiveness. By reciprocal interaction Belsky means to invoke not just Ainsworth's emphasis on contingent and consistent responses to infants' needs and behavioral cues (Ainsworth, Blehar, Waters, and Wall, 1978), but also psychoanalytically based emphases on mothers' sensitivity and appropriate response to their infants' signals, and Brazelton's (Brazelton, Koslowski, and Main, 1974) and Stern's (1974) emphasis on dyadic synchrony as mothers and infants modulate their mutual excitation and affectivity.

Belsky's approach combines operational simplicity with conceptual clarity.

Observers used an interval-recording strategy and checked whenever any of 15 predefined behavioral events occurred within each successive 15-second interval. The codes Belsky used were not startlingly different from codes others have used. For example, his codes included maternal vocalization, infant's looking at the mother, and maternal positive affect. Still, behavioral codes were chosen specifically so that many would index reciprocal interaction, and Belsky was able to show that an index formed by combining individual estimated frequencies was coherent, both conceptually and empirically.

This works as a model for others because frequencies for various codes were reduced to a few indices and these indices were conceptually guided and empirically verified. If Belsky had regarded all of the several codes as indicators of generalized mother-infant interaction and had computed correlations between the several scores and later outcome, rightfully we would not have been impressed. We know too well that when many correlations are computed, some will be significant but few will replicate. Such wholesale computation of correlations is not unknown, but the practice results in studies remarkably similar to the caricature of a study we described earlier.

Belsky provides an excellent alternative to such wholesale approaches. His procedures result in a single score for reciprocal interaction, an important and conceptually grounded aspect of social interaction. Moreover, a measure of maternal involvement has also been derived and internal consistency for both these measures has been demonstrated. We are tempted to recommend that any investigators interested in assessing reciprocal interaction as experienced by infants henceforth adopt Belsky's procedures.

In summary, even a cursory survey of studies concerned with whether early interaction predicts subsequent outcome reveals a welter of measuring instruments, coding schemes, and data reduction strategies. This is brought about in part by a lack of a common conceptual vocabulary and by amorphous notions of interaction. Our argument is not that there is only one aspect of infants' interactive experience—be it reciprocal interaction or contingent responsiveness or any other specific concept—worth further investigation. Most likely, our efforts at prediction will be best rewarded when we take a relatively varied view of social interaction. But discussions of interaction, we argue, would be well-served if we, as a field, carefully constructed measures that closely reflected our understanding of critical aspects of interactions and then subjected ourselves more to the discipline of common concepts and measurements.

At What Ages Should Interaction be Assessed?

A second critical question to ask when designing an effects-of-early-interaction study concerns the age or ages at which interaction should be assessed. Again, we argue for greater conceptual differentiation and specificity. In particular, we think that developmental knowledge should figure prominently in the rationale offered for selecting particular ages to study.

Our caricature study might state simply that interaction will be assessed at one, three, and nine months of age with no further discussion. Yet, from what we know of typical development, the infants' capabilities at these three ages are often dramatically different. Certainly one major watershed in development occurs around two months of age. Emde and Robinson (1979) described in exquisite detail all the ways in which postreflexive infants differ from their earlier reflex-bound incarnations. This burgeoning ability to react not just to external stimulation but also to internal mental events changes both the infant's experience during interaction and the way others react to the infant.

The nature of social interaction again changes in fundamental ways beginning at about six months of age. As the infant's attention turns increasingly towards objects, both the infant's experience of an exchange with another person and the other person's way of interacting with the infant is once again transformed (Adamson and Bakeman, 1982; Trevarthen and Hubley, 1978). Although the changes infants undergo at two and six months of age are not as dramatic as insects' metamorphosis from larva to pupa, there is ample justification for regarding these ages as the boundaries between distinctly different developmental periods.

Until now we have used the phrase "early interaction" quite indiscriminately in this chapter, and so readers might well think we mean events any time within the first year of life. However, just as earlier in this discussion we banned the unadorned use of the term *social interaction,* now we will also banish *early interaction.* Instead, we recommend the use of developmentally sensitive adjectives that explicitly identify developmental phase whenever some aspect of interaction is being discussed.

What adjectives are appropriate? Whereas the first two months of life are commonly called neonatal (Emde and Robinson, 1979), no term in common usage so neatly demarcates the two to six month time interval; yet, this period is one of considerable "primacy." It is regarded as primary from several theoretical points of view, including psychoanalytic, cognitive structuralist, and attachment perspectives. Moreover, from the point of view of interaction, it is a time before infants become much engaged with objects, a time instead when much of their attention seems focussed on engaging and being engaged with primary social partners (Brazelton, Koslowski, and Main, 1974; Tronick, Als, and Adamson, 1979).

Whatever terms become commonly used, and recognizing that preterm infants present special problems, we think the study of the effects early interaction may have on subsequent development would be advanced if we clearly distinguished among measures from the neonatal period, measures from the period of interactive primacy (or primary intersubjectivity, as Trevarthen, 1979, names it), and measures from later infancy. We note that Bakeman and Brown, in an attempt to limit the number of scores analyzed, collapsed data over their 0-, one-, and three-month observations; from our present point of view this seems developmentally unjustified.

Is Any Mechanism Linking Interaction to Outcome Suggested?

A third critical question concerns mechanism. As discussed in the previous two sections, we think investigators concerned with whether social experience during the first six months of life predicts later behavior need to address directly questions concerning the definition and measurement of interaction: Are particular aspects of interaction identified and conceptually justified? Are the ages at which those aspects are assessed developmentally coherent and developmentally justified? A different, but clearly related, unavoidable question concerns process: How might a particular aspect of interaction at a particular period of development work its effects? And what specifically should be affected?

A number of intimately connected questions arise, united by a common demand for conceptual specificity and explicit rationales for the what's and when's of our assessments. Consider outcome. A study similar to the one we caricatured earlier might simply announce that outcome will be gauged with Bayley Mental Development and Stanford-Binet scores. By itself, such a proposed course of action seems problematic. The Bayley is generally regarded as measuring sensorimotor intelligence, whereas the Stanford-Binet is thought to index representational intelligence. Little association is usually found between the two and they may even have quite different genetic roots (Bornstein and Sigman, 1986; Scarr-Salapatek, 1976).

An obvious question is, "Why should early social experience affect cognitive development at all?" Certainly plausible mechanisms could be proposed linking particular aspects of early interaction with subsequent sensorimotor and/or representational intelligence. For example, Lewis and Goldberg (1969) argued that early contingency experiences within social interaction enable infants to develop expectancies that their behavior is effective. These expectancies in turn motivate exploration, learning, and the practice of new skills. Too often, however, it is not clear if investigators have considered the question of mechanism. Instead, we frequently accept what appears to be our field's default outcome, cognitive test scores, without further differentiation or justification (Zigler and Berman, 1983).

If, on the other hand, we being with an idea of a possible mechanism in mind, then we can take full advantage of the guidance provided by theory. Ideally, our theoretical notions should suggest which kind of intelligence, sensorimotor or representational, should be affected and which aspects of early interactive experience in particular should affect that kind of intelligence, thereby providing a rationale for the measurements we then select.

Depending on the particular mechanism suggested, social as well as cognitive outcomes may be suggested, Perhaps the clearest example of this is attachment theory (Ainsworth et al., 1978). Although one might argue about the degree to which the exact mechanism is elaborated, the theory states that the quality of early mother–infant interaction, especially the mother's sensitivity to her infant's cues during the first months of life, should affect the quality of attachment between mother and infant once specific attachments form around one year of age. This claim has been the subject of considerable discussion (e.g., Lamb, Thompson, Gardner, Charnov, and Estes, 1984). But, for present purposes we simply want to note how a strong theoretical statement cleanly identifies not just which aspects of early interaction, but also what kinds of outcome should be assessed.

In addition to the quality of attachment, a second kind of social outcome involves social competence with peers in early childhood. To Bakeman and Brown's credit, they attempted to assess this rather elusive concept. Given a concern with the sequelae of premature birth, it made considerable sense to complement the usual assessments of cognitive ability with assessments of social competence as well. Less clearly justified, however, was their attempt to predict social competence with peers from early interaction with mothers.

Again the question is, what mechanism or developmental process could link early interactive experience with later peer relations? Bakeman and Brown suggested only that mother-infant interaction is somehow the social arena in which social competence first develops, although they also note that Eckerman, Whatley, and Kutz (1975) speculated that young children's responses to peers are generalizations of responses first developed through interaction with familiar adults. Although perhaps not yet a fully elaborated mechanism, this idea at least gives some guidance as to which aspect of early interaction we should attempt to correlate with children's later social competence. The most direct test would seem to be provided by first assessing infants' individual responsiveness during early interaction with mothers and then determining if that correlates with their later responsiveness with peers.

Bakeman and Brown actually had observers rate infants' responsiveness during early mother–infant interaction and, in fact, these rating were correlated, albeit modestly ($r = .32$), with measures of social competence and social participation assessed when the children were three years old. Other measures derived from observing interaction, including the one that most closely captures reciprocal interaction (the probability of coaction), were not significantly associated with social competence. However, because Bakeman and Brown did not explicitly present the reasoning given in the previous paragraph, their study must be regarded as exploratory, not confirmatory.

The point of the preceding discussion is to suggest that an explicit discussion of mechanism can be the glue that holds predictive studies together. Literally hundreds of scores could be derived from observing interaction at various ages during infancy. Dozens of scores describing various facets of outcome are possible. A discussion of mechanism, because it suggests which few aspects of interaction should be considered at which ages, and what kinds of outcome should be affected, provides a much needed focus. Instead of being distracted by exploring perhaps hundreds of correlations, we can instead focus our interpretive energy and ask whether or not a few theoretically justified relations confirm our ideas about mechanism.

HOW MUCH CAN ASSESSMENTS OF INTERACTION PREDICT: STRENGTH OF EFFECTS

The preceding discussion has been concerned almost exclusively with conceptual matters, with concerns that should be addressed before a study begins. We would like to end with a comment or two about how results are presented once the data are in. For the kind of study we have been discussing, predictability between a particular aspect of early interaction and some aspect of subsequent development is sought. Although there is more than one way to define predictability (Cairns, 1979), here we understand the usual individual within-group rank-order stability as indexed with a Pearson product-moment correlation coefficient.

According to some, history is predominately a chronicle of unintended consequences. Imagine, for example, what academic psychology would be like if Karl Pearson had insisted successfully that association be indexed, not by his product-moment correlation, but by its square instead (which indicates proportion of variance accounted for), or better yet by the coefficient of alienation (which indicates the proportion of the original average error remaining after using values of the predictor to compute outcome scores and is defined as the square root of the difference between one and the correlation coefficient squared).

There is a problem with the standard correlation coefficient because its value has no readily apparent meaning. It is in no sense scalable. Thus generations of students have thought quite logically, but falsely, that a coefficient of .50 was somehow halfway there. True, quite weak relations yield satisfyingly big numbers, but to think that .50 is big is like gulping air to feel full. Depending on the number of cases examined, a coefficient of .50 may be significantly different from zero, but the strength of the association it indexes is really quite puny.

Consider the impact of the following three statements, all of which refer to an identical strength of association: (1) The level of contingent responsiveness experienced at three months of age correlates .50 with Stanford-Binet scores at age three years; (2) the level of contingent responsiveness experienced at three months of age accounts for .25 of the variance in Stanford-Binet scores at age three years; (3) the standard error of estimate of Stanford-Binet scores at age three years is 1.00; this becomes 0.87 when the level of contingent responsiveness experienced at three months of age is used as a predictor. In other words, the average error is reduced just by 13%. As McNemar noted some time ago (1969, p. 141), this interpretation of the correlation coefficient "is most useful and at the same time most disturbing."

The best case Bakeman and Brown could make for predictability from measures of interaction during the first six months of life to subsequent development involved a correlation of .32 between infant responsiveness and social competence at age three years. Thus infant responsiveness accounted for 10% of the variance in social competence, leaving 90% unaccounted for. The coefficient of alienation was .95, meaning that the standard error of estimate was reduced just 5% when the early scores were used to predict subsequent social competence. Although the correlation coefficient was significantly different from zero ($p < .05$), the strength of this relation seems considerably less than overwhelming.

If investigators uniformly spoke only in terms of amount of variance for which they can (and cannot) account, or in terms of the proportion of average error reduction accomplished, we wonder if those who cite them would be so quick to claim without any qualification that early interaction affects subsequent development. We recommend that researchers discuss prominently, not just the significance, but the strength of any effects they investigate. This should increase understanding of just how strong (or weak) particular effects are and should reduce the sort of over-simple citation that can too easily promote misunderstanding of research results.

A final but bedrock issue concerns sample size. Should researchers even report many of the statistically significant results that they compute? If we took seriously some of the more recent rules of thumb concerning sample sizes appropriate for multiple regression, much of the published record would be dismissed. For example, Biddle and Marlin (1986) recommended that one not attempt to solve regression problems if the number of variables is greater than $(N/10) - 2$, where N is the number of subjects or cases. Small samples, with their attendant larger random variation in calculating the correlation matrix, have a tendency to yield unreliable regression results.

Thus Bakeman and Brown, with their 40 subjects, should have used only *two* variables in their regression analyses. Although we recognize that somewhat less restrictive rules of thumb are available, at this point we are willing to give credence only to the simple zero-order correlations Bakeman and Brown reported, not to their multiple regression analysis. In general, little weight should be given multiple regression results unless the number of subjects is at least ten times the number of variables.

We conclude that even if all the problems discussed throughout this chapter were addressed in an exemplary fashion, a literature of inconsistent and contradictory findings could still result if sample sizes were not adequate for the number of variables investigated. Given the amount of time that assessing aspects of interaction often requires, especially when microanalytic techniques are employed, this is a sobering thought.

CONCLUSION

Is there predictability between aspects of social interaction assessed during the first six months of life and developmental outcome a few years later? Based only on the Bakeman and Brown study, the answer would be "no." Does this mean that no assessment of mother-infant interaction would have predictive power? Such a conclusion might be premature, but in any event, and this is the main point of our discussion, we think that studies could be designed in ways that would improve our ability to observe whatever predictability may be present. Thus we urge researchers to investigate specific aspects of interaction such as contingent responsiveness or reciprocal interaction, to locate those aspects within a particular developmental period, and to justify the developmental outcomes investigated in terms of a plausible process or mechanism that clearly links those aspects of interaction, assessed at those times, with those outcomes.

If researchers followed these suggestions, would our ability to predict outcome based on early social interaction increase dramatically? We hope so, but frankly we fear not by much. Both empirical evidence and our understanding of the process of development warn us not to be optimistic.

Consider the empirical record. Returning briefly to the Bakeman and Brown study, we note that the strongest consistent correlations occurred between mothers' verbal responsiveness assessed at nine and twenty months of age by the HOME Scale and infants' cognitive competence at three and four years of age (Bradley, chapter 10 in this volume; see also Stevens and Bakeman, 1986). This result is consistent with other reports concerning the predictive validity of the HOME, but note that the HOME is an environmental measure, not an interactive one. It is also a measure that may include, in part, a genetic component (Plomin, chapter 14 in this volume).

In addition, current models of development stress transactional processes and self-righting tendencies (Sameroff and Chandler, 1975), not straightforward unidirectional paths between early environmental or interactional events and subsequent outcome. Such models lead us to expect correlation between measures close in time, perhaps, but not necessarily long-term predictability. This is the usual finding and is also what Bakeman and Brown reported.

Paradoxically perhaps, it is our pessimism about the possibility of future research resulting in strong and general correlations between social interaction during the first 6 months of life and cognitive or social outcomes in early childhood that makes us optimistic about the future of research designed to probe this link. The rewards have not come readily, which has forced us to grapple with the intricacies of early development. In turn, this is beginning to lead us to a better understanding of those particular and perhaps few circumstances for which early interactive experience actually has some impact on subsequent development (e.g., Beckwith and Parmelee, 1986; Brietmayer and Ramey, 1986). Still, the central questions remain How? and How much?

ACKNOWLEDGMENTS

We would like to acknowledge grants MH26131 (NIMH) and HD-11209 (NICHD), which supported the research by Bakeman and Brown discussed here.

REFERENCES

Adamson, L., and Bakeman, R. (1982). Affectivity and reference: Concepts, methods, and techniques in the study of communication development of 6 to 18 month old infants. In T. Field and A. Fogel (Eds.), *Emotion and early interactions* (pp. 213–236). Hillsdale, NJ: Lawrence Erlbaum Associates.

Ainsworth, M. D. S., Blehar, M. C., Waters, E., and Wall, S. (1978). *Patterns of attachment: A psychological study of the strange situation.* Hillsdale, NJ: Lawrence Erlbaum Associates.

Bakeman, R., and Brown, J. V. (1980). Early interaction: Consequences for social and mental development at three years. *Child Development, 51,* 437–447.

Beckwith, L., and Parmelee, A. H. (1986). EEG patterns of preterm infants, home environment, and later IQ. *Child Development, 56,* 777–789.

Belsky, J., Taylor, D. G., and Rovine, M. (1984). The Pennsylvania infant and family development project, II: The development of reciprocal interaction in the mother-infant dyad. *Child Development, 55,* 706–717.

Biddle, B. J., and Marlin, M. M. (1986). Causality, confirmation, credulity, and structural equation modeling. *Child Development, 58,* 4–17.

Bornstein, M. H., and Sigman, M. D. (1986). Continuity in mental development from infancy. *Child Development, 57,* 251–274.

Brazelton, T. B., Koslowski, B., and Main, M. (1974). The origins of reciprocity: The early mother-infant interaction. In M. Lewis and L. Rosenblum (Eds.), *The effects of the infant on its caregiver* (pp. 49–76). New York: Wiley.

Brietmayer, B. J., and Ramey, C. T. (1986). Biological nonoptimality and quality of postnatal environment as codeterminants of intellectual development. *Child Development, 57,* 1151–1165.

Brown, J. B., and Bakeman, R. (1980). Relationships of human mothers with their infants during the first year of life: Effects of prematurity. In R. W. Bell and W. P. Smotherman (Eds.), *Maternal influences and early behavior* (pp. 353–373). New York: Spectrum.

Cairns, R. B. (1979). *Social development: The origins of plasticity of interchanges.* San Francisco: Freeman.

Eckerman, C. O., Whatley, J. L., and Kutz, S. L. (1975). Growth of social play with peers during the second year of life. *Developmental Psychology, 11,* 42–49.

Emde, R. N. (1978). Commentary. In A. J. Sameroff (Ed.), *Organization and stability of newborn behavior: A commentary on the Brazelton Neonatal Assessment Scale.* Monograph for the Society for Research in Child Development, 43, 135–138.

Emde, R. N., and Robinson, J. (1979). The first two months: Recent research in developmental psychobiology and the changing view of the newborn. In J. Woshpitz (Ed.), *Basic Handbook of Child Psychiatry* (pp. 72–105). New York: Basic Books.

Kagan, J. (1984). *The Nature of the child.* New York: Basic Books.

Lamb, M. E., Thompson, R. A., Gardner, W. P., Charnov, E. L., and Estes, D. (1984). Security of infantile attachment as assessed in the "strange situation": Its study and biological interpretation. *Behavioral and Brain Sciences, 7,* 121–171.

Lester, B. M. (1984). Data analysis and prediction. In *Neonatal behavioral assessment scale* (2nd ed., Clinics in Developmental Medicine no. 88). London: Spastics International Medical Publications.

Lewis, M., and Goldberg, S. (1969). Perceptual-cognitive development in infancy: A generalized expectancy model as a function of mother-infant interaction. *Merrill-Palmer Quarterly, 15,* 81–100.

Linn, P. L., and Horowitz, F. D. (1983). The relationship between infant individual differences and mother-infant interaction during the neonatal period. *Infant Behavior and Development, 43,* 135–138.

McNemar, Q. (1969). *Psychological Statistics.* New York: Wiley.

Sameroff, A. J., and Chandler, M. J. (1975). Reproduction risk and the continuum of caretaking causality. In F. D. Horowitz, M. Hetherington, S. Scarr-Salapatek, and G. Seigel (Eds.), *Review of child development research* (Vol. 4, pp. 187–244). Chicago: University of Chicago Press.

Scarr-Salapatek, S. (1976). An evolutionary perspective on infant intelligence: Species patterns and individual variations. In M. Lewis (Ed.), *Origins of Intelligence* (pp. 165–197). New York: Plenum.

Stern, D. N. (1974). Mother and infant at play: The dyadic interaction involving facial, vocal, and gaze behaviors. In M. Lewis and L. A. Rosenblum (Eds.), *The effect of the infant on its caregiver* (pp. 187–214). New York: Wiley.

Stevens, J. H., and Bakeman, R. (1986). A factor analytic study of the HOME scale for infants. *Developmental Psychology, 21,* 1196–1203.

Trevarthen, C. (1979). Communication and cooperation in early infancy: A description of primary intersubjectivity. In M. Bullowa (Ed.), *Before speech: The beginning of interpersonal communication* (pp. 321–347). Cambridge: Cambridge University Press.

Trevarthen, C., and Hubley, P. (1978). Secondary intersubjectivity: Confidence, confiding, and acts of meaning in the first year. In A. Lock (Ed.), *Action, gesture, and symbol* (pp. 183–230). London: Academic Press.

Tronick, E., Als, H., and Adamson, L. (1979). Structure of early face-to-face communicative interactions. In M. Bullowa (Ed.), *Before speech: The beginning of interpersonal communication* (pp. 349–370). Cambridge: Cambridge University Press.

Watson, J. S. (1972). Smiling, cooing, and the game. *Merrill-Palmer Quarterly, 18,* 323–339.

Zigler, E., and Berman, W. (1983). Discerning the future of early childhood intervention. *American Psychologist, 38,* 894–906.

PART II
COMMENTARY

13 Quantitative Methods and the Search for Continuity

Mark I. Appelbaum
Margaret R. Burchinal
Robert A. Terry
University of North Carolina at Chapel Hill

INTRODUCTION

The determination of behavioral continuity (and the related construct of behavioral stability) presents the developmentalist with a series of difficult and profound problems. Two of the most serious involve defining these constructs and selecting methods by which continuity (or its absence) can be assessed in a quantitatively sound manner. These problems, together with that of experimental design, form a triumvirate of thorny issues that must be resolved by the researcher in a consistent fashion before behavioral continuity can be examined reliably. Whatever analytic technique is selected, it is essential that the basic constructs of continuity, experimental design, and quantitative approach together form a consistent package.

Unfortunately, the terms *continuity* and *stability*, together with a host of related and surrogate terms such as plasticity, predictability, and so forth, are not used within developmental psychology in a precise or consistent fashion. Rather than trying to resolve these definitional problems, we simply note that in this chapter we use the terms continuity and stability to refer to the problem of measuring change (or lack of change) in an attribute over time by the use of a mathematically continuous function. Before the fact, there are no restrictions placed on the form of the continuous functions considered—they may be linear functions (with a zero or nonzero slope) as in correlational and regression analysis, or nonlinear functions such as the logistic function in IRT scaling. When measuring change, we may take two different approaches to the problem of anchoring—either by assessing change relative to a group or population (e.g., assessing change relative to standing within a group) or relative to some starting point for the individual (i.e., assessment of individual growth).

In the literature dealing with developmental continuity, three basic quantitative approaches dominate the field. These are correlational and regression approaches, which are used to argue for the existence of behavioral continuity by demonstrating the preservation of relative rank of individuals within a group on some attribute over development (usually time); individual growth curve modelling approaches in which the investigator attempts to argue for continuity of development by showing that a continuous developmental function can be fit that accurately describes the development of the individual; and scaling approaches that are used to attempt to argue for developmental continuity by first providing estimates of developmental level for the individual and then showing that level is a monotonic, continuous function of time or some other metric for the developmental process.

Each of these approaches starts from a somewhat different vantage point and, consequently, has varying focal issues. The correlation/regression approach emphasizes maintenance of relative standing within a group. As a result, the distribution of the attribute within the group, and methods of assessing association are of essential concern. The individual growth curve approach emphasizes the behavior of the individual as a function of time. This approach depends on the ability of the researcher to specify the basic quantitative nature of development and to fit the selected growth curve models to developmental data. The scaling approach emphasizes the measurement of development and has as its basic underlying concern issues generally associated with psychometrics.

In this chapter we consider a number of quantitative issues of importance for each of these approaches with the hope that the developmentalist may achieve some better understanding of these approaches and their complexities. It is not our intention to produce a technical manual (or cookbook) describing how to implement each of these analytic strategies, but rather to identify some of the issues that are of concern when these methods are employed.

CORRELATION AND REGRESSION

By far the most commonly used approach is correlation and/or regression. Most of the foregoing chapters in this volume use this approach. This set of related techniques has a time-honored role in the investigation of developmental continuity, and although they tend to be fairly well-understood by most developmentalists, there are nonetheless several issues that deserve special attention in the context of developmental continuity. Although correlation and regression are highly related, the problems involved in their application to issues of continuity are sufficiently distinct to warrant separate discussion.

Correlation

Appelbaum and McCall (1983) discussed the application of correlational techniques to the problem of developmental continuity as they apply to developmental psychology. Consequently, we do not provide highly detailed accounts of these techniques, but rather attempt to delineate the nature of these problems with the expectation that investigators will consult Appelbaum and McCall (1983) or other cited texts for more detailed discussions.

There are three general problem areas: those dealing with the fact that researchers often obtain many correlations from a single set of data all of which need to be tested for significance; those which arise from the fact that the researcher often wishes to test dependent correlations; and those that arise from the fact that sample sizes in studies of continuity may be small and the data points may include outliers.

It is often the case that the investigator will collect multiple measures on their subjects and will therefore have a matrix of intercorrelations. If p variates have been measured on each subject then the resulting intercorrelation matrix will contain $p(p\text{-}1)/2$ potentially different correlations. Under this circumstance researchers will often proceed to test each of the correlations separately and to discuss the implications of each correlation found to be significant. This strategy is, unfortunately, inappropriate for two reasons. First, the alpha level of the resulting set of tests is very highly inflated. Second, testing each correlation separately ignores the fact that the values of the correlations as a set are constrained. Proper procedures for testing the hypothesis stating that all of the correlations in a correlation matrix are within sampling error of zero have been developed by Bartlett (1954) and are reported in many multivariate texts (e.g., Morrison, 1976). This procedure should be considered the proper omnibus test conducted prior to the search for individually significant correlations. In a similar vein, when testing several populations for the equality of entire correlation matrices, techniques that examine the elements of the correlation matrix one at a time are, in general, inappropriate. For this purpose the procedure developed by Jennrich (1970) for testing the equality of correlation matrices in several populations is best followed.

A second issue becomes relevant when investigators wish to test dependent correlations within a single population. For instance, one may have two indicies of developmental level and may be interested in the question of whether these differentially correlate with some outcome of interest. If we designate the two indices as A and B and the outcome of interest as C, then we wish to test

$$r_{AC} = r_{BC}$$

which is a test of dependent correlations because both correlations involve the same variable C measured on the same subjects. A procedure developed by Olkin

(1967) has been shown by Appelbaum and Cramer (1976) to be an effective method for testing this class of hypotheses, particularly in reasonably large samples.

A third issue of particular consequence to those investigating behavioral continuity using correlational techniques, is one that arises from the fact that our sample sizes are often small and the data points may contain outliers. Correlations, particularly those derived from small samples, tend to be rather unstable and can be greatly influenced by even a very small number of outlying data points. The issue of outliers in bivariate or multivariate data can be a particularly difficult one because visual inspection of the data does not, in general, reveal extreme points as is often the case when one considers variables in a univariate fashion. After considerable work on this set of problems, a number of solutions have been offered concerning ways to minimize the influence of outliers in this context. Although much of the work is technically complex, developmentalists are encouraged to become familiar with these advances. Two particularly good sources are Barnett and Lewis (1984, chapter 9), and Huber (1981, chapter 8). It is unfortunate that relatively few of the techniques discussed in these sources have been incorporated into major computerized statistical packages.

Regression

Although clearly a more complex set of analytic techniques than simple correlational analysis, regression analysis, including multiple regression, seems to be much better understood and to provide fewer problems for the applied researcher. Still, three issues seem to cause difficulties for those researchers employing regression techniques as a method of establishing behavioral continuity: the interpretation of regression coefficients, the influence of outliers in relatively small data sets, and problems encountered when the criterion measure is binary.

Most of the problems in interpretation of regression coefficients and their associated significance tests can be minimized if the researcher understands that multiple regression is a systems approach and that all regression coefficients are partial regression weights. That is, the regression coefficients estimate the contribution of the variables in predicting the criterion given the other variables in the system. Similarly, the tests of regression coefficients are partial tests and test the significance of the variable in question given the other variables in the system. (There is some variation among computer packages as to exactly how these tests are formulated and often within a package there may be more than one option available that governs the formulation of the test.) Where most investigators are prone to error is in the situation where the regression coefficient is small and nonsignificant and this result is expressed in the form "variable *a* makes no contribution to the regression" with the implication that the process underlying the variable is not involved in the outcome. The test actually indicates that, given the other variables in the system (which may tap the same process as underlies variable *a*), no additional prediction is offered by variable *a* in this context. This does not mean that variable *a* would not show a highly significant contribution to the prediction of the outcome if others of the variables in the regression system were deleted. Particular attention must be given to this problem of interpretation when the predictor variables exhibit more than slight intercorrelations. A particularly good discussion of this issue is offered by Mosteller and Tukey (1977, chapter 13).

A second issue of interpretation focuses on the relationship between overall indicies of predictability, usually R^2, and the individual regression coefficients. Any of the following patterns may properly obtain:

(1) Overall regression (R^2) and all betas significant.
(2) Overall regression and some, but not all, betas significant.
(3) Overall regression significant but none of the individual betas significant.
(4) Overall regression nonsignificant, but all of the individual betas significant.
(5) Overall regression nonsignificant and some, but not all, of the individual betas significant.
(6) Overall regression and all of the betas nonsignificant.

A detailed discussion of the interpretation of each of these possible outcomes, including patterns 3, 4, and 5, which are generally found troublesome by applied users of multiple regression, is offered by Cramer (1972).

The treatment of outliers and the influence of individual data points in regression analysis have received far wider treatment than is generally found in correlational analysis. The general term *regression diagnostics* is now commonly used to refer to a set of indices developed for the purpose of quantifying the magnitude of these effects as well as the related issue of the cost of including additional variables in a regression system. Many of the major statistical packages offer regression diagnostics at least as options to their regression programs. Detailed discussion of regression diagnostics are to be found in a number of sources including Cook and Weisberg (1982), Belsley, Kuh, and Welsch (1980), Barnett and Lewis (1984), and Neter, Wasserman, and Kutner (1985), as well as in some of the user's manuals of the major statistical packages. Although generally offered as optional outputs, regression diagnostics should be a central aspect of every regression analysis particularly when sample sizes are relatively small.

Increasingly, researchers are considering issues of continuity where the criterion variable (outcome) is binary; e.g., the presence or absence of a symptom or indicator, mastery or nonmastery to a specified criterion, and so forth, rather than restricting themselves to continuous outcome variables. In this circumstance the basic assumptions of ordinary least squares regression analysis are not tenable, specifically the assumptions of normality of the error term and homogeneity of variance. When the outcome variable is binary a different form of regression analysis, namely logistic regression, is called for. Although this approach to regression analysis is not well known by many developmentalists, it is rather straightforward and is described in many more recent texts on regression analysis, e.g., Neter *et al.* (1985, chapter 10), and Kleinbaum, Kupper, and Muller (1988, chapter 12).

INDIVIDUAL GROWTH CURVES

The existence of continuity in growth of an attribute has quantitative implications for modeling development of the attribute over time. Continuity in growth implies that a continuous mathematical function (a developmental function) can describe the change in an attribute over time for a given individual. This, in turn, suggests that at least one growth curve model that either approximates or represents that mathematical function will provide a good description of the change in the attribute over time. However, the ability to identify an appropriate growth curve model and fit it appropriately and precisely with data depends on at least three factors: (1) how the attribute was measured; (2) the investigator's assumptions about the nature of the attribute's growth; and (3) the type of growth curve model selected and whether the model's assumptions are violated by the data. Each of these issues is discussed in turn after a few general comments regarding growth curve models.

The purpose of this section is to discuss the methodological issues encountered when individual growth curves are estimated from longitudinal data. We assume that the investigator is interested in a multilevel analysis. In these analyses, the developmental functions for the individuals of interest on the attribute of interest are estimated and then correlates of these growth indices are identified. The developmental function is estimated with a growth curve model in the first phase of these analyses, and selected aspects of growth are associated with potential predictors of growth, often in the second phase. Several restrictions are placed on the topics covered in this review. Discussion is limited to methods that model growth of one attribute that displays continuous quantitative change over time from interval- or ratio-level data. These restrictions were placed on the discussion because they present less complicated methodological considerations than fitting more than one attribute simultaneously, using qualitative models, or estimating growth curves from nominal- or ordinal-level data.

Measurement Issues

Measurement issues have been widely discussed by developmentalists so these issues are not discussed in-depth. Longitudinal data are necessary to study intraindividual change that is uncontaminated by interindividual differences. The attribute should maintain the same dimensions over time and be measured with comparable stimulus tasks or tests throughout the developmental period of interest. These two constraints are necessary if scores are to reflect the same aspect of the attribute as it changes during the observational period. Finally, measurement scales are needed that isomorphically represent the level of the attribute during this period of interest when estimation of the underlying developmental function is desired. Norm-referenced scores can be used to distinguish patterns of development, but not to estimate the developmental function(s). This is because they do not reflect the actual level of the attribute as it changes over time.

Assumptions about Growth

Developmentalists have also discussed the types of characteristics an attribute must display in order to qualify as having a developmental function (Bock, 1976; Nesselroade and Baltes, 1979; Wohlwill, 1973). The investigator's assumptions about characteristics of the developmental process will affect the type of growth curve model that is selected. Two general schools of thought have emerged. The "strong concept of growth" is based on the idea that a single developmental function can adequately describe the growth of all individuals on a given attribute. According to this school of thought, the growth curves of any two individuals can have different parametric values, resulting in developmental processes with different onset/offset times, slopes, or asymptotic levels. However, both of their developmental functions would have the same type of functional relation between the observed levels of the attribute and time (i.e., be from the same parametric family). Conversely, advocates of the "weak concept of development" believe in the individuality of growth. Both the functional form of the developmental function and the parametric values of these functions can vary across individuals.

The two views of development are associated with very different approaches to the estimation of individual growth curves. Proponents of the strong concept identify a single class of growth curves to represent the attribute's developmental process. In fact, often a single growth curve, typically the mean profile, is used to represent growth for all individuals within a population. On the other hand, adherents of the weak concept estimate separate growth curves for each individual.

Types of Growth Curve Models

The plethora of growth curve models is probably less familiar to developmentalists than either the measurement issues or assumptions about growth. This may be because these methods have been primarily discussed within the applied statistics literature. These models vary along several dimensions. Classes of growth curve models that present some of the possible cross-classifications of these dimensions are discussed later.

First, models can estimate a single growth curve to describe change for all individuals within a population (aggregate models), estimate a separate growth curve for each individual (individual models), or estimate prototypic growth curves (prototypic models). Variation on the first dimension can be associated with the two types of assumptions about growth. The aggregate models reflect the strong assumption, whereas the individual and the prototypic models reflect the weak assumption.

Second, models can be selected because they represent the parametric family of the developmental function (i.e., the type of functional relation between observed scores and time), approximate this relation, or can provide an indication of this unknown parametric family(s). Selection of a reasonable parametric model can be from models developed through differential equations. These models are based on assumed relationships between growth and time. Nonlinear models are often used when a growth curve model is selected to represent the parametric family because developmental functions are generally monotonically increasing and "S" or "J" shaped, at least during times of acquisition of the attribute. Polynomial growth curve (PGC) models provide interesting approximations of unknown parametric families. Prototypic models are useful when the investigator does not wish to specify any type of parametric family.

The third dimension reflects whether parameters are estimated through ordinary least squares (OLS), weighted least square (WLS), or maximum likelihood methods. OLS assumes that errors under the model are independently and identically (iid) distributed, whereas WLS assumes that the variances and covariances are known. Maximum likelihood assumes both that errors are iid and that an appropriate parametric family has been identified.

Historically, only the simpler models have been widely used. In early attempts to identify patterns of growth, Tucker (1966) suggested using prototypic growth curves as estimated through a type of principal components analysis. This method was applied to the longitudinal IQ data from the Fels sample; patterns of intellectual development were identified and factors that differentiated these identified patterns were located (McCall, Appelbaum, and Hogarty, 1973). Pottoff and Roy (1964) suggested that using a multivariate repeated-measures analysis of a variance model provided an appropriate method for describing change over time and its correlates. This becomes the PGC model when the model involves either powers of the times at which the individuals were observed or orthogonal polynomials. This approach has probably become the standard profiles analysis method. Recently, more complicated models have been discussed and used within the developmental literature. Nonlinear models have been used to describe physical growth (Bock, Wainer, Peterson, Thissen, Murray, and

Roche, 1973) whereas hierarchical PGC models have been used to estimate the effects of Head Start on academic development (Bryk and Weisberg, 1976). In addition, the importance of estimating individual developmental functions when modeling educational or intellectual growth has been strongly advocated by Bock (1976), Nesselroade and Baltes (1979), and Rogosa, Brandt, and Zimowski (1982). Finally, structural equations models (Joreskog, 1979), and models that represent combinations of growth curve models and the structural equations approach, have been developed (McArdle and Epstein, 1987).

Aggregate models. Aggregate growth curve models estimate a single developmental function to describe the growth of all individuals from one population. A single growth curve model can be appropriately estimated from sample data when the individuals' patterns of growth on the attribute vary trivially or when individual differences are uninteresting and can be treated as a source of error. Both nonlinear and PGC aggregate models have been developed.

Various nonlinear models have been used to represent the parametric family of developmental functions. Parameters of these models express interesting characteristics of the growth process. For example, the logistic growth curve (LGC) is often used to represent physical growth. The LGC model is

$$Y_{ij} = \delta \,/\, \{1 + \exp[-\tau(T_j - \alpha)]\} + \epsilon_{ij}.$$

The model states that the i-th individual's score at time j is function of the parameters (δ, τ, α), the j-th time (T_j), and error (ϵ_{ij}). The model's parameters are the asymptotic level of the attribute (δ), the initial rate of growth (τ), and the time at which half of the growth has occurred (α). The group nonlinear function has been estimated both with OLS (Gallant, 1875a) and WLS (Gallant, 1975b).

An aggregate PGC model can be used when the parametric family is unknown and a useful approximation is desired and when it is assumed that individuals vary only trivially. It is assumed that growth can be described by

$$Y_{ij} = \beta_0 + \beta_1 T_j + \beta_2 T_j^2 + \ldots + \beta_q T_j^q + \epsilon_{ij}.$$

This model states that growth is a function of the parameters ($\beta_0 \ldots \beta_q$), the j-th time (T_j), and error (ϵ_{ij}). The parameters of this model consist of β_0 as the level of the attribute when time is zero and $\beta_1 - \beta_q$ as the slopes associated with the linear through the q-th terms (i.e., T_j raised to the first through the q-th power). The order of the model can range between $q = 1$ (a linear model) and $q = p - 1$; generally, a model where $q < p - 1$ is used if $p > 4$. Orthogonal polynomials are typically used rather than the powers of T_j for numerical reasons. It should be emphasized that univariate-corrected (Geisser and Greenhouse, 1958) or multivariate methods (Bock, 1979; McCall and Appelbaum, 1974) should be used to avoid inflated Type I error-rates. Parameters of the multivariate models have been estimated with both OLS (Potthoff and Roy, 1964) and WLS (Rao, 1966).

Individual growth curve models. Individual growth curve models estimate a separate developmental function for each individual. As a consequence of this flexibility the number of observations per individual, the reliability of measurement, and the complexity of the model all severely limit the precision with which the developmental functions can be estimated. Nevertheless, both individual nonlinear and PGC models have been applied to longitudinal data. Typically, OLS methods are used to estimate parameters because the number of observations is too small to permit good estimates of variation that are needed for WLS methods. An example of an individual nonlinear growth curve model is the individual LGC model

$$Y_{ij} = \delta_i / \{1 + \exp[-\tau_i(T_{ij} - \alpha_i)]\} + \epsilon_{ij},$$

and the individual PGC model is

$$Y_{ij} = \beta_{0i} + \beta_{1i}T_{ij} + \beta_{2i}T_{ij}^2 + \dots + \beta_{qi}T_{ij}^q + \epsilon_{ij}.$$

Prototypic growth curves. Prototypic models identify individuals with similar patterns of growth across time without regard for existing classification schemes or specific growth curve models (Nunnally, 1978; Overall and Klett, 1972). Fewer assumptions are made with this approach because a class of growth curve models is not selected a priori to represent or approximate the parametric family of the developmental process. However, the developmental functions themselves are not estimated as they were with the individual and aggregate models. Factor analysis, principal components analysis, and cluster analysis have all been used to estimate prototypic growth curves. Both principal components and cluster analysis identify individuals with similar patterns of growth, whereas principal components analysis also estimates a set of prototypic curves from the data. The growth curve model with these models is

$$Y_{ij} = P_{i1}F_{i1} + P_{i2}F_{i2} + \dots + P_{ir}F_{ir} + E_{ij}.$$

P is a weight matrix such that P_{ik} represents the extent to which the profile of the i-th individual resembles the k-th prototypic curve, and F is a score matrix such that F_{jk} displays the expected value on the j-th occasion under the k-th prototypic growth curve.

Composite growth curve models. Various models have been proposed that combine aggregate, individual, and/or prototypic growth curve models into composite models. These models seek to improve the precision with which parameters are estimated. However, these models tend to make more stringent assumptions than either of the two types of models that were combined to form the composite.

Aggregate and individual models have been combined to form models that estimate separate developmental functions for each individual. Parameter estimates from both the aggregate model fit to the entire sample and the individual model fit to only the individual's data are combined to form the parameter estimates of the composite model. One class of such models, the Empirical Bayesian or hierarchical models, assumes that all individuals have developmental functions from the same parametric family, that the individual parametric values are normally distributed within the population, and that the variances and covariances of these parametric values are known. Nonlinear hierarchical models have been described by Bock (1976) and PGC hierarchical models by Fearn (1975), Laird and Ware (1982), and Strenio, Weisberg, and Bryk (1983).

Other models have been developed from combining group and prototypic models. Growth curves have been estimated by fitting a univariate PGC model to the data and then by submitting the residuals to a principal components analysis (Snee, Acuff, and Gibson, 1979). This model assumes that the relevant between-subject covariates are included in the model and that errors are independently and identically distributed across individuals and time. Recently, a more complicated variation of this class of models including structural modeling was offered by McArdle and Epstein (1987).

Model Selection

Selecting the most appropriate model is a complicated process. Almost all of the models previously described tend to be difficult to fit to the kinds of data collected by developmentalists. In addition, many decisions must be made before the study is conducted in order to select a good model. Model selection should be based on the assumptions made about the characteristics of the growth process and the design characteristics of the longitudinal study. At least four factors must be considered in selecting a model.

First, the investigator's assumptions regarding the nature of individual differences in growth will affect the type of model selected. If it is assumed that individual differences are trivial, then an aggregate model should be appropriate. Otherwise, the investigator must decide whether a sufficient number of observations were collected on each individual to permit estimating separate developmental functions. A recent computer simulation suggested that either a large number of observations ($p > 5$) or highly reliable data are necessary for relatively precise estimation with individual models (Burchinal, 1986). If neither of these conditions is met, then the investigator is forced to choose between imprecise parameter estimates under the individual models or ignoring real and interesting individual differences under the aggregate models.

In addition, selecting among the nonlinear, PGC, and prototypic models involves a number of considerations. A trade-off appears to exist in the choice between the parametric (PGC or nonlinear) models and the prototypic models. Parametric models here refers to growth curve models that estimate parameters describing interesting characteristics of growth (e.g., intercepts, slopes, and asymptotic levels). These models can provide more interesting and powerful analyses for two reasons: the association between these specific aspects of growth and covariates can be tested, and the information in the data can be summarized more succinctly. On the other hand, the prototypic model makes fewer assumptions and, thus, fits well to many types of data. In contrast, the nonlinear and PGC models precisely estimate the growth process well only when the underlying growth function is similar to the selected growth curve model.

Moreover, when a parametric model is selected, choosing between a nonlinear or a PGC model involves several issues. Typically, the nonlinear model is more interesting because the parameters can be easily interpreted, whereas the parameters of the PGC are less obviously interpretable. However, fitting a nonlinear model is an iterative process and will not necessarily find a good set of parameter estimates. This is especially true when either an individual model is fit to a small number of observed values (i.e., when the number of parameters is not much smaller than the number of observations), or when the developmental function has a rather different shape than the selected growth curve model. The nonlinear models appear to be more affected than the PGC models when they are fit to data with developmental functions from parametric families that differ from the selected growth curve model.

Furthermore, violations of certain model assumptions appear to have severe consequences. Fitting an aggregate model that assumes that individual's errors are independent across time can result in highly inflated Type-I errors (McCall and Appelbaum, 1974). Selecting a growth curve model that is very different from the parametric family of the developmental function will produce very imprecise and inappropriate descriptions of growth. Similarly, assuming a simple function when several simple functions are necessary to describe growth throughout the time period of interest will produce poor estimates. For example, physical growth between infancy and adolescence can be well described by a sequence of logistic functions, but not by a single logistic function. Finally, models that use WLS or Empirical Bayesian methods to estimate parameters appear to inappropriately estimate parameters and their variances when sample sizes are small to moderate (Burchinal, 1986).

Thus, the investigator who wishes to use growth curve models to describe growth and especially to estimate individual developmental functions faces many choices. Longitudinal studies must be designed with careful consideration given a priori to how the attribute is measured over time, the assumed nature of change and whether individuals differ, and the type of model that is selected. Nevertheless, despite all of the pitfalls and difficulties, use of growth curve models may be the only way to describe growth for many of the constructs of continuity in development.

SCALING APPROACHES

It has always been hoped that administration of a test, when properly scored, would allow reasonable inferences for locating the position of an individual on a trait or ability, or along a developmental scale. Administration of a single test (or item) would considerably ease the practical task of inferring the level of an examinee along some developmental dimension.

Many researchers have used the classical test theory (CTT) model to approach this particular problem. An estimate of an examinee's level of functioning on some attribute is simply taken as his or her observed score on the test, which is an unbiased estimate of the examinee's true score level. However, classical test theory has been limited in its ability to answer questions of particular interest to developmental researchers, because the foundations of CTT are based on weak assumptions. In particular, no form of the functional relationship between examinee performance on an item and the examinee's trait level on some developmental dimension is assumed.

Other models have been proposed that attempt to remedy some of the shortcomings of the CTT model. These models can be classified as Item Response Theory (IRT) models because all attempt some quantification of the relation between item response probability and a latent characteristic Θ. Furthermore, the particular function relating item response probability and Θ, the developmental or ability level, is known as an Item Characteristic Curve (ICC).

One of the simplest IRT models, and one with some history in developmental psychology, is the Guttman Scale (Guttman, 1950). Figure 13.1a represents a perfect Guttman item, a monotonic single step function relating probability of item response to Θ. If the examinee has ability $\Theta > \Theta_0$, then the probability of successfully responding to the item is 1; otherwise, the probability of correctly responding is 0. By constructing a test consisting of perfect Guttman items, with each successive item requiring more Θ in order for a correct response to occur, a perfect ordering of examinees on Θ can be obtained by simply noting the last item successfully completed.

Although theoretically interesting, it is extremely rare for the deterministic Guttman model to fit actual data. A stochastic IRT model that retains the characteristic of a step-function ICC is the latent-distance model (Torgerson, 1958). An example of an ICC that conforms to this model is given in Figure 13.1b. The latent-distance model in Figure 13.1b, which also contains a discontinuity at one break point, allows for some nonzero probability of responding before the required level of Θ is obtained. Clearly, this model is much closer to actual data,

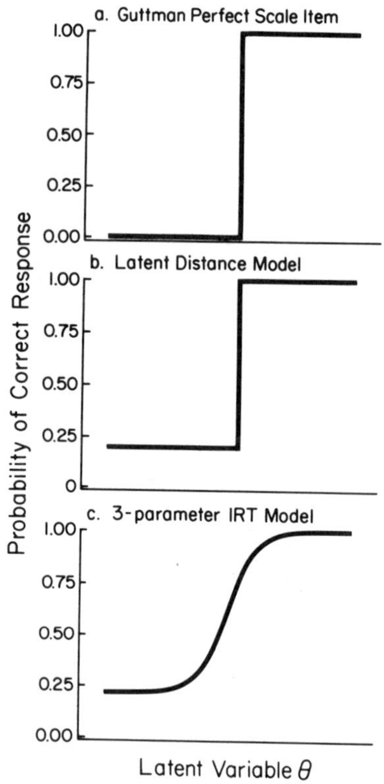

FIGURE 13.1.

because guessing on an item is permissible. However, the slope of the function after the break point seems implausible when considering manifestations of human traits.

Newer IRT models currently enjoy a considerable amount of usage in the field of educational and psychological testing and have been considered as the basis for developmental measurement by Messick (1983). Models representing the ICC as a continuous function have been shown to adequately fit actual data in many circumstances. Figure 13.1c gives an example of an ICC typical of these newer models. Two important features are apparent from the ICC in Figure 13.1c; first, the shape of the ICC is typically assumed to be nonlinear and, second, the relationship between the probability of correctly responding to the item and latent ability Θ is monotonic. Consideration of these two features can lead one to think of these ICCs as somewhat similar in nature to developmental functions. As an examinee increases in ability Θ, the probability of success on some task (item) increases correspondingly. Thus, from a developmental standpoint, discrete events can be seen as probabilistic outcomes of a continuous process.

IRT Models

In order to begin the discussion of IRT models, it is important to consider the natural characteristics of the test item, such as the method of responding to the item. Although some attempts at modeling have been made with respect to polychotomous and continuous choice items, most work has centered around dichotomously scored items. For purposes of exposition, we consider only this type of item.

There are basically two assumptions required for an IRT model. One regards the functional form of the ICC, and the other is a requirement known as the *complete latent space*. The complete latent space requires that all latent traits that influence the responses of a population of examinees to a set of n items be specified. Thus, no other trait that might affect an examinee's response to an item exists within a complete latent space. The assumption of the existence of the complete latent space has several aspects that must be noted. First, we assume that we have, or can construct, items that measure only the traits of interest. Second, we assume that we both know and can specify the population of interest. Finally, we assume that we know the dimensionality of the space measured by the items. It is quite common to assume that the complete latent space is unidimensional with respect to the trait of interest. A single trait is usually of interest to many researchers, so this assumption is not unnecessarily restrictive with respect to theoretical considerations. The question of restrictiveness with respect to empirical considerations is reserved until later.

The consequences of meeting the assumption of the complete latent space are invaluable. First, if a latent space is unidimensional, then all of the items on a test are said to be *locally independent*. This implies that, conditional on Θ, an examinees responses to different items on a test are statistically independent. It does not imply that items are uncorrelated in groups, where Θ varies; it only obtains for a fixed value of Θ. If items are locally independent, then the probability of any particular pattern of item scores for an examinee is the simple product of the probabilities of the individual items. This result is necessary in order to relate an observable item response pattern to the unobservable Θ.

Moreover, if the complete latent space is obtained, then we can interpret the ICC as a regression of item score on a single Θ, without regard to the particular form of the regression. Due to the fact that the probability of a correct response of an individual of ability Θ_0 depends only on Θ_0, it is independent of the distribution of Θ in the population of interest. Thus, the item parameters are *invariant* with respect to the distribution of examinee ability in any particular test administration.

In addition, if the ICC is invariant, then the trait parameter Θ must also be invariant from one test to another, without regard to the items comprising the test, provided they both measure only the single trait Θ. Thus, as a consequence of fulfilling the assumption of the complete latent space, we have a result that item parameters are invariant with respect to the trait level of the group tested, and the trait parameter is invariant with respect to the items comprising a test. This is a clearly a significant departure from the CTT model and the implications are profound.

The other assumption necessary for an IRT model is the specification of the functional form of the ICC. In this respect, many different mathematical functions may be appropriate. The most common form, however, is given by the three-parameter logistic model

$$P_i(\Theta) = c_i + (1 - c_i)/(1 + \exp\{-1.7a_i(\Theta - b_i)\}).$$

In this formulation, Θ is the underlying trait of interest, a_i is an index of item discrimination, b_i indexes item difficulty, and c_i is referred to as the pseudo-chance, or guessing, parameter. $P_i(\Theta)$ is commonly referred to as the probability of a randomly selected examinee at level Θ of the latent trait correctly responding to item *i*.

By dropping the *c* parameter (i.e., assuming it to be 0), we can obtain the two-parameter logistic model, where we expect low ability examinees to have a near zero probability of responding correctly to an item. Furthermore, if we allow the items to have equal discrimination indicies (i.e., the a_is are assumed to be equal), then we obtain the Rasch model (Rasch, 1960). In this model, the only difference in ICCs between items is the difficulty parameter.

Other models, such as a normal ogive formulation, have been suggested as reasonable representations of test item data. Research has shown, however, that a logistic model suitably scaled is similar enough to normal models to justify their use. Another method of expanding the number of useful ICC representations is to allow more parameters to describe the basic function. The rationale is that given more parameters in the model, the better the fit of the model to data. However, the requirements for successful estimation tend to be more stringent.

Relations with CTT

It is important to consider how these new frameworks for solving problems are similar and/or different with respect to the more traditional framework. There are three important issues: (1) the relation between true score and Θ; (2) the relation between item parameters in the two frameworks; and (3) indices of precision of measurement such as reliability.

In CTT, an examinee's true score is defined as the expected value of the examinee's observed score over repeated testings. Lord (1980) showed that an examinee's true score and Θ are the same ability expressed in different metrics. The important difference is that the measurement scale for the true score depends on the items in the test; the measurement scale for Θ is independent of the items in the test, subject to choice of anchoring. Thus, an examinees trait measured in the Θ-metric can be compared across different sets of test items. This can be extremely useful with respect to such testing innovations as adaptive testing, where each examinee receives only partially overlapping tests, with many distinct items or on developmental tests where items change as a function of the age of the subject. In CTT, true scores are comparable only to the extent that parallel forms of the test can be obtained, because true scores depend on the measuring instrument used.

Item Parameters

A we noted earlier, item parameters in an IRT model are invariant with respect to the group of examinees taking the test. Therefore, we can conclude that they are intrinsic parameters of the items they describe. In CTT, the item parameters, such as difficulty and discrimination, are not intrinsic to the items, because they invariably depend on the group tested. For example, the difficulty level for an item in a CTT model will be vastly different depending on whether high-trait or low-trait examinees are tested (i.e., on the nature of the "norm group"). The *b* parameter remains the same, independent of the norm group employed because the ICC is invariant given the complete latent space. Clearly, a framework that provides sample-free calibration of items is preferable to one that has no mechanism for such a procedure.

Precision of Measurement

In IRT models, the accuracy of trait estimates depends only on a quantity known as the information function. Basically, the information function is defined as the reciprocal of the sampling variance of the estimates for Θ for individuals with a common ability Θ. In other words, it is the reciprocal of the squared standard error of the estimated ability level, Θ, given Θ. Under the assumption of local independence, the test information function, I(Θ), is the sum of the item information functions, $I_i(\Theta)$. Therefore, the test information function is a clear indication of the accuracy of estimation, for any given level of Θ. More importantly, it should be noted that the information function can vary for different levels of Θ, depending on the desired measurement requirements of the tests. This last result is important in adaptive testing, where items may be administered to provide a degree of certainty around a specific Θ.

In CTT, the precision of measurement is indexed both by the test reliability and the standard error of measurement. However, because both quantities depend on sample correlations, they are group dependent, and their generalizability is limited (Samejima, 1977). Furthermore, the computation of these quantities depends on the existence of parallel forms of the test. Finally, these indices are aggregate indices, applicable only over the whole range of ability. Clearly, a standard error that is defined locally, as a function of Θ, is to be preferred over one that is not. It is clear that the information function is an intrinsic property of the test, whereas test reliability is not.

Practical Considerations of IRT Models

Having acknowledged some of the advantages of IRT models over CTT models, consideration is turned to problems of estimating the parameters of the model, especially Θ, and to examining ways of testing model assumptions. The question of estimation is particularly relevant to estimation of Θ. When item parameters are known, say through previous calibration, the estimation of Θ is simplified. Simply increasing the number of items will give estimates of Θ with smaller standard errors. Conditional maximum likelihood estimation is the preferred method in this situation, and desirable properties such as consistency and asymptotic normality of the estimators are obtained. The information function is used to determine the precision of measurement. The only potential problem is for examinees with either perfect scores or zero scores. In these two cases, estimates do not exist from maximum likelihood procedures. One can simply assign high and low scores to these individuals, or can employ a Bayesian approach to estimation. The Bayesian approach, however, requires specification of the prior distribution of Θ, which is often not possible.

When both trait parameters and item parameters are unknown, such as in a calibration study, then simultaneous estimation is necessary. Unfortunately, the estimators in these cases may not possess desirable properties. Consider the problems associated with estimation of all parameters simultaneously. If N examinees take a test with n items, then for a three parameter logistic model, $N + 3n - 2$ parameters must be estimated. We know that only 2^n possible response patterns exist from which the $N + 3n - 2$ parameters are to be estimated and not all of these will be observed. Furthermore, any increase in the number of subjects adds to the number of parameters to be estimated.

One solution to the estimation problem is to increase the number of items and examinees simultaneously. Empirical results obtained by Lord (1975) and by Swaminathan and Gifford (1983) indicate that joint estimation by the method of maximum likelihood can give reasonable results with as few subjects as $N = 200$ provided $n \leq 60$. More promising approaches have been recently proposed to deal more directly with the problem of incidental examinee parameters. Bock and Aitken (1981) and Thissen (1982) used marginal maximum likelihood estimation to first produce item parameter estimates. Swaminathan and Gifford (1985) and Mislevy (1986) suggested use of Bayesian techniques to sufficiently estimate all parameters. Although these methods are promising on a theoretical level, the empirical results are not sufficiently available to determine their efficacy.

One communality among all of the estimation methods is the fairly large number of items and examinees required for successful parameter estimation. A conservative rule of thumb, based on current estimation techniques, is to have a minimum of 25 items and 100 examinees in order to produce reasonable estimates. Whichever method of estimation is chosen, a large amount of computer time will be required to obtain the estimates.

Tests of Assumptions

The robustness of IRT methods to the assumption of strict unidimensionality is a controversial one. In actual practice, data sets are not likely to conform to a strict unidimensional model (e.g., a single developmental dimension). It is quite likely that a conglomeration of minor factors will affect item responses. Perhaps a more important consideration is the degree of dominance of the primary factor in relation to the other factors. If the primary factor is dominant, the items are probably sufficiently unidimensional to provide for a robust IRT model. A test of the unidimensionality of the space may be obtained through the application of nonlinear factor analysis (Hattie, 1984; McDonald, 1981). (Ordinary linear factor analysis will tend to give a secondary factor related to difficulty, and thus should not be used.) Furthermore, because the item-trait relation is nonlinear anyway, it makes sense to test it with a nonlinear model.

The assessment of the goodness-of-fit of the specified IRT model to the data has a large literature. Some 80 indices assessing model fit have been suggested (McDonald, 1986). It is unclear which of these are optimal, although likelihood ratio goodness-of-fit tests seem preferred on theoretical grounds.

It is evident that the strong assumptions of IRT theory are subjected to falsifiability in any set of data. The robustness of these models is not clear at this point, although some applications to educational data have proved adequate. Furthermore, procedures for solving the estimation problem are evolving at a rapid pace. Thus, the past difficulties in applying IRT to real data are rapidly being solved.

It is also clear that an IRT formulation can be of extreme theoretical importance to developmental researchers. The conceptualization of ICCs as developmental functions lead to the representation of discrete observable events as probabilistic outcomes of underlying continuous processes. It is also the case that IRT models provide clear practical advantages over CTT models, provided all of the assumptions are met. Sample-free item calibration, item-independent ability estimation, and theoretically optimal ways of test construction are among many of the advantages obtained from these models.

CONCLUSIONS

Progress in the quantitative sciences has yielded new techniques and understanding that allow the developmentalist an expanded array of techniques to investigate behavioral continuity. These new techniques and insights are not simple and will require considerable effort on the part of the applied scientist to gain mastery of their finer points, or will force the formation of alliances with those who regularly deal with such matters. In either case, the gains in understanding of basic developmental processes are likely to be great only if advances in quantitative technique are coupled with careful consideration of the construct of continuity and clever experimental design reflecting the behavioral implications of its existence.

REFERENCES

Appelbaum, M. I., and Cramer, E. M. (1976). *A comparison of several methods for dependent correlation.* Paper presented at the meeting of the Southern Society for Multivariate Experimental Psychology, New Orleans, LA.

Appelbaum, M. I., and McCall, R. B. (1983). Design and analysis in developmental psychology. In P. H. Mussen (Ed.), *Handbook of child psychology* (4th ed., pp. 415–476). New York: Wiley.

Barnett, V., and Lewis, T. (1984). *Outliers in statistical data* (2nd ed.). New York: Wiley.

Bartlett, M. S. (1954). A note on multiplying factors for various chi-squared approximations. *Journal of the Royal Statistical Society* (*Series B*), *16*, 296–298.

Belsley, D. A., Kuh, E., and Welsch, R. E. (1980). *Regression diagnostics: Identifying influential data and sources of collinearity.* New York: Wiley.

Bock, R. D. (1976). Issues in the measurement of change. In de Gruijter and van der Kamp (Eds.), *Advances in psychological and educational measurement* (pp. 75–96). London: Wiley.

Bock, R. D. (1979). Univariate and multivariate analysis of variance of time structured data. In J. R. Nesselroade & P. B. Baltes (Eds.), *Longitudinal research in the study of behavior and development.* New York: Academic Press.

Bock, R. D., and Aitken, M. (1981). Marginal maximum likelihood estimation of item parameters: Application of an EM algorithm. *Psychometrika, 46,* 443–459.

Bock, R. D., Wainer, H., Peterson, A., Thissen, D., Murray, J., and Roche, A. (1973). A parameterization for individual human growth curves. *Human Biology, 45,* 63–80.

Bryk, A. S., and Weisberg, H. I. (1976). Value-added analysis: A dynamic approach to the estimation of treatment effects. *J. of Educational Statistics, 1,* 127–155.

Burchinal, M. R. (1986). *Methods for estimating individual developmental functions.* Unpublished doctoral dissertation, University of North Carolina at Chapel Hill, Chapel Hill, NC.

Cook, R. D., and Weisberg, S. (1982). *Residuals and influence in regression.* New York: Chapman & Hall.

Cramer, E. M. (1972). Significance testis and tests of models in multiple regression. *American Statistician, 26,* 26–29.

Fearn, T. (1975). A Bayesian approach to growth curves. *Biometrika, 62,* 89–100.

Gallant, A. R. (1975a). Nonlinear regression. *American Statistician, 29,* 73–81.

Gallant, A. R. (1975b). Seeming unrelated nonlinear regression. *Journal of Econometrics, 3,* 35–50.

Geisser, S., and Greenhouse, S. W. (1958). An extension of Box's results on the use of the F distribution in multivariate analysis. *Annals of Mathematical Statistics, 29,* 885–891.

Guttman, L. (1950). The basis for scalogram analysis. In S. A. Stouffer *et al. Studies in social psychology in World War II.* Vol. IV, *Measurement and prediction.* Princeton, NJ: Princeton University Press.

Hattie, J. (1984). An empirical study of various indicies for determining unidimensionality. *Multivariate Behavioral Research, 19,* 49–78.

Huber, P. J. (1981). *Robust statistics.* New York: Wiley.

Jennrich, R. J. (1970). An asymptotic chi-square test for the equality of two correlation matrices. *Journal of the American Statistical Association, 65,* 904–912.

Joreskog, K. G. (1979). Statistical estimation of structural models in longitudinal-developmental investigations. In J. R. Nesselroade and P. B. Baltes (Eds.), *Longitudinal research in the study of behavior and development.* New York: Academic Press.

Kleinbaum, D. G., Kupper, L. L., and Muller, K. E. (1988). *Applied regression analysis and other multivariate methods.* Boston: PSW-KENT.

Laird, N. M., and Ware, J. H. (1982). Random-effects models for longitudinal data. *Biometrics, 38,* 963–974.

Lord, F. M. (1975). Evaluation with artificial data of a procedure for estimating ability and item characteristics curve parameters. *Research Bulletin 75-33.* Princeton, NJ: Educational Testing Service.

Lord, F. M. (1980). *Application of item response theory to practical testing problems.* Hillsdale, NJ: Lawrence Erlbaum Associates.

McCall, R. B., and Appelbaum, M. I. (1974). Bias in the analysis of repeated-measures designs: Some alternative approaches. *Child Development, 44,* 401–415.

McCall, R. B., Appelbaum, M. I., and Hogarty, P. S. (1973). Developmental changes in mental performance. *Monographs of the Society for Research in Child Development. 38* (3, Serial No. 150).

McArdle, J. J., and Epstein, D. (1987). Latent growth curves with developmental structural equation models. *Child Development, 58,* 110–133.

McDonald, R. P. (1981). The dimensionality of tests and items. *British Journal of Mathematical and Statistical Psychology, 34,* 100–117.

McDonald, R. P. (1986). Describing the elephant: Structure and function in multivariate data. *Psychometrika, 51,* 513–534.

Messick, S. (1983). Assessment of the child. In P. H. Mussen (Ed.), *Handbook of child psychology* (pp. 477–526). New York: Wiley.

Mislevy, R. J. (1986). Bayes modal estimation in item response models. *Psychometrika, 51,* 177–195.

Morrison, D. F. (1976). *Multivariate statistical methods.* New York: McGraw-Hill.

Mosteller, F., and Tukey, J. W. (1977). *Data analysis and regression.* Reading, MA: Addison-Wesely.

Nesselroade, J. R., and Baltes, P. B. (1979). *Longitudinal research in the study of behavior and development.* New York: Academic Press.

Neter, J., Wasserman, W., and Kutner, M. H. (1985). *Applied linear statistical models* (2nd ed.). Homewood, IL: Irwin.

Nunnally, J. C. (1978). *Psychometric Theory.* New York: McGraw-Hill.

Olkin, I. (1967). Correlations revisited. In J. Stanley (Ed.), *Improving experimental design and statistical analysis.* Chicago: Rand McNally.

Overall, J. E., and Klett, C. J. (1972). *Applied multivariate analysis.* New York: McGraw-Hill.

Potthoff, R. R., and Roy, S. N. (1964). A generalized multivariate analysis of variance model useful especially for growth curve problems. *Biometrika, 51,* 313–326.

Rao, C. R. (1966). Covariance adjustment and related problems in multivariate analysis. In P. R. Krishnaiah (Ed.), *Multivariate analysis.* New York: Academic Press.

Rasch, G. (1960). *Probabilistic models for some intelligence and attainment tests.* Copenhagen: Danish Institute for Educational Research.

Rogosa, D., Brandt, D., and Zimowski, M. (1982). A growth curve approach to the measurement of change. *Psychological Bulletin, 92,* 726–748.

Samejima, F. (1977). A use of the information function in tailored testing. *Applied Psychological Measurement, 1,* 233–247.

Snee, R. D., Acuff, S. K., and Gibson, J. R. (1979). A useful method for the analysis of growth studies. *Biometrics, 35,* 835–848.

Strenio, J. F., Weisberg, H. I., and Bryk, A. S. (1983). Empirical Bayes estimation of individual growth curve parameters and their relationship to covariates. *Biometrics, 39,* 71–86.

Swaminathan, H., and Gifford, J. A. (1983). Estimation of parameters in the three-parameter latent trait model. In D. Weiss (Ed.), *New Horizons in Testing.* New York: Academic Press.

Swaminathan, H., and Gifford, J. A. (1985). Bayesian estimation in the two-parameter logistic model. *Psychometrika, 50,* 349–364.

Thissen, D. M. (1982). Marginal maximum-likelihood estimation for the one-parameter logistic model. *Psychometrika, 47,* 175–186.

Torgerson, W. S. (1958). *Theory and methods of scaling.* New York: Wiley.

Tucker, L. R. (1966). Learning theory and multivariate experiment: Illustration by determination of generalized learning curves. In R. B. Cattell (Ed.), *Handbook of multivariate experimental psychology.* Chicago: Rand McNally.

Wohlwill, J. F. (1973). *The study of behavioral development.* New York: Wiley.

14 Developmental Behavioral Genetics: Stability and Instability

Robert Plomin
College of Health and Human Development
The Pennsylvania State University

INTRODUCTION

When we think beyond description and prediction towards the etiology of stability in development, genetics looms large. Genetic investigations have been slow to enter the mainstream of developmental research because heritability has been associated with stability at a time when the zeitgeist of developmental research favored change. The goal of this chapter is to introduce developmental behavioral genetics, a subdiscipline of behavioral genetics that applies its theory and methods to the study of development (Plomin, 1986a). Developmental behavioral genetics provides a perspective for understanding the genetic and environmental origins of stability and change in individual differences during development.

Developmental behavioral genetics focuses on individual differences in development, their description, prediction, and especially their explanation. For example, when we say that height is heritable, we mean that genetic differences among people play a role in the differences we see in height. Heredity does not speak to the average height of the human species, or to the fact that on average the human species is getting taller, or to the average differences in height between males and females or between the tiny Pygmy and the giant Watusi. These are average group differences; the distinction is critical because behavioral genetics is relevant only to the genetic and environmental causes of individual differences within groups but has little to say about the causes of average differences between groups. For instance, behavioral genetics can inform us about why some children are delayed in their use of language but it cannot tell us why the human species is a natural language user or why girls on average tend to perform better on verbal tests than boys, even though genetics might underlie such group differences. These issues are discussed in detail elsewhere (e.g., Plomin, DeFries, and Fulker, 1988).

Interest in behavioral genetics depends on wanting to know why people differ. There are at least two reasons why developmentalists should be interested in individual differences. First, individual differences are substantial. For example, people differ considerably in scores on vocabulary tests—on most moderately difficult tests, the top scorers in a normal population will get five times as many words correct as low scorers. Individual differences are invariably far greater than average differences between groups. For example, although girls tend to perform better than boys on tests of verbal ability, this average difference accounts for about 1% of the variance of verbal ability (e.g., Plomin and Foch, 1981). In addition, societally relevant issues in the behavioral sciences are usually issues of individual differences. For example, although it is interesting to ask why the human species uses language, more relevant to society are questions such as why some children are delayed in the use of language, why some are reading disabled, and why some people are more verbally fluent than others.

The other chapters in this volume emphasize individual differences in development, especially their ability to predict individual differences later in life. In order to underline this focus on individual differences, the words *stability* and *instability* will be used to refer to developmental changes in individual differences, rather than the words *continuity* and *discontinuity,* which are typically used to connote both mean changes in age and individual differences in the developmental literature. The emphasis on individual differences in many chapters in this volume is compatible with the perspective of developmental behavioral genetics, although their focus tends to be description rather than explanation. The goal of this chapter is to describe concepts and data from developmental behavioral genetics that provide a perspective on the etiology of developmental stability and instability. The chapter begins with an organizational scheme for approaching the description and explanation of individual differences in development.

DESCRIPTION AND EXPLANATION OF INDIVIDUAL DIFFERENCES

As indicated earlier, most developmental research considers average developmental trends or *developmental functions* (McCall, 1979). Appropriate developmental questions are deceptively simple: How do children change on average? What is the earliest age that *X* appears? Can you intervene to get children to do it earlier? Wohlwill (1973) discussed the limitations of such research. The present volume marks a shift back towards an emphasis on individual differences and on stability as well as instability, emphases more characteristic of work before

World War II. However, in contrast to the ease with which questions emerge concerning average age functions, it is not as obvious what we want to know about individual differences. The short answer is that we want to describe, predict, and explain individual difference in development. But what does this really mean? An organizational scheme for answering this question is indicated in Table 14.1. Although this scheme risks stating the obvious, it is useful at least in providing a background for understanding concepts of developmental behavioral genetics.

In thinking about development from an individual differences perspective, the focus of attention is on variance and covariance rather than means. There are three basic issues: age changes in variance, age changes in covariance among variables (factor structure), and age-to-age covariance (stability and predictiveness). Although age-to-age covariance is emphasized in developmental research on individual differences, the other two types of stability and change are also informative about developmental processes. As indicated in Table 14.1, variances and covariances can be described or explained. In this chapter, the word *explanation* refers to genetic and environmental origins of variance and covariance. This is a narrow use of the word explanation—psychologists often use the word to refer to processes underlying outcomes in the sense that elemental cognitive processes could be said to explain more global outcomes such as memory. Throughout this chapter, concepts rather than statistics are emphasized.

AGE CHANGES IN VARIANCE

Description

It is difficult to find research that asks questions about the development of variance. A temporary increase in variance will occur, for example, if individual differences in timing of developmental events are important. More permanent changes in variance might be observed if different processes come to affect a

TABLE 14.1
Description and Explanation of Individual Differences in Development

	Description	*Explanation*
Age changes in variance	Does variance change as a function of age?	Do genetic and environmental components of variance change with age?
Age changes in covariance among variables	Does factor structure change with age?	Do genetic and environmental covariances change with age?
Age-to-age covariance	Is there age-to-age stability? Long-term predictiveness?	Do age-to-age genetic and environmental covariances change?

trait; new processes brought to bear on a trait are likely to magnify extant differences among children. Moreover, increases in variance might be expected simply because older children can do more than younger children. For example, productive vocabulary is not likely to differentiate children much at 12 months when, on average, children say two words, as compared to only one year later when children's vocabularies include hundreds of words.

Nancy Bayley was interested in the topic of developmental changes in variance for mental age; she noticed a sharp drop in variance towards the end of the first year of life and suggested that it is "due to the approach to maturity of the particular processes being measured" (Bayley, 1949, p. 178). Bayley also documented an increase in variance in early adolescence at nine, ten, and eleven years. Increases in variance during early childhood have been posited on theoretical grounds as well. For example, McCall (1981, 1983) proposed a "scoop" model of mental development, at the core of which lies the hypothesis that variance increases substantially beginning at about two years of age and continuing to about six years, which follows from the assumption that mental development during infancy is strongly canalized in the evolutionary sense: "When development is less canalized, the self-righting tendency is weaker, individuals differ from one another to a greater extent, and individual differences are more likely to persist through time because there is less pull by nature to keep her children in single file" (McCall, 1983, p. 114).

Research on changes in variance is so rare that it is difficult to offer any summary conclusion. However, in the Colorado Adoption Project, a longitudinal study of 445 adoptive families and 445 matched nonadoptive families, no evidence emerged in support of the generally accepted hypothesis that variance for cognitive measures increases during infancy and early childhood, although difficulties in comparing variances across ages were acknowledged (Plomin et al., 1988).

Explanation

Although developmentalists rarely consider variance per se, the field of behavioral genetics has virtually fixated on variance, specifically, genetic and environmental components of variance. Heritability is a descriptive statistic that refers to the portion of observed variance for a particular trait that can be accounted for by genetic differences among individuals in a particular population at a particular time. (See Plomin, DeFries, and McClearn, in press, for a discussion of heritability and other issues related to behavioral genetics). It is a descriptive statistic and will change as the population changes in the relative influence of genetic and environmental factors. Populations can change over time because of cohort effects that bring different environmental contingencies to bear or because of genetic changes due to migration or changes in mating patterns.

The point of developmental behavioral genetics is that heritability may also change as a function of age for members of the same population if environmental or genetic influences change during development. For example, heritability will increase if the proportion of phenotypic variance due to genetic influence increases or if the proportion of environmental variance decreases. However, it is possible that the relative amount of phenotypic variance due to genetic variance could remain unchanged, even if completely different sets of genes are transcribed at the two ages. Thus, similar heritabilities at two or more ages do not necessarily imply genetic stability. This issue of age-to-age change in genetic covariance is the topic of a later section.

Although few developmentalists have considered the issue of developmental change in heritability it is reasonable to speculate that, as children develop and experience more diverse environments, environmental variance will increasingly account for phenotypic variance. In other words, heritability will decrease during development. This is explicitly the view among Soviet developmentalists (e.g., Mangan, 1982). However, a review of behavioral genetic data on cognition, personality, and psychopathology from a developmental perspective indicates that, when changes in heritability are found, they increase during development (Plomin, 1986a). For example, twin results and nonadoptive versus adoptive sibling comparisons for height show sharply increasing heritabilities during the first year of life, leading to stable high heritabilities beginning at two years of age (Plomin et al., 1988).

Data from the Louisville Twin Study, a longitudinal study of nearly 500 pairs of twins, indicate that mental development scores also show increasing heritability during childhood, as illustrated in Figure 14.1 for the Bayley Scales of Infant Development through 24 months of age, the Stanford-Binet at 30 and 36 months, and Wechsler tests thereafter (Wilson, 1983). On the whole, these data suggest that heritability is low in infancy and increases in early childhood and especially in the early school years. Heritabilities increase approximately 5% per year, from 10% to 25%, from one to four years; during the early school years, heritability nearly doubles and reaches levels comparable to heritabilities of adult IQ data. The high correlations for both types of twins as compared to nontwin siblings suggest that twin correlations, especially during infancy, are substantially inflated by shared perinatal influences specific to twins.

Other twin studies yield similar results. However, the only study using a design other than the twin design, the Colorado Adoption Project, compared nonadoptive and adoptive siblings and found substantially greater evidence for heritability during infancy for the Bayley test at one and two years of age, perhaps because perinatal influences specific to twins overwhelm genetic factors in the twin data (Plomin et al., 1988). Verbal ability showed the greatest increase in genetic influence in comparisons between nonadoptive and adoptive siblings. Shared environment, as estimated directly by the correlation for adoptive siblings, is essentially zero in infancy and increases during early childhood.

Thus, it is not yet possible to reach a firm conclusion concerning developmen-

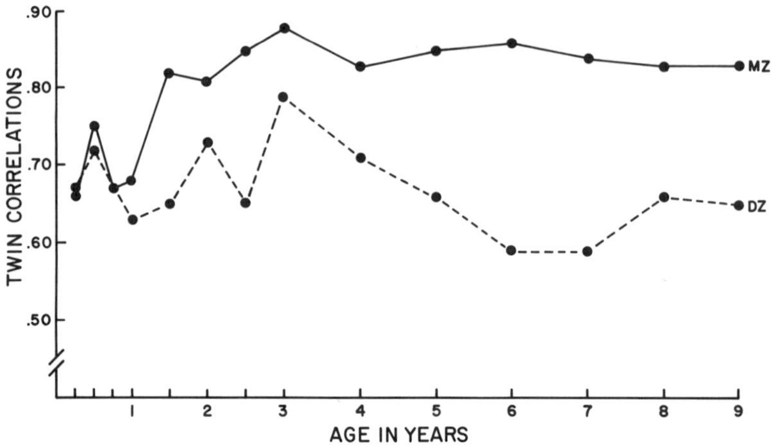

FIGURE 14.1. Correlations for IQ for twins in the Louisville Twin Study (adapted from "The Louisville Twin Study: Developmental Synchronies in Behavior" by R. S. Wilson, 1983, *Child Development, 54,* 298–316.

tal changes in the relative magnitude of genetic and environmental influences in the cognitive realm during development. Although behavioral genetic research focuses on components of variance, developmental change is rarely considered—the vast majority of studies involve a wide age range, often from childhood to adulthood.

COVARIANCE AMONG VARIABLES

Description

Developmental change can also be marked by changes in covariances among variables, which might be expected if constituent processes change during development. For example, language items correlate increasingly with nonverbal cognitive measures during the transition from infancy to early childhood as language begins to assume its symbolic role in communication and becomes an important component of *g,* an index of general cognitive ability (Plomin et al., 1988). When more than a few measures are involved, factor analysis can be used to summarize the pattern of intercorrelations and model-fitting approaches to factor analysis are useful for comparing alternative models of factor structure.

Two aspects of developmental change in factor structure can be examined: Differences in the strength of factors—the amount of variance they explain—and differences in the nature of the factors, seen in the pattern of factor loadings. For example, Werner's (1948) orthogenetic principle states that development is marked by differentiation. Although the orthogenetic principle is phrased in terms of normative development, from an individual differences perspective differentation is seen as a decline in the magnitude of intercorrelations among measures. In a multivariate framework, this can be expressed as a decrease in the amount of variance explained by an unrotated first principal component, an index of *g*, general cognitive ability. For example, items on tests of infant mental development would intercorrelate more highly in infancy than in early childhood if cognitive abilities differentiate. Contrary to this individual differences version of the differentiation hypothesis, the variance explained by a first principal component of mental ability items increases from about 20% in infancy to about 30% in early childhood (Plomin et al., 1988). Although some developmentalists deny any important role for *g* in infancy (e.g., Lewis, 1983), it appears to play a modest role during infancy and is increasingly important in early childhood, at least as assessed by items on the Bayley test. This is not meant to imply that all aspects of cognitive functioning can be described by a single factor. However, more data are available for general cognitive ability rather than specific cognitive abilities such as verbal and memory abilities.

A second aspect of developmental change in factor structure involves changes in the pattern of unrotated and rotated factor loadings. For example, does the nature of general cognitive ability change during the transition from infancy to early childhood? Do relations among receptive and expressive language abilities change during the transition? When do specific cognitive abilities emerge?

The first question has been addressed by McCall and his colleagues in analyses of Gesell items from the Fels study (McCall, Hogarty, and Hurlburt, 1972) and in analyses of the Berkeley Growth Study for the California First-Year Test, the precursor of the Bayley test (McCall, Eichorn, and Hogarty, 1977). In the latter study, comparisons of factor loadings for first principal components for 25 ages from one month to five years led to the conclusion that the most marked changes occur at 8, 13, and 21 months. The nature of the first principal component at the three ages, respectively, was described as separation of means from ends, entity-entity relations, and symbolic relationships (McCall, 1979). Although the first principal components are not easily interpreted, it is clear that unrotated first principal components in the first year largely involve fine motor and gross motor skills; at twenty-four months, the general factor is primarily verbal in nature; the eighteen-month principal component is intermediate. Similar results were obtained in the Colorado Adoption Project at twelve and twenty-four months (Plomin and DeFries, 1985); analyses of three- and four-year Stanford-Binet items also indicate that the nature of *g* is substantially verbal by early childhood (Plomin et al., 1988).

A persistent problem in such comparisons arises when items of a different nature are used at different ages. For example, few language items appear until the second half of the second year. The old saw that "you only get out of factor analysis what you put in" raises the distinct possibility that factor analyses find greater loadings of language items during the second half of the second year simply because it was not possible to include language items earlier. This objection does not, however, make the finding trivial. Although the number of language items is greater in tests towards the end of the second year, these items might not have loaded so highly on the *g* factor—indeed, the few language items included at twelve months do not load highly on *g*.

The nature of rotated factors may also change during development. It would seem reasonable, for example, to posit that specific cognitive abilities differentiate during childhood in the sense that verbal, spatial, and memory abilities become more distinct factorially. However, factor analytic work of this type has rarely been conducted because mental tests in infancy and early childhood emphasize *g*. Stott and Ball (1965) summarized the results of rotated factor solutions for various infant tests administered to a total of 1,926 infants and young children. Comparisons among the factors at different ages was complicated by the necessity of using different tests; nonetheless, Stott and Ball concluded that factor structures change with age although specifics of these developmental changes remained elusive. More recent analyses of this type concur that factor structure changes during the transition from infancy to early childhood, especially in terms of increasing differentation of language-related measures (Lewis, Jaskir, and Enright, 1986; Plomin et al., 1988). Additional work in early childhood suggests the hypothesis that *g* encompasses increasingly diverse cognitive functions while, at the same time, specific cognitive abilities begin to diverge (Plomin et al., 1988).

Explanation

Just as the phenotypic covariance among measures can change during development, genetic and environmental contributions to the phenotypic covariance can also change. Multivariate behavioral genetic analysis is one of the most important advances in the field during the past decade; it disentangles genetic and environmental sources of covariance among traits rather than analyzing the variance of each trait considered individually (DeFries and Fulker, 1986). The essence of multivariate analysis is the decomposition of phenotypic covariance between two traits measured on the same individuals into genetic and environmental sources of covariance. That is, two traits can correlate phenotypically for genetic or for environmental reasons. If the phenotypic correlation is mediated genetically, this means that the genes that affect one trait also affect the other trait. If two traits are highly heritable but uncorrelated phenotypically, this implies that the genes that affect one trait are independent of the genes that affect the other trait. The genetic component of the phenotypic correlation between the two traits is the genetic correlation (r_G) weighted by the product of the square roots of the heritabilities of each of the traits ($h_x h_y$). The genetic correlation is the correlation between genetic deviations that affect one trait and genetic deviations that affect another trait regardless of the heritabilities of the traits. The phenotypically standardized genetic covariance ($h_x h_y r_G$) and the genetic correlation (r_G) thus have different, but equally interesting interpretations and developmental change in either term is noteworthy.

Any behavioral genetic design that can estimate genetic and environmental components of the variance of a single trait can also be used to estimate genetic and environmental components of the covariance between two traits. In effect, however, contemporaneous relations (twins and siblings) are more appropriate than parent-offspring comparisons when parents are adults and offspring are children. As discussed in the following section, parent-offspring correlations are complicated by not knowing the extent to which genetic effects in childhood are correlated with genetic effects in adulthood. In all respects, quantitative genetic analysis of the covariance between traits is parallel to analysis of the variance of a single trait. Using the twin design as an example, instead of correlating one twin's score with the co-twin's score on the same variable, twin cross-correlations are analyzed. A cross-correlation is the correlation between one twin's score on X and the other twin's score on Y. Doubling the difference between identical and fraternal twin correlations for a single trait estimates heritability, the proportion of phenotypic variance that can be accounted for by genetic variance. Doubling the difference between identical and fraternal twin cross-correlations estimates the genetic contribution to the phenotypic correlation (i.e., $h_x h_y r_G$). In traditional univariate analyses of variance, variance not explained by heredity is attributed to environmental factors; similarly, in bivariate analyses of covariance, covariance not explained by heredity is attributed to environmental factors that contribute to covariance between the traits.

Although multivariate behavioral genetic analyses are becoming commonplace, developmentally relevant analyses remain scarce. Preliminary analyses of adoptive and nonadoptive sibling data from the Colorado Adoption Project indicate the promise of such an approach. For example, height and weight are highly correlated—.65, .65, .71, and .65, respectively, at one, two, three, and four years—and both are highly heritable. In effect, multivariate analysis addresses the extent to which genes that affect height also affect weight; the developmental question is whether the extent of genetic covariance between height and weight changes from age to age. The nonadoptive sibling cross-correlations between height and weight at one, two, three, and four years, respectively, are .33, .35, .37, and .46; the adoptive sibling cross-correlations are .00, .00, −.10, and .14. This pattern of results indicates, not surprisingly, that the phenotypic correlations between height and weight are mediated genetically and that genetic mediation of the association between height and weight is stable during infancy and early childhood.

A bivariate issue of long-standing interest is the relation between cognitive and communicative development. The Bayley Mental Development Index and the Sequenced Inventory of Communication Development (SICD) correlate highly, .67 at two years and .63 at three years, and both appear to be influenced by heredity. Cross-correlations are .32 and .04 for nonadoptive and adoptive siblings, respectively, at two years, and .36 and .16 at three years. These results suggest substantial and stable genetic mediation of the association between cognitive and communicative development. A related example concerns the association between expressive and receptive communicative skills as assessed by the SICD at two and three years. The phenotypic correlations are .51 at two and .52 at three; the nonadoptive and adoptive sibling cross-correlations are .25 and −.02 at two and .12 and .11 at three, respectively. These results suggest developmental change in that the phenotypic association between the two variables is substantially mediated by genetic factors at two but not at three years.

Another example involves the association between mental and motor development. The phenotypic correlation between the Bayley Mental Development Index (MDI) and the Bayley Psychomotor Development Index (PDI) correlate .41 at one year and only .18 at two years. To what extent is this relation mediated genetically, and is there evidence for developmental change? At twelve months, the nonadoptive sibling cross-correlation is .23, and the adoptive sibling cross-correlation is −.01, suggesting substantial genetic mediation of the association between mental and motor development. At 24 months, however, the phenotypic correlation is low and the cross-correlations for nonadoptive and adoptive siblings indicate that genetic covariance is also low. The cross-correlations are .01 for nonadoptive siblings and .18 for adoptive siblings. Thus, the data are compatible with a hypothesis of genetic differentiation of mental and motor development during infancy.

At the minimum, these analyses from the Colorado Adoption Project with their diverse but reasonable results exemplify an important direction for research to explore the developmental unfolding of genetic and environmental covariance among traits.

AGE-TO-AGE COVARIANCE

Description

Much developmental research on individual differences describes age-to-age covariance, as evidenced by other chapters in this volume. Two types of data are relevant: short-term and long-term. In addition to simply describing the extent of short-term, age-to-age stability, developmental changes in stability have also been examined. Although problems in interpreting differences in age-to-age correlations are considerable (Bateson, 1978), three types of developmental change in age-to-age correlations have been considered. It is generally accepted that there is more stability later in life and that longitudinal correlations show a simplex pattern in which longer intervals between ages yield lower stability. The third type of short-term developmental change examines the possibility of transitions: If an individual differences transition exists, age-to-age correlations across the transition should be lower than age-to-age correlations before or after the transition. McCall (1983, p. 120) referred to this as "dips in cross-age stabilities of individual differences:"

> It is quite possible that individual differences become rearranged at the advent of new skills, a phenomenon that would be reflected in reduced cross-age stabilities at points in development where major discontinuities in the developmental function occur. Consequently, cross-age stabilities should be higher for periods that do not span a discontinuity, and lower for comparable periods that do embrace a discontinuity in developmental function.

Long-term age-to-age correlations, such as those found in the birth-to-maturity Berkeley and Fels studies, have also been considered, although such data sets are rare for obvious reasons. In addition to simply describing the magnitude of stability, developmental change in such long-term age-to-age correlations can be examined. Conclusions based on short-term age-to-age covariance can of course differ from those reached for long-term predictions.

Height and weight provide useful comparisons for behavioral characteristics because height and weight are more heritable and more stable than behavior. Do age-to-age correlations for height and weight change during infancy and early childhood? Several studies, including new data from the Colorado Adoption Project show: (1) Age-to-age correlations for height increase slightly but steadily, (2) age-to-age correlations for weight do not show systematic change during infancy and early childhood, and (3) stabilities for height and weight are similar in magnitude (reviewed by Plomin et al., 1988). Long-term correlations between childhood and adulthood suggest a somewhat different conclusion. In three studies, long-term predictiveness increases slightly for both height and weight from one to five years and is substantially greater for height than for weight—correlations from childhood to adulthood are about .75 for height and .45 for weight.

Age-to-age correlations for cognitive development suggest greater increases during infancy and early childhood than for height and weight. In a review of nine studies conducted in the 1930s, the average correlation was .50 from one to two years, .68 from two to three years, and .66 from three to four years (Thorndike, 1940). Six major longitudinal studies reviewed by McCall (1979) also yielded a lower correlation (r = .32) from one to two years than from two to three years (r = .59). Although all studies agree that stability for mental test scores increases during infancy and early childhood, it is uncertain whether an abrupt change occurs; the most parsimonious view is that stability increases linearly. Analyses of longer-term correlations predicting IQ in middle childhood or in adulthood also indicate that age-to-age stability correlations increase steadily during infancy and early childhood—correlations from childhood to adulthood are about .25 at one year, .40 at two years, .45 at three years, and .50 at four years (Plomin et al., 1988).

Next to nothing is known about the developmental course of age-to-age covariance for cognitive measures other than IQ. Three studies have suggested that vocalization in infancy yields significant long-term correlations with later IQ, at least for females (Cameron, Livson, and Bayley, 1967; Kagan, 1971; Moore, 1967); however, these studies do not permit developmental comparisons. Recent construction of individual differences measures for the first year of life from experimental psychology paradigms offers considerable promise for yielding greater predictiveness (e.g., Fagan, 1985).

Explanation

Developmental changes in heritability and changes in genetic covariance among variables are cross-sectional etiological concepts. The third concept of developmental change in individual differences is the most important: age-to-age genetic covariance. The concept of age-to-age genetic covariance follows from the simple extension of multivariate analysis to longitudinal data (Plomin, 1986b; Plomin and DeFries, 1981). In longitudinal analysis, genetic correlations (r_G) and genetic contributions to phenotypic stability ($h_1 h_2 r_G$) are especially interesting because they refer to the etiology of age-to-age change and stability, the core issue of developmental behavioral genetics.

In the case of longitudinal data, the phenotypic correlation refers to phenotypic stability between a trait measured at one age and a trait (not necessarily the same trait) measured at another age in the same individuals. This phenotypic stability can be decomposed into genetic and environmental components of stability. In terms of developmental change, to the extent that genetic variance at two ages does not covary between the ages, genetic change is implicated. In this way, low age-to-age genetic correlations indicate genetic change during development. As in the case of multivariate analysis, longitudinal analyses refer to covariance between the genetic deviations that affect traits at two ages. Research in developmental genetics indicates that most developmental change involves modulation of rates at which various genes are transcribed (i.e., coded into RNA) rather than turning different genes on and off (Plomin, 1986a). If many of the genes that affect a particular trait change in this way, age-to-age genetic continuity will be low. However, age-to-age genetic continuity might not map so clearly onto genetic events. For example, the same genes need not be transcribed at the two ages even if genetic stability is 1.0: The relevant genes at age two might no longer be actively transcribed, but their structural legacy (e.g., differences in neural networks) could produce a genetic correlation between age one and age two. Conversely, if genetic stability is low, actively transcribed genes that affect the trait at age one could continue to be actively transcribed at age two if their gene products no longer have the same effects at that time.

Although analyses of age-to-age genetic and environmental covariance will undoubtedly become a hallmark of developmental behavioral genetic analyses in the future, they require longitudinal data and few longitudinal behavioral genetic studies have been conducted. In fact, in addition to the Skodak and Skeels (1949) adoption study of IQ, only two long-term longitudinal behavioral genetic studies have been reported, the Louisville Twin Study (Wilson, 1983) and the Colorado Adoption Project (Plomin and DeFries, 1985; Plomin et al., 1988). The twin design and sibling adoption design provide estimates of genetic and environmental short-term age-to-age covariance; if longitudinal studies of this type are continued for many years, they can also provide analyses of genetic and environmental contributions from childhood to later in life. In addition, the parent-offspring adoption design provides a novel alternative to studying infant-to-adult continuity because, from a genetic perspective, parent-offspring resemblance represents an instant longitudinal study from childhood to adulthood. For example, significant associations between biological mothers and their adopted-away infants can be found only if three conditions are met: The measures are substantially heritable in infancy and in adulthood and the genetic correlation between infancy and adulthood is substantial. Thus, if significant associations are found between biological mothers' scores and scores of their adopted-away infants, some genetic stability between infancy and adulthood is implied.

The longitudinal data from the Louisville Twin Study have not been analyzed in terms of age-to-age genetic correlations. Rather, analyses have employed twin trend correlations based on a repeated-measures analysis of variance; these analyses have been interpreted as supporting an hypothesis of substantial genetic continuity during infancy and early childhood (Wilson, 1983). However, a conceptual problem arises because trend correlations are complex functions of heritabilities at each age and genetic and phenotypic correlations among the ages (Plomin, 1986a). An empirical problem is that the results of analyses of twin trend correlations for longitudinal profiles are generally similar to the average twin results for scores at each age, perhaps because trend correlations include twin similarity both for overall level and for age-to-age changes (Wilson, 1986).

In the Colorado Adoption Project, longitudinal analyses of adoptive and nonadoptive sibling cross-correlations across age have been reported (Plomin et al., 1988). Results indicate that phenotypic stability for height is mediated nearly entirely by genetic factors; however, about 30% of the phenotypic stability for weight is mediated environmentally. Additional analyses indicate that for both height and weight genetic correlations are near 1.0, suggesting complete genetic stability. For Bayley and Stanford-Binet scores, sibling cross-correlations indicate no genetic mediation of stability from one to two years but considerable genetic mediation from two to three and from three to four years. The results for verbal ability are similar. Increasing age-to-age genetic stability corresponds to results for parent-offspring analyses.

Traditionally, behavioral genetic analyses of parent-offspring resemblance have not considered the likely possibility of genetic change from childhood to adulthood (Plomin, 1986b). As mentioned earlier, finding significant parent-offspring resemblance implies not only significant heritability in childhood and in adulthood but also significant genetic continuity between childhood and adulthood. In this sense the parent-offspring adoption design provides an instant longitudinal study from childhood to adulthood. In fact, it would be difficult to detect parent-offspring resemblance unless all three elements are substantial. For height and weight, parent-offspring correlations suggest that phenotypic stability from childhood to adulthood is largely mediated by genetic factors and that child-to-adult genetic stability increases slightly from one to four years.

For cognitive development, the value of the famous study by Skodak and Skeels (1949) is diminished because testing did not begin until after infancy; the average age of the children at their first testing was twenty-six months, and the ages at first testing varied from six months to six years. Figure 14.2 presents Colorado Adoption Project correlations between biological mothers and their adopted-away offspring, which suggest some genetic continuity from infancy to adulthood. Correlations for nonadoptive mothers and their children are similar. On average, the mother/child correlations increase somewhat—from about .10 at one year to about .20 at four years. These correlations suggest an important conclusion: Because the coefficient of genetic relatedness for parents and offspring is .50, the genetic contribution to phenotypic stability from childhood to adulthood appears to be substantial. Results for specific cognitive abilities are also consistent with the possibility of some genetic mediation from childhood to adulthood, although less than for IQ (Plomin et al., 1988).

Although it is useful didactically to present these new concepts of etiological

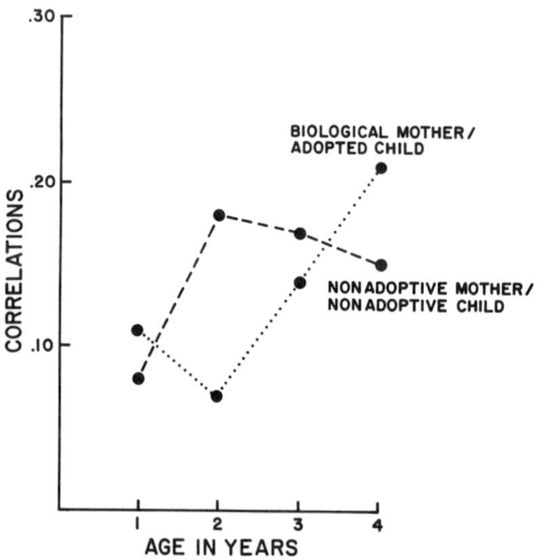

FIGURE 14.2. Parent-offspring correlations for IQ during infancy (Bayley MDI scores) and early childhood (Stanford-Binet IQ scores) for biological mothers and adopted-away children (BM/AC) and control (nonadoptive) mothers and children (CM/CC) in the Colorado Adoption Project. From *Nature and Nurture During Infancy and Early Childhood* (p. 149) by R. Plomin, J. C. DeFries, and D. W. Fulker, 1988, New York: Cambridge University Press.

factors in development at an expository, intuitive level, model-fitting approaches are needed to provide more formal tests of these hypotheses and to utilize all of the data simultaneously from a complex design such as the parent-offspring adoption design of the Colorado Adoption Project, which includes three types of parents, assortative mating, and selective placement. Model fitting—also called causal models, structural models, biometrical models, or path models—is given its name because these procedures test the fit between a model and observed data. Model fitting and the representation of models in terms of path analysis originated over half a century ago for the purpose of genetic analysis (Wright, 1921) and was developed by Jinks and Fulker (1970) to fit behavioral genetic models to a variety of familial correlations. Model fitting represents another major advance in behavioral genetics during the past decade; everything discussed in this chapter could be analyzed in a more sophisticated manner using models that make assumptions explicit, yield parameter estimates given the assumptions of the model, yield standard errors for these parameter estimates, and provide a goodness-of-fit test to aid in the evaluation of alternative models.

An excellent introduction to model fitting in general can be found in Loehlin (1987), and an introduction to model fitting in behavioral genetics is included in Plomin et al. (1988). The model used in analyses of the Colorado Adoption Project, which analyzes data for nonadoptive and adoptive families simultaneously and includes assortative mating and selective placement as well genetic and environmental transmission, is also described in the latter reference, as are multivariate and longitudinal extensions of the model. The longitudinal model is especially relevant to the present discussion because of the complexity of analyzing genetic and environmental sources of developmental change and continuity from childhood to adulthood using the parent-offspring adoption design (DeFries, Plomin, & LaBuda, 1987). The advantage of this model, as compared to the examination of biological mother/adoptee correlations as in Figure 14.2, lies in the simultaneous analysis of data from all three family types, in explicitly testing the significance of the longitudinal genetic correlations, and in modeling the effects of assortative mating and selective placement. Resolution of the model requires independent heritability estimates in childhood and in adulthood, for which twin data were employed.

Model-fitting estimates of genetic correlations (r_G) and genetic contributions to phenotypic stability from childhood to adult IQ ($h_c h_a r_G$) are summarized in Table 14.2. Of greatest interest is the child-to-adult genetic stability represented by the genetic correlation parameter, which is moderate at one year of age but increases to .75 by four years. Despite the large standard error attached to these estimates, the genetic correlation is statistically significant at three and four years; this result was verified more rigorously by means of testing reduced nested models. This suggests that genetic effects on IQ scores in early childhood are substantially correlated with genetic effects on IQ scores in adulthood. These results provide the strongest available evidence for significant genetic stability for IQ from early childhood to adulthood. However, the genetic correlations are not unity, which implies that genetic change might also play a role in the development of cognitive ability.

In addition, these results also imply the ability to predict some phenotypic stability from early childhood to adulthood for IQ. As shown in Table 14.2, the genetic contribution to phenotypic stability is .10 from 1 year to adulthood, .18 from two years, .18 from three years, and .28 from four years. Phenotypic stability from one, two, three, and four years of age to adulthood is about .25, .40, and .50, respectively. Thus, these results suggest that the proportion of phenotypic stability between twelve months and adulthood that is mediated genetically is .40 (that is, .10 / .25). The proportions are .45, .40, and .56 at one, two, three, and four years, respectively. Although a surprising amount of genetic variance that affects IQ scores in childhood covaries with genetic influences on adult IQ, genetic change is also apparent in these results. Across the four years, the average genetic correlation is .58, which means that about half of the genetic variance in childhood does not covary between childhood and adulthood. Thus, phenotypic change during development is also brought about in part by genetic change.

The instant child-to-adult longitudinal feature of the parent-offspring design has been exploited in a study that uses this feature as a means of rapidly screening infant measures for their ability to predict adult cognitive abilities (Fulker, Plomin, Thompson, Phillips, Fagan, and Haith, 1988). A midparent-midtwin design is used to increase the reliability of parent-offspring resemblance and to disentangle genetic and environmental sources of parent-offspring resemblance. Relationships between measures of infant cognitive development at seven, eight, and nine months of age and adult cognitive abilities were assessed for 83 pairs of infant twins and their parents. Infant measures included Fagan's Test of Infant

TABLE 14.2
Genetic Correlations (r_G) and Genetic Contributions ($h_c h_a r_G$) to Phenotypic Stability from Childhood to Adult IQ

	Model-Fitting Estimates	
Parental IQ versus	*Genetic Correlations* $r_G \pm SE$	*Genetic Contributions to Phenotypic Stability* $(h_c) \cdot (h_a) \cdot (r_G) = h_c h_a r_G$
Bayley at 1 year:	.42 ± .50	(.32)(.74)(.42) = .10
Bayley at 2 years:	.61 ± .33	(.41)(.73)(.61) = .18
Stanford-Binet at 3 years:	.56 ± .28*	(.43)(.74)(.56) = .18
Stanford-Binet at 4 years:	.75 ± .27*	(.51)(.74)(.75) = .28

*$p < .05$

Note. From "Genetic Stability of Cognitive Development from Childhood to Adulthood" by J. C. DeFries, R. Plomin, and M. C. LaBuda, 1987, *Developmental Psychology, 23*, 4–12.

Intelligence, Haith's measure of visual reaction time and visual anticipation, selected items from the Bayley Scales of Infant Development, verbal behavior, Bayley's Infant Behavior Record (IBR), and other measures. The infant measures were regressed on midparent IQ to evaluate their likelihood of predicting adult IQ. Most measures appeared to be predictive, but the Fagan, Haith, IBR, and vocalization measures were the best predictors. For a composite of 13 measures, heritability was estimated as .30, and the regressions of midtwin on midparent were .56 ± .12 for parents' adult IQ (Fulker et al., 1988). These results support the notion of substantial genetic stability from childhood to adulthood for general cognitive ability.

CONCLUSIONS

As discussed at the beginning of this chapter, little is known about developmental change from the perspective of individual differences. Change can occur for variances, covariances (factor structure), and for age-to-age correlations. Each facet of developmental change can be approached from the point of view of description or in terms of explanation as in behavioral genetic analyses of variance and covariance.

In terms of description, when developmental changes are found, they tend to indicate increases for all three facets of change. That is, variances increase, covariances increase, and age-to-age stability increases. The changes are not sudden or dramatic; when changes occur, they are linear during infancy and early childhood.

Another major approach to the study of the development of individual differences goes beyond description and prediction to consider genetic and environmental etiology, the forté of developmental behavioral genetics. Even in the absence of descriptive changes in phenotypic variance, within-age covariance among variables, and between-age covariance, genetic and environmental provenances of variance and covariance can change. The etiological analogs are: (1) the magnitude of genetic and environmental components of variance, (2) patterns of genetic and environmental correlations among variables within an age, and (3) genetic and environmental contributions to age-to-age covariance.

The first type of etiological analysis suggests an interesting hypothesis: When heritability changes during development, it increases. Part of the importance of this hypothesis lies in its counterintuitive nature: Most developmentalists would guess that environmental variance, not genetic variance, increasingly explains phenotypic variance as children grow up and experience more and more diverse environmental influences.

The second type of etiological analysis considers the etiology of covariances among measures, rather than the variance of each measure considered individually. For example, height and weight correlate substantially and this phenotypic correlation is mediated nearly completely by genetic covariance; the extent of genetic mediation does not appear to change during infancy and early childhood. The results for the relation between communicative and cognitive development are similar to those for height and weight.

We know least about the most important type of etiological analysis of individual differences in development—changes in age-to-age genetic and environmental correlations—because these analyses require longitudinal data. The surprise is that genetic correlations during infancy and early childhood—and even from infancy and early childhood to adulthood—may be quite substantial for cognitive development as well as for height and weight.

ACKNOWLEDGMENTS

The Colorado Adoption Project is a collaborative project with J. C. DeFries and D. W. Fulker of the Institute for Behavioral Genetics at the University of Colorado at Boulder and is supported by grants from the National Institute of Child Health and Human Development (HD-10333 and HD-18426) and the National Science Foundation (BSN-8643938). Preparation of this chapter was also supported in part by a grant from the National Institute of Aging (AG-04563) and by the Research Program on Successful Aging of the John D. and Catherine T. MacArthur Foundation.

REFERENCES

Bateson, P. P. G. (1978). How does behavior develop? In P. P. G. Bateson and P. H. Klopfer (Eds.), *Perspectives in ethology*. New York: Plenum.

Bayley, N. (1949). Consistency and variability in the growth of intelligence from birth to eighteen years. *Journal of Genetic Psychology, 75,* 165–196.

Cameron, J., Livson, N., and Bayley, N. (1967). Infant vocalizations and their relationship to mature intelligence. *Science, 157,* 331–333.

DeFries, J. C., and Fulker, D. W. (1986). Multivariate behavioral genetics and development: An overview. *Behavior Genetics, 16,* 1–10.

DeFries, J. C., Plomin, R., and LaBuda, M. C. (1987). Genetic stability of cognitive development from childhood to adulthood. *Developmental Psychology, 23,* 4–12.

Fagan, J. F., III (1985). A new look at infant intelligence. In D. K. Detterman (Ed.), *Current topics in human intelligence* (pp. 223–246). Norwood, NJ: Ablex.

Fulker, D. W., Plomin, R., Thompson, L. A., Phillips, K., Fagan, J. F., III, and Haith, M. M. (1988). *Rapid screening of infant predictors of adult IQ: A study of twins and their parents.* Manuscript submitted for publication.

Galton, F. (1875). The history of twins as a criterion of the relative powers of nature and nurture. *Journal of the Anthropological Institute, 6,* 391–406.

Jinks, J. L., and Fulker, D. W. (1970). Comparison of the biometrical genetical, MAVA, and classical approaches to the analysis of human behavior. *Psychological Bulletin, 73,* 311–349.

Kagan, J. (1971). *Change and continuity in infancy.* New York: Wiley.

Lewis, M. (1983). What do we mean when we say "infant intelligence scores"? In M. Lewis (Ed.), *Origins of intelligence: Infancy and early childhood* (pp. 1–17). New York: Plenum.

Lewis, M., Jaskir, J., and Enright, M. K. (1986). The development of mental abilities in infancy. *Intelligence, 10,* 331–354.

Loehlin, J. C. (1987). *Latent variable models.* Hillsdale, NJ: Lawrence Erlbaum Associates.

Mangan, G. (1982). *The biology of human conduct: East-West models of temperament and personality.* Oxford: Pergamon Press.

McCall, R. B. (1979). The development of intellectual functioning in infancy and the prediction of later IQ. In J. D. Osofsky (Ed.), *Handbook of infant development.* New York: Wiley-Interscience.

McCall, R. B. (1981). Nature-nurture and the two realms of development: A proposed integration with respect to mental development. *Child Development, 52,* 1–12.

McCall, R. B. (1983). A conceptual approach to early mental development. In M. Lewis (Ed.), *Origins of intelligence: Infancy and early childhood* (pp. 107–133). New York: Plenum.

McCall, R. B., Eichorn, D. H., and Hogarty, P. S. (1977). Transitions in early mental development. *Monographs of the Society for Research in Child Development, 42,* (171).

McCall, R. B., Hogarty, P. S., and Hurlburt, N. (1972). Transitions in infant sensorimotor development and the prediction of childhood IQ. *American Psychologist, 27,* 728–748.

Merriman, C. (1924). The intellectual resemblance of twins. *Psychological Monographs, 33,* (152).

Moore, T. (1967). Language and intelligence: A longitudinal study of the first eight years. Part I. Patterns of development in boys and girls. *Human Development, 10,* 88–106.

Mussen, P. H. (1983). *Handbook of child psychology.* New York: Wiley.

Plomin, R. (1986a). *Development, genetics, and psychology.* Hillsdale, NJ: Lawrence Erlbaum Associates.

Plomin, R. (1986b). Multivariate analysis and developmental behavioral genetics: Developmental change as well as continuity. *Behavior Genetics, 16,* 25–44.

Plomin, R., and DeFries, J. C. (1981). Multivariate behavioral genetics and development: Twin studies. In L. Gedda, P. Parisi, and W. E. Nance (Eds.), *Twin Research 3, Part B: Intelligence, personality and development* (pp. 25–33). New York: Liss.

Plomin, R., and DeFries, J. C. (1985). *Origins of individual differences in infancy: The Colorado Adoption Project.* New York: Academic Press.

Plomin, R., DeFries, J. C., and Fulker, D. W. (1988). *Nature and nurture during infancy and early childhood.* New York: Cambridge University Press.

Plomin, R., DeFries, J. C., and McClearn, G. E. (in press). *Behavioral genetics: A primer* (2nd ed.). New York: W. H. Freeman.

Plomin, R., and Foch, T. T. (1981). Sex differences and individual differences. *Child Development, 52,* 383–385.

Skodak, M., and Skeels, H. M. (1949). A final follow-up of one hundred adopted children. *Journal of Genetic Psychology, 75,* 85–125.

Stott, L. H., and Ball, R. S. (1965). Evaluation of infant and preschool mental tests. *Monographs of the Society for Research in Child Development, 30,* (101).

Thorndike, R. L. (1940). Constancy of the IQ. *Psychological Bulletin, 37,* 167–187.

Werner, H. (1948). *Comparative psychology of mental development.* New York: International Universities Press.

Wilson, R. S. (1983). The Louisville Twin study: Developmental synchronies in behavior. *Child Development, 54,* 298–316.

Wilson, R. S. (1986). Continuity and change in cognitive ability profile. *Behavior Genetics, 16,* 45–60.

Wohlwill, J. F. (1973). *The study of behavioral development.* New York: Academic Press.

Wright, S. (1921). Correlation and causation. *Journal of Agricultural Research, 20,* 557–585.

15 Intelligence, Stability, and Continuity: Changing Conceptions

David Henry Feldman
Margaret L. Adams
Tufts University

INTRODUCTION

In this commentary, we consider the phenomena of stability and continuity in the development of intelligence. We argue that recent shifts in theory and research suggest a need to reconceptualize notions of intelligence, stability, and continuity, and maintain that these reconceptualizations will advance efforts to understand the course and quality of cognitive development. We begin with some considerations that bear on the meaning of the three key terms—*intelligence, stability,* and *continuity*—as they have been used in psychological research, and then consider some of the more promising reconceptualizations and their implications for the issues at hand.

INTELLIGENCE AS IQ

Tuddenham (1962) pointed out in a useful chapter on the history of intelligence testing that the word *intelligence* is a fairly recent addition to the technical vocabulary of psychology. "As Wechsler notes (1958, p. 3), it [intelligence] did not rate a separate entry in Baldwin's encyclopedic *Dictionary of Philosophy and Psychology,* published in 1901, but was given merely as an alternate to, or synonym of, intellect" (Tuddenham, 1962, pp. 469–470). However, by the 1920s, following the military's dramatically visible effort at assessment of "intelligence quotients" (IQ) in World War 1, intelligence and intelligence testing were firmly entrenched as components of American psychology (Gould, 1981).

Although under attack virtually from the beginning, IQ has nonetheless been a most influential measure of intelligence, and has dominated beliefs about what intelligence is for more than half a century. The notions of IQ and IQ testing have been widely adopted in psychological research and have also had significant impact on applied practice in a number of fields (Herrnstein, 1971).

In reviewing the history of the conception of IQ, it becomes clear that IQ has dominated thinking about intelligence because it is both simple and seemingly precise, appealing to a preference for a clear summary of abilities. In addition, IQ has had a strong hold on the concept of intelligence because IQ tests can be easily and quickly administered: A fairly reliable estimate of IQ can be made in 1 hour or less. Finally, and perhaps of most relevance to the present discussion, the notion of intelligence as IQ has endured because IQ is believed to indicate a person's stable, overall power of mind. Given these qualities, it is small wonder that many professional psychologists continue to support the use of IQ testing (Snyderman and Rothman, 1987).

Despite such support for the continuing use of IQ, there are equally compelling reasons to consider alternative measures of intelligence and to devise new ones. One of these reasons is the central issue under consideration in the present volume: continuity in development. Although it is widely believed that IQ tests measure a trait, and therefore support the notion of stability in intellectual ability, it is not altogether clear that what IQ tests measure is a stable trait (Bayley, 1970; McCall, Applebaum, and Hogarty, 1973). Nor is it clear that the design of traditional IQ instruments even permits the study of continuity in development. McCall (1983), a student of both psychometrics and development, studied these issues with considerable care, and offered the following conclusion:

> . . . just as the correlation between two sets of measurements is independent of the means of those two distributions (if they are symmetric), continuity and discontinuity in a developmental function are also potentially independent of stability and instability in individual differences. This means that evidence for stability does not necessarily imply continuity, and evidence for continuity does not necessarily imply stability. Our failure to understand developmental phenomena comprehensively occurs because we sometimes make generalizations from one realm to the next without ever testing them. (p. 66)

The assumption that the amount of intelligence a person possesses is constant across the life span has rarely been subjected to careful scrutiny. In fact, Alfred Binet, the originator of the modern "mental test," actually made the opposite assumption. Tuddenham (1962) observed that:

> Binet did not live long enough to check the consistency of test performance across appreciable intervals of time, but he rejected the view held by some later workers that intelligence as measured by tests is unchangeable. . . . To prove the contrary,

he and his collaborators developed methods, called by him "mental orthopedics," for raising the intellectual level of the defective. (p. 488)

According to Binet, the mix of elements that indexed intelligence could change with time. Recognizing that such shifts might occur enhanced the flexibility and utility of his technique. This very same notion of change in content and reorganization of abilities is, however, problematic for IQ, which holds that IQ is a stable trait; that view entails the assumption of substantial stability in overall mental power.

THE SEARCH FOR STABILITY

The study of stability in intellectual functioning has often been motivated by practical concerns such as the effects of poverty or retardation on children's development. Much of this research uses applied issues as a basic rationale for investigating whether or not intelligence tends to be roughly stable from birth through adulthood. The earlier that deficiencies and deficits in intelligence can be spotted, the argument goes, the more likely it is that intervention will be effective (Als, 1985; Bornstein and Sigman, 1986; Ramey, Yeates, and Short, 1984; Rose, 1981). It would be difficult to argue with such a rationale for studying IQ, but it should already be clear that it represents a significant departure from the rationale that mobilized the early efforts to construct a stable, reliable, unchangeable estimate of intelligence.

Although it is not always recognized, the basis for the earliest efforts to establish stability in intelligence were theoretical as well as practical. The theoretical construct of general intelligence ("g") was founded on the assumption that the trait being measured was a stable one. For a trait measure to be taken seriously, it had to be able to capture the essential features of the trait it represented not only at a moment in time, but over longer periods of time as well (Feldman, 1974, 1980). Stability was thus an essential assumption in the original conception of intelligence as a general quantity. To prove that this conception was accurate, efforts to establish stability through repeated measurements were absolutely essential. Establishing stability was not Binet's purpose, but it was a priority of English and US research efforts from the beginning (Gould, 1981).

Thus IQ tests were developed to measure the trait of general intelligence, with a central assumption of stability inherent in the effort. Conceived as a differential variable, IQ discriminated among individuals and placed them in ordinal relation to one another. For stability to be firmly established, it was necessary to demonstrate that the ordinal relation in IQ was maintained throughout the life cycle. Although efforts to establish such rigorous stability were never fully achieved, the efforts were motivated by the desire to prove the validity of general intelligence through the establishment of its continuity (defined as stability) over time.

A formidable problem facing those who have attempted to establish this sort of continuity for IQ has been the measurement of intelligence in infancy. Measures from infancy have consistently failed to relate significantly to measures taken at later ages (Bornstein and Sigman, 1986). A number of recent studies using variations of the habituation paradigm have reported substantial predictability from responses in infancy to IQ scores at ages four, five, six, and even later (Bornstein and Sigman, 1986).

Although such predictions are moderate, generally in the .40 to .60 range, they represent a noteworthy improvement in predictive power over earlier measures of infant IQ (Bornstein and Sigman, 1986; Rose, 1981). But how are such correlations to be interpreted? Are they to be seen as evidence for the original conception of an inborn trait that drove the field of IQ testing during its own infancy? If so, they should probably be included in "efficiency of processing" measures as proposed by Jensen (1979) and others. These measures aim to reflect a more or less physiological indicator of pure "*g*" or general reasoning that is so central to traditional theories of intelligence (Jensen, 1979). If such a physiologically inspired measure were found, it would be once again necessary to force the same continuity issues: Should the same variable be measured at each age? On what basis is it reasonable to shift from a more physiological to a more psychological set of measures? In either instance, what would continuity mean?

Identifying a powerful information-processing variable to buttress the construct of general intelligence is not, however, the only purpose that correlating habituation measures with IQ scores could serve. The applied aims of early intervention and ongoing remediation can also be served by using this technique. Let us consider why it might make sense to keep IQ as a measure of intelligence in the effort to predict from earliest infancy to the intellectual standing of older children.

The IQ measure is a robust predictor of the likelihood that a child will thrive in school, at least school as it tends to be practiced in middle-income communities in the Western world. As a rough index of academic talent, IQ has proven to be a serviceable predictor. In particular, scores on individually administered intelligence tests have been useful in identifying children who are at risk for failure in school (Ramey, Yeates, and Short, 1984). As is well known, Binet's test was originally designed to predict failure in the public schools of Paris. As indicators of intellectual retardation and intellectual precocity, IQ test scores are more problematic, but nonetheless widely used (Feldman, 1979, 1982; Feldman and Goldsmith, 1986b). With some 75 years of experience behind us, it seems clear that predicting school difficulty was and still is the most valid purpose for using IQ.

Yet, despite the value of IQ as a predictor of school achievement, it is unlikely that the issue of continuity in intellectual ability will be illuminated until better measures of thinking in infants and young children are available (Bornstein and Sigman, 1986). And if new measures at both infancy and early childhood are needed, we must ask whether the trait conception of intelligence is the best one to guide their development. Considering other conceptions of intelligence may in turn suggest new targets for prediction and measurement. If our purpose is to learn what qualities are present in the earliest days of development, and to see how these qualities persist over time, then it is necessary to look for a more differentiated set of qualities to begin with, and to relate them to a wider array of outcomes in childhood and beyond.

DISCONTINUITY AND INTELLECTUAL DEVELOPMENT

A model of intelligence that has some of the features suggested above and that has had great impact on the field of developmental psychology is the great Genevan enterprise led by Jean Piaget (1952/1963). Psychometric and Piagetian approaches are often viewed as antithetical; the emphasis in IQ is on a differential psychology, whereas the Piagetian focus is on broad cognitive changes that all children experience. But in one sense the two approaches were motivated by similar goals: to characterize common or universal qualities of mind (Elkind, 1967). For Piaget, universal qualities of mind entailed an orderly sequence of changes in reasoning from birth to maturity, whereas for IQ it meant the stability of a trait associated with overall mental power. Both frameworks include the assumption that the mind is best represented as a single complex entity or unified set of processes. Both Piagetian and IQ-based models, then, were quite explicitly motivated by the desire to provide an overall characterization of mind.

Despite this common purpose, the two views diverge in their assumptions about the nature of intelligence. A major premise of the Genevan framework asserts the existence of structural *dis*continuity, that is, a sequence of qualitatively distinct stages. In Piaget's stage theory, regularly occurring shifts in mental organization mark turns in the path of intellectual development from childhood to adulthood. In sharp contrast, psychometric approaches assume that the power of mind is a relatively constant quantity; changes reflect amounts of new information acquired over time, not fundamental reorganizations. They maintain that if intelligence is measured well at one age, it should provide a sufficient index for all ages.

Psychometricians do recognize that mind becomes more sophisticated with age; but according to their position, the increases in complexity and sophistication are more quantitative than qualitative: Increasing sophistication is the result of increased knowledge, not structural or functional reorganization. The rationale for longitudinal research within the psychometric tradition is the assumption that mental power is a constant. For Piagetians, on the other hand, longitudinal research has been driven by the assumption of discontinuity, namely, that there are regular and orderly qualitative shifts in mental structure and function (Piaget, 1954). Given its assumption of regular discontinuity in the succession of stages, it is not surprising that the Piagetian approach has tended to be bypassed by those interested in continuity in intelligence.

Yet, the Piagetian approach, based as it is on assumptions very different from the IQ approach, has raised important issues about the nature of intelligence and has increasingly led to questions about IQ as an adequate representation of this concept. Such questions include a healthy skepticism about the psychometric assumption that intelligence remains stable over the life course. Given a Piagetian perspective, IQ is seen as lacking an account of mental process and actually discouraging close and careful observation of the behavior of children (Gardner, 1983).

Piaget's theory has also served to place the study of continuity in a broader context. This context requires that aspects of intelligence dealing with differences among individuals be complemented by attention to the stages that are common across individuals. From a Piagetian perspective the measure known as IQ, however well refined into a testing instrument, cannot tap or capture many of the critical qualities of what is meant by intelligence, and in particular cannot provide a coherent account of changes in content or organization of the components of intellectual processes (Sternberg, 1984b, 1986).

Partly as a consequence of Piaget's influence, and partly for reasons having to do with problems (such as cultural bias) encountered in the actual use of IQ, a number of investigators have been proposing alternative views of intelligence and intellectual development (Gardner, 1983; Sternberg, 1984b). Each of the alternative conceptions has some connection to previous traditions, but each also departs from these traditions in interesting ways that yield different definitions of intelligence and suggest new measures of intellectual functioning. These more recent accounts also have implications for the study of continuity and stability in development. We now turn to consider the views of Robert Sternberg, Howard Gardner, and David Feldman. Sternberg's and Gardner's theories have received wide attention within the scholarly community and in the popular media. Usually cast as rival viewpoints, they can nonetheless profitably be considered in tandem, for both make important contributions to the changing conception of intelligence. Feldman's work is known primarily within the developmental psychology community; it extends Piaget's framework through its reconceptualization of intelligence.

STERNBERG'S COMPONENTIAL FRAMEWORK

Although Sternberg is a critic of the IQ measure, his componential theory of intelligence is more closely tied to the psychometric tradition than other current reconceptualizations. Sternberg's theory is comprehensive and detailed, with a large number of elements and complicated inner workings. It offers a number of interesting possibilities for studying continuity in intelligence (Sternberg, 1984b, 1986; Sternberg and Davidson, 1986). His theory borrows heavily from an information-processing orientation; the fundamental unit of Sternberg's system is the "component." Although descriptions of the components in different presentations of his theory have been modified and revised, there tend to be three consistent, distinctive types: metacomponents, knowledge acquisition components, and performance components. In a recent description of the system, Sternberg (1986) proposed that nine metacomponents, seven knowledge acquisition components, and four performance components are adequate to carry out most mental functions. These components are assumed to enter the system at different ages and to become strengthened with age.

Metacomponents are the heart of Sternberg's theory. They are the "executive processes" such as planning, devising strategies, and allocating resources for problem solving. They power the entire system; all other components are activated by them. Sternberg maintained that everyone comes to possess the full complement of metacomponents, but that people may differ with respect to how well each metacomponent functions under various circumstances, such as dealing with practical situations versus academic ones. The theory may be considered developmental in certain respects, as some of the metacomponents are not functional until adolescence. Otherwise, it shares little with Piagetian or other developmental perspectives.

Like Binet, Sternberg views intelligence as a rough estimate of an individual's ability to process information at a given point in time. More importantly, Sternberg (1986) maintained that the improvement of almost all aspects of intellectual functioning is not only possible but also feasible. This feature violates the traditional IQ assumption of constancy and suggests that continuity in Sternberg's framework would mean something quite different from continuity as it has been defined in the psychometric tradition. Continuity in Sternberg's framework would probably focus on the continued functioning of the various components throughout the lifespan.

It is important to emphasize, however, that Sternberg's framework is also in many ways concordant with the psychometric tradition. Sternberg conceives of intelligence as a broad, single set of coordinated processes. In his view, the mind can be reasonably described as a centralized executive control system, with a number ofsubcomponents serving the general purposes of adaptation as well as acting to achieve specific adaptive goals. This conception is consistent with the IQ tradition. The various components of the system, however, represent a much more coherent set of processes than IQ.

Sternberg's approach leads to quite different measurement tools than IQ-based instruments. In addition, the specific features of the componential model lead to different predictions about the application of intelligence to practical problems and settings. Indeed, Sternberg (1986) drew implications from the componential model for the improvement of everyday intellectual functioning, a feature most unlikely to emerge from the IQ tradition.

GARDNER'S THEORY OF MULTIPLE INTELLIGENCES

Another recent view of intelligence claiming wide attention is Gardner's theory of multiple intelligences (1983, 1984). Although in many respects similar to the factor theories of the 1940s and 1950s, Gardner's version leans heavily on data derived from clinical neuropsychological evidence that recounts the behavioral effects of strokes, lesions, and other forms of brain damage. Thus, rather than basing his conclusions on rotations in hyperspace of data sets (Gould, 1981), Gardner's proposals for several relatively independent, autonomous "frames of mind" are grounded in assumptions about the functioning of the human brain and nervous system.

Gardner is a strong critic of psychometrics; he is particularly skeptical of the idea that there is a central mental organization that controls the functioning of the child's mind. He asserts that the tendency to view the mind as a single entity or set of coordinated processes lacks plausibility and is unsupported by neuropsychological data. He proposes that these data are better accounted for within a framework positing modular or multiple, relatively uncorrelated intellectual capabilities.

Gardner has proposed seven distinct intelligences: verbal, logical/mathematical, musical, spatial/artistic, kinesthetic, interpersonal, and intrapersonal, with the caveat that this list is subject to modification. The first two intelligences capture much that is represented in traditional IQ tests. The middle three are traditionally associated with the notion of specific talent rather than intelligence. The last two intelligences—interpersonal and intrapersonal—are the farthest afield from what has traditionally been considered to reflect intelligence. Yet Gardner asserts that all seven are well-supported by criteria for achieving the status of an intelligence, including being affected by brain damage in specific areas. Gardner suggests that the failure to award certain of these abilities the status of an intelligence reflects a constraining cultural emphasis on logical, rational thought rather than a scientific conclusion based on evidence.

In the several debates between Gardner and Sternberg, the two have been cast as protagonists in a struggle to redefine the concept of intelligence. Gardner's multiple intelligences are usually seen as the more revolutionary, whereas Sternberg's components are viewed as more precise and process-based aspects of the general intelligence that IQ claims to measure (Gardner, 1984; Sternberg, 1984a, 1984c).

Yet in at least one key aspect, Gardner's framework is more traditional than Sternberg's, and this is in the area of stability. Although he does not address the issue directly, it is reasonable to infer that Gardner considers the relative power of the seven intelligences to be largely a biological matter that remains constant over the life course (Gardner, 1983). In this respect (and perhaps only in this respect), Gardner's theory is more like psychometric conceptions of intelligence than Sternberg's. (Sternberg's theory acknowledges changes in intellectual functioning and describes such changes over time in terms of the activity and strength of different components.) If Gardner's seven intelligences do display stability during development, then it should be possible to assess them in infancy and to predict with substantial accuracy their relative strengths over time, according to the same general research strategies used in psychometric assessments. No modification in the research paradigm would be required other than the existence of an independent measure of each intelligence, a technical problem of substantial difficulty to be sure.

In the search for new measures of intelligence, it is worthwhile to speculate about the feasibility of infant measures of each of Gardner's intelligences, and to gauge their potential power to predict child behavior in each of the seven areas. The intelligences seem sufficiently well-described (with the exception of the personal intelligences) to warrant such an effort, and it would put one aspect of the theory to an appropriate empirical test. Whether or not it affirms stability in the sense that it has been traditionally studied, the information gathered about specific intelligences could be of value for making more informed decisions about enrichment or interventions in the specific areas tested.

Although we know of no efforts to devise infant measures of the seven intelligences, there is currently an effort to develop new assessment techniques for preschool children based in part on Gardner's model (Malkus, Feldman, and Gardner, 1988; Wexler-Sherman, Feldman, and Gardner, 1988). This research, called Project Spectrum, is co-directed by David Feldman and Howard Gardner, and is also based on Feldman's theory of development in nonuniversal domains (discussed in the next section). The objective for Spectrum has been to devise procedures to assess preschool cognitive activity as reflected in bodily-kinesthetic skills, musical talents, social analytic capabilities, natural science abilities, and distinctive styles of work, as well as in the more traditional linguistic and logical/mathematical abilities.

Now entering its fifth year, Spectrum has developed tasks, materials, and observational protocols that could enable teachers to conduct ongoing assessments of children's abilities within a regular classroom context. This range of information promises to offer teachers rich indices of children's interests and capabilities that can be summarized as a kind of cognitive profile describing each child's areas of strength and interest. These profiles are expected to be useful guides for the child's future teachers. They are also intended to help parents recognize and appreciate the distinctive qualities and capabilities that characterize their child, and to suggest the potential appropriateness of pursuing particular enrichment opportunities.

Although its primary purpose was to develop a new applied assessment procedure, Spectrum's system also promises to have research applicability. In particular, it offers the means for empirical tests of stability in intelligences across a wide range of cognitive dimensions. The Spectrum system allows an examination of stability not only in terms of specific cognitive capacities but also in terms of *patterns* of competencies. Changes in these patterns would not necessarily imply that cognitive development is discontinuous, but may suggest that dimensions interact in ways that enable new patterns to emerge.

Spectrum represents a radical alternative to traditional intelligence research, both theoretically and in terms of techniques of assessment. Where traditional IQ-based research was designed to predict children's school success, Spectrum has set a broader agenda from its inception, deliberately aiming to define and measure intelligence in ways that are as relevant for the nonacademic world as for school performance. Furthermore, Spectrum begins with the assumption that each child has a unique set of strengths. Its assessment system is designed to reveal these individual qualities rather than locate children along a unidimensional continuum of ability.

Although quite promising as a more diverse set of measures of capability in childhood than traditional IQ tests, the Spectrum process has not been tested in the field for its predictive value. And in particular, it has not been tested as an indicator of stability over time. The techniques are currently limited in their application to a 4-year-old population. It is not known if the qualities revealed in 4-year-olds, however valid, would appear in younger children if attempts were made to measure them, nor do we know if these qualities would continue to appear as children develop. In order to assess the practical value of Spectrum, it will be necessary to do studies in both directions, namely predicting from infancy forward toward 4 years and predicting from 4 years forward into later childhood and beyond. Clearly, these will be time-consuming and expensive efforts. But, if there is consensus that it is desirable to assess a wider range of capabilities in children, these efforts are well justified (Feldman and Gardner, 1987).

FELDMAN'S THEORY OF NONUNIVERSAL DEVELOPMENT

Although not a theory of intelligence per se, David Feldman's work on nonuniversal domains of development has implications for discussions of both intelligence and continuity. The concept of nonuniversal developmental domains broadens the scope of developmental psychology to include bodies of knowledge previously considered part of what Piaget called "mere learning," and therefore supposedly of little interest to developmentalists (Feldman, 1980, 1981).

Nonuniversal development is described by many of the same criteria as universal development (e.g., qualitative reorganization, positive direction, and hierarchical integration), but is subject to greater cultural influence and modification. The "universal to unique" continuum proposed as part of this framework (see Figure 15.1) is intended to encompass the range of domains individuals might try to master, including many that have not previously been characterized as developmental in the traditional constructivist sense of the term. It is assumed within this framework that individuals differ with respect to the number of domains within which they may become active, as well as the progress they might make in each. Thus, Feldman's conception of nonuniversal development includes possibilities for individual differences in ability at the same time that it is fundamentally developmental in nature.

The study of nonuniversal development is relevant to considerations of intelligence and stability in a number of ways. Rather than viewing intelligence as an estimate of an individual's relative standing on some test of overall mental power, the source of individual differences is considered to lie in the potential for mastery of various domains, and in the variety of domains made available and accessible to the individual. Intelligence in the context of nonuniversal development is an estimate of how well a process is advancing, not a quantity to be tested and scored.

Feldman's framework is guided by the assumption that individuals possess the possibility of expressing their potential in uniquely satisfying ways (Feldman with Goldsmith, 1986a). To the extent that they are moving toward such expression in optimal ways, the process can be seen as positive. Less than optimal movement in the direction of expression of potential implies a less successful process, and hence a less intelligent one. The more the various aspects of development are in optimal coordination (the aspects are called "co-incidence forces" in this framework), the more likely they are to lead to optimal states of developed potential.

Continuity, then, becomes a variable in the overall process of coordination of developmental forces. To the extent that there is coherence and direction in where the process is going, continuity in development can be perceived (Sroufe and Jacobvitz, 1987). On the contrary, when there is fragmentation, disorder,

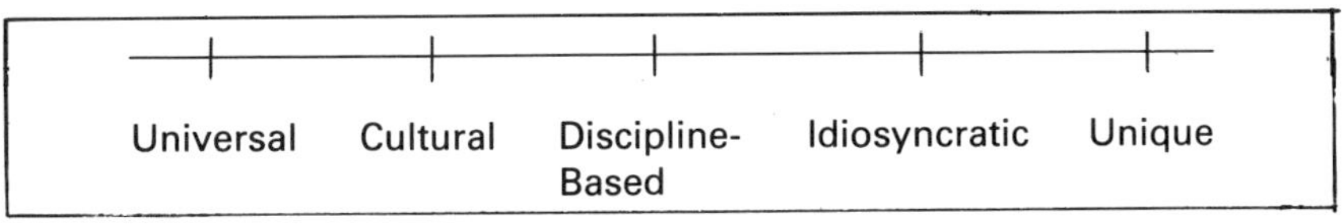

FIGURE 15.1. Developmental regions from universal to unique.

and lack of direction, continuity is lacking. Paradoxically, normal periods of disruption and disorganization are to be expected as an individual moves through various levels of mastery of domains, because progress requires constructive reorganization. Such disruptions may seem to be signs of a process gone awry, but are actually normal, even essential, phases in development and do not, in themselves, signal discontinuity.

More subtle analytic categories than are currently available are needed to reliably distinguish between healthy disorganization and more seriously disruptive disorganization. Sometimes it may not be possible to determine whether disorganization is part of a positive change or a sign of a process gone awry until later in the process. Hindsight may well provide acuity not possible during a transition itself. Conceptually, though, the distinction between disorganization in the service of development versus disorganization that signals a breakdown in progress is clear enough.

Research on Child Prodigies

Feldman's research on child prodigies' progression through various nonuniversal domains illustrates the interplay of factors contributing to development in cases of extreme talent, with the assumption that in such extreme cases developmental processes are more sharply etched than in more typical situations (Feldman, 1980, 1986; Feldman with Goldsmith, 1986a). The child prodigy has been little studied, due in part to the influence of the psychometric tradition that assimilated the unique gifts of the prodigy to the IQ continuum. Viewed as a child of exceedingly high IQ, psychometricians apparently did not see that the phenomenon merited separate study (Feldman, 1982, 1986). In fact, the prodigy seems to have some quite distinct qualities that make him or her an appropriate research subject. In particular, in addition to good (but not necessarily overwhelmingly powerful) general intellectual ability, prodigies seem to have an exceptionally powerful talent in (usually) one specific area of expertise such as music, chess, or mathematics.

For the past decade we have been involved in a study of six child prodigies and their families (Feldman with Goldsmith, 1986a). The primary goal was to study the intellectual development of each of the six boys whose special areas of expertise were, at initial contact, chess (two children), music, science, writing, and languages. The children and their families were studied through interviews, observations, consultations with experts and school personnel, reviews of school records, and assessments of Piagetian reasoning.

Most striking about the children was their almost uncanny ability to perform at a very high level within a particular area of special interest. In general, the child's ability in his area of interest far outdistanced his general academic talent and his general developmental level as measured by Piagetian tasks (Feldman, 1979). All the children were bright and for the most part performed well in school, but they were not academically more exceptional than thousands of other American school children. Accordingly, if they had been assessed with only IQ tests, their areas of special capability would have almost certainly been missed, because these domains are not sampled by most standard testing instruments.

The unevenness of capability in the prodigy is extreme, although not as much so as in the idiot savant (Miller, 1987a, 1987b). Both phenomena—prodigies and savants—tend to support theories of intelligence indicating modularity of specific functions as critical features (Gardner, 1983). Without denying the need to recognize general academic talent as an aspect of intelligence, research on prodigies strongly indicates that certain vital additional aspects of intellectual functioning must be taken into account before a comprehensive theory of intelligence and its development can be successfully articulated.

For example, in describing relations between intellectual development and adult professional success or life satisfaction, it seems that specific areas of intellectual achievement are as relevant as measures of general ability. Were any of the six prodigies in the Feldman study lacking general intellectual ability, the opportunities to follow their specific areas of ability may have been vastly reduced. But given adequate ability to do well in most academic situations, the more critical variables in their success revolved around pursuits in specific domains. And although raw talent in these specific areas may be relatively constant, its sustained expression is continually challenged by the dynamic and recursive interplay among both individual factors and complex social systems. When all of the relevant developmental forces are carefully coordinated, a prodigy may emerge. But unless this coordination is productively sustained, the individual's expression of talent reverts to the level of potential.

With regard to stability, we have informally noted that the general academic ability of the prodigies has remained relatively constant over the ten or more years we have observed them. In contrast, their specific capabilities and interests have changed. Two children gave up chess as a major focus of activity; two other children became focused in musical pursuits. One stayed involved in science, and one stayed involved in music but shifted his focus from composition to performance. These changes in focus of interest and effort would have been missed had we only attended to the children's general intellectual abilities, or even to how well they performed in school.

Co-incidence

Feldman proposed a "co-incidence" process to account for how extremely gifted individuals come to express their specific talents. As a theoretical framework, co-incidence draws attention to the major sets of variables that contribute through their complex interplay to the realization of potential by shaping the degree to which talent is expressed.

Prodigy research suggests that a very delicate coordination of several processes is necessary for even the most gifted child to develop his or her given talents sufficiently to be recognized as a prodigy. Once such status has been achieved, the "co-incidence" forces must continue to be productively orchestrated or even the most exceptional prodigy's talents will stall or falter. Thus, although the prodigy may seem to be a case study in continuity of ability, there is almost constant shifting and correcting of the forces underlying and supporting the prodigy's development.

This description of prodigies illustrates that continuity in intelligence engages a much more complicated set of issues than the literature generally acknowledges. The following are among the variables that must be considered when describing the sort of co-incidence process that sustains the development of prodigies' extreme potential: the features and demands of the specific domain in which the individual's talent manifests itself; the availability of master teachers and appropriate educational technologies; parents' interest, commitment, and ability to support their children; family traditions that value the domain in which the child excels (Feldman with Goldsmith, 1986a); and historical and cultural contexts' recognition of early prodigious achievements (Csikszentmihalyi, 1988; Simonton, 1984).

Randomly occurring events may also be catalytic or disruptive to the expression of an individual's potential. These forces all operate in addition to the particular intellectual and personal qualities of the child. These qualities include passion, confidence, dedication, persistence, and joy in achievement, as well as a strong interest and talent for a particular domain. Clearly, the course of development for prodigies is a complicated one to assess; although it may seem less complicated for less exceptional children, we believe that the same forces involved in the co-incidence process for prodigies are critical in the intellectual development of all individuals.

The study of prodigies reveals that intelligence defined in terms of IQ tells only part of the story of ability, for it leaves us unable to account in any satisfactory way for the phenomenon of a prodigy. Adopting a much more complex and dynamic process model, we are able to begin to understand what nonetheless remains incredible when encountered. If the goal of continuity research is to better predict the course of development and, by virtue of this, to better understand the conditions that facilitate further development, then the scope of relevant research questions will have to be considerably broadened. This seems to be as true, perhaps more so, for less talented children as it does for prodigies (Feldman with Goldsmith, 1986a).

CONCLUSION

Having considered both traditional and a few more recent theories of intelligence and related areas that bear on stability, continuity, and development, we see several new and promising directions in the study of intellectual development. In particular, we maintain that theories of intelligence emphasizing practical uses of potential and specific areas of capability, and conceptions of development that consider development in a wide range of domains, hold the most promise for further research. We believe that predicting school performance is only part of what can be gained from studying stability in intelligence, and possibly not the most critical part. Broadening what is meant by intelligence will mean more complicated research designs replete with measurement challenges and conceptual problems. First and foremost among these conceptual challenges is the sorting out of what use to make of the concept of stability.

Except for such facts as date of birth, name, and eye color, there are very few qualities that in any reasonable sense can be said to stay constant (Maccoby, 1987), and even these qualities are changed under certain circumstances. The question to be answered is what sorts of changes are to be considered signs of a coherent developmental process, proceeding toward comprehensible goals, and what sorts of changes indicate that a process has been abnormally disrupted. When put this way, continuity in development may well include certain kinds of changes that are now taken as signs of discontinuity, as for example the Piagetian sorts of stage changes. There are no obvious or easy answers to the questions that we may pose about continuity, but there are a number of promising avenues of investigation.

It continues to be of great interest to know to what degree there are distinctive qualities of individuals, how early these can be detected, and how stable they tend to be. For practical reasons as well as for their intrinsic interest as goals of psychological inquiry, it is likely that there will be increasing research effort devoted to the study of the stability and continuity of intellectual development. Based on the kinds of theoretical research efforts now ongoing in fields of cognitive and developmental psychology, there are promising new directions for research to take, particularly for purposes of more differentiated and diverse measurement of a wider range of talents and abilities. Although only briefly touched upon in the present discussion, we believe that they will find increasing use as frameworks within which issues of stability and continuity in intellectual development will be studied.

ACKNOWLEDGMENTS

The support of the Jessie Smith Noyes Foundation, the Andrew W. Mellon Foundation, and the Spencer Foundation is gratefully acknowledged. Also, the members of our research team, the Developmental Science Group, made important contributions: thanks to Lynn T. Goldsmith, Ellen Band, Ann Benjamin, Jie-Qi Chen, Carol Mockros, Martha J. Morelock, Mark Ogonowski, and

Ronald E. Walton for their help and support. For their comments, we also thank Marc H. Bornstein and Norman A. Krasnegor.

REFERENCES

Als, H. (1985). Patterns of infant behavior: Analogues of later organizational difficulties? In F. H. Duffy and N. Geschwind (Eds.), *Dyslexia: A neuroscientific approach to clinical evaluation* (pp. 67–92). Boston: Little, Brown.

Bayley, N. (1970). Development of mental abilities. In P. H. Mussen (Ed.), *Carmichael's manual of child psychology* (3rd ed., Vol. 1, pp. 1163–1209). New York: Wiley.

Bornstein, M. H., and Sigman, M. D. (1986). Continuity in mental development from infancy. *Child Development, 57,* 251–274.

Csikszentmihalyi, M. (1988). Society, culture, and person: A systems view of creativity. In R. J. Sternberg (Ed.), *The nature of creativity.* Cambridge, England: Cambridge University Press.

Elkind, D. (1967). Piaget and Montessori. *Harvard Educational Review, 37,* 535–545.

Feldman, D. H. (1974). Universal to unique: A developmental view of creativity and education. In S. Rosner and L. Abt (Eds.), *Essays in creativity* (pp. 45–85). Croton-on-Hudson, NY: Ablex.

Feldman, D. H. (1979). The mysterious case of extreme giftedness. In H. Passow (Ed.), *The gifted and the talented: Yearbook of the National Society for the Study of Education* (pp. 335–351). Chicago: University of Chicago Press.

Feldman, D. H. (1980). *Beyond universals in cognitive development.* Norwood, NJ: Ablex.

Feldman, D. H. (1981). Beyond universals: Toward a developmental psychology of education. *Educational Researcher, 10,* 21–31.

Feldman, D. H. (1982). Transcending IQ in the definition of giftedness. *Early Childhood Review, 23,* 15–18.

Feldman, D. H. (1986). Giftedness as a developmentalist sees it. In R. J. Sternberg and J. E. Davidson (Eds.), *Conceptions of giftedness* (pp. 285–305). Cambridge: Cambridge University Press.

Feldman, D. H., and Gardner, H. (1987). *Third Annual Report submitted to the Spencer Foundation.* (Available from Project Spectrum, Longfellow Hall, Harvard University, Cambridge, MA 02138)

Feldman, D. H., with Goldsmith, L. T. (1986a). *Nature's gambit.* New York: Basic Books.

Feldman, D. H., and Goldsmith, L. T. (1986b). Transgenerational influences on the development of early prodigious behavior: A case study approach. In W. Fowler (Ed.), *Early experience and the development of competence: New directions for child development* (pp. 67–85). San Francisco: Jossey-Bass.

Gardner, H. (1983). *Frames of mind: The theory of multiple intelligences.* New York: Basic Books.

Gardner, H. (1984). Assessing intelligences: A comment on 'Testing intelligence without I. Q. tests.' *Phi Delta Kappan, 65,* 699–700.

Gould, S. J. (1981). *The mismeasure of man.* New York: Norton.

Herrnstein, R. J. (1971, September). IQ. *Atlantic Monthly,* 43–64.

Jensen, A. R. (1979). *Bias in mental testing.* New York: Free Press.

Maccoby, E. E. (1987, April). *Person constancy within developmental change.* Paper presented at the meeting of the Society for Research in Child Development, Baltimore, MD.

Malkus, U., Feldman, D. H., and Gardner, H. (1988). Dimensions of mind in early childhood. In A. D. Pellegrini (Ed.), *Psychological bases for early education* (pp. 25–38). New York: Wiley.

McCall, R. B. (1983). Exploring developmental transitions in mental performance. In K. W. Fischer (Ed.), *Levels and transitions in children's development: New directions for child development* (pp. 65–79). San Francisco: Jossey-Bass.

McCall, R. B., Applebaum, M. I., and Hogarty, P. S. (1973). Developmental changes in mental performance. *Monographs of the Society for Research in Child Development, 38*(3), Serial No. 150.

Miller, L. K. (1987a). Determinants of melody span in a developmentally disabled musical savant. *Psychology of Music, 15,* 76–89.

Miller, L. K. (1987b). Sensitivity to tonal structure in a developmentally disabled musical savant. *American Journal of Mental Deficiency, 91,* 467–472.

Piaget, J. (1954). *The construction of reality in the child.* New York: Basic Books.

Piaget, J. (1963). *The origins of intelligence in children.* New York: Norton. (Original work published 1952)

Ramey, C. T., Yeates, K. O., and Short, E. J. (1984). The plasticity of intellectual development: Insights from preventive intervention. *Child Development, 55,* 1913–1925.

Rose, S. A. (1981). Lags in the cognitive competence of prematurely born infants. In S. L. Friedman and M. Sigman (Eds.), *Preterm birth and psychological development* (pp. 255–269). New York: Academic Press.

Simonton, D. K. (1984). *Genius, creativity and leadership.* Cambridge, MA: Harvard University Press.

Snyderman, M., and Rothman, S. (1987). Survey of expert opinion on intelligence and aptitude testing. *American Psychologist, 42,* 137–144.

Sroufe, A. L., and Jacobvitz, D. B. (1987, April). *Diverging pathways, developmental transformations, multiple etiologies and the problem of continuity in development.* Paper presented at the meeting of the Society for Research in Child Development, Baltimore, MD.

Sternberg, R. J. (1984a). Fighting butter battles: A reply. *Phi Delta Kappan, 65,* 700.

Sternberg, R. J. (Ed.). (1984b). *Mechanisms of cognitive development.* New York: W. H. Freeman.

Sternberg, R. J. (1984c). Testing intelligence without I.Q. tests. *Phi Delta Kappan, 65,* 694–698.

Sternberg, R. J. (1986). *Intelligence applied: Understanding and increasing your intellectual skills.* San Diego: Harcourt Brace Jovanovich.

Sternberg, R. J., and Davidson, J. E. (Eds.). (1986). *Conceptions of giftedness.* Cambridge: Cambridge University Press.

Tuddenham, R. D. (1962). The nature and measurement of intelligence. In L. Postman (Ed.), *Psychology in the making* (pp. 469–525). New York: Knopf.

Wechsler, D. (1958). *The measurement and appraisal of adult intelligence, 4th Edition.* Baltimore: Williams and Williams.

Wexler-Sherman, C., Feldman, D. H., and Gardner, H. (1988). A pluralistic view of early assessment: The Project Spectrum approach. *Theory into Practice, 27,* 77–83.

About the Authors

MARGARET L. ADAMS is a doctoral student at the Eliot-Pearson Department of Child Study, Tufts University. She earned her A.B. from Duke University and her M.S. from George Peabody College. She is an honorary Jessie Smith Noyes Fellow and a member of the Developmental Science Group.

LAUREN B. ADAMSON is an Associate Professor of Psychology at Georgia State University. She received her B.A. from Swarthmore College and her Ph.D. from the University of California, Berkeley. Her research interests include early communication development and the emergence of cultural differences in social behavior.

HEIDELISE ALS is Associate Professor of Psychology in the Department of Psychiatry at Harvard Medical School, and Director of Neurobehavioral Infant and Child Studies and Associate in Psychiatry at The Children's Hospital, Boston. She is also Research Associate in Newborn Medicine at Brigham & Women's Hospital, Boston. She received her undergraduate degree summa cum laude from the University of Wurzburg and the Padagogische Hochschule in Eichstatt, West Germany, and her Master's and Ph.D. degrees from the University of Pennsylvania. She spent a year as Visiting Scientist at the University of London and was Director of Research at the Child Development Unit of Children's Hospital Boston for seven years prior to her current position. She is a clinically licensed psychologist and is the senior author of the Assessment of Preterm Infants' Behavior (APIB). Her extensive scientific research publications have focused on the development of assessment methodologies for the neurobehavioral and social emotional functioning of the newborn infant and the young child as well as on parent-infant interaction in normal and at-risk pairs.

MARK I. APPELBAUM, Gordon and Bowman Grey Professor of Psychology, has been a faculty member in the Psychometric Laboratory of the Department of Psychology of the University of North Carolina at Chapel Hill since receiving his Ph.D. in Measurement Psychology from the University of Illinois in 1968. He has written on the application of statistical and psychometric methods to developmental and educational issues.

NATHLIE BADIAN is Research Fellow in the Department of Neurology, The Children's Hospital, Boston, and consulting teacher in the Holbrook Public Schools. She received her B.A. and M.A. in Ancient Greek Literature from the University of New Zealand and her M.S. and Ed.D. in Special Education from the State University College at Buffalo and the Boston University. She is a reading specialist and the developer of the Holbrook Preschool Screening Battery. Her scientific publications focus on the prediction of learning disabilities and, specifically, reading disabilities, and she works diagnostically and therapeutically with children from preschool through the high school years.

ROGER BAKEMAN is Professor of Psychology at Georgia State University. He received his B.A. from Antioch College and his Ph.D. from the University of Texas at Austin. Bakeman is currently on the editorial boards of *Child Development* and *Infant Behavior and Development.* For some time he has been interested in effective and meaningful ways to analyze social interaction and its effects, and is coauthor with John M. Gottman of *Observing Interaction: An Introduction to Sequential Analysis.*

LEILA BECKWITH is Professor of Pediatrics at the University of California, Los Angeles. She received her B.A. and Ph.D. from the University of Chicago. She is currently on the editorial board of *Infant Behavior and Development.* Her research interests are in the development of at-risk infants, and the influence of early social relationships on later development.

RICHARD Q. BELL is a Professor of Psychology at the University of Virginia, Charlottesville. He received his Ph.D. from Stanford University and spent most of the intervening years in the intramural research program of the National Institute of Mental Health where he was the Chief of the Child Research Branch and directed a longitudinal study of early marriage, mother-infant interaction, and preschool development. His scientific publications have involved congenital contributors to early development, the effect of children on adults, and the methodology of longitudinal and risk research. He is the coauthor of *Child Effects on Adults.*

MARC H. BORNSTEIN is Senior Research Scientist and Head, Section on Child and Family Research, at the National Institute of Child Health and Human Development. He holds a B.A. from Columbia College and M.S. and Ph.D. degrees from Yale University. Bornstein has received the C. S. Ford Cross-Cultural Research Award from the Human Relations Area Files and the B. R. McCandless Young Scientist Award from the American Psychological Association; he was also a J. S. Guggenheim Foundation Fellow. Bornstein has held visiting positions in Munich, London, Paris, New York, and Tokyo. Bornstein coauthored *Development in Infancy* (with M. E. Lamb) and *Perceiving Similarity and Comprehending Metaphor* (with L. E. Marks and R. J. Hammeal). He is general editor of *The Crosscurrents in Contemporary Psychology Series*, including *Psychological Development from Infancy* (with W. Kessen), *Comparative Methods in Psychology, Psychology and Its Allied Disciplines* (Vols. I–III), *Sensitive Periods in Development*, and *Interaction in Human Development* (with J. S. Bruner). He also coedited *Developmental Psychology: An Advanced Textbook* (with M. E. Lamb). Bornstein has contributed more than 100 papers in the areas of human experimental, methodological, comparative, developmental, cross-cultural, and aesthetic psychology.

ROBERT H. BRADLEY received his Ph.D. in Educational Psychology from the University of North Carolina in 1974. He is currently Professor and Director of the Center for Research on Teaching and Learning, University of Arkansas at Little Rock. Bradley is developer, along with Dr. Bettye Caldwell, of the HOME Inventory, a widely used measure of the quality of children's environments. Bradley's primary areas of research include the relation of family environments to children's health and development, early education, and evaluation of educational programs, in which he has contributed more than 100 publications.

SARAH H. BROMAN is Research Psychologist and Health Scientist Administrator at the National Institute of Neurological and Communicative Disorders and Stroke, Division of Convulsive, Developmental and Neuromuscular Disorders, Developmental Neurology Branch. She received her A.B. degree from Vassar College and her M.A. and Ph.D. degrees from Tulane University. Broman's major interest is in cognitive development. She is coauthor of *Preschool IQ: Prenatal and Early Developmental Correlates, Low Achieving Children: The First Seven Years,* and *Retardation in Young Children: A Developmental Study of Cognitive Deficit.*

JOSEPHINE V. BROWN is currently associated with the Psychology Department, Georgia State University, after having worked for a number of years at the University of Bielefeld, West Germany. She received her B.A. and Ph.D. from Emory University. Her research interests include sensorimotor development of newborn infants and preventive intervention with high-risk infants and their families.

MARGARET R. BURCHINAL is an investigator at the Frank Porter Graham Child Development Center at the University of North Carolina in Chapel Hill. She received her B.S. from Iowa State University, her M.A. and Ph.D. from UNC-CH, and spent a postdoctoral year at the University of Leiden in the Netherlands. Burchinal is interested in longitudinal methodology and cognitive development, with special emphasis on estimation of individual growth curves and in the efficacy of early intervention on the cognitive development of poverty children.

SARALE E. COHEN is Associate Professor of Pediatrics in the division of child development at the School of Medicine of the University of California, Los Angeles. She received her B.S. and M.S. degrees at the University of Washington and her doctorate at the University of California, Los Angeles. Her scientific publications have centered on longitudinal studies of infants born at biological or social risk.

BRUCE A.B. COOPER received his Ph.D. from the University of California, Berkeley and is currently a visiting postdoctoral research psychologist at the Cardiovascular Research Institute of the University of California, San Francisco. Research interests include statistical methods for longitudinal research and methods for assessing family functioning. He is a co-author, with N. Haan and E. Aerts, of *On Moral Grounds: The Search for Practical Morality*.

FRANK H. DUFFY is Associate Professor of Neurology at Harvard Medical School, and Associate in Neurology, Director of Developmental Neurophysiology, and Director of the BEAM Laboratory at The Children's Hospital, Boston. He received a B.S. degree in Electrical Engineering and Mathematics from the University of Michigan and his M.D. from Harvard Medical School. After his surgery internship at Yale and neuro-surgical and neurology residencies at Harvard, he was a neurology research fellow for two years at Harvard Medical School. He has received numerous awards, such as Scientist of the Year and Men of Science. He is a pioneer in the field of topographic mapping of brain electrical activity and invented the Brain Electrical Activity Mapping (BEAM) methodology. His scientific work spans basic animal electrophysiological studies in somatosensory and visual cortex, kindling phenomena, and clinical investigation of the brain base of the epilepsies, learning disabilities, schizophrenia, depression, Alzheimer's disease, tumor recurrence, and the normal developmental process from the newborn period on. He is editor of *Dyslexia*.

MELVIN ELDRIDGE is a graduate student at Georgia State University. He received his B.A. from the University of Tennesee, Knoxville, and his M.A. from The College of William and Mary. His interests include family interaction research.

DAVID HENRY FELDMAN is Professor of Developmental Psychology at the Eliot-Pearson Department of Child Study, Tufts University. He earned his Ph.D. from Stanford University. He is Director of the Jessie Smith Noyes Fellowship Program and the Developmental Science Group. He is author of *Beyond Universals in Cognitive Development* and *Nature's Gambit*.

JANE V. HUNT is Research Psychologist at the Institute of Human Development and administrator of the Harold E. Jones Child Study Center at the University of California, Berkeley. She holds a research appointment in the Department of Pediatrics, University of California, San Francisco. Her Ph.D. is from the University of California, Berkeley. Hunt's research interest has been in longitudinal studies of mental development in infancy and childhood. Her major research is focused on high-risk preterm infants, with special interest in neonatal status and subsequent development.

NORMAN A. KRASNEGOR is Chief of the Human Learning and Behavior Branch of the National Institute of Child Health and Human Development. He received his undergraduate degree from Boston University, his Master's degree from Columbia University, and his Ph.D. from the University of Maryland. He is a clinically licensed psychologist and is senior editor of *Child Health Behavior: A Behavioral Pediatrics Approach* and *Perinatal Development: A Psychobiological Perspective*. One of Krasnegor's main scientific interests is in promoting interdisciplinary research to better define biological and behavioral factors that underpin development.

MARVIN W. LEE is a postdoctoral fellow at the Frank Porter Graham Child Development Center at the University of North Carolina. He received his B.A. from the University of North Carolina, his M.S. from Indiana University, and his doctorate from the University of California, Los Angeles. Lee's work has focused on the effect of daycare and early intervention on children's social and cognitive development and its implications for policy.

GLORIA B. MCANULTY is Research Associate in Neurology at Harvard Medical School and at The Children's Hospital, Boston. She received her B.A. and Ph.D. in Psychology from the State University of New York at Albany and has taught statistics at the undergraduate level. She is a clinically licensed neuropsychologist and the recipient of the A.C. Bennett Neuropsychiatric Research Foundation Award. Her scientific publications focus on the neuropsychological and neurophysiological relations in the learning disabilities, Alzheimer's disease, and early child development.

ARTHUR HAWLEY PARMELEE is a Professor of Pediatrics in the School of Medicine, University of California, Los Angeles. He received his B.A. and M.D. degrees from the University of Chicago. After serving four years in the Navy during World War II he obtained pediatric training at Yale Medical School and the University of Southern California. He spent three years in the private practice of pediatrics before joining the pediatric faculty at UCLA. There he developed the Division of Child Development for teaching of children's behavioral development to medical students and pediatricians and for biosocial research in infants and young children.

ROBERT PLOMIN is a Professor of Human Development in the College of Health and Human Development at The Pennsylvania State University. He received his doctorate at the University of Texas at Austin and until 1986 was Professor of Psychology and Behavioral Genetics at the Institute for Behavioral Genetics at the University of Colorado at Boulder. His research applies behavioral genetic strategies to the study of genetic and environmental sources of change as well as continuity in development throughout the life course.

CRAIG T. RAMEY is Professor of Pediatrics and Associate Director of the Frank Porter Graham Child Development Center at the University of North Carolina at Chapel Hill. He is also Director of the Carolina Early Intervention Program. Ramey received his A.B., M.A., and Ph.D. from West Virginia University with a concentration in life-span developmental psychology. This was followed by postdoctoral work at the University of California at Berkeley. His empirical and theoretical work is focused on the role of environments in enhancing or retarding cognitive and social functioning. His most recent book which he co-edited is entitled *The Malleability of Children.*

SUSAN A. ROSE is Professor of Pediatrics and Psychiatry at Albert Einstein College of Medicine. She received her B.A. from the University of Massachusetts, her doctorate from New York University, and was a postdoctoral interdisciplinary research fellow at Albert Einstein College of Medicine. Rose is currently on the editorial boards of *Developmental Psychology* and *Infant Behavior and Development,* the steering committee of the International Society for Infant Studies, and the Review Committee for Cognition, Emotion, and Personality of the National Institutes of Mental Health. Her scientific publications have centered on perceptual and cognitive development in infants and young children. She is co-author of *The Language of Learning: The Preschool Years* and *Preschool Language Assessment Instrument (PLAI): The Language of Learning in Practice*. She has been a Visiting Professor at the Sorbonne and an Indo-American fellow for the Council for the International Exchange of Scholars.

LINDA S. SIEGEL is a Professor of Special Education at the Ontario Institute for Studies in Education in Toronto, Ontario, Canada. She received her doctorate from Yale University. She has been associate editor of *Child Development*. She has published articles on language and cognitive development, early identification of developmental problems, learning disabilities, reading, attentional deficit disorder, and social history.

MARIAN SIGMAN is Professor of Psychiatry and Psychology at University of California, Los Angeles. She received her B.A. from Oberlin College and her Ph.D. from Boston University. She is on the editorial board of *Child Development* and the *Journal of Abnormal Child Psychology*. She is co-editor of two volumes, *Preterm Birth and Psychological Development* and *Children with Emotional Disorders and Developmental Disabilities*.

ROBERT A. TERRY is a graduate student in the Quantitative Psychology program at the University of North Carolina. He is particularly interested in the application of statistical and psychometric methods to problems in developmental psychology.

INA Č. UŽGIRIS is Professor of Psychology at Clark University, Worcester, MA. She received her Ph.D. from the University of Illinois at Champaign-Urbana and remained there to work with J. McV. Hunt on developing the Ordinal Scales before moving to Clark University. Her research has focused on cognitive and social development during infancy. She is coauthor of *Assessment in Infancy: Ordinal Scales of Psychological Development,* coeditor of *Infant Performance and Experience: New Findings with the Ordinal Scales,* and editor of *Social Interaction and Communication during Infancy*. She spent a semester at the University of Utrecht as a Fulbright Research Scholar.

MARY F. WALDROP is retired in Bethesda, Maryland, but remains active as a resource person and in helping investigators carry out research on minor physical anomalies. She received her Ph.D. in Child Development from the University of Maryland, and was director of the research nursery school in the intramural research program of the National Institute of Mental Health during the period in which preparatory studies were being carried out for a longitudinal study of early marriage, mother-infant interaction, and preschool development. Her interests also include the effect of family size and density on development in early infancy.

Author Index

Numbers in *italic* denote reference citations.

Subject Index